AF553144

SP
Pvt. Ltd.

Growth of Indian Economy
in the New Millennium

by

Zeba Sheereen
Department of Economics
Aligarh Muslim University
Aligarh – 202 001

2019

Studium Press (India) Pvt. Ltd.

Growth of Indian Economy
in the New Millennium

ISBN: 978-93-85046-46-9

Published by:

Studium Press (India) Pvt. Ltd.
4735/22, 2nd Floor, Prakash Deep Building
(Near Delhi Medical Association),
Ansari Road, Darya Ganj, New Delhi-110 002
Tel.: + 91-11-43240200-15 (15 lines); Fax: 91-11-43240215
E-mail: pubdir@studiumpress.in

Printed at India

About the Editor

Dr. Zeba Sheereen is Professor in Economics at A.M.U. She is the recipient of gold medal for securing first position in M.A Economics and was also awarded NET-JRF by the University Grants Commission. She has been actively engaged in teaching and research for almost three decades. She has taught Development Economics, Money and Banking, Indian Economy and Agriculture Economics at graduation and post-graduation level .Her field of interest is agriculture economics and economics of education. She has contributed articles in several national and international journals. She was also co-investigator in a Major Research Project by UGC. She is life member of Indian Economic Association and Uttar Pradesh - Uttarakhand Economic Association. Besides, she has also supervised several research works leading to the award of the degree of Ph.D.

Acknowledgement

I would like to take this opportunity to acknowledge all those people who have helped to put together this edited book. To my colleagues for helping me as and when needed.

This book would not have been possible without the support of my researchers. A special thanks to Sohrab Ansari for taking the responsibility of this book. He was as important to this book getting done as I was. Also a sincere gratitude to Arbiya Naseem Ansari, Jigisha Singh and Parvez Ahmad for extending their hands to support me and assist me in the editing and proofreading for compilation of the book.

I greatly appreciate and acknowledge all the authors for taking interest and contributing papers in their respective field of specialization.

Lastly to my family for giving moral support and encouraging me in all my pursuits.

Editor's Note on the Book

The beginning of the new millennium in 2000 brought India in to the league of fastest growing economies of the world and now she stands as the fourth fastest growing country. In terms of purchasing power parity, India is the third largest economy and further aspires to better the lives of its citizens to become a high middle income country by 2030.

India has witnessed diversification in agriculture sector which has led to increase in productivity and rise in farmers income. The dismantling of various controls under the reform has liberalized the financial institutions. Many new measures and schemes taken up have improved infrastructure, health, education, taxation and energy sectors.

Keeping in view of several growth forces since the beginning of the new millennium, this book provides deep insights into various macroeconomic variables with the help of 22 well-authored chapters.

November 2018

Zeba Sheereen
AMU Aligarh

List of Contributors

Aastha Dhingra: *Research Scholar*, Civil Engineering Department, Jamia Millia Islamia, New Delhi, India.

Abid Ahmad Koka: *Research Scholar*, Jiwaji University, Gwalior.

Abid Sultan: *Faculty*, Department of Management Studies,University of Kashmir, Srinagar, Kashmir, J&K, India.

Anil Kumar Biswas: *Assistant Professor*, Department of Political Science, The University of Burdwan, Burdwan, West Bengal.

Arbiya Naseem Ansari: *Research Scholar*, Department of Economics, Aligarh Muslim University, Aligarh.

Arshad Hussain: *Associate Professor*, Civil Engineering Section, University Polytechnic, AMU, Aligarh, India.

Divya Mahajan: *Assistant Professor*, UBS, Guru Nanak Dev University Amritsar.

Fazlollah Changani: *Assistant Professor*, Department of Environmental Health Engineering, Tehran University of Medical Science, Tehran.

Imran Ali Baig: *Research Scholar*, Department of Economics A.M.U Aligarh-202002.

Ishfaq Hamid: *Research Scholar*, Shri Mata Vaishno Devi University, Jammu and Kashmir.

Izharul Haq Farooqi: *Professor*, Civil Engineering Department, Aligarh Muslim University, India.

Jigisha Singh: *Research Scholar*, Department of Economics, Aligarh Muslim University, Aligarh.

Kanchan Kumari Sharma: *Assistant Professor,* Department of Economics, Arunachal University of Studies, Arunachal Pradesh.

Khursheed Hussain Dar: *Research Scholar in Economics*, Central University of Jammu, Jammu and Kashmir.

Kumkum Mukherjee: *Professor* (Retired), Indian Institute of Social Welfare and Business Management (IISWBM), Kolkata.

Mahammad Habeeb: Guest Faculty at Dept of Economics, Raichur University (Proposed), Raichur, State: Karnataka, India.

Mohd Faishal: *Research Scholar*, Department of Economics, Aligarh Muslim University, Aligarh.

Mohammad Arif: *Assistant Professor*, Department of Arts, KLE, University, Vijayawada - 522502, India.

Madhurima Basu: *Research Scholar*, M.Phil in Management, Indian Institute of Social Welfare and Business Management (IISWBM), Kolkata.

Nadeem A Khan: *Research Scholar*, Civil Engineering Department, Jamia Millia Islamia, New Delhi, India.

Nighat Mukhtar: *Junior Statistical Assistant*, Department of Planning and Statistics, J&K.

Pabitra kumar Jena: *Research Scholar*, Shri Mata Vaishno Devi University, Jammu and Kashmir.

Rejimon P. M.: *Assistant Professor*, Department of Economics, University of Calicut, Kerala.

Rubeenah Akhter: *Research Scholar*, School of Economics, Devi Ahilya Vishwavidyalaya, Indore.

Shazia Banu: *Research Scholar*, Department of Economics, Aligarh Muslim University, Aligarh.

Sirajuddin Ahmed: *Professor*, Civil Engineering Department, Jamia Millia Islamia, New Delhi, India.

Saroj Kumar Yadav: *Research Scholar*, Department of Economics University of Allahabad, Allahabad.

Suraj Walia: *Assistant Professor*, Department of Economics R.K.S.D. (PG) College, Kaithal (Haryana).

Sampurna Goswami: *Research Scholar,* Department of International Relations, Jadavpur University, Kolkata.

Tariq Ahmad Bhat: *Research Scholar* in Economics, Vikram University of Ujjain, Ujjain (M.P.).

Uday Chatterjee: *Assistant Professor,* Department of Geography, Bhatter College, Dantan, Paschim Medinipur, West Bengal.

Zeba Sheereen: *Professor*, Department of Economics, Aligarh Muslim University, Aligarh.

Preface

The Indian economy experienced considerable changes in the new millennium that were initiated in the early 1990s through the economic reforms. The beginning of the new millennium had witnessed the emergence of new opportunities, better governance and various favorable changes that helped the economy to boost further ahead.

This book consists of research papers by distinguished scholars in their field and provides an insight into the changes that the economy is undergoing through. The contributors have covered the topics on various sectors such as agriculture, migration, food security, taxation, infrastructure and development, energy and environment, health, education, and also sheds light on serious issue regarding the hospital waste water management. The researchers have also suggested various perspectives and ways that could help the economy to tackle the issues concerned under various categories. We wish that this work would be of great help to the general reader, graduate and undergraduate students.

The new millennium ushered in an era of growth and transformation of various institutions. The agriculture sector has undergone substantial changes in its food grains sector, with horticulture and high value crops gaining popularity. The diversification towards horticulture is generating higher income and employment in Bihar thereby improving the food security status in the state. The study on Jammu and Kashmir shows that the infrastructural development contributes equally for the agricultural growth. Irrigation, regulated markets storage and roads are positively associated with the agricultural development. Development of economics is also changing the lifestyles of people in the economy and has accelerated the growth of food processing industry in India. The state of Jammu & Kashmir (J&K) also faces huge power deficits during the winter and the summer season, as a study on supply and demand of electricity in J&K reveals.

Public Distribution System (PDS), one of the most important delivery system is crucial for National Food Security Act (NFSA) success and improving the food security in India and the states. One of the chapters deal with the working of PDS in India and Uttar Pradesh and tries to evaluate its present working status in the state.

Another aspect of development is migration and here the focus is especially on the seasonal migration of rural people and its impact on marginalized Scheduled Tribe (ST) in Bengal. Migration is observed during the lean season of agriculture as a livelihood mechanism and needs the attention of the policy makers to address the issue.

Good and Service Tax (GST); a historic taxation reform has widened the tax base of both the Centre and the States. The impact of this reform has been on many spheres, including the customers, traders, businessmen, and the economy at large. But there are many challenges that need to be addressed such as the impact of GST on agriculture sector and the issues to be faced by the farmers.

Education is associated with high rates of return and it enhances the productivity and development of the nation's stock of human capital. Haryana has made tremendous progress in overall education including higher education, but a proper balance between quantity and quality of higher education is needed. Regarding health and nutrition in rural India, the condition of health of women in the states like Chhattisgarh, Madhya Pradesh, Jharkhand, Uttar Pradesh, Assam, Gujarat, Rajasthan, Bihar and Orissa is found to be the worst.

Thus, the beginning of new millennium and the 21st century was beset with many development issues like infrastructure, taxation, food security, health and education, etc. This book is an attempt to bring these issues in notice through recent datum as per their availability and also through the primary surveys. This book is just an attempt to serve the students to enhance and polish their knowledge regarding the concerned topics.

Table of Contents

1

Emerging Trends in Cropping Pattern and Growth Performance of Major Crops in Bihar

SHAZIA BANU[1*]

ABSTRACT

Agricultural economy of Bihar is marked by structural rigidity in area allocation among various crops and this reflects the traditional character of the agriculture in the state. The cropping pattern is dominated by production of food grains and there has not been any substantial change in last few decades. However, within the food grains sector, substantial changes have taken place. In recent years there has been some reorientation in the cropping pattern through diversification policy, enhanced cropping intensity and use of modern technologies. The state has taken a quantum jump in production of various crops but has also witnessed high coefficient of variation implying instability in production. Of late the horticultural and other high value crops is gaining popularity and the state has been diversifying towards high value crops generating higher income, increasing employment in high value added food-processing industry and improving the food security scenario in the state.

***Key words*:** Diversification, Cropping pattern, Subsistence, Income, High value crops.

INTRODUCTION

Agriculture and allied sectors are considered as the backbone of Bihar economy. The percentage of population employed in agricultural production system is estimated to be seventy six percent, which is much higher than the national average. Nearly twenty two percent of gross domestic product of the state has been from agriculture sector, including forestry and fishing.

[1] Department of Economics, Aligarh Muslim University, Aligarh, UP (202001).
**Corresponding author:* E-mail: shaziabanuamu@gmail.com

High concentration of population, largely dependent on agriculture coupled with low yields of the major cereal crops, is main reason for high poverty ratio in the state (Economic Survey, 2010). According to 2011 Census, the population of the state is 100.4 million and growing at the rate of more than two percent per annum. This has led to many socio-economic problems including food insecurity, income insecurity, malnutrition and migration of agricultural laborers to other states. It is therefore important to attain self-sufficiency in food grain production with rate of growth higher than population growth rate. Agriculture is not only the source of livelihood but also it generates raw material for the agro-based industries which has immense potential in the state (Bihar's Agriculture Development, 2008).

The state best endowed with fertile gangetic alluvial soil with abundant water resources, particularly ground water resources, forms the basis of agriculture in Bihar. With total geographical area of 93.6 lakh hectares and fertile soil, good rainfall, plenty of water resources and agro-climatic conditions, the farmers in Bihar grow three crops a year and almost all types of crops. The gross and net sown area in the state is estimated at 76.4 lakh hectare and 54.0 lakh hectare, respectively (Agricultural Statistics at a Glance, 2014) though rice, wheat and maize are the major crops, the state also produces pulses, oilseeds, fiber crops, sugarcane, fruits, vegetables and various other crops. Recently, there has been a diversification in production and the farmers have also taken interest in growing flowers because of its increasing demand, both domestic and external. Hence, there is need to stabilize the rate of growth of agriculture through introduction of modern techniques and spread of irrigation.

Unfortunately, agricultural and allied sector witnesses wide fluctuations in Bihar mainly due to the vagaries of monsoon, which tend to cause upswing and downswing in the rate of growth of agriculture and the remaining sectors of the economy. The year-to-year variation in rainfall tends to create adverse climatic conditions like drought and floods in the state. Apart from loss of human and animal lives, this causes serious damage to agricultural production and affects the state economy in several ways. As a result, the performance of agriculture sector in Bihar has been constantly poor by national standard. It has not been able to exploit its potential of agricultural growth and its resources remained untapped due to poor planning and agricultural policies. Bihar lags behind in agricultural performance in comparison to other states of India because of its traditional cropping patterns and poor incentives. But in recent years, the state government is trying to re-orient agriculture through diversification policy and other measures such as enhanced cropping intensity, change in cropping pattern, improvement in seeds of high yielding varieties, cultivation practices and with the availability of better post-harvest technology etc.

I. CHANGES IN CROPPING PATTERN

Foodgrains dominate the cropping pattern in Bihar. There has not been any substantial change in this regard over the period of last decade or so. Table 1 reveals that the agricultural economy of the state is very much tilted in favour of the subsistence sector, since the acreage under foodgrains, even after a decrease in recent years, is more than 90 percent. The share of cereals is around 85 percent and that of rice being around 45 percent has shown a marginal increase at the cost of area under pulses. The percentage of area under pulses has shown a marginal decline from around 7 percent in 2010–11 to 6 percent in 2015–16. The non- food sector (oilseeds, fibre, sugarcane etc.) account for only 7 percent of the total area under cultivation and their individual shares in the total cropped area show only marginal changes. The average cropping area under sugarcane has increased marginally at the cost of oilseeds and fibres. The cropping area for fibre crops (Jute and Mesta), has diminished from 2.1 percent in 2001–02 to 1.6 percent in 2015–16. The cropped area under sugarcane shows a rise from 1.90 percent in 2009–10 to 3.46 percent in 2015–16.

Table 1: Cropping pattern in Bihar (figures are percentage of gross area sown).

Years	*Cereals*	*+ Pulses*	*= Foodgrains*	*Oilseeds*	*Fibres*	*Sugarcane*
2001–02	84.92	9.38	94.30	1.90	2.10	1.50
2002–03	85.10	9.30	94.40	1.80	2.30	1.40
2003–04	85.20	9.20	94.40	1.90	2.40	1.40
2004–05	84.80	9.40	94.20	1.90	2.20	1.40
2005–06	85.80	8.60	94.40	1.90	2.10	1.50
2006–07	85.90	8.40	94.30	1.90	2.10	1.60
2007–08	86.50	8.00	94.40	1.90	2.10	1.50
2008–09	86.80	8.00	94.70	1.80	1.90	1.50
2009–10	86.30	8.00	94.30	1.90	1.90	1.90
2010–11	84.03	8.03	92.06	1.94	2.27	3.73
2011–12	85.73	7.28	93.01	1.85	2.11	3.03
2012–13	85.90	7.11	93.02	1.59	1.94	3.46
2013–14	85.80	7.08	92.89	1.74	1.71	3.66
2014–15	86.16	7.09	93.25	1.63	1.56	3.51
2015–16	86.18	7.07	93.27	1.69	1.58	3.46

Source: Economic survey of Bihar (various issues)

II. GROWTH PERFORMANCE OF MAJOR AGRICULTURE CROPS

Agricultural economy of Bihar has marked a measure of structural rigidity in area allocation among various crops and that reflects the traditional character of the state agriculture. The gross and net sown area in the state has increased marginally and estimated at 76.4 lakh ha and 54.0 lakh ha respectively and cropping intensity of 1.42 in 2011–12. The foodgrains have remained predominant since the early 1950s and occupied high percent of the gross cropped area in the last two decades also (Table 2). It occupied as high as 89.9 percent of the gross cropped area in 1990–91 and this reflects the impact of the widespread demand structure of food crops such as paddy, maize, bajra, jowar, barley, wheat, ragi, gram and arhar which are cultivated in Bihar. However, within the foodgrains sector, substantial changes have taken place (Table 3).

Table 2: Area under major crops in Bihar since 1999–00 to 2015–16 ('000 hectares).

Year	*Rice*	*Wheat*	*Maize*	*Coarse cereals*	*Pulses*	*Oil-seeds*	*Sugar-cane*	*Jute & Mesta*
1999–00	3596	2081	368	57	712	157	94	966
2000–01	3657	2067	621	55	717	154	94	929
2001–02	3552	2126	594	53	694	143	113	877
2002–03	3585	2131	604	64	697	137	107	932
2003–04	3578	2077	616	47	681	141	104	970
2004–05	3188	2022	627	42	649	137	104	872
2005–06	3251	2002	661	47	593	138	101	809
2006–07	3463	2069	647	47	610	142	117	835
2007–08	3477	2131	659	43	449	142	120	857
2008–09	3495	2104	625	31	585	130	111	767
2009–10	3124	2116	641	31	565	135	73	791
2010–11	2845	2100	654	30	538	130	251	805
2011–12	3324	2142	675	28	524	134	218	829
2012–13	3299	2208	693	29	516	128	250	781
2013–14	2563	2149	732	30	500	123	258	673
2014–15	3262	2154	706	32	505	116	254	617
2015–16	3233	2099	704	30	499	119	244	613
CAGR	–0.66	0.05	4.14	–3.93	–2.20	–1.72	6.14	–2.80
ST.DEV	287.94	49.93	79.28	11.71	87.36	10.94	71.36	108.12
MEAN	3323.06	2104.59	636.88	40.94	590.24	135.65	153.71	819.00
C.V	8.67	2.37	12.45	28.61	14.80	8.06	46.42	13.20

Source: Economic survey of Bihar (various issues); *CAGR is in percentage;* C.V= (STDEV/MEAN)*100

Table 3: Percentage share of various agricultural crops in gross sown area.

Commodity	*1990–91*	*1995–96*	*2000–01*	*2005–06*	*2010–11*	*2015–16*
Rice	44.96	48.89	44.09	42.77	38.69	42.87
Wheat	22.15	19.58	24.92	26.34	28.56	27.83
Maize	6.4	7.74	7.49	8.7	8.89	9.34
Coarse cereals	0.76	0.8	0.66	0.62	0.41	0.4
Pulses	11.49	9.65	8.64	7.8	7.32	6.62
Oilseeds	1.99	2.04	1.86	1.82	1.77	1.58
Sugarcane	1.69	1.58	1.13	1.33	3.41	3.24
Jute & Mesta	10.56	9.72	11.20	10.64	10.95	8.13

Source: Computed from data in Table 2

Table 4: Production of major crops in Bihar since 1999–00 to 2015–16 ('000 tonnes).

Year	*Rice*	*Wheat*	*Maize*	*Coarse cereals*	*Pulses*	*Oil-seeds*	*Sugar-cane*	*Jute & Mesta*
1999–00	5547	4584	1427	57	620	115	3989	1266
2000–01	5444	4437	1497	58	622	131	3988	1380
2001–02	5203	4391	1488	53	547	120	5211	1101
2002–03	5086	4041	1350	51	561	105	4521	1094
2003–04	5448	3689	1474	43	557	124	4286	1286
2004–05	2625	3280	1490	39	471	116	3769	1371
2005–06	3709	2821	1520	44	454	134	4240	1472
2006–07	5131	4149	1754	45	451	141	5416	1505
2007–08	4459	4977	1803	39	473	144	4027	1453
2008–09	5771	4639	1702	31	536	123	4811	1073
2009–10	3640	4404	1544	29	460	141	3444	1271
2010–11	3113	5094	2108	37	467	142	11828	1310
2011–12	8188	6531	2557	38	520	175	11289	1739
2012–13	8322	6174	2756	35	543	183	12741	1717
2013–14	6650	6135	2904	28	522	157	12882	1745
2014–15	8242	3570	2479	31	429	127	15499	1637
2015–16	6802	4736	2517	27	421	127	11914	1631
CAGR	1.28	0.20	3.61	–4.56	–2.39	0.62	7.08	1.60
ST.DEV	1731	1012	529.17	9.96	61.82	20.74	4227.50	224.47
MEAN	5493	4568	1904	40.29	509	136.00	7286	1415
C.V	31.50	22.15	27.79	24.72	12.14	15.29	58.03	15.87

Source: Economic survey of Bihar (various issues); *CAGR is in percentage;* C.V= (STDEV/ MEAN)*100

The production levels of most significant crops of Bihar for the period 2000–01 to 2015–16 are presented in Table 4. The total cereal production in the state has significantly increased to 143.21 lakh tonnes in 2014–15, compared to 114.3 lakh tonnes in 2000–01. This quantum jump in production figure is largely due to remarkable increase in rice production because of the use of new System of Rice Intensification (SRI) technique and use of newer agricultural implements during the period 2011–12 and 2012–13. The level of rice production prior to 2011–12 has not been consistent and there exist much variation in the production level. This is because around fifty percent of net sown area is bereft of irrigation and dependent on rainfall. The average production figure was around 50 lakh tonnes. However, from 2010 onwards rice production has registered an impressive growth with CAGR of 27.56. The CAGR of rice production is 1.28, but has high coefficient of variation implying instability in production. Table 5 presents the percentage share of various agricultural crops in total production.

The production levels of wheat and maize have recorded a positive trend during the period 2005–06 to 2009–10 and 2005–06 to 2014–15 respectively. The average annual wheat production level was 40–45 lakh tonnes and that of maize is around 15 lakh tonnes. The production level drastically declined

Table 5: Percentage share of various agricultural crops in total production.

Commodity	*1990–91*	*1995–96*	*2000–01*	*2005–06*	*2010–11*	*2015–16*
Rice	25.91	29.99	31.01	25.77	12.92	24.14
Wheat	18.08	19.74	25.27	19.6	21.14	16.81
Maize	4.88	7.11	8.53	10.56	8.75	8.93
Coarse cereals	0.34	0.37	0.33	0.31	0.15	0.1
Pulses	4.05	2.77	3.54	3.15	1.94	1.49
Oilseeds	0.58	0.64	0.75	0.93	0.59	0.45
Sugarcane	40.01	32.4	22.71	29.46	49.08	42.29
Jute & Mesta	6.16	6.98	7.86	10.23	5.44	5.79

Source: Computed from above Table 4.

to 35.70 lakh tonnes during the period 2014–15. The maize has impressive growth rate of 3.61 percent and wheat has registered minimum growth rate of 0.20 percent but coefficient of variation is high for both wheat and maize. The production level of pulses showed a continuous decline with CAGR of –2.39 percent and a low coefficient of variation. Whereas Oilseeds have low growth rate of 0.62 percent, fibres has been grew at the rate of 1.60 percent. The CAGR for sugarcane is 7.08 percent. The growth and variations in yield of various crops are presented in Table 6 below.

Table 6: Yield of major crops in Bihar since 1999–00 to 2015–16 (kgs/ha).

Year	*Rice*	*Wheat*	*Maize*	*Coarse cereals*	*Pulses*	*Oil-seeds*	*Sugar-cane*	*Jute & Mesta*
1999–00	1543	2203	2235	1	869	735	42029	1311
2000–01	1489	2147	2413	1.05	867	825	42635	1485
2001–02	1465	2065	2504	1	788	841	45938	1256
2002–03	1419	1896	2236	0.8	804	765	44141	1173
2003–04	1523	1776	2390	0.91	818	881	41370	1326
2004–05	923	1622	2378	0.93	726	850	36084	1573
2005–06	1141	1409	2298	0.94	766	974	41884	1821
2006–07	1482	2005	2712	0.96	740	944	46092	1803
2007–08	1282	2335	2735	0.91	1053	1015	33558	1695
2008–09	1651	2205	2724	1	915	941	43417	1399
2009–10	1165	2081	2411	0.94	833	1043	47228	1608
2010–11	1094	2426	3225	1.23	868	1094	47184	1627
2011–12	2463	3049	3788	1.36	991	1308	51713	2099
2012–13	2523	2797	3975	1.21	1052	1431	50896	2198
2013–14	2110	2855	3966	0.93	1044	1279	49916	2594
2014–15	2526	1657	3508	0.97	848	1093	60938	2651
2015–16	2104	2256	3571	0.9	844	1059	48826	2660
CAGR	1.96	0.15	2.97	–0.66	–0.18	2.31	0.94	4.52
STDEV	515.00	444.16	637.75	0.14	105.6	194.69	6279.02	492.36
MEAN	1641	2164	2886	1.00	872	1005	45521	1781.1
C.V	31.38	20.53	22.10	13.99	12.10	19.38	13.79	27.64

Source: Economic survey of Bihar (various issues); *CAGR is in percentage;* C.V= (STDEV/MEAN)*100

III. GROWTH PERFORMANCE OF MAJOR HORTICULTURE CROPS

The state of Bihar, best endowed with very fertile plain land and agro-climatic diversity with high rainfall distributed over a five-month monsoon and a reasonably long and moderate winter, holds a vast potential for growing a large variety of horticultural crops. A wide range of fruits and vegetables, a variety of roots and tuber crops such as potato, medicinal and aromatic plants, flowers and spices are grown in the state with great ease and success. Presently fruits and vegetable crops cover 1.15 million ha accounting for roughly 19.5 percent of the net cropped area and 14 percent of gross cropped area. Spices and medicinal and aromatic plants cover 15.35 thousand hectare (Agricultural statistics at a Glance, 2009). Horticulture sector is gaining popularity owing to the high value of horticulture produces than agriculture crops. It provides a strong base for a vibrant and high value added food-processing industry in the state. Further, it provides foods security, prevents malnutrition and generates continual source of income to the farmers.

Bihar has the opportunity to have varied types of agro climatic conditions, congenial for growing almost all the horticultural crops India (Indian Horticulture Database, 2009). The area production and yield of major horticulture crops are presented in Table 7. These crops are currently grown over an area of 11.90 lakh hectares consisting of 3.5 lakh hectares under fruits and 8.4 lakh ha under vegetables. The state now ranks third in fruit production and first among all the states in terms of vegetable production in the country. The state is also one of the leading producers of spices for which there is good demand for domestic as well as foreign markets. Presently the total area under different fruit crops in Bihar is 2.85 lakh ha with a production of 40.62 lakh tonnes, the annual productivity being 14.24 mt/ha. Apart from major fruit crops, the agro-climatic conditions in the state are well suited for the production of vegetables and Bihar also produces a variety of vegetables. The Gangetic alluvial soil is a major boon for the vegetable producers of the state. Bihar ranks first among all the states in terms of vegetable production, and vegetables are exported to far- off states. The total area under different vegetable crops in Bihar is 8.23 lakh ha with a production of 142.84 lakh tonnes, the annual productivity being 17.37 mt/ha. Many spices are grown commercially in the state which includes Ginger, Turmeric, Chilly, Coriander, Garlic and Methi. At present Bihar produces about 1 lakh tonnes of spices annually from an area of nearly 46,590 ha. The total area under spices which was recorded 11.10 thousand hectare with a production of 12.30 million tonnes in 2006–07, increased to 12.75 thousand hectare and 14.98 million tonnes in 2008–09. The productivity was also increased from 1.10 MT/ha to 1.174 MT/ha during the same period (Annual Action Plan, 2009–10). Recently, the farmers of Bihar are also taking interest in floriculture. The commercial production of flowers is taking place in the state in view of its rising demand. Flower production in the state has increased, providing immense opportunity of employment and income in rural areas. The major flower crops cultivated in the state are Rose, Marigold, Jasmine (Bela), Tuberose Gladiolus and many others. Patna, Jehanabad, Gaya, Muzaffarpur, Samastipur and Vaishali are major flower producing districts in the state.

Table 7: Area, production and yield of major horticultural crops.

Area – 000' Hectares			*Production – 000' Tonnes*			*Yield Tonnes/Hectare*			
Year	***Fruits***			***Vegetables***			***Flowers***		
	Area	***Prod.***	***Yield***	***Area***	***Prod.***	***Yield***	***Area***	***Prod.***	***Yield***
2001–02	269	2877	10.7	709	10220	14.4	NA	NA	NA
2002–03	271	2890	10.7	720	10285	14.3	NA	NA	NA
2003–04	272	2992	11.0	765	11452	15.0	NA	NA	NA
2004–05	274	3056	11.2	790	12280	15.5	NA	NA	NA
2005–06	276	3068	11.1	805	13357	16.6	NA	NA	NA
2006–07	279	3426	12.3	824	13613	16.5	NA	NA	NA
2007–08	286	3252	11.4	824	14068	17.1	0.44	4.57	10.4
2008–09	291	3723	12.8	827	13385	16.2	0.59	5.95	10.0
2009–10	294	3465	11.8	836	13951	16.7	0.63	6.63	10.6
2010–11	296	3912	13.2	845	14630	17.3	0.69	7.11	10.3
2011–12	299	3946	13.2	853	15503	18.2	0.80	8.82	11.0
2012–13	295	3835	13.0	849	14898	17.5	0.75	7.64	10.2
2013–14	304	4458	14.7	806	15132	18.8	0.79	8.83	11.1
2014–15	347	3980	11.5	843	14498	17.1	0.82	8.92	10.8
2015–16	285	4062	14.3	823	14285	17.4	0.85	9.02	10.7
CAGR	0.41	2.49	2.07	1.07	2.42	1.34	8.48	8.87	0.30
St. Dev.	19.52	496.55	1.28	44.65	1664.96	1.30	132.91	1571.36	0.37
Mean	289.2	3529.5	12.19	807.93	13437.13	16.57	706.33	7496.56	10.57
C.V.	6.75	14.07	10.49	5.53	12.39	7.88	18.82	20.96	3.53

Source: Economic survey of Bihar (various issues); CAGR is in percentage

CONCLUSIONS

The agriculture sector in Bihar, over the past few decades, has not undergone any substantial change. The cropping pattern is marked by structural rigidity in area allocation and is still dominant by subsistence level food crops. But in recent years there has been some reorientation in the cropping pattern through diversification policy, enhanced cropping intensity and use of modern technologies. The state has taken a quantum jump in production of various crops but has also witnessed high coefficient of variation implying instability in production. The lack of stability in growth brings forth the poor infrastructural development and heavy reliance of agriculture production on monsoon rainfall. Of late the horticultural and other high value crops is gaining popularity and the state has been diversifying towards high value crops generating higher income, increasing employment in high value added food-processing industry and improving the food security scenario in the state.

REFERENCES

Government of Bihar (2010). Bihar Economic Survey. Ministry of Finance.

Government of India (2008). *Bihar's Agriculture Development: Opportunities & Challenges; A Report of the Special Task Force on Bihar*. New Delhi.

Government of India (2009). *Agricultural statistics at a Glance*. Ministry of Agriculture and Cooperation. *www.agricoop.nic.in*

Government of India (2009). *Economic Survey 2009–10*. Ministry of Finance, New Delhi.

Government of India (2009). *Indian Horticulture Database*. Ministry of Agriculture, New Delhi. *www.nhb.gov.in*

Government of India (2014). *Agricultural Statistics at a Glance*. Ministry of Agriculture, Department of Agriculture and Cooperation, Directorate of Economics and Statistics, New Delhi.

2

Linkages Between Agriculture Infrastructure and Agriculture Development

RUBEENAH AKHTER[1*]

ABSTRACT

Agriculture growth cannot be achieved in isolation without the development of infrastructure, thus an attempt has been made in this paper to analyse the impact of infrastructure on agricultural development in Jammu and Kashmir by employing secondary data. The results indicated that development of irrigation, availability of regulated markets and storage facilities and agricultural development are positively associated. While as road length and agricultural growth are negatively associated this means that farmers who are not connected to markets face high transportation costs to bring their produce to market which is major constraint to the development of agriculture. On the basis of findings, this study suggests that the pace of growth in development of the agricultural economy has to be accompanied by consistent growth in infrastructural variables.

Key words: Infrastructure, Isolation, Regulated markets, Road length.

INTRODUCTION

Agriculture is the primary activity by which humans live and survive on the earth. Agriculture is the backbone and main component of Indian economy. It plays a vital role in the development of Indian economy, particularly in rural economy. Agriculture is specifically linked to many facets of sustainable development, like wise poverty reduction, sustainable utilization and production, administration of natural resources, technological transfer and capacity building as well as trade and market access. Agri

[1] Research Scholar, School of Economics, Devi Ahilya Vishwavidyalaya, Indore, Madhya Pradesh.

**Corresponding author:* E-mail: economicsruby@gmail.com

business will be essential analytics and general advancement system, serving towards it. For achieving the inclusive growth, it is essential to reduce disparity likewise social inequality, regional disparities etc. Infrastructure plays significant role in improving the agricultural productivity, inadequate infrastructure can be big constraint to growth and productivity. Improving agricultural productivity reduces the food prices, benefits both urban and rural inhabitants who are net food buyers and hence has significant poverty-reduction effects (Acharya & Akhter, 2018).

Infrastructure is considered pre-requisite for take-off and for attracting various economic activities like agriculture, agro based industries. Moreover, it incidentally provides basic amenities that help to improve the standard of life. Varying levels of infrastructural and policy environment coupled with varied agro-climatic conditions and resource endowment determines differential growth performance of agriculture across regions. Warton (1996) highlighted that agricultural infrastructure are categorized into:

- ***Capital intensive*** - like irrigation roads, bridges.
- ***Capital extensive***- like extension services.
- ***Institutional infrastructure*** - like formal and informal institutions

However, agricultural infrastructure primarily includes wide range of public services that facilitate production, procurement, processing, preservation and trade. It can be grouped under below categories:

- ***Input based infrastructure*****:** seed, fertilizer, farm equipments and machinery etc.
- ***Resource based infrastructure*****:** water/irrigation, farm power/energy.
- ***Institutional infrastructure*****:** Agriculture research, extension and education technology, financial services, marketing etc.

A study conducted by Singh (1983) pointed out that among various infrastructural facilities; agricultural development was strongly correlated with agricultural infrastructural index followed by index of transport and communication. Moreover, while employing regression, (Majumdar, 2002) found that among physical infrastructure, it was transport infrastructure that affected significantly and positively the agricultural output and agricultural development index (ADI). He observed that agriculture and transport infrastructure were important components of agricultural output and agricultural development index (ADI). Similarly, (Thorat & Sirohi, 2002) attempted to analyse the impact of infrastructure on agricultural development using time series data and covered ten explanatory variables of infrastructure. The study indicated that transport, power, irrigation and research infrastructure were crucial determinants that influenced agricultural productivity. The other infrastructure facilities like access to fertilizer sale points, markets, credit, extension services also developed with development of transport infrastructure. Furthermore, (Dhawan, 1998), (Shah, 1993), (Vaidyanathan, 1999) observed that irrigation infrastructure increases the land use and cropping intensity, which provides incentives to farmers to use high yielding enhancing inputs and thus results in higher agricultural output. They highlighted that rural electrification increases the energisation of pump sets, which helps to increase the irrigated area using groundwater and the output of crops cultivated underground irrigation is always higher than those under canal or tank irrigation, because of its better reliability and controllability. Another study conducted by Fan *et al.* (2000) observed that the impact of government expenditures on agriculture research and development, irrigation, roads, education, power, soil and water conservation on agriculture growth and rural poverty. The study also explicit that government expenditure on roads had largest impact on poverty reduction and growth in agriculture productivity.

The development of infrastructural variables like roads increases the diffusion of agriculture technology by improving access to markets, enhances more efficient allocation of resources, reduces the transaction costs as well as helps the farmers to realise better input and output prices (Ahmed & Donovan, 1992; Van de walle, 2002). Moreover, improved road infrastructure increases the transport facility through which the rural farm households are able to get better health care, education and credit policy, reduces transport costs of inputs and outputs, thereby increasing the profit margin. However, as pointed out by (Binswanger *et al.,* 1993) that institutional infrastructure such as markets and credit facility play crucial role in agriculture growth. Poor access to market faces higher transaction cost in buying from or selling to national economy. Thus, it can be concluded that rural-urban linkages are developed through road development which also helps in strengthening the backward and forward linkages in agricultural linkages.

METHODOLOGY ADOPTED

The whole analysis of the study is based on secondary data. The agricultural output is determined by a number of infrastructures.

MULTIPLE REGRESSION MODEL

Multiple regression technique was used to analyse factors affecting the agricultural productivity. The equation 1 is represented as:

$$logNSDP = b_0 + b_1 log\ rl + b_2 log\ irrigntn + b_3 log\ storage + b_4 log\ villageselectrfd + b_5\ log\ working\ captl + \varepsilon$$

Where,

Y_i – dependent variable (NSDP); b_0 – intercept;

b_1, b_2, b_3, b_4, b_5, b_6, b_7, b_8, b_9, ... Regression coefficients;

Breusch-Pagan-Godfrey test was used to check the heteroscedasticity in the data set.

The data is represented in Annexure Tables A, B, C and D.

RESULTS AND DISCUSSION

Stationarity of Data

The time series properties of variables given in Eq. (1) are analysed by applying two types of unit root tests for data. The, ADF Fisher Chi Square, and PP unit root tests perform null hypothesis of a unit root. ADF and PP assumes individual unit root process across cross-sections and assumes an alternative hypothesis of no unit root. The results of these tests for the given data is given in Table 3 that all the series in Eq. (1) indicates to have unit root in their levels, but stationary in their first difference, assuming that they are integrated of order one, *i.e.*, I (1), (refer Table 1).

Table 1: Stationarity of data

Variable	*Augmented-Dickey*		*Phillips-Perron*	
	Level	*First difference*	*Level*	*First difference*
Log irrigation	1.06	2.80*	5.183	–0.331
Log NSDP	–1.46	–0.67	–0.478	–0.605
Log road length	–2.73	0.152	–0.590	–4.691*
Log storage	–2.22	–4.947*	–2.197	–4.947*
Log villages electrified	–0.771	–2.166*	–0.820	–2.015
Log working capital	–4.36*	–5.864*	–6.177*	–11.789*

Source: Compiled from data

Infrastructure plays a noteworthy role in improving the agricultural output. Infrastructure like other public investments, improves agricultural productivity, which in turn induces growth especially in rural areas. It will bring higher agricultural wages and opens a new opportunity for non-farm labour. Moreover, improved infrastructure leads to expansion of markets, economies to scale and improvement in factor market operations. In other words, we can say that agricultural development is affected by different infrastructural variables differently because of the fact that the role played by each variable is different. The result of regression presented in Table 2 clearly shows that among five infrastructural variables, the impact of irrigation, road facility and storage affects the agricultural output in our study area.

Table 2: Multiple regression model results of factors affecting agricultural development.

Explanatory variable	*Coefficient*	*Std. error*	*t-statistic*	*Prob.*	*R-square*
Log road length	–0.136570	0.285593	–0.478197	0.0494**	0.863
Log irrigation	3.540547	0.785191	–4.509154	0.0041*	
Log storage facility	0.015501	0.052383	0.295923	0.0773***	
Log villages electrified	1.203508	0.523108	2.300688	0.6110	
Log working capital	0.073461	0.114184	0.643353	0.5438	
Constant	9.830410	1.587557	6.192163	0.0008	

Note: Significance level; * ($p \leq 0.01$); ** ($p \leq 0.05$); *** ($p \leq 0.10$); Dependent variable-Log NSDP

Stability Diagnostic Test

Stability Diagnostic Test was measured by applying CUSUM test, the results indicate that data set was stable. Thus, it indicates consistency in our results.

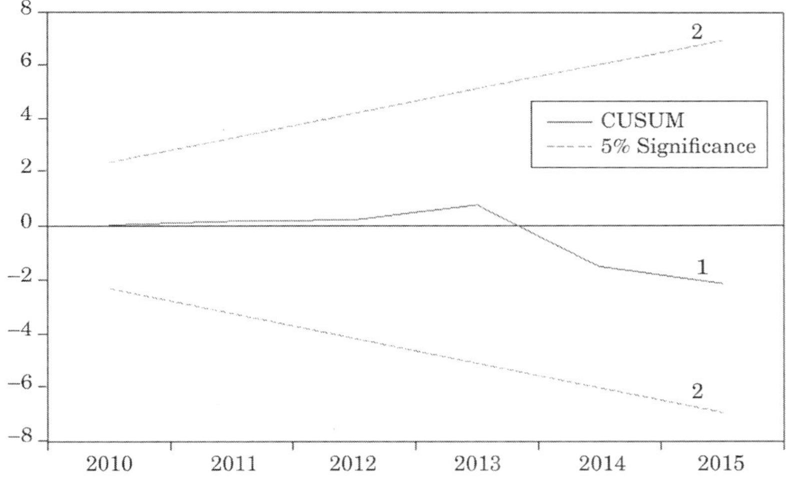

The analysis reveals that road length was found to affect the agricultural development significantly and negatively. Thus, the agricultural development and road length are inversely associated with each other. It is due to the fact that farmers that are far-away from the market face high costs of transportation to bring their produce to market and in such cases farmers prefer either to grow for household consumption or keep their lands uncultivated. The existence of road facility plays important role in encouraging agricultural development of any region and is pre-requisite for development of modern marketing system. Proper infrastructure especially road connectivity provides better opportunity to farmers to market their produce. Accesses to markets induce farmers to shift their cultivation of variety of crops which could yield higher income. Road investment in agriculture can increase intensity of land use and can prevent loss of crops between farm gate and consumers (World Bank, 1997). Moreover, it reduces rural poverty through productivity growth and also through increased non-agricultural employment opportunities and higher wages. Road facility has yet more importance in hilly areas where it helps in increasing accessibility to non-farm jobs (Baba *et al.,* 2010). Thus, it is obvious that once the farmers are connected through improved all-weather roads to markets, the higher agricultural production, lower inputs and transportation costs, improved cropping pattern and increased output prices are expected.

Irrigation facility is another most important technological component which has remarkable impact on agricultural output of any region. From the results, it is evident that access to irrigation influences significantly and positively agricultural output. This finding could be explained by the fact that access to irrigation helps the farmers to do cultivation in Rabi as well as in kharif season. It not only facilitates farming in Rabi season but also use high yielding crops and chemical fertilizers, which in turn increase the productivity of crops. Moreover, agriculture is a risky business in terms of production as well as market prices and thus inadequate irrigation facility may expose farmers to higher risks. Also efficient and effective water management through irrigation is essential for raising agricultural productivity levels and achieving food security. Irrigation has several potential pathways through which it can influence nutrition and health outcomes. (1) It may encourage crop diversification and the production of more diverse food for household consumption. (2) It may provide higher income through sale of cash crops. (3) It may improve water supply, sanitation and hygiene.

Finally, one of the important marketing functions is storage, which involves holding and preserving goods from the time they are produced until they are needed for consumption. It helps to protect the quality of perishable and semi-perishable products like fruits, vegetables etc from deterioration. It provides employment and income through price advantages. It is found from the results that the development of infrastructural variable like storage facility is positive determining factor leading to agricultural development.

The economic impact of improved infrastructure and agricultural development are: (a) increase in cropping intensity, (b) changes in cropping pattern, (c) increase in yield, (d) saving of wastage in marketing, (e) introduction of new activities. The effect of other variables *viz;* electrification and working capital found to be non-significant while analysing the impact of infrastructure on agriculture development in Jammu and Kashmir.

Breusch-Pagan-Godfrey test was used to check the heteroscedasticity in the data set and the results confirm that there was no such a problem in the data set. Hence our OLS results are consistent and free of bias.

Heteroskedasticity Test: Breusch-Pagan-Godfrey
Null hypothesis: Homoskedasticity

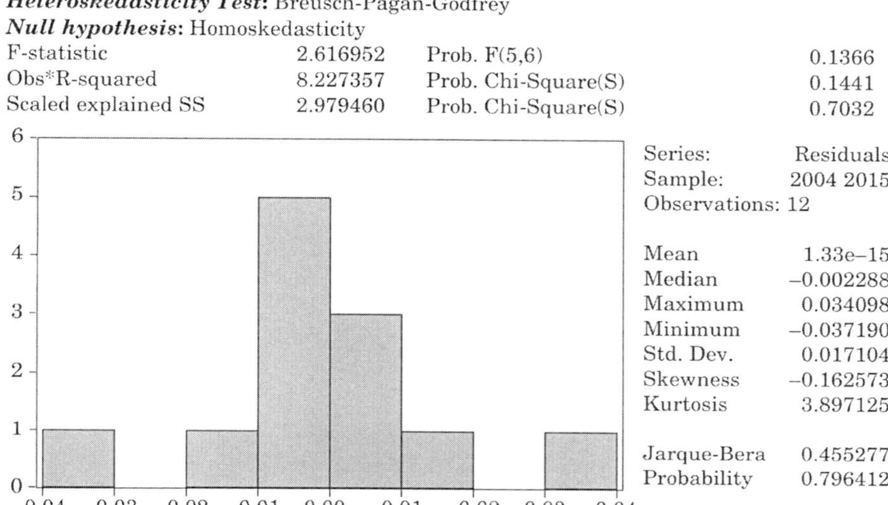

F-statistic	2.616952	Prob. F(5,6)	0.1366
Obs*R-squared	8.227357	Prob. Chi-Square(S)	0.1441
Scaled explained SS	2.979460	Prob. Chi-Square(S)	0.7032

CONCLUSIONS

Jammu and Kashmir economy is primarily an agriculture based economy. Agriculture is the vital source of income in the state, thus an attempt was made to investigate the influence of selected infrastructural variables on agricultural productivity in the state. From the forgoing analysis by using multiple regression model, the linkage between infrastructure and agriculture development has been analysed during the period 2004–2015. The analysis reveals that the infrastructural development play a noteworthy role in improving the agricultural productivity while as inadequate infrastructure can be big constraint to growth and productivity. The study suggests that for remarkable progress in agriculture field, there is need to increase irrigated area, availability of better roads, regulated markets and storage facilities which is possible only by improving the share of public investment on agriculture. Following policy suggestions emerge on the basis of findings:

- Jammu and Kashmir is facing severe problem due to lack of infrastructural facilities such as transportation and communication especially in hilly areas. The farmer's produce to the market normally account huge transportation cost for agricultural inputs and outputs. Thus, transport infrastructure will improve farmers' access to markets, thereby increasing their earnings and improving their livelihoods.
- Rural godowns should be established and promoted for storage of both grains as well as seeds. Storage facility is one of the constraints to agricultural development. High value crops are subject to residual production risk due to weather, disease and marketing to crops perishability.

- The irrigation facilities should be expanded in view of their crucial role in the improvement of agricultural development. Moreover, existing irrigation structures should be made functional by removing obstructions and through regular maintenance.

The failure investment in rural infrastructure would be critical bottleneck for future agriculture and as well as economic growth and poverty alleviation especially in rural areas. Government spending on production related aspects likewise irrigation, storage facility, roads etc. helps to increase the rural production, income and employment which will contribute to reduction in rural poverty and agriculture growth.

ANNEXURE

I. Irrigation Infrastructure

Table A: Net irrigated area from different source (000 hac.)

Year	*Canals*	*Tanks*	*Wells*	*Other sources*	*Total*
2003–04	282.41	3.87	1.06	19.19	306.53
2004–05	286.28	3.93	1.08	19.60	310.89
2005–06	289.28	4.21	1.05	17.57	312.11
2006–07	286.64	4.24	1.04	17.52	309.44
2007–08	285.78	4.22	0.99	17.05	308.04
2008–09	287.77	4.84	3..80	17.32	313.73
2009–10	287.80	5.11	4.33	20.03	317.27
2010–11	288.48	6.22	11.65	14.28	320.63
2011–12	285.40	7.11	7.42	19.33	319.63
2012–13	285.35	8.03	10.42	21.29	325.09
2013–14	288.59	7.71	8.95	18.02	323.27
2014–15	289.96	7.53	8.61	18.40	324.51
2015–16	320.41	7.26	8.84	19.48	355.99

Source: Digest of statistics, 2015–16, Directorate of Economics and Statistics, Government of Jammu and Kashmir.

II. Electricity Infrastructure

Table B: No. of villages electrified.

Year	*No. of villages*	*Year*	*No. of villages*
2003–04	13158	2004–05	13550
2005–06	13620	2006–07	13814
2007–08	13998	2008–09	14047
2009–10	15201	2010–11	17426
2011–12	17477	2012–13	17547
2013–14	17655	2014–15	17690
2015–16	17766		

Source: Digest of statistics, 2015–16, Directorate of Economics and Statistics, Government of Jammu and Kashmir.

III. Cooperation

Table C: Godowns/ Storage capacity.

Year	*No. of godowns*	*Storage capacity (MTs)*
2003–04	–	–
2004–05	687	63016
2005–06	930	37382
2006–07	961	39526
2007–08	711	73772
2008–09	709	109646
2009–10	597	66159
2010–11	727	157230
2011–12	710	77926
2012–13	723	84954
2013–14	691	67053
2014–15	683	65608
2015–16	651	57409

Source: Digest of statistics, 2015–16, Directorate of Economics and Statistics, Govt; of Jammu and Kashmir.

IV. NET STATE DOMESTIC PRODUCT

Table D: Net state domestic product.

Year	*NSDP*
2003–04	546706
2004–05	546232
2005–06	554363
2006–07	563038
2007–08	576175
2008–09	574435
2009–10	627323
2010–11	637926
2011–12	624799
2012–13	663854
2013–14	556124
2014–15	440556

***Source*:** Digest of statistics, 2015–16, Directorate of Economics and Statistics, Government of Jammu and Kashmir.

V. Road Length

Table E: Road length (Kms)

Year	*Surfaced road*	*Unsurfaced road*	*Total road*
2003–04	12745	2368	15113
2004–05	13423	2049	15472
2005–06	13885	1883	15768
2006–07	14183	1996	16179
2007–08	15560	2808	18368
2008–09	15868	3093	18961
2009–10	16838	3178	20016
2010–11	18788.1	3030.63	21818.73
2011–12	20699.5	2605.15	23304.65
2012–13	21545.22	2577.24	24122.46
2013–14	21591.52	4441.13	26032.65
2014–15	17118.97*	9824.69	26943.66
2015–16	17479.66	10012.67	27492.33

***Source*:** Digest of statistics, 2015–16, Directorate of Economics and Statistics, Government of Jammu and Kashmir; *Metalled road has been included under unsurfaced category from 2014–15

REFERENCES

Acharya, R. and Akhtar, R. (2018). An analysis on agriculture infrastructure and its impact on agricultural output in India. *International Journal of Research*, 5(1): 3342–3353.

Ahmed, R. and Donovan, C. (1992). *Issues of Infrastructural Development: A Synthesis of the Literature,* International Food Policy Research Institute, Washington, D.C., U.S.A.

Binswanger, H.P., Khandker, S.R. and Rosenzweig, M.R. (1993). How Infrastructure and Financial Institutions Affect Agricultural Output and Investment in India. *J. Dev. Econ.*, 41(2): 337–366.

Borbora Soundarya and Mahanta Ratul (2002). "An Analysis of inter-district disparity in agricultural development in Assam". *Indian Journal of Regional Science*, XXXIV(2): 28–36.

Dhawan, B.D. (1998). Irrigation in India's Agricultural Development: Productivity, Stability, Equity, New Delhi: Sage Publications India Pvt.

Fan, S., Hazell, P. and Thorat, S.K. (2000). "Government Spending, Growth and Poverty in Rural India". *American Journal of Agricultural Economics*, 82(4): 1038–1051.

Majumder, R. (2002). Infrastructure and Economic Development: A Regional Analysis, Unpublished PhD Thesis at Jawaharlal Nehru University, New Delhi.

Shah, T. (1993). Groundwater markets and irrigation development. Political Economy and Practical Policy, New Delhi: Oxford University Press.

Singh, K.M., Chaudhari, J.N. and Singh, R.K.P. (1993). "An analysis of compound growth rates and factors affecting area, production and productivity of gram in Bihar". *Agricultural Situation in India*, XLVII(11): 841–846.

Thorat, S.K. and Sirohi Smita (2002). Development of Rural Infrastructure in India: Trends and Emerging Issues, State of Indian Farmer: A Millennium Study. Ministry of Agriculture, Government of India, New Delhi.

Vaidyanathan, A. (1999). Water Resource Management: Institutions and Irrigation Development in India. New Delhi: Oxford University Press.

Van de Walle, D. (2002). Choosing Rural Road Investments to Help Reduce Poverty. *World Development*, 30(4): 575–589.

3

Structural Changes in the Food Processing Industry of India

Abid Sultan[1*]

ABSTRACT

The increasing economic development in India has increased employment avenues across the different states of India and has also increased women participation in the workforce. Further, the westernization of Indian societies and changing lifestyles of people has accelerated the growth of food processing industry in India. This has been further increased by the various government initiatives like National food processing Mission, Make in India campaign etc. Food processing industry is a promising industry of Indian manufacturing sector and offers multiple entrepreneurial opportunities across the different states of India. Keeping in view the potential and growth of this industry in India, the article describes the structural changes in the selected parameters of Indian food processing industry. The results of structural changes reflect the growth of the food processing industry in India. The selected parameters have positive percentage increase at both aggregate and disaggregate levels, except in employee's generation parameter. The study also makes a comparative assessment of growth in Indian manufacturing sector and food processing sector. The study can be beneficial to the policy makers and academicians in understanding the structural changes in the food processing industry during 2008–09 to 2015–16. It can also provide policy makers cues for drafting specific policies that can strength and accelerate the growth and development of food processing industry in India.

***Key words*:** Food processing industry, Structural change, India, Indian manufacturing sector.

---

[1] Department of Management Studies, University of Kashmir, Srinagar, Kashmir, J&K.

**Corresponding author:* E-mail: abidsultan2012@gmail.com

INDIAN MANUFACTURING SECTOR

Economic development of a nation is strongly influenced by the performance of its manufacturing sector. The significance of manufacturing sector is very crucial for the growth and development of both developing and developed economies. In developing economies like India, manufacturing sector has been the central focus of every economic reforms and policies. The economic reforms of 1991 in India aimed at improving the competing capabilities of the manufacturing firms of India along with increasing the living standards of its citizens. Reforms also favored increasing employment generation and reduce poverty levels in the country. Manufacturing sector of India has contributed to the socio-economic development in India.

Indian manufacturing sector has been a thrust area of every government policy right from the independence of India. It was strongly advocated for the rapid growth and development of the manufacturing sector in every five year plan of the government of India. Indian manufacturing sector have witnessed three growth phases *i.e.,* from 1950's to mid-1960's; mid 1960's to late 1970's and 1980's onwards (Thomas, 2008). Indian manufacturing sector witnessed huge reforms in 1991. Reforms of 1991 opened the gateways of Indian economy to the new era of manufacturing characterized by great thrust on competition; technology; quality etc. Indian manufacturing is diverse in its spread and operations. Indian manufacturing sector is broadly classified into registered and unregistered manufacturing. Registered manufacturing in India is diverse in its operation and database about registered manufacturing in India is maintained by the Central Statistical Organization (CSO) of India and is published on year wise basis in the form of annual survey of Industries (ASI).

During 2015–16, there have been around 233116 manufacturing factories in India. Indian Manufacturing sector has grown with CAGR of 5.21 percent between the period of 2008–09 to 2015–16. Total fixed capital invested in Indian manufacturing sector has increased from Rs. 105596614 in 2008–09 to Rs. 280964722 in 2015–16, with CAGR of 13.01 percent. The working capital structure of the Indian manufacturing sector reported CAGR of 9.61 percent. While as Gross Value Addition (GVA) and Income reported CAGR of 9.61 and 9.1 respectively. Employment generation in Indian manufacturing sector has grown with CAGR of 2.96. The performance of Indian manufacturing sector on the selected parameters is given the Table 1.

Indian manufacturing sector has grown significantly during the period 2008–09 to 2015–16. Structural changes in Indian manufacturing on the selected parameters are given in the Table 2. The fixed capital per factory in Indian manufacturing sector has been Rs. 679.9(lakhs) during 2008–09 which increased to Rs. 1205.3(lakhs). The working capital per factory has increased from Rs. 200.4(lakhs) to Rs. 317.7(lakhs) during 2008–09 to 2015–16. GVA per factory has increased from Rs. 393.6(lakhs) to Rs. 546.2(lakhs) from 2008–09 to 2015–16. Income generation per factory has increased from Rs. 289.3(lakhs) to Rs. 386.8(lakhs) from 2008–09 to 2015–16. Employment generation per factory has decreased from 72.9 to 61.3 during 2008–09 to 2015–16. All the selected indicators except employment reported positive increase during the study period 2008–09 to 2015–16 (refer to Table 2).

Table 1: Performance of Indian manufacturing sector on the selected parameters during 2008–09 and 2015–16.

Parameters	*2008–09*	*2015–16*	*CAGR*
Number of factories	155321	233116	5.21
Fixed capital	105596614	280964722	13.01
Working Capital	31123298	74052998	11.44
GVA	61131148	127327968	9.61
Income	44932732	90165276	9.1
Employees	11327485	14299710	2.96

Source: Annual Survey of Industries for the period 2008–09 and and 2015–16

Table 2: Per factory basis performance of Indian manufacturing sector on the selected parameters during 2008–09 and 2015–16.

Parameters	*2008–09*	*2015–16*	*Percentage increase/decrease*
Fixed capital	679.9	1205.3	77.27
Working capital	200.4	317.7	58.52
GVA	393.6	546.2	38.77
Income	289.3	386.8	33.7
Employees	72.9	61.3	–15.88

Source: Author's estimation based on the data of annual survey of Industries for the period 2008–09 and 2015–16

With 5.21 percent of CAGR, Indian manufacturing sector is on growth trajectory. Except employment parameter, all other studied parameters reported positive increase on per factory basis. Although the employment generation in Indian manufacturing has increased with CAGR of 2.96, however, on per factory basis it has reported a negative percentage decrease, which is a concern for the policy makers and researchers. Indian manufacturing sector is a huge and complex with manufacturing activities diverse. Food processing industry is a prospectus industry of Indian manufacturing with huge scope for growth and development. The present study aims at understanding Indian food processing industry, its key parameters and their structural change.

Indian Food Processing Industry

Indian food processing industry is a growing and promising industry of Indian manufacturing sector. It offers multiple economic opportunities ranging from primary processing to value processing. Indian food processing industry is defined through eight segments, as per NIC-2008, *i.e.,* Processing and preserving of meat (101), Processing and preserving of fish, crustaceans and molluscs (102), Processing and preserving of fruit and vegetables (103), Manufacture of vegetable and animal oils and fats (104), Manufacture of dairy products (105), Manufacture of grain mill products, starches and starch products (106), Manufacture of other food products (107) and Manufacture of prepared animal feeds (108). India holds a distinction of being second largest producer of food products in the world. Food processing sector offers huge prospects in food processing and related activities. In Indian context, food processing industry has huge value chain starting with farmers cultivating agriculture and horticulture crops, selling of the produce in the local markets and mandi's, from mandi's to the national corporation purchasing produce and using it for processing (Kumar, 2015).

During 2008–09, there were around 25856 manufacturing units in India, which increased to 37098. Indian FPI has grown with CAGR 4.62 during 2008–09 to 2015–16 (refer to Table 3).

Table 3: Performance of Indian food processing industry on selected Parameters during 2008–09 and 2015–16.

Parameters	*2008–09*	*2015–16*	*CAGR*
Number of factories	25856	37098	4.62
Fixed capital	6812392	17809486	12.76
Working capital	2282426	8199581	17.33
GVA	3706996	8585292	11.07
Income	2187280	5380513	11.91
Employees	1439620	1599818	1.33

Source: Author's estimation based on the data of Annual Survey of Industries for the period 2008–09 and 2015–16.

The share of Indian food processing industry in the Indian manufacturing sector is given in the Table 4. In 2008–09, the share of Indian food processing industry in the Indian manufacturing sector was around 16.64 percent which has decreased to 15.91 percent in the year 2015–16. The working capital share of FPI has increased from 7.33 percent to 11.07 percent during 2008–09 to 2015–16.

Table 4: Share of Indian food processing industry in Indian manufacturing sector on selected parameters during 2008–09 and 2015–16.

Parameters	*2008–09*	*2015–16*
Number of factories	16.64682	15.91397
Fixed capital	6.451336	6.338691
Working capital	7.333497	11.07258
GVA	6.064005	6.74266
Income	4.867899	5.967389
Employees	12.70909	11.18777

Source: Author's estimation based on the data of Annual Survey of Industries for the period 2008–09 and 2015–16.

Structural Changes in the Food Processing Industry of India

According to Haraguchi and Rezonja (2010), "the term 'structural change' most commonly refers to long-term changes in the composition of an aggregate....." The present study has selected six parameters for understanding the structural changes in Indian food processing industry during 2008–09 to 2015–16. The six parameters include fixed capital per factory, working capital per factory, GVA per factory, income per factory and employees per factory. The structural changes in these six parameters have been studied at two levels *i.e.,* aggregate level (food processing as a whole) and disaggregate levels (across eight segments of food processing industry of India). The results of aggregate and disaggregate levels are discussed below:

At Aggregate Level (Food Processing Industry as a Whole)

At aggregate levels the number of factories involved in food processing industry in India increased from 25856 in 2008–09 to 37098 2015–16. The fixed capital per factory increased from 263.47(lakhs) to 480.06 (lakhs), with a percentage increase of 82.21 percent. The working capital per factory reported an increase of 150.38 percent from 2008–09 to 2015–16. GVA per factory in Indian food processing industry enhanced from 143.37(lakhs) to 231.42(lakhs), an increase of around 61.4 percent. Income per factory also reported an increase of 71.44. However, employment per factory has decreased from 55.67 to 43.12, a decrease of 22.52 percent (refer to Table 5).

Table 5: Per factory basis performance of Indian food processing industry on the selected parameters during 2008–09 and 2015–16.

Parameters	*2008–09*	*2015–16*	*Percentage increase/decrease*
Fixed capital	263.4743193	480.0659335	82.21
Working capital	88.27452042	221.02488	150.38
GVA	143.370823	231.4219634	61.4
Income	84.59467822	145.0351232	71.44
Employees	55.67837252	43.12410373	(–) 22.52

Source: Author's estimation based on the data of Annual Survey of Industries for the period 2008–09 and 2015–16.

In comparison to the Indian manufacturing sector, food processing industry of India reported better performance on the studied parameters. Fixed capital per factory in Indian manufacturing sector increased with 77.27 percent during 2008–09 to 2015–16. While as in food processing industry fixed capital it increased with 82.21 percent during same period (refer to Table 6). Except employees per factory Indian food processing industry has a better performance on the studied parameters in comparison to Indian manufacturing sector.

Table 6: Comparison of per factory basis performance of Indian food processing industry and Indian manufacturing sector on the selected parameters during 2008–09 and 2015–16.

Parameters	*Percentage increase/decrease in Indian manufacturing sector*	*Percentage increase/decrease in Indian food processing industry*
Fixed capital	77.27	82.21
Working capital	58.52	150.38
GVA	38.77	61.4
Income	33.7	71.44
Employees	–15.88	(–) 22.52

Source: Author's estimation based on the data of annual survey of industries for the period 2008–09 and 2015–16.

At Disaggregate Level (Segment Wise) Fixed Capital per Factory

The fixed capital investment in the eight segments of Indian food processing industry increased from Rs. 6812392 (lakhs) to Rs. 17809486 (lakhs) during 2008–09 to 2015–16. It has grown with a CAGR of 12.76 percent. The fixed capital per factory in India has increased from Rs. 263.47 (lakhs) in 2008–09 to Rs. 480.06 (lakhs) in 2015–16. Segment-wise fixed capital per factory is given in Table 7. Among the eight segments, segment 108 reported highest percentage increase of 299.81 percent and 104 reported lowest percentage increase of 28.92 percent.

Table 7: Segment-wise fixed capital per factory of Indian food processing industry during 2008–09 and 2015–16.

Segments	*2008–09*	*2015–16*	*Percentage increase*
101	1133.056	1750.061	54.45
102	289.5824	784.2846	63.08
103	389.0804	576.4203	32.5
104	347.8827	448.496	28.92
105	498.06	1150.779	131.05
106	70.70189	138.3301	95.65
107	586.411	1005.499	71.47
108	163.4826	653.6133	299.81

Source: Author's estimation based on the data of Annual Survey of Industries for the period 2008–09 and 2015–16.

Working Capital per Factory

Segment-wise working capital per factory is given in Table 8. Among the eight segments, segment 103 reported highest percentage increase of 927.65 percent and 107 reported lowest percentage increase of (–) 44.78 percent.

GVA per Factory

Percentage increase of GVA per factory is reported highest by segment 103 followed by segment 108, and 102. While as lowest is reported by 104, a percentage increase of 8.86 percent (refer Table no 9).

Table 8: Segment-wise working capital per factory of Indian food processing industry during 2008–09 and 2015–16.

Segments	*2008–09*	*2015–16*	*Percentage increase/decrease*
101	618.8111111	2371.837838	283.29
102	116.8892045	480.8127341	311.34
103	101.6149506	1044.24245	927.65
104	152.7426925	493.9256435	223.37
105	135.47	344.5182707	154.31
106	45.84642755	151.5351572	230.53
107	133.8360955	73.9086656	(–)44.78
108	126.2157221	464.1623094	267.75

Source: Author's estimation based on the data of Annual Survey of Industries for the period 2008–09 and 2015–16.

Table 9: Segment-wise GVA per factory of Indian food processing industry during 2008–09 and 2015–16.

Segments	*2008–09*	*2015–16*	*Percentage increase*
101	942.0444	1364.236	44.81657
102	211.571	592.03	179.8256
103	94.60226	384.3221	306.2505
104	267.0655	290.7452	8.866626
105	375.8055	562.8348	49.7676
106	61.53032	70.03029	13.81428
107	224.5171	404.401	80.12033
108	141.3254	446.4107	215.8743

***Source*:** Author's estimation based on the data of Annual Survey of Industries for the period 2008-09 and 2015-16.

Income per Factory

Segment 103 reported highest percentage increase of Income per factory among the eight segments of food processing industry of India and lowest is reported by segment 106 a percentage decrease of (–)12.99 percent (refer to Table 10).

Table 10: Segment-wise income per factory of Indian food processing industry during 2008–09 and 2015–16.

Segments	*2008–09*	*2015–16*	*Percentage increase/decrease*
101	767.5333	1089.466	41.94383
102	105.0114	432.764	312.1116
103	17.1213	277.4773	1520.656
104	191.8596	213.8049	11.4382
105	289.7964	409.3109	41.24085
106	34.83163	30.30453	(–)12.99709
107	112.1645	243.3305	116.9407
108	104.4534	327.2353	213.2836

Source: Author's estimation based on the data of Annual Survey of Industries for the period 2008–09 and 2015–16.

Employees per Factory

Employees per factory has been observed highest in segment 102 followed by segment 101 and 108. Except these three segments, rest eight segment reported percentage decrease. Highest decrease of (–) 33.06 percent was reported by segment 106 and lowest decrease of (–) 9.29 percent by segment 105 (refer to Table 11).

Table 11: Segment-wise employees per factory of Indian food processing industry during 2008–09 and 2015–16.

Segments	*2008–09*	*2015–16*	*Percentage increase/decrease*
101	161.6222	194.8784	20.57648
102	93.9233	123.2678	31.24304
103	63.47109	50.9849	–19.6722
104	43.96871	30.38481	–30.8945
105	92.95	84.31034	–9.29495
106	24.67827	16.518	–33.0666
107	115.9789	85.35938	–26.4009
108	51.91042	59.80174	15.20181

Source: Author's estimation based on the data of Annual Survey of Industries for the period 2008–09 and 2015–16.

The analysis of selected parameters reveals the growth of food processing industry in India at both aggregate and disaggregates levels. Except, employees per factory parameter, all other reported positive percentage increase. All the stakeholders involved with food processing industry in need to collaborate and synchronize their efforts for the strategic growth and development of this industry in India. Indian states like Jammu and Kashmir, Himachal Pradesh etc. with their rich agriculture and horticulture resource bases offers immense potential towards accelerating the growth of this industry in India.

CONCLUSIONS

India is agriculture and horticulture based country that offers multiple economic opportunities through primary processing, value processing, grading etc. India with its diverse climatic and soil texture has rich resource base that can be leveraged upon. Indian rich agriculture and horticulture base offers advantageous inputs to the food processing industry and therefore, policymakers, academicians and entrepreneurs need to deliberate and discuss for the long term growth of this industry in India. The analysis of selected parameters reveals encouraging growth among the different parameters. The present study offers beneficial cues towards this direction and therefore can help in understanding the structural changes happening in this industry both at aggregate and disaggregate levels.

REFERENCES

Annual Survey of Industries 2008–09 to 2015–16, available at *http://www.csoisw.gov.in/cms/cms/Feedback.aspx*, accessed on 10th August, 2018.

Kumar, D. (2015). Economic Reforms and Productivity of Indian Manufacturing: A Study of Food Product Sector. *Abhinav National Monthly Refereed Journal of Research in Commerce & Management*, 4(1): 17–24.

Thomas, J.J. (2008). Financial sector reforms and manufacturing growth in India: A preliminary analysis. Presented at the Money and Finance Conference, Indira Gandhi Institute of Development Research, available at *http://www.igidr.ac.in/conf/money/mfc_10/Jayan%20Jose%20Thomas_submission_69.pdf,* accessed on 16th August, 2018

4

Assessing the Impact of Seasonal Migration on Rural Livelihood – A Critical Review on Bhalukhundi Village, Hirbandh Block, West Bengal

UDAY CHATTERJEE[1*]

ABSTRACT

Detention of work opportunities in a particular season, hostile circumstances for cultivation allied with least scope of irrigation, inaccessibility regarding various forms of employment, minimal wage rate and climatic extremities are played the role of push factors for migrating rural people towards new locations. Present study was undertaken to assess the status of seasonal migration and its socio-economic impacts on marginalized Schedule Tribe (ST) people of the Bhalukhundi Village of Hirbandh Block in Bankura District, West Bengal. Household survey by pre-formulated questionnaire, focus group discussion, key informant interviews and physical observation were employed in data collection. A total of 160 households were chosen for accumulation of socio-economic data in 2016. The paper magnifies the role of women participation in the process of seasonal migration and superficial impact on family welfare as well as socio-economic development of the marginalized tribal region.

Key words: Rural migration, Income sources, Marginalization, Impact, West Bengal.

[1] Department of Geography, Bhatter College, Dantan, Paschim Medinipur – 721426, West Bengal.

**Corresponding author:* E-mail: raj.chatterjee459@gmail.com

1. INTRODUCTION

The seasonal migration means when the nomads travel to the place of destinations during the period of transplantation and harvesting of the agricultural crop. In fact these migrants migrate to the place of terminus with the aim of accumulating resources, which they can spend in social functions and pay their debt to the local money lenders. In lean season (the period when job is not available in the place of origin of the migrants), people simply waste their time with various non-productive activities in their respective areas. In case of Bhalukhundi, many villagers migrate to the Bardhaman and Hooghly districts for various jobs related mainly to the agriculture and allied activities. Some districts of West Bengal are still considered as the poorest regions among India. The economy of West Bengal is predominantly agricultural and the performance in this sector is crucial to the development of the state. The prevalence of small farmers having small sized land holdings, seasonal unemployment, the non-application of modern technology in agriculture in West Bengal had forced the people to search for alternate sources of livelihood. People of the rural areas migrate to urban areas within and outside their districts and also to the neighbouring states. Some literatures have been reviewed in this regard which will surely be considered as very pertinent to apprehend the further study.

Fields (1975), Gugler and Flanagan (1978) and Kelly William (1984) highlighted the discrepancy access to information for rural workers and urban residents, the cost of living and education levels when computing the possibility of migrant securing an urban job.

Srivastava (1999) focussed on the circumstance that migration develops a better consciousness among the migrants concerning conditions of work at their ultimate destination. Furthermore, the migrants to transfer to urban areas achievement the knowledge the importance of the education for their children.

Rao's (2001) exertion on migration on labour in Andhra Pradesh discriminates between the migration for endurance and that for getting additional income. He perceived that people in Rayadurga district in Andhra Pradesh take the decision on migration for survival in 1970s but changed their attitude in 1990s. In the later their decision of migration was only because of earning additional wage.

Francis Thonippara (2005) discussed Malayali migration to Bangalore and their life styles in the city. According to him better employment and educational opportunities as well as health care facilities are the factors that attracted Malayalees in to the town. According to him Malayalees have a good base in this state; some of them have become political leaders and even some ministers also in this state.

Saikia (2011) has examined the economic conditions of the in-migrant workers in Kerala. Informal information networks through acquintances plays important role in 45 migration of workers to Kerala. Poor economic conditions along with several other overlapping factors have been identified as the reason of migration.

2. OBJECTIVES

Present study was undertaken to delineate the causes and consequences of seasonal migration among the village dweller of Bhalukkhund and to examine the socio-cultural and economic impacts of migration to the marginalized people of the said village. In this study, the role and perceptions of migrants regarding such periodic relocations and imply some policy recommendations have also been discussed.

3. BACKGROUND OF THE STUDY AREA

The study was carried out in the western part of West Bengal. However, specifically it was confined to the Bhalukhundi Village of Hirbandh Block in Bankura District of West Bengal (Fig. 1). Geographically the district of Bankura is located in between 22°42'35" North to 23°42'0" North latitude and 85°49'25" East to 86°54'37" East longitude. Much of the terrain is Undulating, so that the run-off is too rapid and naturally the soil moisture content is low across this region. The district is dominated mainly by Schedule Tribes.

Agriculture is mostly based on rain water and the prime crops are paddy, sesame, mustard, wheat, potato, oil seeds, pulses etc. Migration is rampant due to the unavailability of irrigation facilities and single crop agriculture. The forest was depleted and the villagers were not allowed to be depended on forest products. The people migrated in search of jobs for eight months and stayed back for four months. Meanwhile there was no good connectivity. Besides, the water level was very low since there was no scope for water harvesting. So the villagers had to be dependent on the monsoonal rainfall for the production of crops.

Malnutrition was very usual phenomenon. Due to seasonal migration the village dwellers did not take care of their common property resources. In summer, most of the villagers had to bring drinking water from 2 to 3 kilometers away from the perennial channels of rivers or nallahs. Total population of the study village is 186 (Table 1) where male population (39.78 percent) is less then female (43.54 percent) population.

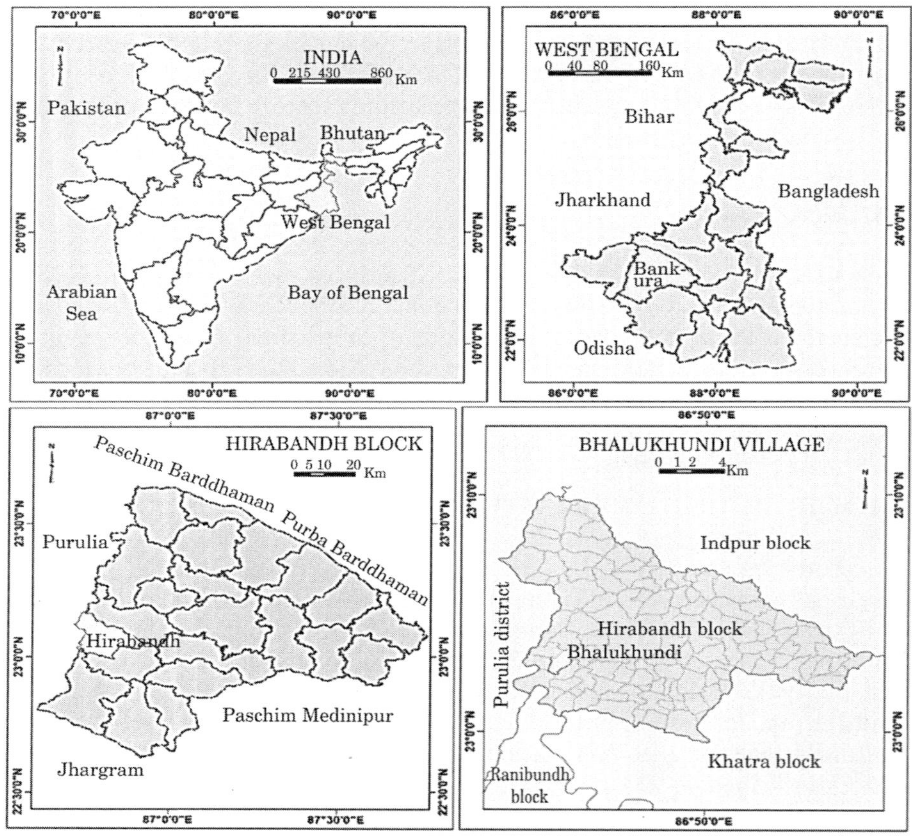

Fig. 1: Location map of the study of area. ***Source:*** Computed by authors

Table 1: Demographic profile of the study area.

Total Population	186
Males	74
Percentage of Males	39.78
Females	81
Percentage of Females	43.54
Children (Males)	17
Percentage of Children (Males)	9.13
Children (Females)	14
Percentage of Children (Females)	7.52

Source: BLRO Office of Hirabandh block, West Bengal.

4. RESEARCH DESIGN AND METHODOLOGY

The data were collected from 160 labour migrants in Bhalukhundi Village of Hirbandh Block in West Bengal. The information has been gathered randomly by taking face-to-face interviews and at times through telephonic conversations from the respondents of the aforesaid of the study area. The required information was obtained from the people on the basis of a pre-structured questionnaire during the field survey. The questions were arranged in such a fashion so that it was helpful to find out the answers of the basic objectives of the study. Secondary data was collected from Panchayat Office, Moshira, Block Development Office, Hirbandh, and Primary Health Centre (PHC), Simlabandh for the period between 2006 and 2016.

5. RESULTS AND DISCUSSION

Factors Influencing the Migration Pattern

The factors which push the villagers of Bhalukhundi to migrate in surrounding suburbans and cities are more or less found similar as general patterns that takes place across the country .The reduction of personalized dependencies or 17 interlocked relationships may also accelerate labour mobility and migration aslabourers seek out alternative sources of cash income (Srivastava 1987; Breman 1974 & 1985; Mosse *et al.,* 1997).

The causes of migration has been divided into five categories, such as, education, employment, amenities or landlessness, marriage and away from the parental residenecs. Our results shows that more than 55% migration is caused due to employment of the study village for the period between 2006 and 2016. The second highest migration in the village is caused due to marraige. However, the percent of migration due to amenities or landlessness is very less, almost negligible in the study village. As such, the frequency of the migration is increaing year after year in the study village (Table 2). As it happens most of the times that the investments are concentrated mainly within the cities from the perspectives of profit maximization which ultimately encourages the regional disparities. In a recent paper, Ghosh and Chakraborty (2010) has mentioned that migration from Bihar, Orissa and Uttar Pradesh to West Bengal played a key role in the history of interstate population movement in India during the 20th

Table 2: The key drivers of migration in Bhalukhudi village.

Year	2006	2012	2016
Total population	156	167	186
Causes of Migration			
Education (% of total population)	01 (0.64%)	–	01 (0.54%)
Employment (% of total population)	92 (58.97%)	103 (61.68%)	111 (59.68%)
Amenities or landlessness (% of total population)	–	–	01 (0.54%)
Marriage (% of total population)	3 (1.92%)	2 (1.20%)	06 (3.22%)
To stay and join with the relatives (% of total population)	1 (0.64%)	1 (0.60%)	02 (1.08%)
Total (% of total population)	97 (62.18%)	106 (63.47%)	121 (65.05%)

***Source*:** Local Panchayat and Primary Health Centre, Hirbandh block

century. The paper also reveals that the out migrating regions of Bihar, Orissa and Uttar Pradesh are almost same throughout the 20th century and the reasons for migration are primarily economic.

During the period of 2006 to 2016 the key causes for migration from the study area were in search of job opportunities and later the trend was gradually increased to assess higher wages for economic stability. Most of the people from the working age group of 25–44 years *i.e.*, 76 person migrated (Table 3 and Fig. 2) from the study area because of less work chances, political instability, to obtain better livelihood and to betterment of the futures of their children (Fig. 2).

Table 3: Classification of causes for migration in different age groups.

Age groups	*Causes of migration*					
	Education	*Employment*	*Amenities*	*Marriage*	*To stay and join with the relatives*	*Total*
10–14	1	18	1	0	2	22
15–19	0	4	0	6	0	10
20–24	0	5	0	0	0	5
25–29	0	18	0	0	0	18
30–34	0	23	0	0	0	23
35–39	0	18	0	0	0	18
40–44	0	17	0	0	0	17
45–49	0	5	0	0	0	5
Above 50	0	3	0	0	0	3

Source: Field investigation by author

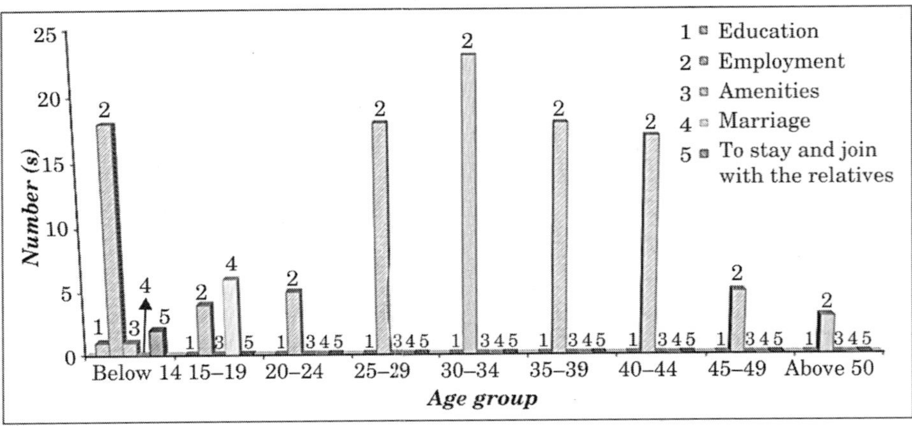

Fig. 2: Classification of causes for migration in different age groups. *Source:* Field investigation by author

6. IMPACT OF MIGRATION IN THE STUDY AREA

The impact of migration on the migrated families has been found very precarious. To some extent it seems better for them but on the other hand it's associated with irregular remittance; it tends to enhance the physical, financial and emotional burdens on the migrated.

Persons irrespective of genders. Migration trends (Table 4) from 2012 to 2016 in the study area reflects that the distress of migrated people in the area of origin (Fig. 3).

Table 4: Temporal variations of migration rate from Bhalukhundi.

Total population (2012)	*No. of migrators (%)*	*Total population (2014)*	*No. of migrators (%)*	*Total population (2016)*	*No. of migrators (%)*
156	97 (62.18%)	167	105 (62.87 %)	186	120 (64.52%)

Source: Local Panchayat and Primary Health Centre.

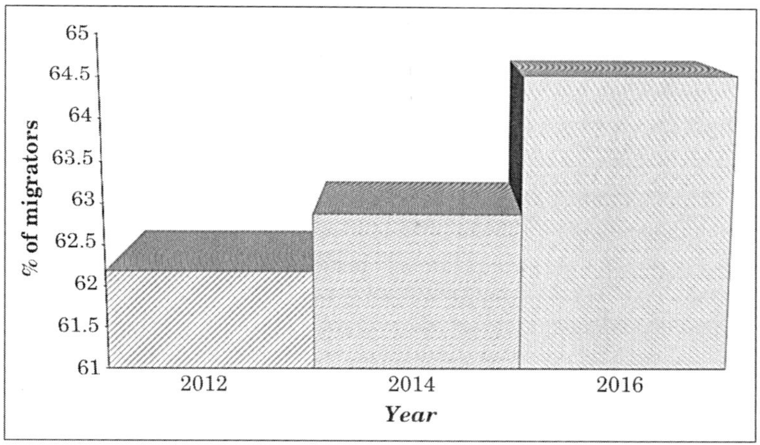

Fig. 3: Temporal variations of migration rate from Bhalukkhundi.

Table 5: Gender wise distribution of migrators.

Gender wise distribution	*No. of migrators*	*Percentage of migrators*
Male	52	42.98
Female	69	57.02

Source: Field investigation, 2016 by author

The Table 5 reflects that female trend of migration is greater (57.02 percent) than male (42.98 percent). Woman plays a dominant role to maintain her family. This areas migration trends reflect the self-esteem and empowerment of women headed household.

6.1. Economic Impact

In the absence of the female members in the family, the males suffer economically in the women headed households. The advance money given to the migrant households is utilized to repay the loans, debts and a very small amount is given to the husband. It is the responsibility of the woman to maintain the family. There is no monthly remittance from the husbands and the women heading the households who stay back have to struggle for fooding, clothing, and education, etc.

6.1.1. *Impact of migration on different age groups*

The impact of migration on children either of migrant families or of women headed households is a matter of great concern. Basic human rights of children such as nutrition, health and education have been violated repeatedly overtimes. Deprived of their childhood and education, the children of the migrating parents are in the same path as that of their parents. Child labour is found extensively in the brick kilns such as in Indpur, Khatra, Simlapal, Burdwan, Hoogly etc. The children who accompany their parents to the brick kilns are engaged in the work along with the family members. The children those who are dropped out from the schools indicating the adverse impact of migration on those families. Those children who migrate with their parents, discontinue their schooling for 6 months and after returning home, they continue in the same class. It is found that the children are continuing for three to four years in the same class. The impact of migration on old women is also an inordinate stuff of worry. Elderly women from migrating families most of the times are left behind in the native village. And as a result they have to encounter many challenges both socially as well as economically. The old and the infirm are not in a position to take care of themselves and without the support of their near and dear ones; their survival itself faces a tremendous hurdle. The children of the migrants are affected socially and emotionally. Overall there are two major scenarios which have emerged in case of migration. In one situation, the children migrate with their parents. In such a situation when their mothers work in the agricultural activity like paddy cultivation in Burdwan District, brick factories and other allied activities they stay in the temporary home near the workplace. There is nobody to look after them and they wander here and there. The small babies are kept in the custody of the elder children. Even the mothers are afraid to feed their small babies by stopping work. Both the mothers and the small children are physically and emotionally exploited. The children in the migrated locations are not in a position to continue their education.

6.1.2. *Family expenses*

To meet the family expenses, the women do go for wage work but it is not available after the cultivation period. Whatever work is available, it is predominantly done by the male members of the villages. The wages for the work is very low (Rs 185/- to Rs 200/-). Due to arid weather conditions, drought and lack of water facilities, kitchen garden, and livestock rearing or any other home based activity is rarely undertaken. Infact the women sell the goats, hens and utensils to meet the urgent needs of the family. For the women who migrate, income generation is possible in the short run but it does not lead to economic independence or an improvement on the status of migrant women. They have no control over their own income. As family income is taken into calculation, individual income doesn't have any relevance. There is heavy workload at workplace and the work environment is stressed, living condition is not up to the mark. They also need to perform the domestic activities, childcare and health care after working.

Table 6: Monthly income comparison between pre and post migration period.

Monthly income (Rupees)	*Number of families involved*	
	Pre-migration phase	***Post-migration phase***
Below 1000	43	5
1000–3000	39	4
3000–5000	30	10
5000–7000	9	74
7000 and above	0	28

Source: Local Panchayet and Primary Health Centre, Hirbandh block.

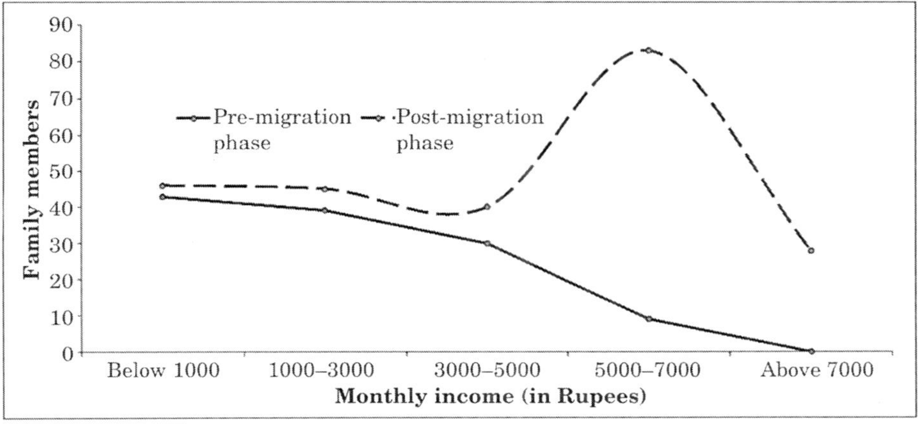

Fig. 4: Monthly income comparison between pre and post migration period. ***Source***: Local Panchayet and Primary Health Centre, Hirbandh block.

The Table 6 derives the fact that before migration income of the majority of people in the study area within 3000 rupees and after migration from the origin to destination this income level increases to 5000 to 70000 per month (Fig. 4). The below table (Table 7) shows that migratory family member expend more money after their migration for their family welfare.

Table 7: Monthly expenditure of the family members of the Bhalukhundi village.

Monthly income of rupees	*Before migration*	*After migration*
Below 1000	43	3
1000–3000	39	6
3000–5000	30	10
5000–7000	9	74
Above 7000	–	28

Source: Local Panchayet and Primary Health Centre, Hirbandh block.

Table 8: Monthly family savings of the migrants.

Monthly savings (Rupees)	*Number of families involved*	
	Pre-migration phase	*Post-migration phase*
Below 1000	61	49
1000–3000	36	23
3000–5000	14	31
5000 above	8	14

Source: Local Panchayet and Primary Health Centre.

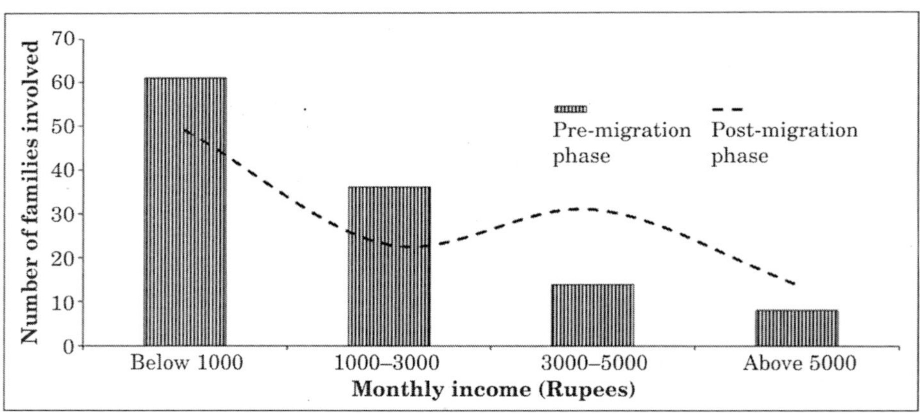

Fig. 5: Monthly family savings of the migrants. ***Source***: Local Panchayet and Primary Health Centre, Hirbandh block.

Table 8 and Fig. 5 explore the monthly family savings before and after migration from the study area, as per their income increases after migration they savings more money for their better livelihood in future. More than 30 family save at least 5000 thousand per month.

6.2. Social Impact

In absence of male members in the women headed households, the women are alienated and feel a loss of identity. As their husbands are away, nobody gives them any importance. For example, they are ignored while getting BPL rice or other items on time, below table (Table 9) shows their better housing condition, satisfied income level and better standard of living.

Table 9: Changes in socio-economic variables during pre and post migration period.

Socio-economic parameters	*Extent of changes*	
	Pre-migration phase	*Post-migration phase*
Housing condition	2	3
Sanitary condition	2	3
Health improvement	3	2
Income level	2	4
Standard of living	2	4
Change in house assets	2	3
Child education	3	2

Source: Local Panchayet and Primary Health Centre, Hirbandh block.

Given score depicts that's the qualitative changes of socio-economic variables 1 = very poor, 2 = poor, 3 = average, 4 = high, 5 = very high

6.2.1. *Dependency on others*

During the period of non-appearance of male members, the women and elderly persons are almost forced to depend on others in every aspects of their life. In case of purchasing basic goods, in taking care of their health, education of children, they need the help of their neighbours. But it shouldn't expect that the others will always be ready to facilitate them whenever they require. Frequent dependency on others has created depraved social relations among the households. So the women are always alert about these issues and always try to do the work by themselves.

6.2.2. *Health status*

Continuous work in the sun and insufficient food, the women migrants often become ill. The employer provides medicine to them, but does not give them any time for taking rest. On the other hand, constant work without taking any rest during sickness leads to further ill-health and suppression. The pregnant women and the small babies of such workers suffer much at the migration places. They are destitute of immunization, and other facilities. Hard work during pregnancy make the women migrants very prone to complications or even still births. ICDS (Integrated Child Development

Services) facilities are not transferable and there by the Migrant women cannot avail any benefits. Migration is a matter of survival and has Tran's generational presence. Young women who had migrated in their youth are left behind today when old, as their children migrate. There is no social net for the old. Widows are especially vulnerable. They facing food insecurity, burdened with old age and its health problems.

7. POLICY RECOMMENDATIONS

To eliminate the distress of migration in the study area some policy recommendation should be implied, these are as follows-

i. A long-term and comprehensive political will at national level is very much required to tackle the problem of distress migration and to ensure the sustainable livelihood at the place of origin of migration.
ii. Supplementary sources of income for women should be enhanced and strengthened. Policy at national and state level is required for the prevention of distress migration and a law specific to migration with focus on women taking into consideration the emerging issues such as Women headed Households.
iii. To prevent migration in Bhalukhundi village Sustained availability of work at the grass root level, conservation of forest resources, restoration of traditional water supply system should be taken up to increase the productivity. Irrigation facilities should be provided so that the production of two crops can be done.
iv. Distress paddy selling should be avoided by giving correct price.
v. Employment opportunities should be created at village level to check migration.
vi. Women Self Help Groups (SHGs) should be encouraged so that women are able to earn a sustainable amount of the year from the SHG activities.

8. CONCLUDING REMARKS

The present study it was observed that the influence of 'push' and 'pull' factors on the migrants was determined by the socio-economic conditions of the household of origin. Better employment and higher wages as the crucial variables in attracting rural people to the place of destination. Migration brought out significant changes in the economic status of the migrants in terms of higher income and savings. Migration is not a positive sign for economic development of the any region. Government need to generate work opportunity and provide them MGNREGS (Mahatma Gandhi National Rural Employment Guarantee Scheme) schemes related works like digging pond, integrate the fishing activities on the community basis to provide agricultural activities and strong livelihood security to the landless people in their respective villages so that they don't migrate. They need to provide childcare and better educational facilities for the children who migrate along. So that they can cope with mingle with the mean stream. If government of West Bengal recommended some policy to transform the rural areas holistically such as Bhalukhundi village, by making available socioeconomic and infrastructural amenities, health services, sanitation, good housing condition, electricity, small and medium scale industries trough National Policy Frameworks this would assistance their better livelihood.

REFERENCES / SUGGESTED READINGS

Hugo Graeme (1993). 'Migration and Rural-Urban Linkages in the ESCAP Region 'Migration and Urbanisation in Asia and the Pacific: Inter relationships with Socio-economic Development and Evolving Policy Issues, United Nations, New York.

Iyer K. Gopal (*ed.*) (2003). Migrant Labour and Human Rights in India, Kanishka Exploitation". *Economic and Political Weekly*, India.

Kabeer, N. (2000). 'The Power to Choose, Bangladeshi Women and Labour Market Decisions in London and Dhaka 'Verso Press, London and New York.

Khan, Shahzad A. (2001). CDS, University of Swansea, Wales; Paper Presented at the Conference Livelihoods and Poverty Reduction: Lessons from Eastern India.

Kumari Hema, T.A. and Tataji, U. (1996). Migrant Labour: The Gender Dimension - A Study of Women Migrant Workers in Coastal AP, CWDS, New Delhi, India.

Migration in Development Policies, Social Development Report, Hans Asha, Amrita (2000).

Patel and Das Minakshi (2003). Violence against Women in Orissa, School of Women's Studies, Utkal University, Bhubaneswar.

5

Economic Profile of Short-Term Migrant Labourers: A study of Hyderabad-Karnataka Region

MAHAMMAD HABEEB[1*]

ABSTRACT

Short-term migration is a transfer of an economic activity but not the usual residence. There are number of studies in the field of migration in India as well as abroad. Majority of the studies conducted are confined to either macro level or based on secondary source of data. But the problem with secondary source of data is, it does not cover the short term movements like circular and seasonal out migration. In the present context of unavailability of secondary source of information on short-term movements like seasonal and circular migration the micro level investigation like this is very useful. Macro level studies may help us to understand the trend, reason and pattern of short-term migration but it will not help us to understand the real issues at the grassroots. Present study has been conducted in a second largest arid regions of the country i.e., Hyderabad-Karnataka region of Karnataka state. It has focused on the background of the short-term migrants with special reference to economic capabilities. The present study tried to analyse short-term migration as a livelihood mechanism of the rural labourers in the lean season of agriculture with the intention to provide significant inputs to policy makers engaged in the design and execution of labour or employment policies.

Key words: Short-term migration, Labour: Hyderabad-Karnataka region.

[1] Department of Economics, Raichur, University (Proposed), Raichur, Karnataka.
**Corresponding author:* E-mail: mahammadhabeeb@gmail.com

1. INTRODUCTION

It has been perceived for some time by migration experts that internal short-term population movements ranging from every day commuting to seasonal migration have become common all over Asia. India is one such nation where internal migration is more vital than cross border (international) movements as far as the number of individuals involved and possibly even the volume of remittances (Deshingkar, 2009). Internal migration is essential and unavoidable segment of the economic and social existence of the nation, given regional imbalances and labour deficiencies, and safe migration ought to be promoted to boost its benefits (UNESCO, 2012). It assumes an essential part in enhancing the economic and social status of the population (Devi, 2012).

In fact, migrants are inadequately endowed all-round: they belong to poor families where access to physical, financial and human capital is restricted and where prospects for enhancing living standards are compelled by their substandard social and political status (Srivastava, 2003). Migration in India is basically of two sorts: long term migration and short term migration. Long term migration brings about the relocation of an individual or family and short term includes forward and backward movement between a source area and destination (UNESCO, 2012). Internal migration in India constitutes a large population of 309 million or 30 percent of the total population (Census of India, 2001) and by more recent estimates 326 million or 28.5 percent of total population (NSSO, 2007–2008). Within internal migration, short term migration constitutes nearly 12.24 million and 15.2 million people out of total population as per NSSO 55th and 64th Round respectively. According to the National Commission on Rural Labour (NCRL, 1991; cited in Korra, 2010) the number of circular migrants in rural areas alone accounted around 10 million (including roughly 4.5 million inter-State migrants and 6 million intra-State migrants). It also stated that the dominant part of seasonal migrants are employed in farming and plantations, brick-kilns, quarries, construction industry and fish processing units. Further, large numbers of seasonal migrants work in urban unorganised sector, construction, services or transport industry, employed as casual labourers, head-loaders, rickshaw pullers and hawkers (cited by: Deshingkar & Start, 2003).

In order to study the economic profile of the short-term migrant labourers of Hyderabad-Karnataka region the information has been collected on various aspects and discussed below in detail. This research article is based on the primary data collected from the study area. The detailed information on demographic characteristics, household assets, income, expenditure and savings of short-term migrant labourers' households has been presented.

2. OBJECTIVES OF THE STUDY

The present study has following broad objectives.

1. To examine the economic background of short-term migrants.
2. To propose suitable remedial measures for solving the problems faced by short-term migrants.

3. METHODOLOGY

The methodological section envelops a brief discussion of the study area, sample design, nature and sources of data and analytical framework employed in the present study, for addressing the set of objectives.

3.1. Study Area

The present study has been undertaken in two Taluks of H-K Region of Karnataka state for an in-depth analysis. The selection of the H-K Region and Taluks was purposive for following reasons.

The H-K Region has suitable background for the study due to its backwardness in terms growth and development, this region comprises maximum number of most backward and backward taluks of the state. The labour migration from H-K Region is common. The semi-skilled and most of unskilled labourers are migrating from the Region. Devadurga taluk of Raichur district and Jewargi taluk of Kalburagi district are the two taluks where household survey was conducted. These two taluks were selected based on the rankings allotted by Dr. D.M. Nanjundappa's Committee Report. As per the Report out of 175 taluks, Jewargi stands 174th rank and Devadurga stands 175th rank. These two taluks are most backward taluks not only in H-K Region but also in the State.

Against this background, H-K Region has become an ideal choice for conducting the present study on economic profile of short-term migrant labourers.

3.2. Sources and Collection of Data

The present study is based on primary sources of data. Primary data have been collected from two Taluks of H-K Region *i.e.,* Devadurga and Jewargi. The selection of villages in both the Taluks have been made based on the information collected from key informants (Village Accountants, Grama Panchayat Members, PDO's, Journalists, Civil Society Organisations and Local people of the respective taluks). Six villages from each Taluk were selected based on the same criteria used for selection of villages. While selecting the villages due attention has been given to villages which are located in dry land areas of the Taluk. The selection of villages is also guided by the distance criteria. Out of six villages selected from each Taluk, three villages are located within a distance of 10 KM from the Taluk headquarters, whereas remaining three villages are located between the distances of 10 to 20 KM of the taluk headquarter.

3.3. Sampling

Hence the size of the population of the study is unknown, total 200 households were selected for the survey, 100 from each Taluk. Number of households from each village for household survey is selected based on the information collected from key informants of the respective villages. Purposive Sampling Approach has been adopted for the selection of sample of migrants' households.

3.4. Time Period

The survey was conducted in the month of October, 2016. The researcher purposively conducted the survey in the peak season of agriculture so that migrant labourers could be available easily.

3.5. Data Analysis and Interpretation

The data collected during the time of enquiry has been scrutinized and tabulated. To fulfill the specific objectives of the study based on nature and extent of availability of data the basic statistical tools like percentage and averages have been used.

4. HOUSEHOLD PARTICULARS

The household particulars of sample households are presented below in detail.

4.1. Demographic Characteristics of Sample Households

Involvement in the process of short-term migration by labourers of rural areas is largely influenced by demographic, social and economic factors of the households. Size and occupational diversification of the household tends to influence the decision to migrate for a short term in search of employment opportunity. The greater the size of households, greater is the chance of migrating for a short period of time from rural areas especially of dry zone/ arid regions.

4.1(a) *Family structure*

Details on family structure of the sample households are presented in Table 1. Types of family in India are viewed as; Nuclear and Joint. Nuclear family is composed of a man, his wife and his unmarried children whereas joint family is said to be a composition of two or more than two nuclear families living under the same shelter by using a same kitchen and a common purse. It is seen from the figures presented in the Table 1 that nuclear type of family is dominant among sample households and across the social category. Type of family plays an important role in decision making in every aspect of life. Joint families are characterized by diversification in occupation whereas it is not same in case of nuclear families. In joint families capacity to divert economic risks during recession of family is more than nuclear families. Larger the household size, the lower will be the probability of migration (Gurung & Yogendra, 2012). So, in this respect there are two kinds of links between migration and type of family or especially joint family. First one, if a family is joint it can avoid its members from migrating for a short period or distress kind of migration because the chances of smooth consumption are more in joint families due to income from diversified occupations, assets etc. The second one is joint family is advantageous for migration since there are other members to look out the left behind's, there would be less obstacles for migration especially related to left behinds.

Table 1: Distribution of households by social category and family type (in percentage).

Social category	***Migrants HH***		
	Nuclear	***Joint***	***Total***
SC	69.05	30.95	100 (84)
ST	61.54	38.46	100 (52)
OBC	79.55	20.45	100 (44)
Minority	85.71	14.29	100 (14)
Others	50.00	50.00	100 (6)
Total	70.00	30.00	100 (200)

Source: Field study. *Note*: Figures in the parentheses are actual number of households.

4.1(b) *Population and sample households*

Table 2 presents the details of sample households by social category. The total number of households selected is 200. Across the social groups it has been observed that households belong to SC's are dominant among sample households. As Dwivedi (2012), found that labourers from vulnerable and marginalised class of the society are more migratory in nature. In this connection figures in the Table 2 clearly shows that people from oppressed, vulnerable and marginalised classes are more prone to migrate for short-period of time.

Table 2: Distribution of sample households by social category (in percentage).

Social category	Migrant HH
SC	42.00 (84)
ST	26.00 (52)
OBC	22.00 (44)
Minority	07.00 (14)
Others	03.00 (6)
Total	100 (200)

Source: Field study. *Note*: Figures in the parentheses are actual number of households.

The data presented in the Table 3 indicate that total percentage of male population is greater than female population not only among migrants' households but also across different social categories. As it is observed during the field survey, rural economy is more favourable for female labourers, where female labourers get more number of days of employment than male labourers. This is because most of the activities in the agriculture field can be done by both male and female labourers. There are fewer activities reserved only for men. The reason behind female labourers getting more number of days of employment compared to male labourers is the low wage rates. Figures in this Table 3 also support the assumption that more number of male labourers involved in short duration migration for employment purpose.

Table 3: Distribution of total household population by social category (in percentage).

Social category	Migrant HH		
	Male	Female	Total
SC	51.9	48.1	100 (616)
ST	53.4	46.6	100 (382)
OBC	52.6	47.4	100 (302)
Minority	61.8	38.2	100 (89)
Others	50.0	50.0	100 (46)
Total	53.0	47.0	100 (1435)

Source: Field study. *Note*: Figures in the parentheses are actual number of households.

4.1(c) *Age composition of the household members*

The data provided in the table 4 indicate that the share of the population in the age group of 15–24 and 25–34 years is estimated to be larger compared to other age groups of sample households of migrants. It is seen from the Table 4 that population less than 14 years and above 65 years has accounted less. Directly or indirectly these estimates supported the notion that the working age population is in highest number in India.

Table 4: Gender and age-group wise distribution of household population (in percentage).

Age group of HH population	*Migrant HH*		
	Male	*Female*	*Total*
0–6	15.11	13.65	14.43
7–14	13.27	14.39	13.80
15–24	19.97	20.62	20.28
25–34	22.47	20.62	21.60
35–44	9.46	10.39	9.90
45–54	7.23	8.61	7.87
55–64	8.15	7.42	7.80
65 & Above	4.34	4.30	4.32
Total	100 (761)	100 (674)	100 (1435)

Source: Field study. *Note:* Figures in the parentheses are actual number of population.

4.1(d) *Marital status*

Marriage is a socially recognized union of male and female. It is difficult to live without marrying in a country like India where marriage is a must in practice and without marriage life is incomplete. The proportion of married population helps us to understand the dependency ratio of the family. The dependency level increases with an increase in the number of married population in the household especially in Indian context. If dependency ratio increases then there will be a more economic pressure on bread winner of the family. In these situations if they do not get employment at their place of origin due to single cropping system and distress situations or lean agricultural periods, households automatically adopts migration as a livelihood strategy.

Table 5: Distribution of household population by social category and marital status (in percentage).

Social category of HH population	*Migrants' HH*			
	Married	*Unmarried*	*Widow*	*Total*
SC	51.0	45.0	4.1	100 (616)
ST	49.0	46.3	4.7	100 (382)
OBC	52.0	44.4	3.6	100 (302)
Minority	41.6	53.9	4.5	100 (89)
Others	45.7	47.8	6.5	100 (46)
Total	49.9	45.9	4.3	100 (1435)

Source: Field study. Note: Figures in the parentheses are actual number of population.

Details on marital status of household population is presented in Table 5. It is observed that large portion of population is married among sample households. Married population across the different social categories is found to be more among OBC's and unmarried population is more among minorities.

4.1(e) *Educational background*

Educational background of the members of the sample households' is presented below in detail.

Literacy rate of population by gender is depicted in Figure 1. Rate of percentage and Gender is presented on vertical and horizontal axis respectively. An effort has been made to estimate the literacy level of sample population of 6 and 6+ years by gender and social category. The data presented in the Fig. 1 reveals that the rate of literacy among males is more compared with female population among sample households.

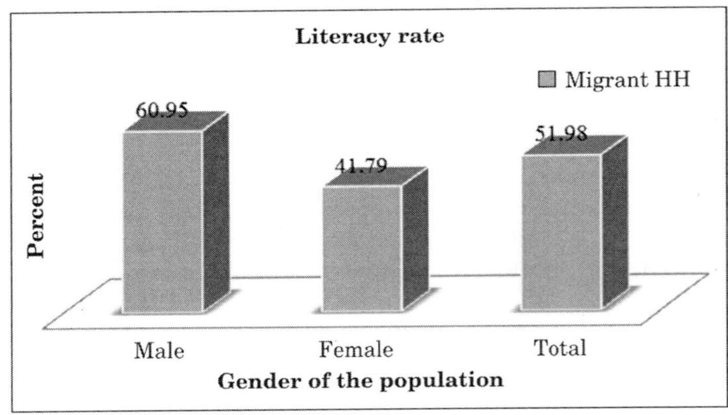

Fig. 1: Distribution of household population by literacy rate (in percentage). ***Source*:** Field study.

4.1(f) *Occupational structure*

Main occupation by social category

Occupational structure of the rural household is generally classified into following broad categories: Casual Wage Employment in Agriculture, Cultivator/Farm Activities, and Casual Wage Employment in Non-Agriculture, Non-Agriculture Self Employment, and Regular salaried /Wage employment (Biradar, 2014).

The data provided in the Table 6 indicate that majority of the migrants' household labourers belong to different social categories are casual labourers in agriculture. It is found that among casual wage employment in agriculture SC's are in majority followed by ST's. Studies by Dwivedi, R. (2012) and Deshingkar, P. (2010) found that people from marginalized groups and poor background are more likely to migrate in search of employment because people from these groups are highly dependent on farm activities because neither they have land nor alternate source to lead their life in the absence of farming activity.

Table 6: Distribution of household population by social category and main occupation (in percentage).

Main occupation of the HH member	***Migrants***					
	SC	***ST***	***OBC***	***Minority***	***Others***	***Total***
Casual wage employment in agriculture	73.49	66.96	62.50	61.70	60.00	68.51
Cultivator/farm activities	21.26	25.55	30.36	31.91	28.00	25.00
Casual wage employment in non-agriculture	3.41	5.73	4.17	4.26	4.00	4.25
Non-agriculture self employment	1.05	1.32	1.79	2.13	8.00	1.53
Regular salaried/wage employment	0.79	0.44	1.19	0.00	0.00	0.71
Total	100 (381)	100 (227)	100 (168)	100 (47)	100 (25)	100 (848)

Source: Field study. *Note:* Figures in the parentheses are actual number of households.

4.2(a) *Household Conditions*

It is important from the point of the view of the present study to focus on short-term migrants households' basic conditions like, status of poverty, housing condition, electricity, drinking water, sanitation etc, all these details are presented in Table 7. It is observed that majority of the sample migrants households are economically poor. With regard to housing conditions of the sample migrants households it is found that more than 50 percent of houses are Kacha. One of the most important basic facilities of a household electricity is accessible to majority of the households under Bhagyajyothi Scheme under which a household is allowed to use one bulb at free of cost. This scheme is for the people belong to economically poor section. Another basic need of a day to day life *i.e.,* drinking water is supplied through public tap followed by bore-well or hand pump.

Though few years ago the maximum importance has been given to cleanliness first time since independence, 99 percent of migrant's households have no toilet facility in their house premises. It shows the poor condition of the rural sanitation facility. Rural areas not only need sanitation facility but also the awareness against open defecation. Recent programmes like

'Swachh Bharat' mission should reach to rural masses as it is reached to urban masses in some extent and created awareness. Based on these conditions one can easily draw the conclusion that most of the rural labourers involved in short term migration are having poor household conditions.

Table 7: Distribution of households by household conditions and social category (in %).

Particulars	***Social category***					
	SC	***ST***	***OBC***	***Minority***	***Others***	***Total***
(1) Housing condition						
Katcha	59.52	53.85	38.64	71.43	33.33	53.50
Pucca	40.48	46.15	61.36	28.57	66.67	46.50
Total	100 (84)	100 (52)	100 (44)	100 (14)	100 (6)	100 (200)
(2) Electricity condition						
No electricity	11.90	7.69	4.55	0.00	0.00	8.00
Electrified (own)	10.71	23.08	38.64	14.29	50.00	21.50
Bhagyajyoti scheme	77.38	69.23	56.82	85.71	50.00	70.50
Total	100 (84)	100 (52)	100 (44)	100 (14)	100 (6)	100 (200)
(3) Drinking water						
Public tap	26.19	69.23	47.73	28.57	16.67	42.00
Private tap	10.71	19.23	15.91	0.00	16.67	13.50
Open well/ tank	15.48	9.62	18.18	28.57	50.00	16.50
Bore well /hand pump	47.62	1.92	18.18	42.86	16.67	28.00
Total	100 (84)	100 (52)	100 (44)	100 (14)	100 (6)	100 (200)
(4) Sanitation						
Open defection	100.00	100.00	97.73	100.00	100.00	99.50
Community toilet	0.00	0.00	2.27	0.00	0.00	0.50
Total	100 (84)	100 (52)	100 (44)	100 (14)	100 (6)	100 (200)
(5) Poverty status						
No card	1.19	0.00	2.27	0.00	0.00	1.00
BPL	96.43	96.15	90.91	92.86	83.33	94.50
APL	1.19	1.92	6.82	7.14	16.67	3.50
AAY	1.19	1.92	0.00	0.00	0.00	1.00
Total	100 (84)	100 (52)	100 (44)	100 (14)	100 (6)	100 (200)

***Source*:** Field study. *Note:* Figures in the parentheses are actual number of households.

4.2(b) *Household Assets*

Assessing the information on household assets of migrant's households is very important from the point of view to understand their economic conditions. The information collected from the field survey in this regard is presented in Table 8 which has revealed that majority of the houses in which migrants living are provided by government. One of the important household asset *i.e.* vehicle, is not possessed by 78.50 percent of migrants' households. This information is supportive for tracing the economic background of migrants' households. Another important asset is television because in rural areas it is still treated as luxury, though the percentage of sample households with television has crossed 50 percent there are still a section of people living without television due to poverty. This is really a shame to know that the number of households with television is higher than the number of households with toilet facility. The study has also observed that the possession of commercial plot among migrants' household is not at all impressive, it is even worst across the different social categories. One of the important and must have asset of the household nowadays is a cell phone, almost all the households possess cell phones.

Table 8: Distribution of households by assets and social category (in %).

Particulars	***Social category***					
	SC	***ST***	***OBC***	***Minority***	***Others***	***Total***
Ownership of house						
Own	89.29	84.62	95.45	71.43	100.00	88.50
Govt. provided	10.71	15.38	2.27	28.57	0.00	11.00
Rent	0.00	0.00	2.27	0.00	0.00	0.50
Total	100 (84)	100 (52)	100 (44)	100 (14)	100 (6)	100 (200)
Possession of vehicle						
No vehicle	82.14	71.15	72.73	92.86	100.00	78.50
2 wheeler	15.48	26.92	25.00	7.14	0.00	19.50
3 Wheeler	2.38	1.92	2.27	0.00	0.00	2.00
Total	100 (84)	100 (52)	100 (44)	100 (14)	100 (6)	100 (200)
Possession of television	57.14	55.77	72.73	71.43	50.00	61.00
Possession of commercial plot	2.38	7.69	20.45	0.00	0.00	7.50
Possession of cell phone	78.57	90.38	90.91	85.71	100.00	85.50

***Source*:** Field study. *Note:* Figures in the parentheses are actual number of households.

5. SIZE, DISTRIBUTION AND CLASSIFICATION OF LAND HOLDINGS

Details on possession of land, classification of land holdings, and type of land holdings are presented in this section.

5.1. Possession of Land

Land is an important asset of the poor in rural areas, provided it is cultivable. Distribution of land in rural areas is not equal and the households with limited access to land are in large number. Figure 2 depicts information on sample households with possession of land. The data in the Fig. 2 indicate that households' access to land across social categories among sample households is higher among minorities followed by ST's and lower among 'Others'.

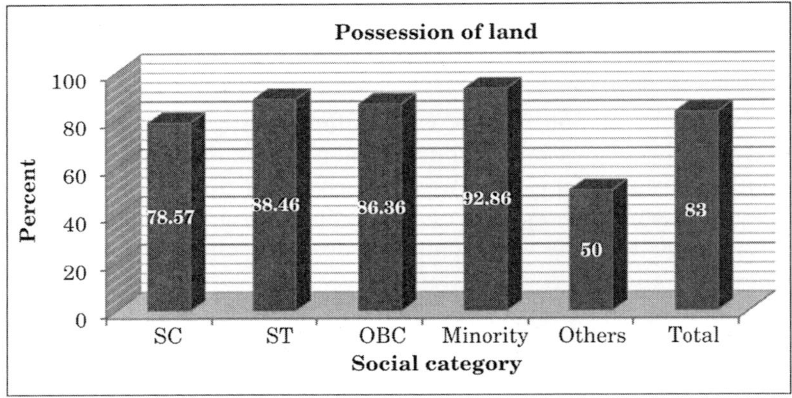

Fig. 2: Distribution of HH by social category and possession of land (in percentage). ***Source:*** Field study.

Table 9 provides details of irrigated land by size and social category. It is found that majority of the sample households don't have access to irrigated land. Observations across the social groups and size reveals that marginal, small, medium and large landholdings are dominated by ST's, Minorities, ST's and Others respectively. It is also observed that majority of the households possess marginal land holdings. From this background it can be stated that households with low access to irrigated land are economically weaker than those with high access.

Table 9: Distribution of household by social category and size of land holdings (irrigated) (percent).

Irrigated land in Acre	***Migrant HH***					
	SC	***ST***	***OBC***	***Minority***	***Others***	***Total***
No Land	95.24	78.85	86.36	92.86	83.33	88.50
Marginal (2.5<)	1.19	11.54	11.36	0.00	0.00	6.00
Small (2.5–5)	3.57	1.92	2.27	7.14	0.00	3.00
Medium (5–10)	0.00	3.85	0.00	0.00	0.00	1.00
Large (10<)	0.00	3.85	0.00	0.00	16.67	1.50
Total	100 (84)	100 (52)	100 (44)	100 (14)	100 (6)	100 (200)

***Source*:** Field study. *Note:* Figures in the parentheses are actual number of households.

Table 10 presents the details on possession of dry land among sample households' by size and social category. Majority of the households have access to dry land. Though households possess dry land, majority of the households possess only marginal and small size of holdings. The figures across the social categories are almost same with small variations. It is observed from the field survey that most part of the land in the surveyed area is dry in nature where a single crop system prevails.

Table 10: Distribution of households by Social category and size of land holdings (dry) (in percentage).

Dry land in Acre	***Migrant HH***					
	SC	***ST***	***OBC***	***Minority***	***Others***	***Total***
No land	23.81	19.23	22.73	21.43	66.67	23.50
Marginal (2.5<)	29.76	40.38	29.55	14.29	0.00	30.50
Small (2.5–5)	32.14	34.62	29.55	50.00	16.67	33.00
Medium (5–10)	13.10	5.77	15.91	14.29	16.67	12.00
Large (10<)	1.19	0.00	2.27	0.00	0.00	1.00
Total	100 (84)	100 (52)	100 (44)	100 (14)	100 (6)	100 (200)

Source: Field study. *Note:* Figures in the parentheses are actual number of households.

6. ECONOMIC BACKGROUND OF THE SAMPLE HOUSEHOLDS

This section deals with the income details, expenditure, borrowing and savings details of sample households of the study area.

6.1. Major Source of Income

Major source of income of the sample households is presented in Table 11. It is found that wages are the major source of income whereas income from own business/petty shops is quite less. Across the social categories too major source of income is from wages except for the households categorized under others. Remittances also having a considerable share in major source of income among sample migrants' households within this 'Others' are getting major share of remittances than rest of the social groups.

Table 11: Distribution of households by social category and major source of income (in percentage).

Social category	***Migrants' HH***				
	Farming	***Wage***	***Remittance***	***Own business/petty shop***	***Total***
SC	29.8	59.5	9.5	1.2	100 (84)
ST	25.0	53.8	17.3	3.8	100 (52)
OBC	27.3	43.2	25.0	4.5	100 (44)
Minority	35.7	50.0	14.3	0.0	100 (14)
Others	50.0	16.7	33.3	0.0	100 (6)
Total	29.0	52.5	16.0	2.5	100 (200)

Source: Field study. *Note:* Figures in the parentheses are actual number of households.

Around 93 percent of sample migrants' households are involved in agriculture and allied activities in study area (see Table 6). With this background of the sample households in the study area, this study tried to find the contribution of agriculture and allied sector in households' income. The data presented in Table 12 shows that majority of sample households' income from agriculture and allied sector falls below Rs. 25000/-. Negative income is also reported by households. This is too a push factor for short-term migration in search of employment opportunities. The percentages of households are very less in the income slabs of more than Rs. 50000/- from agriculture and allied sector. As it is mentioned earlier the percentage of households dependent on this sector is high but the return is very less, it is a clear sign that agriculture and allied sector is no more profitable, in these circumstances people from rural areas try to search new sources to lead life.

Table 12: Distribution of sample households by social category and income from agriculture and allied activities (in percentage).

Income	*SC*	*ST*	*OBC*	*Minority*	*Others*	*Total*
Migrant HH						
Negative Income	13.10	3.85	9.09	14.29	0.00	9.50
0 to 25000	71.43	76.92	61.36	64.29	50.00	69.50
25001 to 50000	11.90	7.69	20.45	14.29	33.33	13.50
50001 to 100000	2.38	5.77	6.82	0.00	0.00	4.00
100001 to 200000	1.19	1.92	2.27	0.00	0.00	1.50
200001 to 400000	0.00	3.85	0.00	0.00	16.67	1.50
Above 400001	0.00	0.00	0.00	7.14	0.00	0.50
Total	100 (84)	100 (52)	100 (44)	100 (14)	100 (6)	100 (200)

***Source*:** Field study. *Note:* Figures in the parentheses are actual number of households.

6.2. Expenditure Profile of Sample Households

The expenditure level depends on the size and composition of the family, stages of family life cycle, occupation of the family members, needs and objectives of the family, resources of the household, social and religious traditions. In Table 13 sample households are distributed by social category and total expenditure. The maximum number of sample households' total expenditure falls between the ranges of Rs. 50001 to Rs. 200000.

6.3. Borrowings Details of Sample Households

Volume of borrowing depends on many issues like level of household income, consumption, and assets and many more.

Table 13: Distribution of sample households by social category and total expenditure (yearly) (in percentage).

Total expenditure	*SC*	*ST*	*OBC*	*Minority*	*Others*	*Total*
Migrant HH						
0–50000	20.24	23.08	15.91	7.14	0.00	18.50
50001–200000	55.95	57.69	59.09	50.00	50.00	56.50
200001–350000	19.05	17.31	18.18	35.71	33.33	20.00
350001–500000	2.38	1.92	2.27	0.00	0.00	2.00
Above 500001	2.38	0.00	4.55	7.14	16.67	3.00
Total	100 (84)	100 (52)	100 (44)	100 (14)	100 (6)	100 (200)

***Source*:** Field study. *Note:* Figures in the parentheses are actual number of households.

Sample households are distributed by social category and the size of borrowings. It is seen from the Table 14 that majority of sample households have borrowed less than Rs. 25000. It is also observed that the percentage of households borrowed up to 1 lakh is in majority. The reason behind this is very clear that the size of borrowings depends on economic capacity of the household. The amount borrowed by households indirectly gives the details on the economic capacity of a household. Because nobody lends crores together to a person with no assets, money lenders follow the criteria of repaying capacity before lending money.

Table 14: Distribution of households by social category and amount borrowed (in percentage).

Amount	*SC*	*ST*	*OBC*	*Minority*	*Others*	*Total*
Migrant HH						
Below 25000	23.81	38.46	34.09	0.00	0.00	27.50
25001 to 50000	22.62	19.23	9.09	35.71	0.00	19.00
50001 to 100000	26.19	30.77	15.91	21.43	33.33	25.00
100001 to 200000	15.48	9.62	25.00	7.14	0.00	15.00
200001 to 400000	11.90	1.92	9.09	35.71	50.00	11.50
Above 400001	0.00	0.00	6.82	0.00	16.67	2.00
Total	100 (84)	100 (52)	100 (44)	100 (14)	100 (6)	100 (200)

***Source*:** Field study. *Note:* Figures in the parentheses are actual number of households.

6.4. Source of Borrowings

Source of loan of sample households by different social categories is presented in Table 15. The maximum numbers of sample households have borrowed from private money lenders. Borrowing from institutional sources is roughly around 20 percent of sample households. It is found that the institutional sector has unable to reach to the larger section of the sample households of the study area; this is a clear challenge against the success of financial inclusion. The informal sector in India is still dominated in rural areas, even after the seven decades of independence. It is really a major issue of concern, if large section of the rural masses continues to depend on non-institutional sector for borrowings

Table 15: Distribution of households by social category and source of Loan (in percentage).

Social Category	*Source of Borrowing*						
	Bank	*Private Money Lenders*	*Coope-rative Societies*	*Micro finance*	*Self Help Groups*	*Friends and Relatives*	*Total*
Migrants HH							
SC	19.44	70.83	0.00	0.00	4.17	5.56	100 (72)
ST	18.92	72.97	5.41	0.00	0.00	2.70	100 (37)
OBC	12.12	72.73	6.06	6.06	0.00	3.03	100 (33)
Minority	7.14	85.71	0.00	0.00	7.14	0.00	100 (14)
Others	0.00	83.33	0.00	16.67	0.00	0.00	100 (6)
Total	16.05	73.46	2.47	1.85	2.47	3.70	100 (162)

Source: Field study. *Note:* Figures in the parentheses are actual number of households.

6.5. Purpose of Borrowings

Sample households are distributed by social category and purpose of loan in Table 16. It is seen from the estimated values that maximum number of sample households have borrowed for marriage purpose followed by the purpose of taking up of agricultural activities. The study also found other purposes such as health, education, construction of house, business, consumption and purchase of land. Across the social categories too, majority of the households have borrowed to meet the expenses involved in marriage.

Table 16: Distribution of households by social category and purpose of loan (in percentage).

Social Category	*Purpose of loan*									
	Agriculture	*Marriage*	*Health*	*Education*	*Construction of house*	*Business*	*Consumption*	*Alcohol consumption*	*Purchase of land*	*Total*
Migrants HH										
SC	23.61	47.22	13.89	6.94	4.17	0.00	2.78	0.00	1.39	100 (72)
ST	35.14	35.14	10.81	0.00	5.41	0.00	8.11	5.41	0.00	100 (37)
OBC	21.21	36.36	15.15	0.00	18.18	3.03	6.06	0.00	0.00	100 (33)
Minority	21.43	42.86	21.43	0.00	7.14	0.00	0.00	0.00	7.14	100 (14)
Others	0.00	33.33	16.67	0.00	16.67	0.00	16.67	0.00	16.67	100 (6)
Total	24.69	41.36	14.20	3.09	8.02	0.62	4.94	1.23	1.85	100 (162)

Source: Field study. **Note:* Figures in the parentheses are actual number of household.

6.6. Details on Households' Savings

Details of savings of sample households are provided in the Table 17. It is seen that majority of sample households recorded with no savings. Some households recorded the savings but the amount saved is less than Rs. 25000/-. The details of savings across the different social categories also placed in the Table 17 where majority of households belonging to marginalized and backward categories do not have any savings.

Table 17: Distribution of sample households by social category and total savings (in percentage).

Total savings	***Social category of sample HH***					
	SC	***ST***	***OBC***	***Minority***	***Others***	***Total***
Migrants HH						
Nil	67.86	84.62	63.64	85.71	66.67	72.50
Below 25000	29.76	9.62	29.55	14.29	33.33	23.50
25001 to 50000	1.19	5.77	4.55	0.00	0.00	3.00
100001 to 200000	1.19	0.00	2.27	0.00	0.00	1.00
Total	100 (84)	100 (52)	100 (44)	100 (14)	100 (6)	100 (200)

***Source*:** Field study. **Note:* Figures in the parentheses are actual number of households.

7. FINDINGS, POLICY IMPLICATIONS AND CONCLUSIONS

Directly or indirectly, short term migration is an outcome of regional disparities in terms of growth and development, employment generation, literacy rate, occupation and structural changes etc. these inequalities led to concentration of growth and development in urban areas of the country. In India majority of the population still depends on agriculture sector but the agriculture sector has failed to fulfill the needs of dependents even at subsistence level, it is because agricultural sector is majorly depends on monsoon and because of this there is only a single crop in the study area, the situation in dry land areas is worst especially in areas like Hyderabad-Karnataka Region of Karnataka state which is the second largest arid region of the country, where, if monsoon fails there will be no work in rural areas for rest of the year and leads to drought like situation. In these circumstances rural people opt to move temporarily to other places in search of employment opportunities. The labourers are migrating from rural areas because they don't get employment at their places during lean season of agriculture. This could be avoided if the household members of the rural areas are involved in diversified occupations. Majority of the population involved in short term migration fall in the working age category *i.e.,* young age population, so that there is a need of training programmes to the rural youths which would help them to create alternate source of income to the households during the lean season of agriculture. Economic background of the migrant's households reveals that their literacy rate is very low, they work as casual labourers, they possess small size of dry land, their expenditure is more than their income, they borrow money from non-institutional sources, their savings are zero, in-short they are economically distressed and socially deprived. On the one hand the capacity of employment generation is decreasing in rural areas, on the other hand, working age population is at its peak, in this situation, poor, non literates and unskilled population opt to migrate to nearby urban places in search of work, this trend attracted the labourers unemployed during the lean season of agricultural sector. This trend has both positive as well as negative consequences. The positive side is people will get employment by migrating and the negative side is in this kind of migration is not by-choice, it is by-force, the second type pushes people to go somewhere in search of their livelihood otherwise their survival will be in trouble. To overcome the negative side of migration there is a need to create employment opportunities other than agriculture sector in dry land areas like Hyderabad-Karnataka Region, this will help in creating diverse occupations in rural areas. Employment creation will generate income to the rural people which in turn boost the rural economy. The study found that the background of the migrant's families in the study area is economically poor and socially backward, so the migration from this area is distress in nature. Distress migration is not good for any economy.

REFERENCES

Biradar, R.R. (2014). *Dynamics of Non-Farm Activities in Karnataka: A Study in Two Different Agro-Climatic Conditions,* Unpublished Report, ICSSR, New Delhi.

Census of India (2001). *Migration Data 'D' Series.* Government of India, New Delhi. Retrieved from: *http://censusofindia.gov.in*

Deshingkar, P. and Start, D. (2003). *Seasonal Migration for Livelihoods in India: Coping, Accumulation and Exclusion* (Working Paper 220). London: Overseas Development Institute, United Kingdom. Retrieved from *www.odi.org.uk/resources/docs/74.pdf*

Deshingkar, P. (2009). *Circular Internal Migration and Development in India.* London, Overseas Development Institute, United Kingdom. Retrieved from *http://essays.ssrc.org/acrossborders/wp-content/uploads/2009/08/ch8.pdf*

Devi, P.A. (2012). "Remittance model on migration". *Journal of Radix International Educational and Research Consortium,* 1(5).

HPCFRRI (2002). High Power Committee on Redressal of Regional Imbalances in Karnataka (DM Nanjundappa Committee), Government of Karnataka.

Keshri, K. and Bhagat, R. (2010). "Temporary and seasonal migration in India". *Genus Journal of Population Sciences,* 66(3).

Keshri, K. and Bhagat, R. (2012). "Socio-economic Determinant of Temporary Labour Migration in India: A Regional Analysis". *Asian Population Studies,* 9(2): 175–195. Retrieved from *http://dx.doi.org/10.1080/17441730.2013.797294*

Keshri, K. and Bhagat, R. (2012a). "Temporary and Seasonal Migration: Regional Pattern, Characteristics and Associated Factors". *Economic & Political Weekly,* XLVII(4): 81–87.

Korra Vijay (2010). Nature and Characteristics of Seasonal Labour Migration: A Case Study in Mahabubnagar District of Andhra Pradesh (Working Paper 433). India: Centre for Development Studies, Thiruvananthapuram. Retrieved from *www.cds.edu/wp-content/uploads/2012/09/wp433.pdf*

Korra, Vijay (2011). "Labour Migration in Mahabubnagar: Nature and Characteristics". *Economic and Political Weekly,* XLVI(02): 67–70.

Kumar Shashi, S.K. (2004). *"Theories of Internal Migration"*, *In*: Iyer Gopal, K. (*ed.*), Distressed Migrant Labour in India: Key human rights issues, Kanishka Publications, India.

Lusome, R. and Bhagat, R.B. (2006). *Trends and Patterns of Internal Migration in India,* 1971–2001. Paper presented at the Annual Conference of Indian Association for the Study of Population (IASP) Thiruvananthapuram, Kerala, India.

Mihra, S.K. (1981). Factors and Process of Migration in Developing Economy. *In*: Mandal, R.B. (*ed.*), *Frontiers in Migration Analysis.* Concept Publishing Company, New Delhi.

National Sample Survey Organisation (NSSO) (2010). Migration in India, Report No. 533, Ministry of Statistics and Programme Implementation, Government of India, New Delhi. Retrieved from: *http://mospi.nic.in/mospi_new/upload/533_final.pdf*

Roy, B. and Nijim, B. (1991). On the Questions of Migration in India: Challenges and Opportunities. *Geo Journal,* 23(3): 257–268. Retrieved from *http://www.jstor.org/stable/41145096.*

Smitha (2008, nd). *Distress Seasonal Migration and its Impact on Children's Education. Research Monograph,* 28. Consortium for Research on Educational Access, Transitions and Equity and National University of Educational Planning and Administration (NUEPA). Retrieved from *http://www.create-rpc.org/pdf_documents/PTA28.pdf*

Srivastava, R. and Sasikumar, S.K. (2003, nd). *An overview of migration in India, its impacts and key issues.* Paper presented at the Regional Conference on Migration, Development and Pro-Poor Policy Choices in Asia. The Refugee and Migratory Movements Research Unit, Bangladesh, and the Department for International Development, UK, in Dhaka, Bangladesh. Retrieved from *www.livelihoods.org*

6

Revisiting Public Distribution System in India: A Glimpse on Uttar Pradesh

ZEBA SHEEREEN[1] AND ARBIYA NASEEM ANSARI[1*]

ABSTRACT

The Public Distribution System in India has always been the topic of concern for various economists, for ensuring food security to the nation. This paper deals with the working of PDS in India and Uttar Pradesh and tries to evaluate the present status of the scheme, using the latest data up-to 2017. For some purpose, the data of only upto 2011–12 have been considered due to the unavailability of any recent ones.

Key words: Public distribution system, NFSA, Food security.

INTRODUCTION

Post–Independence, Indian agriculture followed the Bengal famine of 1943 and food scarcity during the time of Second World War (1939–45). It was during this time of war that the concept of public distribution system (PDS) was evolved around 1942 as a war-time rationing measure, due to shortage of food grains in the country. The PDS in India is among the most significant anti-poverty and government welfare, state-administered food-subsidy programme, aiming to provide subsidized food grains to the poor population. It is operated under the joint responsibility of the centre and the state governments. While the central government, through Food Corporation of India (FCI), assumes the responsibility of procurement, storage, transportation and bulk allocation of food grains to the states, the state governments extend the hands for the distribution of food grains to its ultimate beneficiaries through the established network of approximately 5 lakh fair price shops (also called ration shops). The system of procurement

[1] Department of Economics, Aligarh Muslim University, Aligarh, UP (202001).

**Corresponding author:* E-mail: naseemarbiya4368@gmail.com

is also used by the Government of India to provide minimum support prices (MSPs)[1] to the farmers to sustain farm output and income. Major commodities that come under the PDS system includes wheat, rice, sugar, and kerosene. Some States/UTs (Union Territories) also distribute additional items such as spices, iodized salt, pulses, edible oils, etc.

Till 1992, PDS was universal in its coverage. However, this programme was revamped, and The Revamped Public Distribution System (RPDS) was introduced in June 1992 to strengthen its reach based on area approach. The revamped system planned to give its preference to the population living in the most difficult areas of the country, such as drought-prone areas, tribal areas, hilly areas, desert areas, and urban slum areas, etc. The PDS was criticized for its urban bias and its failure to serve the poorer sections of the population effectively. It was also criticized for its minor coverage in the states with the maximum population of the rural poor and also bcause of the lack of transparent and accountable arrangements for delivery (Planning Commission, 2002–2007, Vol. II, p. 368).

Subsequently, in June 1997, the government of India launched the Targeted Public Distribution System (TPDS) with focus on the poor. Under this programme, the whole population was categorized into two forms, namely Below Poverty lines (BPL) and Above Poverty Lines (APL). The state governments were entrusted with the task of stripping down the PDS by issuing special cards (ration cards) to BPL families and selling essential items under TPDS to them at specially subsidized prices, with better functioning of the delivery system. The TPDS sells significant food grains, mainly rice and wheat, through Fair Price Shops (FPSs) at remarkably lower prices than the market. Different states have adopted different measures to strengthen its TPDS operations. Though the TPDS feeds more than 65 million low-income families of the nation, it had been criticized for its poor identification of the targeted beneficiaries and inefficient delivery and leakages. During 1997, several states have adopted for Decentralized Procurement Scheme (DPS) under which food grains were procured from the farmers and were distributed by the state governments themselves.

In September 2013, Parliament authorized the National Food Security Act, 2013. The Act depends largely on the existing TPDS to deliver the food grains as the legal entitlements to the poor households. This marks a shift by making the right to food a justiciable right. The Act provides for coverage of up to 75% of the rural population and up to 50% of the urban population for receiving subsidized food grains under the Targeted Public Distribution System (TPDS), thereby covering about two-thirds of the population. Under the NFSA, eligible beneficiaries are legally entitled to receive 5 kg of foodgrains at highly subsidized prices from the TPDS. In the case of non-supply of the entitlement, the centre commits to giving a food security allowance. Based on population coverage and the distribution commitment, TPDS forms the largest component of the NFSA.

LAWS AND REGULATIONS GOVERNING TPDS

The Table 1 highlights the developments regarding the TPDS since its birth and the various laws and regulations that govern its Implementation.

Table 1: Timeline of PDS: 1930s to present

Evolution of PDS	*Timeline*	*Details*
PDS	1940s	Launched as general entitlement scheme
TPDS	1997	PDS was revamped to target poor households
Antyodaya Anna Yojana	2000	Scheme launched to target the poorest of the poor
PDS Control Order	2001	The government notified this Order to administer TPDS
PUCL *vs.* Union of India	2001	The ongoing case in Supreme Court contending that "right to food" is a fundamental right
National Food Security Act	2013	Act to provide a legal right to food to the poor

ESSENTIAL COMMODITIES ACT AND PDS (CONTROL) ORDER

TPDS is operated under the Public Distribution System (Control) Order 2001, notified under the Essential Commodities Act, 1955 (ECA). The ECA monitors the production, and distribution of essential commodities including edible oils, food crops such as wheat, rice, and sugar, among others. The PDS (Control) Order, 2001 stipulates the anatomy for the implementation of TPDS. It accentuates the major aspects of the scheme including the method of identification of beneficiaries, the issue of food grains, and the mechanism for distribution of food grains from the centre to the states.

PUCL *vs.* UNION OF INDIA, 2001

In 2001, the People's Union for Civil Liberties (PUCL) filed a writ petition in the Supreme Court confronting that the "right to food" is indispensable to the right to life as given in Article 21 of the Constitution. During the ongoing prosecution, the Court had issued several interim orders, including the implementation of eight central schemes as legal grants. These include PDS, the Mid-Day Meal Scheme, Antyodaya Anna Yojana (AAY), and Integrated Child Development Services (ICDS). In 2008, the Court ordered that the Below Poverty Line (BPL) families be sanctioned to 35 kg of food grains per month at subsidized prices.

NATIONAL FOOD SECURITY ACT, 2013

Ministry of Consumer Affairs, Food and Public Distribution achieved new milestone during 2013 with the enactment of historic National Food Security

Act. The National Food Security Act gives statutory support to the TPDS. This legislation marks a shift in the right to food as a legal right rather than a general entitlement. The Act classifies the population into three categories: *excluded* (*i.e.*, no entitlement), *priority* (entitlement), and *Antyodaya Anna Yojana* (AAY; higher entitlement). The Act provides for coverage of up to 75% of the rural population and up to 50% of the urban population for receiving subsidized food grains under Targeted Public Distribution System (TPDS), thus covering about two-thirds of the population. Persons belonging to eligible households will be entitled to receive 5 Kilograms of food grains per person per month at subsidized prices of Rs. 3/2/1 per Kg for rice/wheat/coarse grains provided that existing Antyodaya Anna Yojana (AAY) households, which falls into the category of the poorest of the poor, will continue to receive 35 Kgs of foodgrains per household per month. In case of non-supply of entitled food grains or meals, the beneficiaries will receive food security allowance. The Act also contains provisions for setting up of grievance redressal mechanism at the District and State levels. Separate provisions have also been made in the Act for ensuring transparency and accountability.

Identification of Eligible Households Under Existing TPDS

APL and BPL

Under TPDS, beneficiaries were divided into two categories:

- Households below the poverty line (BPL), and
- Households above the poverty lines (APL).

BPL beneficiaries that are currently covered under the TPDS were identified through a detailed process when TPDS was initially launched. The Planning Commission calculated state-wise estimates of the total number of BPL beneficiaries that would be covered under TPDS. Each state government was responsible for identifying eligible BPL households by inclusion and exclusion criteria evolved by the Ministry of Rural Development. Such households were entitled to receive a BPL ration card. APL households were not specifically identified, and any household above the poverty line could typically apply for an APL ration card.

Antyodaya Anna Yojana (AAY)

The AAY scheme was launched in December 2000 for the poorest among the BPL families. Individuals in the following priority groups are entitled to an AAY card, including: (i) landless agricultural labourers, (ii) marginal farmers, (iii) rural artisans/craftsmen such as potters and tanners, (iv) slum dwellers, (v) persons earning their livelihood on a daily basis in the informal sector such as porters, rickshaw pullers, cobblers, (vi) destitute, (vii) households headed by widows or terminally ill persons, disabled persons, persons aged 60 years or more with no assured means of subsistence, and (viii) all primitive tribal households.

As per under the NFSA, it proposes to cover up to 75% of rural and 50% of the urban population. However, the major issues that pinch the concerned act are that the government has not set any specific guidelines or methods for the identification of priority households, mainly the homeless people, the state migrants, tribals and the destitute, etc. Also, it is not clear that on what grounds the rural and urban population is categorized under NFSA.

CONSUMPTION FROM PDS

Table 2: Per capita consumption and percentage of households reporting consumption from PDS of rice, wheat/*Atta*, sugar and kerosene during 2004–05, 2009–10 and 2011–12, all-India.

Item	*2004–05*			*2009–10*			*2011–12*					
	Monthly per capita consump-tion(Kg)		*% Share of PDS in qty consu-med*	*Monthly per capita consump-tion(Kg)*		*% Share of PDS in qty consu-med*	*Monthly per capita consump-tion(Kg)*		*% Share of PDS in qty consu-med*	*% of HHS reporting consumption from PDS for 30 days*		
	PDS	*Other Sources*		*PDS*	*Other sources*		*PDS*	*Other sources*		*2004 –05*	*2009 –10*	*2011 –12*
(1)	*(2)*	*(3)*	*(4)*	*(5)*	*(6)*	*(7)*	*(8)*	*(9)*	*(10)*	*(11)*	*(12)*	*(13)*
Rural												
Rice	0.839	5.537	13.2	1.408	4.594	23.5	1.670	4.306	27.9	24.4	39.1	45.9
Wheat /atta	0.307	3.885	7.3	0.619	3.625	14.6	0.744	3.544	17.3	11.0	27.6	33.9
Sugar	0.062	0.587	9.6	0.097	0.563	14.7	0.113	0.603	15.8	15.9	27.8	33.7
Kero-sene*	0.477	0.142	77.1	0.511	0.081	86.3	0.431	0.103	80.8	72.8	81.8	75.6
Urban												
Rice	0.530	4.181	11.3	0.814	3.706	18.0	0.882	3.605	19.6	13.1	20.5	23.3
Wheat /atta	0.167	4.192	3.8	0.371	3.706	9.1	0.406	3.605	10.1	5.8	17.6	19.0
Sugar	0.054	0.763	6.6	0.080	0.700	10.3	0.084	0.732	10.3	11.5	18.7	20.6
Kero-sene*	0.350	0.268	56.6	0.295	0.169	63.6	0.230	0.166	58.1	32.8	33.0	30.0

(*) represents quantity in litres. ***Source:*** NSS Report No. 558; 68th Round

The above Table 2 shows that the consumption of the population, dependent on PDS has increased over the years in the rural and urban area. In rural India, the percentage share of PDS in monthly consumption of rice, wheat and sugar has almost doubled and that of kerosene has increased by about 4%. Likewise in urban area, the consumption of rice, wheat, sugar and kerosene through PDS, has also increased but the increase in consumption of urban mass is much less than that of the rural population.

Similarly, the number of households (HHS) benefitting consumption from PDS for the items mentioned above have also increased much more in the rural region than the urban population. In case of kerosene intake, the percentage of rural households beneficiaries have swelled up by 2.8%, as opposed to 2.8% shredding of the urban household beneficiaries. Bhattacharya *et al.* (2018) showed that the public distribution system reaches about 800 million individuals who consume subsidized commodities through fair price shops.

A Note to the PDS in Uttar Pradesh

Uttar Pradesh, the largest state in India in terms of population, is host to the largest network of public distribution system of the nation. Automation of PDS as per National Food Security Act (NFSA) - 2013 has been introduced in Uttar Pradesh with the name "AAPURTI" with the objective of providing essential commodities to underprivileged sections of the society at subsidized rates. It is the largest network of PDS in India with more than 3.40 crore ration card holders, 15 crore beneficiaries and 81088 Fair Price Shops (FPSs). Uttar Pradesh was under the DCP (Decentralized Procurement Scheme) mode of operations from 1999–2010. The purpose of PDS is always questioned in the Indian context because of the high level of inclusion and exclusion errors during identification of beneficiaries. The exercise of deletion of bogus/ ineligible cards and the inclusion of eligible families is a continuous process and the State Governments are to carry out the same periodically. As per the reports, 4170894 fraudulent cards have been deleted from Uttar Pradesh ration card list during the year 2013–2017[1].

Table 3: Offtake of foodgrains under NFSA (up to July 2018) from central pool against the annual allotment of 2018–19.

Figs. In '000 Tonnes

State / Total	*Wheat*						*Rice*						*Total (wheat + rice)*		*Total % of lifting*
	Allotment			*Offtake*			*Allotment*			*Offtake*			*Allotment*	*Offtake*	
	NFSA	*Other than NFSA*	*Total*	*NFSA*	*Other than NFSA*	*Total*	*NFSA*	*Other than NFSA*	*Total*	*NFSA*	*Other than NFSA*	*Total*			
UP	5795.81	0.00	5795.81	1866.81	0.00	1866.81	3945.77	0.00	3945.77	1253.71	0.00	1253.71	9741.58	3120.32	32
India	23295.18	707.02	24002.20	7016.39	227.30	7243.69	29332.00	2081.52	31413.52	9554.52	873.28	10427.81	55415.72	17671.50	32

Source: www.fci.gov.in

Table 3 illustrates the total offtake of foodgrains by the Food Corporation of India (FCI) under NFSA, from the allotment made by the Centre during the year 2018–19. The allocation made to the states depend upon their offtakes during the three consecutive previous years. The offtake of foodgrains by the UP Government is much less than that of the total allocation made by the centre; the state does only 32% of lifting. One of the reasons behind the low offtake is the storage capacity problem. Currently, the state's existing total storage capacity is only around 56 lakh MT (Million Tonnes) against the peak demand of 70 lakh MT. "There is a critical gap of around 15 lakh MT due to which wheat procured from farmers has to be often kept in the open, which often ends up getting drenched[2]. The low offtake leads to rotting of the huge amount of foodgrains lying in the godowns. The poor procurement of wheat and rice in Uttar Pradesh is primarily due to weaknesses of the state procurement machinery (Verma, Gulati & Hussain, 2017).

Leakages in the PDS

'Leakages' in welfare schemes have consistently increased India's expenditure on the welfare of these schemes. The biggest issue and problem faced in the functioning of PDS is the wide prevalence of pilferage/leakage of rations into the open market. The Planning Commission had stated in its 2005 report, "For every Rs. 3.65 spent on the PDS, only Re. 1 reaches the poor", and "about 70% of the PDS food grain does not reach the intended people".

Table 4: Leakages of foodgrains as evaluated under various studies since 1999–2000 to 2011–12.

States /India	*1999–2000**	*2001–02**	*2004–05**	*2006–07**	*2007–08**	*2009–10*	*Rice*	*2010–11 Wheat*	*Total*
UP	31.1	69.7	58 (83.9)	50.5	26.7 (52.1)	43.5	34.76	59.93	47.92
India	23.9	39	54 (54.8)	46.7	43.9 (42.8)	41.2	36.15	62.88	46.72

*From Khera (2011); Value in parenthesis are as calculated by Himanshu and Sen (2011)
Source: NSSO and Foodgrains Bulletin

The leakage of the foodgrains acts out in different ways such as the pilferage or damage during the transportation of foodgrains, diversion to non-beneficiaries through the issue of ghost cards[3], and, or exclusion of people entitled to foodgrains, etc. Table 4 illustrates the percent of leakages of foodgrains (rice and wheat) from the PDS during the year 1999–2000 to 2011–12. This table has been extracted from the ICRIER (Indian Council For Research on International Economic Relations) original working paper 294 (2015 The PDS leakage in India declined by 7% from 54% in 2004–05 to 46.72% in the year 2011–12. While in Uttar Pradesh, it shows a decline of around 10% during the period as mentioned earlier.

However Drèze and Khera (2015) claim this calculation to be wrong and state that the leakage in UP (Uttar Pradesh) PDS has shown virtually no progress and had decreased only by 1%, from 58.0% in 2004–05 to 57.6% in the year 2011–12. UP is still among the states that are suffering from higher leakage issue where more than even 50% of the subsidized foodgarins does not reach its intended beneficiaries. Drèze and Khera also claim that the main source of leakage is the above poverty line (APL) quota population. Because of being phased out under the NFSA, they make their way to get the benefit by somehow getting themselves added to the beneficiaries list.

Leakages remain to be high in various states, but there is clear evidence of refinement in some states, including Bihar, whose PDS system was once stated as the most corrupted PDS. These states have undertaken bold PDS reforms and it proved to be fruitful. The UP government also needs to learn from such recovering states and adopt the similar steps in order to improve the poor functioning of the existing public distribution system. Many economists suggest universalizing the benefits to get over the problem of leakagaes. Much of the efforts have already been taken by the government, like that of the end-to-end computerization of the TPDS scheme. Under this scheme, UP government have achieved 100% digitalization of the rations cards, whereas, 85% of the ration cards have so far been linked with Aadhar in order to keep a check on the leakage and keep a track on the foodgrains that are intended to reach its beneficiaries. Transparency portal has been launched which shows the online allocation of the foodgrains and also many FPSs have been installed with ePOS (Electric Point of Sale) to ensure the eligibility of the beneficiaries through their bio-metric and also to link the update of the transactions to the central server.

CONCLUSIONS

India's Public Distribution System is the largest distribution network aiming to provide subsidized food and fuel to the beneficiaries and to solve the issue of food security of the country. As India's 400 million urban populations is expected to expand to 600 million by 2030, food security will become an even bigger challenge (Ashok Gulati, 2015). This paper evaluates the working of the PDS in India and Uttar Pradesh and it can be concluded that the PDS is working well at the macro level, but at the state level it still has to go a long way to ensure and improve the food security. Food storage capacity needs to be enlarged for improving the offtake and also to find a way to nail the leakages in the process of PDS. Many economists suggest opting for the DBT (Direct Benefit Transfer) scheme and some others for food coupons. The significant improvement in Bihar's PDS shows a hope that even worst governed states are capable of improvement. A lot can be learned from the success stories of Tamil Nadu and Chhattisgarh PDS working. Based on the data concerned, not much improvement has been experienced in UP's PDS but is still showing some betterment steadily. Despite its various weaknesses, the PDS system is still a key determinant of the food security in India and the states. However, the high percentage of pilferage form the APL quota remains a critical issue and the government needs to ensure their inclusion under the beneficiaries coverage and further improve the food security scenario of the state.

NOTES

[1] Rajya Sabha Unstarred Question No. 2334, dated on 04.08.2017.
[2] As reported on www.hindustantimes.com
[3] Ghost cards are made in the name of non-existent people, which indicate diversion of foodgrains from deserving households to the open market.

REFERENCES

Annual Report (2017–18). Department of Food & Public Distribution, Ministry of Consumer Affairs, Food & Public Distribution.

Dreze, J. and Khera, R. (2015). Understanding Leakages in the Public Distribution System. *Economic and Political Weekly*.

Gulati, A. and Saini, S. (2015). *Leakages from Public Distribution System (PDS) and the Way forward,* ICRIER.

NSSO (2014). Report 558 - Household Consumption of various goods and services in India 2011–12. NSSO.

Parashar, B.K. (2018). Increasing food storage capacity in UP: Private companies to set up modern silos. Retrieved from *https://www.hindustantimes.com/lucknow/increasing-food-storage-capacity-in-up-private-companies-to-set-up-modern-silos/story*

7

Impact of GST on Sustainable Development Goals - A Case Study of India

DIVYA MAHAJAN[1*]

ABSTRACT

Around 160 countries have implemented GST so far. India has one of the lowest 'tax to GDP' ratio among the emerging economies in the world. In India, GST has been implemented with the aim of broadening the ambit of taxpayers. This paper is an attempt to provide a bird's eye view about the implications of GST for Sustainable Development Goals particularly in India. GST bill is passed to create a common market across the country and accelerate economic growth. The expected benefits of GST include widening of the tax base of both Centre and states and significant improvement in the ease of doing Business. This paper is an attempt to spectacle GST effects that India is going to witness in the immediate future. The paper is divided into three parts. In the first part, GST is studied in the context of Sustainable Development Goals and vice versa. The second part presents contribution of the Indian GST model and its implications for UN SDGs. In the third part, an attempt is made to speculate on the possible impact of GST on Sustainable Development Goals for India.

***Key words*:** GST, Millennium development goals, Sustainable development goals, Cascading of tax, Input tax credit.

JEL Classification: I1, I2, I3, H2, H21, H22, H25, J16, L67, L69, O, Q, QO1, Q5

[1] UBS, Guru Nanak Dev University Amritsar, Punjab.

**Corresponding author:* E-mail: mahajandivya12@gmail.com

INTRODUCTION

In order to achieve something, whether at small or large scale, it is very important to develop an Action Plan. These Action plans work as a roadmap to reach the set goals. In order to run an economy, it is very important to set goals so that action plans can be directed to achieve the same. For that matter governments design various policies to target various objectives. The different types of policies framed by government are popular by the names of Five Year Plans, National Plans, Industrial Policies, Economic policies, etc.

But the goals that have become very significant in the recent origin are Millennium Development Goals (MDGs) and Sustainable Development Goals (SDGs). Generally, goals and objectives are designed to cater to all the aspects of an economy. These aspects include Independence objective, Economic objective, Efficiency objective, Resource Conservation objective, Stability objective and Equity objective. The above mentioned goals seem to take all these critical aspects into it's ambit.

Journey from Millennium Development Goals to Sustainable Development Goal

"The Millennium Development Goals (MDGs) are the world's time-bound and quantified targets for addressing extreme poverty in its many dimensions which include income, poverty, hunger, disease, lack of adequate shelter, and exclusion-while promoting gender equality, education, and environmental sustainability. They are also basic human rights-the rights of each person on the planet to health, education, shelter, and security" – UNDP. MDGs were decided for a particular time period, *i.e.,* to be achieved till 2015. These goals were mainly designed for the developing world. With the main focus on reducing extreme poverty, the world leaders at large gathered and adopted the UN Millennium Declaration at the Millennium Summit in September 2000.

Introduction to Sustainable Development Goals

As compared to MDGs, SDGs have a wider scope. Also, where the Millennium Development Goals were designed to cater the needs of Developing Nations, the SDGs are universal in nature, *i.e.,* they are for all nations, not just for the developing world. Thus, resource mobilisation for implementing the SDGs will focus on nations' capacities instead of the traditional categorisation of 'developed' or 'developing' nations. "The Sustainable Development Goals (SDGs), officially known as Transforming our world: the 2030 Agenda for Sustainable Development is a set of 17 "Global Goals" with 169 targets between them"- UNDP. SDGs are means to reach the end *i.e.,* "The Future We Want". Where Poverty eradication and health, were the main target of MDGs, SDGs contribute towards Education, Shelter, Economic Growth, Worldwide Peace and Justice, Industrial Growth, Fostering Innovation and Building Infrastructural Facilities, issues related to aquatic species (life under water), etc. leading to a wider coverage. Thus, for the first time, specific goals on economic indicators were designed under SDGs. These targets will be discussed one by one.

Introduction to Goods and Services Tax – GST

GST in the backdrop

In the year 2000, NDA government, under the chairmanship of Asim Das Gupta set up an empowered committee to design GST model. The then Finance Minister, Mr. P.Chidambaram, proclaimed the implementation of GST. In the budget of 2007, he manifested that GST should be implemented by April 2010 and proclaimed to set up an empowered committee of state Finance ministers to work with center for the same. For that matter, on 10 May 2007 Joint Working Group was set up by empowered committee of state finance ministers. In Nov 2009, first detailed discussion paper on structure of GST was introduced by empowered committee with the objective of generating a debate and getting the inputs from all stakeholders. It suggested a dual GST Module along with a GST Council.

Finally in March 2011, constitution 115th amendment bill was introduced to draw up laws for implementing GST. But the proposed 115 amendment bill was lapsed with dissolution of 15th Lok Sabha. On 19 Dec 2014 after making slight changes in GST Bill, NDA government redefined it in 16th Lok Sabha as 122nd amendment of constitution. On 6 may 2015 it passed in lower house of government. Ultimately, the 122nd constitutional amendment was stranded on in Rajya Sabha where it has to be passed with 2/3rd majority in order to be implemented from 1 April 2016.

Thus, Goods and Services Tax was introduced in the 101st Amendment of the Constitution Act 2016 which came into operation from 1st July, 2017.

Thus, Goods and Services Tax is a revolution introduced and implemented in the Indian Tax System. It can be regarded as the one of the biggest tax reform since Independence. The GST has proposed uniformity in the Tax across the country. (Thus, different tax rates have been introduced for different sectors).

Purpose

The purpose behind introducing the Goods and Services Tax was to abolish multiplicity of taxes *i.e.,* to abolish the cascading effect of taxes. (Wikipedia), (Refer Table 1).

It is framed to replace complicated taxes like State Value Added Tax, Central Excise, Service Tax, Octroi, etc. Thus, GST combines all the taxes like those of state, local tax, entertainment tax, excise duty, surcharge, etc.

Table 1: Cascading effect of Tax (VAT).

***For example*:** A government levies a 2% cascade tax on all goods produced and distributed. A company sells Rs. 1,000 worth of stone for a tax-inclusive price of Rs. 1,020 (1000 + 2% cascade tax) to an artist. The artist makes a sculpture out of the stone and wants to make Rs. 2,000 when he sells it to an art dealer, so he adds this figure to what he paid for the stone to get Rs. 3,020, and then adds on the cascade tax to bring the total to get Rs. 3,080 (3020 + 2%). The art dealer wants to make Rs. 5,000 for the sculpture, adding this to Rs. 3,080 for a pre-tax Rs. 8,080. She then adds the 2% cascade tax for a total price of Rs. 8,242. The government collected taxes of Rs. 242, which is actually a rate of 3.025% (242/ 8,000).

***Source*:** Investopedia *http: / / www.investopedia.com / terms / c / cascade-tax.asp*

Research Methodology

Data collection technique

Being an explanatory research Secondary Data Collection technique has been used to collect the information. An extensive literature review has been done to collect all the necessary information. During the collection, various Journals, Articles including Trade Journals, Magazines, Books, Conference proceedings, Government Reports and corporate reports, Working Papers, etc have been studied.

Rationale of the study

While going through the literature, studies related to Sustainable Development Goals and GST were available. But no contribution has been made in building the relationship between the two aspects. The present study is an attempt to build a quality relationship between the two aspects. Thus, Sustainable Development Goals have been studied in the light of Goods and Services Tax and *vice versa*.

Objectives of the Study

The present study has been conducted to:

1. To understand the concept of Sustainable Development Goals;
2. To understand the concept of Goods and Services Tax;
3. To understand the working of GST;

4. To study the contribution/ impact of GST on Economy and Sustainable Development Goals;
5. To find out Advantages and Disadvantages of GST for Sustainable Development Goals.

GST and the Sustainable Development Goals

GST and the 1st sustainable development goal: Reducing poverty

Reducing poverty has been the topic of discussion in almost India's every economic policy. It will remain the pivotal objective of every economic policy. Thus, GST has also contributed towards achieving the Zero poverty Goal by levying no tax on basic food items so that every person has an easy access to food. As the food will be available at affordable prices, the poor people will be benefitted in two ways:

- Benefit due to increase in real purchasing power leading to increase in their income levels (as food will be available at relatively low prices, this will increase the real purchasing power of the poor people which will in other ways increase their income).
- Benefit due to reduction in the prices of the products consumed by them.

GST and the 2nd sustainable development goal: Zero hunger

As discussed earlier, prior to GST, there were many indirect taxes that were levied on the products and services before reaching the ultimate customers that led to increased tax rates (Cascading of tax). Every state had its own tax rates. Thus, GST is aimed at bringing a uniform tax regime Pan India. But, it is very important to check, the purpose for which this tax was introduced is fulfilled or not. The goods and services fall under various tax slabs under GST. The government has categorized approximately 1211 items under tax slabs (Economic Times, 2017).

The tax slabs will be as follows: "5 percent (necessities/ essential items), 12 percentand 18 percent (standard goods/ services), 28 percent (luxury and sin tax items)". (SDG datalabs, 2017).

Food items (Most of these) will be taxed at the rate of 0 %. "Food items such as fresh meat, fish chicken, eggs, milk, butter milk, curd, natural honey, fresh fruits and vegetables, flour, besan, bread, prasad, salt, Cereal grains hulled, Palmyra jiggery, etc will not be taxed. Thus it will make food available to people at affordable prices" (Economic Times, 2017).

However, it is a step towards providing food to all reducing poverty from the country.

GST and the 3rd sustainable development goals: Good health and well being

Under the GST Tax structure, Health care is exempt from any tax. Thus, Indian Government has taken a fruitful step towards promoting healthcare services by providing access to healthcare services to all the Citizens tax free. Thus GST has again proved to promote Sustainable Development in the country by laying positive impact on it's 3rd SDG *i.e.,* Good health and well being (For simplification, healthcare and hygiene have been discussed separately).

GST and the 4th sustainable development goals: Quality education

The education aspect has been included as the Fundamental Right in our constitution as "Right to Education". As per the 86th Amendments made in The Constitution of India, the Government of India implemented the law to provide free and compulsory education to all children in age group of 6–14 years. However, the contribution of GST is no less. Finance Minister in his statements mentioned to exempt the education services from taxation so that quality education at low cost can be provided to all. Thus GST will have a positive impact on achieving the 4th Sustainable Development Goal *i.e.,* Quality education.

GST and the 5th sustainable development goals: Gender equality

The complex tax structure has been simplified by introducing a Tax that works on a formula of "one nation, one tax, one market" - GST. Although Women empowerment has always been a matter of discussion while designing any policy, still it is very difficult to include this issue in every policy.

At the very outset, it is important to mention that the GST council does not include any women as its member. As a result of it, Gender Equality comes to question in its very council structure. Also, the list that has come under the purview of GST tax include so many items to be used/ consumed by women that it is not proving very favourable for women. Garments and Jewellery, Cosmetics and Beauty Products, Household Appliances and Meals, Domestic Appliances and Health Products, etc have come under the ambit of GST Tax Structure.

(Central Board for Excise and Customs; Hindustan Times, 2017).

Products such as sanitary napkins, tampons, towels etc have been taxed under the tax slab of 12%. However, it is an irony to state that condoms and other items like sindoor, bindi etc are kept tax free. Most underprivileged women don't even use the sanitary napkins because of its cost, instead, they use old clothes even though they know that they are risking their health (refer Table 2).

Table 2: Some of the excerpts of the GST tax rates are mentioned in the table below: (Hindustan Times, 2017).

Product/ Service	***Tax rate***
Beauty or make-up: Preparations and preparations for the care of the skin (other than medicaments), including sunscreen or sun tan preparations; manicure or pedicure preparations.	28%
Cosmetics: Scent sprays and similar toilet sprays, and mounts and heads therefore; powder-puffs and pads for the application of cosmetics or toilet preparations.	28%
Garments: Artificial fur; Artificial fur as trimmings and embellishments for garments, made ups, knitwear, plastic and leather goods.	18%
Precious stones: (Other than diamonds) and semi-precious stones, but not strung, mounted or set; ungraded precious stones (other than diamonds) and semi-precious stones, temporarily strung for convenience transport.	3%
Silver: (Including silver plated with gold or platinum), unwrought or in semi-manufactured forms, or in powder form.	3%
Gold: (Including gold plated with platinum) unwrought or in semi-manufactured forms, or in powder form.	3%
Health products: Products such as sanitary napkins, tampons, towels etc have been taxed heavily.	12%
Domestic Appliances: Electro-mechanical domestic appliances with self-contained electric motor, other than vacuum cleaners.	28%
Stoves: [Other than kerosene stove and LPG stoves], ranges, grates, cookers (including those with subsidiary boilers for central heating), barbecues, braziers, gas-rings, plate warmers and similar non-electric domestic appliances, and parts thereof, of iron or steel.	28%

Source: Hindustan times, 2017

"The National Family Health Survey (NFHS), 2015–16 survey pegs the number for women using hygienic means of managing menstruation in India at 78% in urban areas, 48% in rural areas and 58% overall". *(https://thelogicalindian.com/health/menstruation-in-rural-india/).*

GST has become controversial as the step to tax necessary items like sanitary napkins and keeping condoms tax free has gone "Anti Gender Equality". Thus, it can be said, GST has had a negative impact on achieving the Goal of Gender Equality (Hindustan times, 2017).

Thus it is clear from the table that tax rates are going to upset the Female category of consumers. GST is not so promising as far as Gender Equality is concerned.

GST and the 6th sustainable development goals: Clean water and sanitation

Clean water and sanitation is covered under "Swachh Bharat Abhiyan". In order to find out the impact of GST on the former, one can study the impact of GST on Swachh Bharat Abhiyan.

Thus, one positive aspect that has come into limelight with the emergence of GST is that impositions in the form of cess/surcharge by the government including the Swachh Bharat cess have been ruled out.

As per the data revealed by NDTV news, since the implementation of Swachh Bharat Cess on November 2015, "an amount of approximately *Rs.* 9,851.41 crore has been collected till October 2016, aiming at building nearly 12 crore toilets, along with undertaking programmes related to solid and liquid waste management, waste segregation and spreading awareness about sanitation, etc" (*http://swachhindia.ndtv.com/gst-impact-on-swachh-bharat-abhiyan-abolition-of-swachh-bharat-cess-and-high-tax-rates-on-sanitation-products-9319/*); (Hindustan Times, 2017), it is matter of concern that how will the government fill up the financial void being created due to abolition of all the other taxes and cesses. To show it even worse, GST has imposed a high tax rate of "18% on soaps and toiletries compared to the existing 12%" (*http://swachhindia.ndtv.com/gst-impact-on-swachh-bharat-abhiyan-abolition-of-swachh-bharat-cess-and-high-tax-rates-on-sanitation-products-9319/*). It is portraying, the necessities (sanitary napkins, soaps, etc) are being charged like luxuries and the luxuries or other non essentials like condoms, bindis, sindoor, etc have been exempted from tax like these are the necessities.

"Sanitary equipment such as urinals, commodes and flushing cisterns will fall under the 12.5 percent bracket and become more expensive. This will essentially translate to the whole exercise of toilet building becoming slightly more expensive for individual toilet constructions". (*http://swachhindia.ndtv.com/gst-impact-on-swachh-bharat-abhiyan-abolition-of-swachh-bharat-cess-and-high-tax-rates-on-sanitation-products-9319/*); (Dutta, 2017).

"Sanitary napkins, soaps, hand wash, etc should be charged at lower tax rates so that more and more people can buy. Else it will go against the spirit of Swachh Bharat Abhiyan. The price of these items must be kept as low as possible to ensure that more people are encouraged to buy and use these products" - Praveen Khandelwal, Secretary General, Confederation of All India Traders (CAIT). *(http://swachhindia.ndtv.com/gst-impact-on-swachh-bharat-abhiyan-abolition-of-swachh-bharat-cess-and-high-tax-rates-on-sanitation-products-9319/*).

Thus GST appears to be negatively affecting the 6th Sustainable Development Goal.

GST and the 7th sustainable development goals: Affordable and clean energy

GST has proved to be promising for the energy sector. As per the GST tax Rates, sale of solar equipment – panels, modules and inverters will be taxed at 5 percent. However, it was rumored that these equipments will fall under the tax slab of 18 percent. It is a big relief to the energy sector. However, the situation is not hunky dory for the residential sector.

The small residential installations of 100 KW and solar inverters will fall under the Tax Slab of 28 percent, highest among the GST tax slabs. In case of Wind energy, Sale of turbines and other equipment fall under the Tax slab of 5 percent (prior to GST, VAT was also charged @ 5 percent on such equipments).

However, "most wind equipment manufacturers also take on the task of setting up projects for developers, and this being a service, will attract 18 percent GST, up from 12 percent tax on engineering services earlier". (*https://economictimes.indiatimes.com/industry/energy/power/gst-shines-on-renewable-energy-sector/articleshow/59432031.cms*); (Chandrasekaran, 2017)

GST and the 8th sustainable development goals: Decent work and economic growth

One of the aims of sustainable development goals is to encourage and ensure a sustainable economic growth, which can be achieved by ensuring higher levels of productivity and technological innovation (decent work). There is a need to design such policies which provide a platform to boost up sustainable development. According to UNDP, along with wiping out "human trafficking, slavery and forced labour", giving wings to policies like entrepreneurship and job creation are key to this.

Economic development is closely related to technology. Progress/ advancement of/ through technology paves way for economic development. Heavy taxes levied on technology will slow down the growth of the economy which will also affect the employment generation. As for instance, prior to GST, packaged software attracted VAT at around 5 percent during the sale in most states and service tax rate is 15 percent and Excise duty in the case of manufacturing of IT products. (*https://cleartax.in/s/impact-of-gst-on-it-sector*).

Software Services provided by software companies will attract 18% GST in the IT sector. It has been estimated that for purely software services, the cost of such services will increase under GST.

All businesses, large or small are under extreme pressure to get their accounting systems and ERPs in tandem with GST. This will bring about changes in business systems increase in infrastructure costs. Most large companies have set up teams consisting of their own technical experts, finance experts, and an expert from their GST software vendor *(https://cleartax.in/s/impact-of-gst-on-it-sector)*.

They will have to pay these teams and experts a higher remuneration for dealing with the hassles of GST. But on the contrary, GST will positively affect the companies which are software developers as the demand for such softwares will increase pan India.

Free lancers will be negatively affected. Those providing designing, app development, website designing services etc., will attract 18 percent service tax under GST which was 15 percent earlier.

It takes time for every policy to prove it's intentions. Similar is the case with GST.

The following impacts of GST are expected to be seen on companies:

- Restructure their operations;
- Compulsory furnishing of invoices by the suppliers /Vendors;
- Compliance cost for small firms may relatively increase, etc.

According to some experts, GST may lead to inflation in the short run, but it will lead to economic growth in the medium to long run. One promising and propelling step that can ensure economic growth is that through GST, more and more companies, even the smaller ones will come into the tax net. Indian Government is hopeful that GST will eventually reap benefits in terms of economic Growth in the long run (Ray, 2017; undp.org; India Infoline News Service, 2016).

GST and the 9th sustainable development goals: Industry, innovation and infrastructure

Infrastructure is the backbone of every economy. In India also, infrastructure sector is showing signs of growth.

As per the government, "total infrastructure spending is expected to be about 10% of GDP (gross domestic product) during the 12th Five-Year Plan (2012–17), up from 7.6% during the previous Plan".

(https://www.livemint.com/Opinion/RNcufKfrRXehYaj2af1mfN/GST-impact-on-the-infrastructure-sector.html); (Live Mint, 2017).

This shows Indian Government is taking propelling steps in case of infrastructure sector. According to the Ministry of Road Transport and Highways, a total of 6,604 km has been constructed out of the 15,000 km target set for national highways in 2016–17. *(https://www.livemint.com/Opinion/RNcufKfrRXehYaj2af1mfN/GST-impact-on-the-infrastructure-sector.html).*

Following Initiatives are taken by Government for the growth of Infrastructure Sector:

- "The Airports Authority of India plans to develop city-side infrastructure at 13 regional airports, with help from private entities for building of hotels, car parks and other facilities".
- "Significant allocations have been made to power, urban development and inland waterways sectors." (*https://www.livemint.com/Opinion/RNcufKfrRXehYaj2af1mfN/GST-impact-on-the-infrastructure-sector.html*); (Livemint, 2017).

But, the Post GST era shows some different aspects. There is an apprehension that infrastructure projects will be taxed under the tax slab of 18%. Well, this will result in increased incidence of tax on infrastructure projects. "Seemingly, there will also be a change in the cost of construction materials. A higher GST rate of 28% imposed upon cement would adversely impact construction cost. Similarly, electricity is not within the ambit of GST and input tax will be an additional burden for the infrastructure industry" (*http://www.financialexpress.com/opinion/gst-impact-on-infrastructure-it-will-cut-multiple-taxes-but-will-affect-cost-of-construction/758032/*); (Financial Express, 2017).

GST will boost the sector by eliminating multiple taxes and simplifying the law, but it will also impact the cost of goods and services used in construction and increase compliance costs (*http://www.financialexpress.com/opinion/gst-impact-on-infrastructure-it-will-cut-multiple-taxes-but-will-affect-cost-of-construction/758032/*). But, such concerns will be set off by Input Tax Credit. Thus, "GST impact on infrastructure sector seems to be a mixed bag—predictability and efficiency are key advantages while higher GST rates and non-inclusion of sub-sector are negatives" (*https://www.livemint.com/Opinion/RNcufKfrRXehYaj2af1mfN/GST-impact-on-the-infrastructure-sector.html*); (Bhoomi College, 2017).

Country shall wait till it concretises. The infrastructure sector with get a boost with the introduction of input tax credit (ITC) and elimination of ´tax on tax' and the (Financial Express, 2017).

Innovation is directly related to Ecommerce. Both go hand in hand. As far as Innovation is concerned, GST has shown some definitional problems while defining what all will fall under the ambit of different business models.

It has also been confirmed by "Internet and Mobile Association of India (IAMAI), the industry lobby group which represents companies like Flipkart, Snapdeal and Amazon." (*http://www.business-standard.com/article/economy-policy/gst-may-stifle-innovation-in-e-commerce-space-iamai-116062901066_1.html*); (Srivastava, 2016).

This can have a detrimental impact on innovation in the e-commerce space. Internet and Mobile Association of India (IAMAI) stated "For instance, the definition of 'aggregator' suggests it applies only for services and that too, only for 'listing' of sellers. The GST bill defines 'aggregator' as a service that lists 'persons providing service 'X' under the brand name or trade name of the said aggregator. However, under this definition, online classifieds like Naukri will not qualify as 'aggregator', because jobs listed on Naukri are actually offered by other companies in their name". Similar issue that arises is that Online Travel Aggregators (OTA) like Make My Trip and Yatra can be wrongfully qualified as 'operators' rather than 'aggregators', as they facilitate payments and supply of services, as opposed to listing 'persons providing service of a particular kind under the brand name or trade name of the said aggregator'. Even the recognition of online classifieds such as Olx and Quikr is also undefined. Thus these hassles make things little difficult for innovation to progress.

GST and the 10th sustainable development goal: Reduced inequalities

The basic purpose behind implementing any indirect tax is to contribute effectively towards building of social infrastructure. Under the earlier tax regime, the indirect tax charged on goods and services was credited to the state where the goods/ services were manufactured *i.e.,* the origin state. As a result, those states where the consumers paid tax on account of consumption of the good was not benefitted at all as the tax used to get transferred to the state from where the good has been imported. As for example, if the goods manufactured by a manufacturer in Maharashtra are sold in Meghalaya, tax paid by the Meghalaya consumer is collected by Maharashtra.

As a result, these states develop on the cost of development of other states. The benefit of infrastructure development that would have been available to Meghalaya on account of tax being paid by the consumers in the event of goods being purchased, is transferred to Maharashtra. This leads to an unequal development of states in India. That means people of a particular state pay tax to government for infrastructural development but they are not benefitted as the tax collected is transferred to the state where the goods were manufactured. GST will put an end to this uneven and loop sided tax regime. Thus GST is more than a mere Tax Regime. It can be regarded as a socio-economic regime (Menon, 2015).

Another comparable aspect between pre GST era and Post GST era is that the previous tax system was vague. VAT (value added tax), entertainment tax, sales tax, service tax, entry tax, etc and all were under different administrations earlier. A sales tax commissioner doesn't talk to an excise commissioner. Even within the same circle, a service tax commissioner doesn't communicate with the excise commissioner. As a result, there was a huge discrepency between goods/services manufactured and consumed. As a result of it, black money was generated. Thus, under GST everything is taxed under one roof leaving no scope for black money and corruption. Every organization, big or small, will be taxed, thereby reducing the gaps between the rich and the poor. Thus GST will help reduce inequalities existing between different sections of society.

GST and the 11th sustainable development goal: Sustainable cities and communities

India is Urbanising rapidly. By 2030, India is expected to be home to six mega-cities with populations above 10 million. According to 2013–14 figures, 68% of the country's total population live in rural areas, while 17% of the country's urban population live in slums. The Government of India is doing it's part in the form of Smart Cities Mission, the Jawaharlal Nehru National Urban Renewal Mission, and the Atal Mission for Rejuvenation and Urban Transformation (AMRUT) are working to address the challenge of improving urban spaces. The prime minister's Pradhan Mantri Awas Yojana aims to achieve housing for all by 2022. But all these efforts require funds which can be raised through taxes. Thus a positive hope is expected to arise out of implementation of GST. Government should decide about the allocation of funds raised through taxes for making cities sustainable and worth living for the community on the whole. But on the contrary, imposing heavy taxes on infrastructural facilities may lead to relatively more negative impact in making cities sustainable and overall benefit of the community.

GST and the 12th sustainable development goal: Responsible consumption and production

Population is also growing with accelerating urbanisation. As a result, there will be more and more people to feed on but less and less water, energy and food available for them. Thus there is a need to bring in sustainability in consumption and production patterns so that basic necessities are available for future generations to come. The sad part is, on one hand, one third of the food produced in the country is wasted while close to 800 million people on the planet are chronically hungry.

It is important that producers grow more food while reducing negative environmental impacts such as soil, water and nutrient loss, greenhouse gas emissions, and degradation of ecosystems. "It was estimated that 12 percent GST will be charged on fertilisers, up from the 4–8 percent. As per certain estimates, the prices for urea, an important fertiliser, may increase by 300 to 400 per tonne. At the same time, the retail prices for other fertilisers such as di-ammonium phosphate (DAP) can increase as much as 3,000 per tonne in States such as Punjab, Haryana and Uttar Pradesh, which has no taxes on the farm nutrients". (*https://www.thehindubusinessline.com/opinion/not-really-a-green-and-sustainable-tax/article9799146.ece*). *"But at present, taxes on fertilisers are in the range of 0 to 6 percent across states. A 12 percent increase in fertilisers would have seen the retail prices going up from Rs. 30 to Rs. 120 per bag (50 kg) on Urea, Di ammonium Phosphate (DAP) and Potash in states like Punjab, Haryana and Andhra Pradesh where there is zero tax on soil nutrients". (https://timesofindia.indiatimes.com/business/india-business/government-lowers-gst-on-fertlisers-just-ahead-of-launch/articleshow/59389136.cms)*; (Times of India, 2017).

Lowering GST rates will bring down the prices to current effective rate which will be beneficial for overall productivity.

GST and the 13th sustainable development goal: Climate action

What is the goal all about?

The 13th Sustainable Development Goal aims to "mobilize $100 billion annually by 2020 to address the needs of developing countries and help mitigate climate-related disasters like earthquakes, tsunamis, tropical cyclones and flooding count in the hundreds of billions of dollars, requiring an investment of US$ 6 billion annually in disaster risk management alone" (UNDP).

Climate change is a global phenomenon and we all are responsible for the same. Ever since late 90s, this issue has occupied an important place while discussing sustainability. The harm, caused by humans to climate is immense and affects many generations to come. Human actions have eroded climate to that extent that it had lead to many natural calamities. Where government should take serious steps towards it's conservation, policies don't seem to do anything for it. The scope of climate conservation covers many aspects. As for example, clean air, no pollution, clean energy like solar, wind, water energy, etc.

AN INDIAN SCENARIO

India's vulnerability profile is increasing. As far as the data related to number of deaths, missing persons and directly affected population due to disasters impacts are concerned, it is found to be conflicting. According to the

(UNISDR, 2016) report, "India was among the top three most disaster hit countries in 2015, with economic losses amounting to $ 3.30 billion". (*http://www.socialwatch.org/sites/default/files/swindia/2017-Civil-Society-Report-on-SDGs-Agenda-2030-INDIA.pdf*).

The report of the UNISDR titled "Human Cost of Weather Related Disaster," says that India had 19 disaster events including floods, droughts and heat waves in 2015. (*http://www.socialwatch.org/sites/default/files/swindia/2017-Civil-Society-Report-on-SDGs-Agenda-2030-INDIA.pdf*). Human activities are one of the major causes of the vulnerability.

As far as India is concerned, it is running low on finances which is the main reason behind slow progress and adaptation." A meager sum of INR 3.5 billion for the National Adaptation Fund for the financial years 2015–16 and 2016–17, has been allocated by government of India." (*http://www.socialwatch.org/sites/default/files/swindia/2017-Civil-Society-Report-on-SDGs-Agenda-2030-INDIA.pdf*).

Impact of GST

Impact of GST on fuel

Diesel is out of the ambit of GST, and that is why its price is high. At the very outset, it not being a clean fuel will affect the climate negatively; further 5 percent GST on road transport will escalate the prices of fuel; then, to make the condition even worse, there is no provision to promote a cleaner fuel mechanism like CNG which emits lower carbon. All these not so promising policies are going to worsen the climatic conditions even more.

Impact of GST on solar/ wind energy

Where government should promote climate conservation alternatives like solar energy, considering there is no dearth of Sunlight in India, situations are somewhat frustrating. The present situation is quite the opposite. Solar and wind energy will attract a tax rate of 15 percent which is quite high.

Impact of GST on coal

"The carbon tax (or coal cess) will now feed the GST Compensation Fund — a fund meant to compensate various state governments for any loss in revenue arising out of the goods and services tax because the costs for coal is projected to fall by almost 7 percent. The GST regime clearly shows positive "terms-of-trade" as far as coal is concerned". (*https://www.thehindubusinessline.com/opinion/not-really-a-green-and-sustainable-tax/article9799146.ece*).

GST and the 14th sustainable development goal: Life below water

The 14th Sustainable Development Goal relates to "Conserving and sustainably using the oceans, seas and marine resources to achieve sustainable development"- UNDP.

The targets to be achieved under Sustainable Development Goal 14 includes: (*Frangoul, 2017*)

- Preventing and significantly cutting marine pollution by 2025;
- Minimizing and addressing the impacts of ocean acidification; and
- Conserving at least 10 percent of coastal and marine areas by 2020.

We, the humans have acted very selfish and have destroyed almost every sphere of environment. Our unscrupulous, unprincipled, undisciplined, dishonourable and unethical actions have led to environmental problems, contributing towards polluting oceans and seas, probably the most. All the problems have been created by us. But it is the time to turn the tide. With informed decisions, coordination and congruent global actions, we can solve these problems by focusing on reducing pollution in the form of chemicals, particles, industrial, agricultural, and residential waste, noise (*UNDP, 2015*).

The institutions at National and international level are doing their part. The United Nations Ocean Conference of 2017 sought to find ways and call for the implementation of Sustainable Development Goal 14. (undp.org)·

But there is a huge requirement to amend our activities at personal level also.

"It is a curious situation that the sea, from which life first arose should now be threatened by the activities of one form of that life. But the sea, though changed in a sinister way, will continue to exist; the threat is rather to life itself." - Rachel Carson.

Some regulatory actions are required to control emissions and promote developments in renewable energy. As such, no direct relationship can be formed between GST and the 14th sustainable development Goal, still the contribution of GST towards overall sustainability can be one of the driving force for achieving the target.

GST and the 15th sustainable development goal: Life on land

It relates to "Protect, restore and promote sustainable use of terrestrial ecosystems, sustainably manage forests, combat desertification, and halt and reverse land degradation and halt biodiversity loss".

(*https://sustainabledevelopment.un.org/content/documents/211617%20 Goals%2017%20Partnerships.pdf*); (UNDP, 2015) (refer Table 3).

Table 3: Targets to be achieved under goal 15 include: (undp.org).

- Ensuring the conservation, restoration and sustainable use of terrestrial and inland freshwater ecosystems and their services, etc by 2020;
- Halt deforestation, Restoration of degraded forests and substantially increasing afforestation and reforestation globally by 2020;
- By 2030, ensure the conservation of mountain ecosystems, including their biodiversity, in order to enhance their capacity to provide benefits that are essential for sustainable development
- Take urgent and significant action to reduce the degradation of natural habitats, halt the loss of biodiversity and, by 2020, protect and prevent the extinction of threatened species
- Take urgent action to end poaching and trafficking of protected species of flora and fauna and address both demand and supply of illegal wildlife products
- By 2020, introduce measures to prevent the introduction and significantly reduce the impact of invasive alien species on land and water ecosystems and control or eradicate the priority species
- By 2020, integrate ecosystem and biodiversity values into national and local planning, development processes, poverty reduction strategies and accounts
- Mobilize and significantly increase financial resources from all sources to conserve and sustainably use biodiversity and ecosystems
- Mobilize significant resources from all sources and at all levels to finance sustainable forest management and provide adequate incentives to developing countries to advance such management, including for conservation and reforestation

Source: *https://sustainabledevelopment.un.org/content/documents/211617%20Goals %2017%20Partnerships.pdf*

To make life livable on land it is important that both UNDP and man's untiring efforts go hand in hand to preserve the environment.

As far as taxation system is concerned, there seems to be no direct link between GST and the 15th Sustainable Development Goal.

GST and the 16th sustainable development goal: Peace, justice and strong institutions

The 16th Sustainable Goal proves to be a necessary achievement in order to ensure attainment of other SDGs. Ensuring equality and sustainability in the world is only possible if our societies are more inclusive and peaceful. Prerequisites for ensuring everything written above include efforts towards reducing crime, violence, and exploitation, etc. putting an end to illegal arms and drug trade is also essential. Also, more and more transparency, effectiveness and accountability is required on the part of Public institutions that we all rely on.

Table 4: Ensuring peace and justice includes working towards the following agendas: (Civil society report, 2017).

- Ensuring that all Forms of Violence and Related Death Rates Everywhere, are reduced· Efforts are made to put an end to Abuse, Exploitation, Trafficking and All Forms of Violence and Torture of Children;
- Ensure that every citizen has an Equal Access to Justice for *i.e.* Justice for All;
- Reducing smuggling and the Illicit Financial and Arms Flows, and Combat Crime;· Reducing Corruption and Bribery in all their Forms;
- Developing Effective, Accountable And Transparent Institutions At All Levels;
- Ensure Responsive, Inclusive, Participatory and Representative Decision-Making at All Levels;
- Broaden and Strengthen the Participation of Developing Countries in the Institutions of Global Governance;
- By 2030, Provide Legal Identity For All, Including Birth Registration;

Ensure Public Access to Information and Protect Fundamental Freedoms, in Accordance with National Legislation and International Agreements;

***Source*:** http://www.socialwatch.org/sites/default/files/swindia/2017-Civil-Society-Report-on-SDGs-Agenda-2030-INDIA.pdf

As such, no direct relationship can be found between GST and the 16th SDG. The onus of it's achievement lies with several other institutions like United Nations Development Programme (UNDP).

GST and the 17th sustainable development goal: Partnerships for the goals

To ensure attainment of sustainable development agenda, it is important that partnership between government, private sector and civil society grows. Attainment of Goal Congruency is possible only when there is Group Cohesiveness *i.e.,* a healthy partnership between governments, the private sector and civil society. It is essential so that these partnerships comprising of principles and values, a shared vision, and shared goals that place people and the planet at the centre, can contribute effectively at the global, regional, national and local level.

Mobilization, redirection and unlocking the transformative power of trillions of dollars of private resources to deliver on sustainable development objectives is the need of hour. Huge and Long term Investments in the form of foreign direct investment, are needed especially in developing countries in many critical sectors. This includes focusing on information and communications technologies, besides sustainable energy, infrastructure and transport. There seems to be a linkage that can be drawn between GST and the 17th Sustainable Development Goal *i.e.,* Partnerships for the Goals. GST can contribute positively towards attracting Foreign Direct Investment. It is expected that GST will lead to more and more tax compliance that will attract more foreign direct investments across sectors including heavy engineering and automotive sectors (www.thehindubusinessline.com) because of transparency and ease in doing business.

Table 5: GST ready India, 2017

According to a survey conducted by Feedback Business Consulting Services across 67 Indian companies, majority believed that the GST implementation would be constructive for the Indian economy. Around 72 percentage respondents reverted that they believed investments would increase across different sectors and a significant portion of that would be in the form of FDI, especially in the automotive and heavy engineering sector.

Source: *(http: / / www.gstreadyindia.com / gst-implementation-attract-foreign-direct-investment /*

The President of Asian Development Bank, Takehiko Nakao stated "For India to grow faster, FDI is important... For that purpose, the Indian economy should be integrated as truly one single economy and rationalisation of tax, the GST, as the government is seeking, is very important reform. I hope it can be successful". (*https: / / www.thehindubusinessline.com / economy / macro-economy / gst-will-integrate-indian-economy-attract-fdi-adb-chief / article8352436.ece*);

Thus, GST will prove be a boon for ensuring partnerships for achieving Sustainable Development Goals

CONCLUSIONS AND READINGS

Governments may make policies and policy changes in response to the change in economic conditions. Governments keep a constant eye on how the economy is affected by the policies made by them although policies take their own time to prove the intentions. These regulations are frequently used to engineer economic growth or prevent negative economic consequences. Normally, during periods of weak growth, interest rates are lowered to encourage borrowing and restore economic growth according to Keynesian school of thought. To curb inflationary rise in prices, governments may decide to increase interest rates. Government policies may also use various tax incentives/ strategies to direct economic conditions also. The active use of these strategies demonstrates government interest in amending economic circumstances for economic well-being. But this time there is more to the government policy of introducing one country one tax by the name of GST. GST is going to show its performance in the long term, like other policies. But several conclusions can be easily estimated. With the advent of GST, following things are expected to happen:

- Cascading effect of taxes will come to an end;
- Excessive taxes at various stages of the product value chain is eliminated;
- The slogan of one nation one tax will be formalized;
- Coordination and Integration amongst various Markets, Processes, Institutions, Organizations is expected, etc.

GST is apprehended to considerably show positive impacts on the following aspects:

1. ***Inflation Will See a Fall***: It is expected that food grains, household consumer items and essential services will either be exempt or kept lower under GST, so, it is expected that inflation will fall.
2. ***Reduction in Non Productive Expenses***: The most peculiar feature of GST is that all the other indirect taxes like entry tax, service tax, etc are going to be subsumed in GST. As a result of it, there will be reduction in the cost associated with logistics and warehousing cost. "But this cost reduction by the producers many not necessarily be passed on to the consumers in terms of lower prices. GST may appear to be loop sided". (*http://www.financialexpress.com/opinion/gst-impact-on-inflation-here-is-all-you-want-to-know/749504/*).
3. ***Reducing Income Inequalities***: GST is a sure shot step towards reducing the income disparities. Where it's main focus is on providing food to all, reducing poverty, ensuring zero hunger, etc, at the same time it is working towards reducing the gap between the "haves" and "have nots".

   For this, the luxuries have been taxed at the rate of 28%, highest under the GST tax structure. As prescribed under GST list of items like "*bidis, molasses, chocolate not containing cocoa, waffles and wafers coated with chocolate, pan masala, aerated water, paint, deodorants, shaving creams, after shave, hair shampoo, dye, sunscreen, wallpaper, ceramic tiles, water heater, dishwasher, weighing machine, washing machine, ATM, vending machines, vacuum cleaner, shavers, hair clippers, automobiles, motorcycles, aircraft for personal use, will attract 28 % tax*". (*https://economictimes.indiatimes.com/news/economy/policy/a-quick-guide-to-india-gst-rates-in 2017/articleshow58743715.cms?utm_source=contentofinterest&utm_ medium=text&utm_campaign=cppst*) ; (Bhatia, 2017).

   'Compensation Cess' will be charged by the Government tobacco, coal, aerated water, motor cars etc., which will be costing the customers to pay high. (*http://www.sdgdatalabs.org/2017/06/14/gst-boon-or-bane-to-sustainable-development-goals/*)
4. ***Benefitting the Ultimate Consumers:*** GST is purported to reduce the burden of taxation on ultimate consumers through the concept of Input Tax Credit, etc. Also, with the abolition of other taxes like State Value Added Tax, Central Excise, Service Tax, Octroi, local tax, entertainment tax, excise duty, surcharge, etc, products and services are expected to be available at comparatively reasonable prices. The following hypothetical example will prove to be benefitting the ultimate consumers.

Table 6: Benefit to ultimate consumers with the introduction of GST.

	The distribution network from manufacturer to ultimate consumer	*Scenario of Tax in case of VAT*	*Scenario of Tax in case of GST*
i.	Cost of production	1000000	1000000
ii.	Profit margin	500000	500000
iii.	i+ii (Cost of Production + Profit Margin)	1500000	1500000
iv.	Central excise duty @ 12% of iii	180000	N/A
v.	iii+iv (1500000+180000) and (1500000+N/A)	1680000	1500000
vi.	VAT @12.5 % of v. (12.5% of 1680000)	210000	N/A
vii.	Add central GST @ 12% of v (12% of 1500000)	N/A	180000
viii.	State GST @ 8% of v. (8% of 1500000)	N/A	120000
ix.	Total sale price	(iii+iv+vi)	(v+vii+viii)
	(*Source:* Compiled from various souraces in google)	1890000	1800000

As is clear from the example, with the application of tax under GST regime, the consumer will be benefitted with an amount of Rs. 90,000. It is because the central Excise duty @12% and VAT @ 12.5% will be not applicable and the product will be available at reasonable price comparatively. Earlier, when VAT was charges, the price at which the product was available to the consumer was Rs. 1890000. In the GST regime, the same product will be available at a price of Rs. 1800000. A consumer saves Rs. 90,000.

Where GST is expected to bring about root level changes in the country, it may also shake the very roots of the country. Things are going to be Topsy Turvy in the coming future.

GST may Negatively Affect the Following Aspects

1. ***Economic growth will take place at a slower pace*:** Since companies will have to restructure their processes, businesses, internally as well as externally, Economy will take time gearing up towards growth. GST in itself is a big revolution in the history of tax regime in India. Almost everything in the market has to undergo a change to meet the requirements of this tax. The internal processes have to be changed, supply chain and value chains are to be altered, internal as well as external restructuring is required, new softwares, which are in tandem with the requirements of GST have to be installed, new workforce may have to be employed to incorporate GST completely in the business, and the like. Where large firms can still bear the shock, small firms are going to lose revenue at least in the near future. It is hoped that this situation is only for short period of time and the condition will be conducive in the medium-long term.
2. ***Shaking up corporate operations*:** As stated earlier, corporate will have to undergo forced restructuring as far as their business operations are concerned. Where large companies may not find it too

difficult to make alterations, it will be more challenging for the small firms to restructure them as their compliance cost is going to increase. Big companies have their supply chains in order and may also benefit from input tax credit.

3. ***Forced instructions on vendors/ suppliers*:** Where companies, big or small are challenged in terms of changes to be made in their existing structures, vendors and suppliers also cannot escape from the clenches of GST. They have to furnish invoices of all the transactions made because if the companies want to take the benefit of Input Tax Credit, (ITC), they will have to show all the invoices of the taxes already paid on the inputs purchased by them from the vendors or suppliers. As a result, when vendors will have to show the invoices of each and every transaction, it will become nearly impossible for them to evade tax, which is a good thing but may lead to turbulence in the beginning. Thus vendors will be bound to furnish the invoices.
4. ***Vague anti-profiteering clause*:** Passing on the benefit of lower tax may not be practiced by the producers which may violate the very reason for which GST is implemented. The GST council, headed by Finance Minister, Mr. Arun Jaitley is promising that companies will pass on the benefit of lower taxes to consumers but assuring about the same is doubtful.
5. ***Inflationary rise in prices*:** GST will lead to inflation. "Many items are not covered by the GST regime. Potable alcohol, crude oil, natural gas, aviation fuel, diesel, petrol, electricity and real estate are out of GST's ambit, and states will levy their own taxes on these". (*http://www.financialexpress.com/opinion/gst-impact-on-inflation-here-is-all-you-want-to-know/749504/*). There are chances that states may pose heavy taxes on these products, thereby leading to rise in transportation/ logistics cost, etc. Therefore it may lead to inflationary threat.

Table 7

"We believe that while corporates would pass on the direct benefits of GST (like a lower tax rate), they would aim to retain partly (if not fully) the indirect benefits from the saving in logistics costs, streamlining of business processes and the seamless flow of input credits," Nomura said in a report.

While GST laws include anti-profiteering measures—the benefits of the reduction in the tax rate and input credit shall be passed on by a commensurate reduction in prices—such measures are difficult to implement and would be a retrograde step, similar to price controls, if implemented in haste, **Nomura added**.

***Source*:** *https://www.hindustantimes.com/business-news/gst-impact-on-economy-five-things-to-watch-out-for/story-vlIqCqYPX8vzlIZvsJG55M.html*

Evaluation of GST from the Perspective of Sustainable Development

GST and reducing poverty

- GST is expected to positively contribute towards achieving the Zero poverty Goal by levying no tax on basic food items;
- The poor people will be benefitted due to increase in real purchasing power leading to increase in their income levels and reduction in the prices of the products consumed by them;

GST and zero hunger

- Under GST, most of the food items will be taxed at the rate of 0 %;
- Food items such as "fresh meat, fish chicken, eggs, milk, butter milk, curd, natural honey, fresh fruits and vegetables, flour, besan, bread, prasad, salt, Cereal grains hulled, Palmyra jiggery, etc will not be taxed". (*https://economictimes.indiatimes.com/news/economy/policy/a-quick-guide-to-india-gst-rates-in-2017/articleshow/58743715.cms?utm_source=contentofinterest&utm_medium=text&utm_campaign=cppst*).
- It is expected that GST will aid the Government in reducing the problem of hunger to zero.

GST and good health and well being

- Health care is exempt from any tax under GST Tax Proposal;
- GST will positively contribute towards achieving 3rd Sustainable Development in the country.

GST and quality education

- Education Sector has been marked as one of the most important sector under GST Tax Structure;
- To make education accessible for everyone, education services are exempted from tax so that quality education at low cost can be provided to all;
- Thus GST will have a positive impact on achieving the 4th Sustainable Development Goal *i.e.,* Quality education.

GST and gender equality

- The GST council does not include any female as it's member;

- Garments and Jewellery, Cosmetics and Beauty Products, Household Appliances and Meals, Domestic Appliances and Health Products, etc which are used mainly by women have come under the ambit of GST Tax Structure. (Central Board for Excise and Customs and Bhatia, Gurman, 2017)
- Products such as sanitary napkins, tampons, towels etc have been taxed under the tax slab of 12%;
- Condoms, sindoor, bindi etc are kept tax free.
- This is an "Anti Gender Equality" step;
- GST has had a negative impact on achieving the Goal of Gender Equality.

Table 8: Some of the excerpts of the GST tax rates are mentioned in the table below: (Bhatia, 2017).

Product/ Service	***Tax rate***
***Beauty or make-up*:** Preparations and preparations for the care of the skin (other than medicaments), including sunscreen or sun tan preparations; manicure or pedicure preparations.	28%
***Cosmetics*:** Scent sprays and similar toilet sprays, and mounts and heads therefore; powder-puffs and pads for the application of cosmetics or toilet preparations.	28%
***Garments*:** Artificial fur, artificial fur as trimmings and embellishments for garments, made ups, knitwear, plastic and leather goods.	18%
***Precious stones*:** (other than diamonds) and semi-precious stones, but not strung, mounted or set; ungraded precious stones (other than diamonds) and semi-precious stones, temporarily strung for convenience transport.	3%
***Health products*:** Products such as sanitary napkins, tampons, towels etc have been taxed heavily.12%	12%
***Domestic appliances*:** Electro-mechanical domestic appliances with self-contained electric motor, other than vacuum cleaners.	28%

(***Source:*** Bhatia, 2017)

GST and clean water and sanitation

- As discussed earlier, clean water and sanitation is not directly covered under GST;
- In order to find out the impact of GST on the former, one can study the impact of GST on Swachh Bharat Abhiyan;
- "GST has implemented a high tax rate of 18% on soaps and toiletries compared to the existing 12%". (*https://twitter.com/ndtv/status/880367671098789889*). Sanitary napkins, soaps, etc are being charged like luxuries and the luxuries or other non essentials like condoms, bindis, sindoor, etc have been exempted from tax like these are the necessities;

- Thus GST appears to be negatively affecting the 6th Sustainable Development Goal.

GST and affordable and clean energy

- Sale of solar equipment – panels, modules and inverters will be taxed at 5 percent contrary to the proposed tax slab of 18 percent;
- It is a big relief to the energy sector;
- The small residential installations of 100 KW and solar inverters will fall under the Tax Slab of 28 percent, highest among the GST tax slabs;
- The position to expect Affordable and Clean Energy stands topsy-turvy.

GST and decent work and economic growth

- Heavy taxes on technology will slow down the growth of the economy which will also affect the employment generation;
- The cost of purely software services will increase under GST;
- All businesses will alter their accounting systems and ERPs to bring them in tandem with GST, thereby increasing Infrastructural Costs;
- The Freelancers will be taxed at the rate of 18 percent which was earlier only 15 percent (for software services like website designing, app designing and the like);
- Thus because of GST economic growth will take place at a slower pace.

GST and industry, innovation and infrastructure

- "The infrastructure projects will be taxed under the tax slab of 18% and GST rate of 28% will be imposed upon cement"; (*http://www.indialawjournal.org/impact-of-gst-on-infrastructure.php*)
- This will adversely impact construction cost;
- Cost of goods and services used in construction will increase thereby increasing the compliance costs;
- A considerable boost is expected to be given to the infrastructure sector by eliminating multiplicity of taxes and introducing input tax credit (ITC)".
- GST will have a detrimental impact on innovation in the e-commerce space.
- Online classifieds and Online Travel Aggregators (OTA) like Naukri, Olx and Quikr and Make My Trip, Yatra, respectively will also be detrimentally impacted because of these falling under vague and undefined categories;

GST and reduced inequalities

- The Tax paid by the consumer will be credited to the state where the consumer lives, rather than transferring the benefit of tax to the state where the goods were manufactured." *(https://economictimes.indiatimes.com/opinion/interviews/gst-is-not-just-a-tax-reform-but-it-is-a-socio-economic-reform-sachin-menon-kpmg/articleshow/47618950.cms?utm_source=contentofinterest&utm_me dium=text&utm_campaign=cppst)*
- Many states will have more funds for development and the inequalities of the distribution of income will reduce.
- It can be regarded as a socio-economic regime.
- Everything will be taxed under one roof leaving no scope for black money and corruption, unlike previous fragmented tax structure;
- Every organization will be taxed, thereby reducing the gaps between the rich and the poor, helping reduce inequalities existing between different sections of society.

GST and sustainable cities and communities

- By 2030, India is expected to be home to six mega-cities with populations above 10 million.
- A positive hope is expected to arise out of implementation of GST. However, the GST is expected to increase tax revenues;
- Government should decide about the allocation of funds raised through taxes for making cities sustainable and worth living for the community on the whole;
- But on the contrary, imposing heavy taxes on infrastructural facilities may lead to relatively more negative impact in making cities sustainable and overall benefit of the community.

GST and responsible consumption and production

- Bringing sustainability in consumption and production patterns is all what is needed for an ever increasing population;
- Fertilisers will have an increased percentage of tax on them;
- The retail prices for Fertilizers like Urea, Di-ammonium phosphate (DAP) will increase.
- These increased prices will be recovered from farmers, which will ultimately affect the productivity.

GST and climate action

- Diesel prices would have come down if GST was applicable on it and a 15 percent tax on solar and wind energy will be implemented. Both of these steps will prove to be detrimental for deteriorating climate;
- Costs for coal is projected to fall by almost 7 percent under GST which will show a positive terms of trade.

GST and life below water

- The United Nations Ocean Conference of 2017 sought to find ways and call for the implementation of Sustainable Development Goal 14; (www.undp.org)
- As such, no direct relationship can be formed between GST and the 14th sustainable development Goal, still the contribution of GST towards overall sustainability can be one of the driving force for achieving the target.

GST and life on land

- "UNDP is contributing towards making life worthliving on land";
- As far as taxation system is concerned, there seems to be no direct link between GST and the 15th Sustainable Development Goal.

GST and peace, justice and strong institutions

- As such, no direct relationship can be found between GST and the 16th SDG.
- The onus of it's achievement lies with several other institutions like United Nations Development Programme (UNDP)

GST and partnerships for the goals

- To ensure attainment of sustainable development agenda, it is important that partnership between government, private sector and civil society grows;
- GST will positively contribute towards 17th Sustainable Development Goal by attracting Foreign Direct Investment;
- It is expected that GST will lead to more and more tax compliance that will attract more foreign direct investments across sectors including heavy engineering and automotive sectors because of transparency and ease in doing business.

REFERENCES

A Civil Society Report. Sustainable Development Goals: Agenda 2030 (2017). Wada Na Todo Abhiyan. Retrieved from: *http://www.chsj.org/uploads/1/0/2/1/10215849/civil_society_report_on_sdgs.pdf*

A quick guide to India GST rates in 2017 economic times (2017). The Economic Times. Retrieved from: *http://economictimes.indiatimes.com/articleshow/58743715.cms?utm_source=contentofinterest&utm_medium=text&utm_campaign=cppst*

Bhatia Gurman (2017). From eating out to mobile phones. Find out the GST rate for over 1,700 goods and services. Retrieved from: *http://www.hindustantimes.com/interactives/gst-rate-complete-list/*

Bhoomi College (2017). A reality check of menstruation in rural India.

Retrieved from: *https://thelogicalindian.com/health/menstruation-in-rural-india/*

Cascade Tax. Investopedia. Retrieved from: *http://www.investopedia.com/terms/c/cascade-tax.asp.*

Cascade Tax. Wikipedia.Retrieved from: *https://en.wikipedia.org/wiki/Cascade_tax.*

Central Board for Excise and Customs.

Chandrasekaran Kaavya (2017). GST shines on renewable energy sector. ET Bureau. Retrieved from: *http://economictimes.indiatimes.com/industry/energy/power/gst-shines-on-renewable-energy-sector/articleshow/59432031.cms*

Dutta Saptarshi (2017). GST Impact on Swachh Bharat Abhiyan: Abolition of Swachh

Bharat Cess and High Tax Rates on Sanitation Products.

Retrieved from: *http://swachhindia.ndtv.com/gst-impact-on-swachh-bharat-abhiyan-abolition-of-swachh-bharat-cess-and-high-tax-rates-on-sanitation-products-9319/*

Frangoul Anmar (2017). "UN Secretary General Guterres says world's oceans are facing unprecedented threat", *CNBC.*

Goal 15: Life on land *(2015) UNDP.*

GST impact on economy: Five things to watch out for. Hindustan Times. Retrieved from: *http://www.hindustantimes.com/business-news/gst-impact*-on-economy-five-things-to-watch-out-for/story-vlIqCqYPX8vzlIZvsJG55M.html

GST Impact on Infrastructure Sector (2017). Live Mint. Retrieved from *http://www.livemint.com/Opinion/RNcufKfrRXehYaj2af1mfN/GST-impact-on-the-infrastructure-sector.html*

GST impact on infrastructure: It will cut multiple taxes but will affect cost of construction (2017). Financial Express. Retrieved from: *http://www.financial express.com/opinion/gst-impact-on-infrastructure-it-will-cut-multiple-taxes-but-will-affect-cost-of-construction/758032/*

GST Ready India. GST Implementation to Attract Foreign Direct Investment (2017). Retrieved from *http://www.gstreadyindia.com/gst-implementation-attract-foreign-direct-investment/*

GST to boost job creation; hiring to increase by 11% (2016). India Infoline News Service, Mumbai. Retrieved from: *http://www.indiainfoline.com/article/news-top-story/gst-to-boost-job-creation-hiring-to-increase-by-11-116112800226_1.html*

GST will integrate Indian economy, attract FDI. Press Trust of India. Retrieved from: *http://www.thehindubusinessline.com/economy/macro-economy/gst-will-integrate-indian-economy-attract-fdi-adb-chief/article8352436.ece*

Highlights of Telecom Subscription Data (2015) TRAI.

Implementation of Goods and Services Tax (GST) in India: Boon or Bane for Sustainable Development Goals? (2017). SDG datalabs. Retrieved from: *http://www.sdgdatalabs.org/2017/06/14/gst-boon-or-bane-to-sustainable-development-goals/*

Implementation of GST to attract more FDI (2016). The Economic Times.

Retrieved from: *http://economictimes.indiatimes.com/articleshow/54310069.cms?utm_source=contentofinterest&utm_medium=text&utm _campaign= cppst*

India's budget for climate adaptation is too low, activists say. Retrieved from: *http://in.reuters.com/article/india-climatechange-budget-idINKCN0X805H*

Menon Sachin (2015). GST is not just a tax reform but it is a socio-economic reform. The Economic Times, KPMG ET Bureau. Retrieved from: *http://economictimes.indiatimes.com/articleshow/47618950.cms?utm_source=contentofinterest&utm_medium=text&utm_campaign=cppst*

One Hundred and First Amendment of the Constitution of India. Wikipedia. Retrieved from: *https://en.wikipedia.org/wiki/One_Hundred_and_First_Amendment_of_the_Constitution_of_India*

Ray, K.R. (2017). GST impact on economy: Five things to watch out for. Hindustan Times. Retrieved from: *http://www.hindustantimes.com/business-news/gst-impact-on-economy-five-things-to-watch-out-for/story-vlIqCqYPX8vzlIZvsJG55M.html*

Retrieved from: *http://envfor.nic.in/sites/default/files/pressreleases/Indian_Country_Paper_Low_Res.pdf*

Retrieved from: *http://www.in.undp.org/content/india/en/home/post-2015/sdg-overview/goal-8.html*

Retrieved from: *http://www.undp.org/content/undp/en/home/sustainable-development-goals/goal-15-life-on-land/targets/*

Retrieved from: *http://www.thehindubusinessline.com/opinion/not-really-a-green-and-sustainable-tax/article9799146.ece*

Retrieved From (2016, 11th April) Livemint, *http://www.livemint.com/Politics/xBROsTMzIdFIvMDhN/Indias-bud-get-for-climate-adaptation-inadequate.html*

Retrieved from: *https://sustainabledevelopment.un.org/content/documents/211617%20Goals%2017%20Partnerships.pdf*

Sengupta Ramarko (2017). Government lowers GST on fertilizers just ahead launch. The Times of India. Retrieved from: *http://timesofindia.indiatimes.com/business/india-business/government-lowers-gst-on-fertlisers-just-ahead-of*launch/articleshow/59389136.cms

Sinha Rajani (2017). GST impact on inflation: Here is all you want to know. Financial Express. Retrieved from: *http://www.financialexpress.com/opinion/gst-impact-on-inflation-here-is-all-you-want-to-know/749504/*

Srivastava Moulishree (2016). GST may stifle innovation in e-commerce space. IAMAI business standard, Mumbai . Retrieved from: *http://www.business-standard.com/article/economy-policy/gst-may-stifle-innovation-in-e-commerce-space-iamai-116062901066_1.html*

The Hindu. 2017. "GST will increase tax revenue: Official". Retrieved from: *http://www.thehindu.com/news/cities/Visakhapatnam/GST-will-increase-tax-revenue-Official/article17363677.ece*

The impact of GST on Small Business in Queensland: A Report for the Queensland Department of State Development (1999). Ernst & Young.

8

Goods and Services Tax: A Reformed Taxation Model of Post Globalized India

ANIL KUMAR BISWAS[1*]

ABSTRACT

After the initiation of the concept of 'globalization' in the world economy, it needed to reform their existing taxation system for sustaining in the globalized era. India is one of the fastest growing economy in the world. India's Gross Domestic Product (GDP) grew at 7.5% during 2015–16. But due to demonetization this growth slightly slowdown, yet it is hopeful. Demonetization is strong steps of present Narendra Modi led Central Government against illegal money in markets. At the same time initiation of GST, Goods and Services Tax is another strongest initiative for taxation reform in India after independence. The 122nd Constitutional Amendment Act 2016 will go down in India's political-economic history as a watershed; it gives the country the most historic tax reform up to date since independence. Goods and Services Tax amendment act is a historic taxation reform in the era of globalization in India which turns in to taxation under one umbrella as an inclusive technique for financial governance. Before the introduction of GST, there were two types of taxes collected by the government: one is the direct tax and another is the indirect tax. The tax structure before the introduction of GST; it is the tax on tax making goods and services rather expensive for the ultimate consumer while making life hard for the trade and industry. GST is a reformed technique of inclusive financial governance which includes all taxes into a single tax for the consumer. Goods and services tax would be subjected to taxes only on value addition at each stage, thus bringing down the overall tax burden for the consumer; which smother financial governance. The main objective of this study is to analysis the taxation reform in India in the globalized era in general and various dimensions of Goods and Services Tax in particular.

[1] Department of Political Science, The University of Burdwan, Burdwan, West Bengal.

*Corresponding author: E-mail: bappa_anil@rediffmail.com

This study has analysis to the prospects and challenges of the new types of the taxation system. This study also critically analyse the impacts of this reforms on consumers, traders and businessmen in particular and country's economy in general and also gives some policy recommendations for removing challenges.

Key words: Goods, Services, Globalization, Governance, Taxation, Inclusive, Financial.

INTRODUCTION

Developing countries of the world are assigned on tax reform in recent year. Such initiative of tax reform in developing countries mostly influenced by some local factors as such as international factors. After the initiation of the concept of 'globalization', it needs to reform their existing taxation system for sustaining in the globalized era. It is true that foreign investment in a country depends mostly on her simple taxation system. Enhancing competitiveness and attracting foreign investment require minimizing both efficiency and compliance costs of the tax system. Due to the impact of globalization, countries are losses their revenue from customs within the existing system of taxation. So there is the need for taxation reform of a country which helping to fulfil maximum needs with domestic tax (Rao & Rao, 2009). Under these circumstances, India has taken various initiatives for her taxation reform by discarding old aged multifarious critical nature of taxes. The fiscal crisis of 1991 had created a situation; under which country realised an urgent need for her taxation reform. Since then various initiatives have been taking for unifying the country under one taxation system replaced by multifarious taxation by major reform. Introduction of Value Added Taxes (VAT), 2005 replaced by sale taxes was the biggest step for unifying sale taxes in the country. As a result, after the introduction of the VAT, all states are moved towards the reformed taxation system. Goods and Services Tax (GST) is one of the major tax reforms after independence introduced in 2017. After the introduction of GST, the multifarious indirect tax regime is disappearing step by step from the life of the Indian nation.

NATURE OF INDIAN ECONOMY

India is one of the fastest growing economies in the world. India's Gross Domestic Product (GDP) grew at 7.5% during 2015–2016. But in terms of the global outlook, real GDP of the world at large grew at 2.8% during the period. The rich countries of the world grew at a rate of about 2% while the developing countries as a whole grew at a rate of about 4.4%, India's growth rate in the past year, in comparison to the major countries of the world, were particularly gratifying (Nayek, 2016). During the half century prior to independence, the growth rate of India's GDP was under 1%. After independence, the onset of Nehruvian Socialism India grew at an average rate of around 3.5% to 4%. In the early 1980s economist are realised that the Indian economy needs to be opened up. The new opening of the Indian economy increased up against the average economic growth rate to the range of about 5% to 5.5%. In late 1980, due to political populism country has facing fiscal profligacy both at the centre as well as in the states. The combined fiscal deficit of the centre and the states were in the range of almost 10% of GDP at that time. On that situation, P.V. Narasimah Rao assumed charge as prime minister in June 1991. He was the man who was heartily wanted to prevent the economy from falling precipitously into utter ruination. He was the lucky man to have the acquiescence of Manmohan Singh to join as the finance minister to carry out the reform agenda. For the reform initiatives of Narashima Rao government, the overall growth rate of the economy moved up to about 6% in the decade of the 1990s. It is the second decade of the new millennium the growth rate of the Indian economy touched 7.5% of GDP in 2015–2016 and is projected at 7.6% at the end of the financial year 2016–2017; although the growth rate fixed in 7.2% after the end of this financial year. Demonetization of high value notes the biggest initiatives for curbing black money from the market was taken by the present government in the last quarter of that financial year. So due to the short impact of demonetization growth slightly decline; although this economic growth is a gigantic growth in the world economy. The fastest growing country China's growth was 7.1% for that year. GST, Goods and Services Tax is one of the biggest steps of the Narendra Modi led NDA government for taxation reform in India. Under this historic reform, India's economic growth should be high and hope the Indian nation can move forward very fast.

What is Goods and Services Tax (GST)?

The 122nd Constitutional Amendment Act 2016 will go down in India's political-economic history as a watershed; it gives the country the most historic tax reform up to date since independence. Goods and Services tax amendment act is a historic taxation reform in India, which shall boost up Indian economic growth rapidly and also shall be able to improve social growth of our country and move forward nation faster toward development. "Goods" is defined in the bill as every kind of movable property other than money and securities but include actionable claim. "Services" is defined as anything other than goods. The multi-staged tax structure before July 2016 has been charged from the state and union government separately, leading to cascading effect of taxes. In India, the power to levy taxes and duties has been divided among Central, State and Local governments. Personal income taxes except for income from agriculture and corporations taxes have been levied by the Central government. In the case of indirect taxes, the Central government has the authority to impose excise duties on production or manufacture and service tax on service provided. The state government has assigned the power to levy the tax on the sale of goods and some other taxes. The state government has also power to levy the sales tax, stamp duty, state excise, land revenue, tax on entertainment and professional tax. Local bodies have the power to levy the tax on properties like building, octroi, tax on markets and tax for utilities such as water supply, drainage (Chakravarty, 2016). These types of taxes were collected by the government for development of the nation before the introduction of GST was divided into two categories. One was direct tax like the professional income tax, which is covering a small fraction of the population. Another one was indirect tax like as excise duty, customs, service tax, value added tax or sales tax, entertainment tax, octroi, entry tax, purchase tax, luxury tax and different surcharges. These taxes lead to the increased tax burden on the products affecting the prices and sales in the domestic as well as in international markets. While direct taxes are affected on the small portion of the population, indirect taxes affected each and every Indian. In the case of indirect taxes rich and poor, both have paid the same. For tax collection, there is a separate machinery of the central and state government for collecting taxes from the people before the introduction of GST. But for central excise and VAT, most of the taxes get calculated on a base which itself has been subjected to taxation at some or the other stage of manufacturing value chain. So, it is a tax on tax making goods and services rather expensive for the ultimate consumer while making life hard for the trade and industry (Chawla, 2016). GST is a reformed version of taxation which includes all taxes into a single tax for the consumer. Goods and Services taxes would be subjected to taxes only on value addition at each stage, thus bringing down the overall tax burden for the consumer.

Types of Goods and Services Tax (GST)

The 122nd Constitutional Amendment Act provides provisions for two types of GST. One is Central Goods and Services Tax (CGST), the tax levied on consumption of goods or rendering of service is split 50:50 between Centre and States. Another one is State Goods and Services Tax (SGST), which levied and collected by the state on all transition within the respective state boundary. The input tax credit of Central Goods and Services Tax (CGST) is available for discharging the CGST liability on the output at each stage. As similarly, credits of State Goods and Services Tax (SGST) paid on inputs are allowed for paying the SGST on output. There is also Integrated GST (IGST). It is levied on the inter-state supply of goods or services collected by the centre. Import of goods or services would be treated as inter-state supplies and would be subject to IGST in addition to the applicable customs duties. Union Territory Goods and Services Tax (UTGST) is another type of GST for Union Territories. Rates of taxes of all categories are decided by the GST Council. Under GST, taxes are levied at the destination level. But previous taxation system taxes such as excise and central sales tax were levied on manufacturing at factory level or on inter-state movement of goods. Under this new system gains favoured for consuming states and loss for manufacturing states. On that ground for the implementation of the new system, the government has to provide compensation for the losses to the states for first five years. For this, the GST (Compensation to States) Bill 2017 was passed.

Monitoring Mechanism of GST

There is a provision in the 122nd Constitutional Amendment Act that there is a GST Council which would monitor the GST. In the Constitutional amendment, there is no mention of the GST rate, which is very important. This act mentioned that the GST rate would be decided by the council. GST council is formed comprising with Cabinet Finance Minister and all Finance Ministers of states and union territories. Union finance minister would act as a chairman of this council as per GST act. According to the active decision of the Goods and Services, Tax Council would require three fourth approval of the council. As per Constitutional provision the states would have two-thirds of the voting powers and the centre have one-third. The GST Council as it stands will now take its decisions or the basis of the above-mentioned majority. This provision gives the union a veto power over every decision of the GST Council.

Taxation Patterns under GST

GST council recommended for four-tier tax structure. This tax structure is 5%, 12%, 18% and 28%. GST Council meeting which was held on 18–19 May 2017 in Srinagar, where the crucial issue of the fitment of various goods and services in different slabs was taken up. Most of the services were fitted in the 18% slab and very few items of service tax were fitted in slabs other than 18%. Luxury items like high-end cars and demerit goods including tobacco, pan masala and aerated drinks, dining in restaurants, paying utility bills booking tickets were taxed at the highest. With the view of safeguarding the interest of poor and keeping inflation under cheek, half the items which are very essential for daily consumption like were under two standards of 12% and 18%. For the relief of common people, food articles are presently totally exempted from GST. Common uses items are kept under 5% tax rate. Soap, oil, shaving stick, toothpaste and such products will move down from higher slabs to 18% slabs. This act makes distinguish between car and luxury car, cars are kept in slabs of 28% and luxury cars are fall in 30–31% slabs. This act making distinguished between footwear up to Rs. 500/- and above; footwear costing below Rs. 500/- taxed at 5% and above it fitted at the 18% rate. Yarn and fabric fitted at tax slab under 5% for the boosting up cotton industries. GST on any item has charging inclusively excise duty plus VAT. There are also some items exempted from GST such as electricity has been kept out of the GST ambit. There was a provision in GST for exemption of sale of land and buildings in its initial stage. But now it is under included under GST.

Prospects of the GST

GST is a historic taxation reform in India in the era of globalization. It would reduce the burden of taxes from the consumers and will be able to increase foreign investment. It has combined all taxes under one umbrella mechanism. It has made life easier for the trade and industry and more importantly reduce the cost of goods and services for the consumers, without compromising on the revenues of either the centre or the state. IMF in its latest Asian Pacific Regional Economic update declared that the adoption of the goods and services tax is poised to boost India's medium-term growth. Progress on reforms of India could ignite business investment and further be boosting domestic demand. IMF also indicates that "further progress on reforms will boost sentiment and the incipient recovery of private investment is expected to help broaden the source of growth amid gradual fiscal consolidation and broadly neutral monetary policy". Global Financial Services reported that on-going reform of Indian economy, like GST, inflation targeting, a new bankruptcy code, financial inclusion, liberalization of FDI measures to curb black money and encouraging digitalization which making Indian economy more transparent. Asian Development Bank said in July 2017, that the implementation of the GST is expected to improve ease of doing business and facilitate the growth of the country. For taxation reforms growth has continued to benefit from the large improvement in the terms of trade, positive policy actions including implementation of key structural reforms, gradual reduction of supply-side constraints and a rebound in confidence. Manufacturing sectors remained constant at around 15% to 16% over a long span. But manufacturing sectors recognised to be the most dynamic of all sectors, and it has the highest potentiality of generating jobs which will be able to absorb much labour. In India employment in manufacturing has remained stagnant and possibly declined in the organised sectors. But hope it; under this new initiative, the standard GST could be much lower than the present excise and state levies. In this background growth of manufacturing sectors would increase and absorbing much labour which also creates much consumption and boosts up the all-over growth of the nation. It should be the antidote to inflation and would thus be people-friendly along with industry-friendly. Asian Development Bank said in the middle of 2017 that "inflation in India is now expected to average 4% in the financial year 2017 (2017–18), well below the forecast of 5.2% in Asian Development Outlook (ADO) 2017, before rising to 4.6% in the financial year 2018 (2018–19)". It also will be able to bridging up unorganised sectors with mainstream economics. It will be able to increase the resources available for poverty alleviation and development of the country. It will be able to minimise the centralising tendency of the centre under the dual tax system. It will be reduced various tax barriers such as check posts and toll plazas and also minimising road blocking, wastage of items in roads and warehousing costs, time-killing under a single taxation system. A single taxation on producers would also translate into a lower final selling price, which benefits the common consumers. For instance, before GST, if the cost of a Television was Rs. 20,000 it was charged by the customer at final stage Rs. 24,900 including 24.5% taxes (Excise duty + VAT). But under new taxation policy, it is reduced by Rs. 23,600 fixed by 18% slab because it is inclusive. At the same time before the introduction of GST the cost of a pair of footwear priced from Rs. 500/- to 1000/- attracts 6% excise duty plus the state's VAT; so finally taxed levied on a footwear was 20% before GST, now it is 18%. GST will also be removed customs duties on exports. So under this system, our foreign markets would also increase on account of lower cost of the transaction. So think it that under the new reign of taxation our nation would be moved forward inclusively faster than past. Collection of taxes is increased under this new taxation regime. A Finance Ministry statement reported that country collected Rs. 7.41 lakh crore taxes in the first year of GST ending the March 2018. It is a positive significance of the collection of taxes in the first year of the GST regime. Various evidences are found that small traders are not victims of GST. They are not sufferers; they are dealing their business under GST by same faith and earn their livelihood honestly.

Challenges of the GST

An initiative of Narendra Modi led NDA government for taxation reforms is a historic milestone in the field of financial sectors in the era of post globalization. GST is a historic step of the present government in financial sectors of the country. Therefore, there are some challenges are identified in the newly born taxation reform initiatives. The first challenge of the GST is there is no clear idea and consensus about the GST rate among the members of the GST Council. But it is very important for even economic growth across country for the interest of federation. According to the provision of GST, rate of the GST is decided by the GST Council. Presently this rate is fixed at 5%, 12%, 18% and 28%, which creates confusion among the members of the council and also traders and common people. There was a hope that the GST Council meeting which was held on 18–19 May 2017 in Srinagar before roll out of GST nationwide making consensus on GST rate and fitment of various goods and services in different slabs. But that meeting was not able to make consensus among the council members about slabs of the new tax. Even till date, there is no consensus between the members of the Council on slabs of taxes. So different slabs of tax have creates difficulties among members of the GST Council, traders and consumers. This criticality is a serious challenge to the proper understanding on GST. There is a big lacuna in the GST because any decision of the GST will be taken by the basis of majority. A majority is defined as three-fourths of those present in meeting and voting, with the union having one-third weight of all the votes. This provision effectively gives to the union a veto power over every decision of the GST Council. On that case, if all states want a highest GST rate, but if union gives a veto so states are bound to levy the GST at a lower rate decided by veto. Under this situation, the union have power to imposed veto over the state's fiscal policies. Under this circumstance, the Indian federal structure turns into a new model called 'controlled federalism'. Country's present economic growth slightly decline due to the impact of demonetization; it was 7.2% in 2015–16 before demonetization, but after demonetization, it slows down to 5.2%, but it is increasing to 6.3% during July-September quarter in 2017 after the introduction of GST acts hope it will be boom up. As per report delivered by Finance Ministry GST collection has been put at Rs. 7.41 lakh crore in the first financial year of the new taxation which was ending on 31st March 2018. Hope it will be boom up although 'social growth' of the country is not hopeful compare to its economic growth. So it is very necessary to booming up country's 'social growth' for faster movement of the nation toward the highest stage of all-round development. Another big challenge of the act is, it is not able to ensure the revenue neutral rate. If any major deviation from Revenue Neutral Rate (RNR) it would be counter productive either for inflation or for fiscal prudence. Under this circumstance states and centre both facing the challenge of getting actual Revenue Neutral Rate (RNR). Under this system, taxation is divided into centre and state. So there is no opportunity of local governments for taxation because of under mutually formula between state and centre local bodies will have to deal with a huge fiscal gap once local body tax, Octroi and other entry taxes are scrapped. So due to the impact of GST local government will be more dependent on central and state government. This dependency may decreased the importance of decentralized governance. So think it is a big challenge to the strengthening the local government as a self-institution due to the present structure of GST. The real estate sector generates a lot of black money. But this sector was exempted from GST at the time of roll out of GST. So it was a serious challenge to gaining actual benefit from GST and minimizing corruption and black money from the society. But now real estate sector is in under GST ambit. There is also no clear provision on land sealing issues. There is also a need for inclusion of land selling under GST. There are also some complexities in the inter-state transactions proposed under the GST. Various common goods are now under high slabs; this is a serious challenge for the livelihood security of the poor people. So there is a need to examine present slabs very carefully by the council and fitted items in under actual slabs which will be able to relief poor people of the society. Lack of technical knowledge on GST collection of tax by small businessmen creates a big threat to the implementation of GST. Lake of knowledge on GST of consumers is also another challenge to the implementation of the new tax system. GST approve a serious challenge by increasing burden of taxes on people of the country through more opening markets to foreign traders for the impact of globalization. If it happens this will be the most serious challenge to the common people of the country.

CONCLUDING OBSERVATIONS

India is now one of the fastest growing nations in the world. India's GDP was 7.5% in 2015–16 and it was projected 7.6% at the end of the current financial year 2016–17. But due to short-term impact of demonetization of the high value of currency notes from November 2016 GDP was not touched projected 7.6%; although it did not decline dramatically, it slightly slipped from projection and fixed on 7.2% on the last quarter of the financial year 2016–17. It slightly jumps down to 5.2% in the same financial year; but it is very interesting that it is increased to 6.3% in the last quarter of the financial year 2016–17. So it is hopeful that it will be increasing in nature after the short-term impact of demonetization. India is a second populous nation in the world. So it is very necessary to move the growth rate (economic and social) of the nation as faster. India follows the taxation system which was implemented by the British Indian government since their role. After independence, there was not a big initiative for all-around reforms of the taxation system. But in the era of globalization, it is very necessary to reform its taxation system for the need of the world. India accepts new liberal economy; so it is very necessary to reform its economy. As a result, various initiatives have been taking for economic reform since the initiation of the new liberal economy. Present Narendra Modi led NDA government has to take various bold initiatives for reforms in social and economic sectors for the fastest move of the Indian nation. GST is one of the historic initiatives of the present Narendra Modi led NDA government for booming up India's GDP which will be able to faster movement of the nation. So it is right to say that which financial reform was started in the 1990s is shaped in under the present Modi government. But it was a very challenging task of government to take this bold initiative for economic reform. So it was a daunting task to the Modi government to making consensus within the various national and regional political parties. It is his great success to manage consensus within all political parties and passing 122nd Constitutional Amendment Act for taxation reform of the country. Hope it, this act able to integrating taxation system within one umbrella. GST actually is a people friendly taxation system. Hope it will be able to reduce overburden of the taxes from common people and inspired industrialist to set up people friendly industrial units which will be able to create more and more jobs. It will be able to mainstream unorganised sectors, which will be boosting up the country's economic growth. Under increasing economic growth social growth of the country also boomed up, which will be able to promote the living standards of the people of our country. There is a need for a provision in GST for tax sharing between centre, state/territory and local governments. Because local government is being now called back boon of the grassroots development on the basis of sustainability and inclusiveness. Hope it that

GST council will be provisions for this. There is an urgent need for inclusion of real estate sector under GST; because it deals a huge amount of black money. Need to minimizing complexities in the inter-state transaction in a meeting on GST Council. There is a need for the introduction of various training including techniques for traders for understanding the GST. There is also a need for the introduction of various sensitization programmes for consumers for understanding GST. For this electronic media, newspapers, NGOs, are will be able to take a positive role on the various aspects of GST. Primarily traders are facing some complexities, but hope in the long term they will easily able to get benefit from the new structure of the taxation. Small and medium level unorganised traders are mostly affected during the initial stage of the implementation of GST. So it is very necessary to take appropriate measures for protecting their interest. But various observations of the grassroots level have shown that small businessmen are not badly affected under this new system. As per their version they are not worst affected by the GST. Consumers' version is also the same as per small traders. On the other hand various report of the government showing that the collection of GST and SGST is increasing from the date of implementation of the new tax system. So, hopefully, it will be able to boom up the GDP of the country by decreasing complexity and burden of the tax on common people of the country. Actually, GST is an antidote to inflation and it is a people friendly along with trade and industry-friendly initiative. Hope it discarding all challenges this reformed model of inclusive financial governance act will be able to boost up country's growth rate and will be able to free people from the overburden of the present taxation and turn India towards 'one nation one tax' concept. Hope, under this new taxation system foreign trader will be more attractive on the Indian market for investment; which will be able to boost up India's economy.

REFERENCES

Chakravarty, M. (2016). India's Tax System: Increasing Progressivity. *Yojana*, 60: 12–14.

Chawla, P. (2016). GST- A game – changer for India. *Kurukshetra*, 64(11): 20–21.

Mehta, R. (2016). GST: Game Changer for Indian Economy? *Yojana*, 60: 35–39.

Nayak, Pulin B. (2016). Revisiting India's Growth and Development. *Economic and Political Weekly*, LI(34): 43–48.

Prasanna, A.K. (2016). Goods and Services Tax An Exercise in 'Controlled Federalism? *Economic and Political Weekly*, LI(34): 10–11.

Rao, Govinda M. and Rao, Kavita K. (2009). Tax Reform in India. Initiative for Policy Dialogue Working Paper Series, National Institute of Public Finance and Policy.

Roy, Chowdhury J. (2016). GST and the Constitution Conundrum. *Yojana*, 60: 41–43.

9

Goods and Service Tax: It's Impact on Agricultural Sector

IMRAN ALI BAIG[1*]

ABSTRACT

Goods and services tax is a single a broad based tax levied on goods and services consumed in an economy. The main aim of GST is "One Nation, One Tax and One Market'. Globally, it is simple, efficient and will help to improve the economic growth of the country by eliminating several taxes of state and central such as VAT, Excise and Services etc. The implementation of Goods and Services Tax (GST) is expected to facilitate of National Agricultural Market on account of subsuming all kinds of taxes and cess on marketing of agricultural production as well as it would ease interstate movement of agricultural commodities which would improve marketing efficiency, facilitate development of virtual markets through Warehouses and reduce overhead marketing cost. In this paper we study about the impact of GST on agricultural sector and also focused on the problem likely to be faced by the farmers (agricultural price, production etc.) which has been the root of Indian economy and it contributes to around 17.4 percent to GDP. About 52 percent of the totcl rural livelihood depends on this sector as their primary means of livelihood, so this paper is helpful in bringing out the light on Impact of GST on Agriculture Sector.

Key words: Goods and Services Tax, VAT, Agricultural sector, Agricultural price, Production.

[1] Aligarh Muslim University, Aligarh, UP (202001).
**Corresponding author:* E-mail: ialibaig043@gmail.com

INTRODUCTION

Farming is a standout among the most basic parts of the Indian economy. Development and advancement of farming and unified segment straight forwardly influences prosperity of individuals everywhere, country thriving and work and structures a vital asset base for various agro -based ventures and agro-administrations (Kanwal, 2017). The agribusiness division in India has experienced noteworthy auxiliary changes as decline in offer of GDP from 30 percent for every penny in 1990–91 to 17.4 percent in 2015–16 (Annual Report, 2015–16) demonstrate a moving from the conventional agrarian economy towards an administration overwhelmed one. In any case, this abatement in agribusiness' commitment to GDP has not been joined by a coordinating decrease in the offer of horticulture in work. Around 52 percent of the aggregate workforce is as yet utilized by the homestead part which makes the greater part of the Indian populace reliant on farming for sustenance (NSS 66th Round). Esteem expansion in agriculture, accordingly, holds gigantic potential for improving the expectation for everyday comforts of greater part of the general population. Enhanced agriculture promoting offers a noteworthy chance to accomplish this target. Merchandise and administration assessment will have both negative and positive effect on farming. The cost of farming items will go down, as already the rural products are accused of various costs inside the state, between state and in generally speaking nation. GST would prompt proficient portion of assets. Terms of exchange move in the support of Agriculture when contrasted with assembling area. This will expand costs of a few items like drain, tea, and so on in this way, shelter the a large number of ranchers in India (Chaurasia & Singh, 2016). In nutshell we can state that it will impact straightforwardly and in a roundabout way to horticulture division.

GST IN INDIA

GST was first time presented on 28th February 2006 in the Budget Speech of the year 2006–07 by Finance Minister Sh. P. Chidambaram. A message was left by the Finance Minister in the Union Budget 2007–08 that GST will be presented with impact from first April 2010. Local and State Governments will be cooperate to set up a guide for the presentation of GST in India. They wanted to present GST or "supplanting the past VAT and Service Tax" on first April 2010, yet a portion of the States were not prepared to actualize the GST. After that on first April 2012, again Government would present GST, yet because of some administration and foundation issues it was not presented. Back Minister Arun Jaitley presented the 122nd Constitution Amendment Bill in Parliament and expects to execute GST change by first April 2016. The GST structure will display a straight forward framework which will be useful to diminish the weight of falling impact and it will likewise enhance the Tax compliances and Tax accumulation. GST will demonstrate the consistency of Taxes in everywhere throughout the nation.

Table 1: Taxes at the centre and state level are being subsumed into GST.

Sl. no.	*CGST*	*SGST*
1.	Central Excise duty	VAT/Sale Tax
2.	Additional Excise duty	Entertainment Tax
3.	Service Tax	Octroi and Entry Tax
4.	Additional custom duty	Purchase Tax
5.	Surcharge and Cess	Luxury Tax

http://www.gstcouncil.gov.in/brief-history-gst

Table 1 shows rundown of charges focus and state level are being subsumed into GST Keeping as a primary concern the government structure of India, there will be two parts of GST– Central GST (CGST) and State GST (SGST). Both Center and States will at the same time exact GST over the esteem chain. Duty will be collected on each supply of merchandise and enterprises. Focus would exact and gather Central Goods and Services Tax (CGST), and States would impose and gather the State Goods and Services Tax (SGST) on all exchanges inside a State. The information impose credit of CGST would be accessible for releasing the CGST risk on the yield at each stage. Also, the credit of SGST paid on sources of info would be taken into account paying the SGST on yield. No cross usage of credit would be allowed.

The expense became effective from July 1, 2017, GST as a change on the VAT framework, a uniform GST is relied upon to make a consistent national market. GST is by all accounts more exhaustive, compliable, basic, orchestrated and advancement arranged assessment system. From the buyer perspective, the greatest preferred standpoint would be as far as a lessening in the general taxation rate on merchandise, which is right now evaluated to associate with 25–30 for each penny (Central Board of Excise and Custom). The charge rates, standards and directions are represented by the Goods and Services Tax Council which includes back priests of focus and every one of the states. GST improved a large number of backhanded expenses with a brought together assessment and is in this manner anticipated that would significantly reshape the nation's 2 trillion dollar economy.

The execution of GST isn't just to raise government's income however it additionally enables more income dissemination to low-wage worker, along these lines making the hole of the economies littler between the general population (Awang, 2011). GST is a wide based utilization assess which covers all exchanges including imported merchandise and enterprises with the exception of the products and ventures that are named zero evaluated supply and excluded supply which will be exempted by the Government (Fatt, CK

& Ling, 2006). It implies that the expense is charged on each supply of assessable merchandise and ventures at all levels in the inventory network during the time spent creation, assembling, discount and retail. The duty is paid by clients when they buy products and ventures (Alapatt, 2015). Other than that, GST will be imposed and charged on the assessable supply of merchandise and enterprises made in the course or promotion of business in India by an assessable individual. In other word, it influences customers in all cases including poor people and penniless (The Edge, 2013).

Table 2: List of some Asian countries implemented VAT/GST.

Sl. no.	*Name of countries*	*Implementation year*	*GST rate (%)*
1	South Korea	1977	10
2	Taiwan	1986	5.0
3	Japan	1989	5.0
4	Pakistan	1990	16.0
5	Bangladesh	1991	15.0
6	China	1994	17.0
7	Nepal	1997	13.0
8	Jordan	2002	16.0
9	Lebanon	2002	10.0
10	Sri Lanka	2002	12.0
11	Iran	2008	5.0
12	Tajikistan	2007	20.0
13	India	2017	5–18

Sources: *http://gst.customs.gov.my/en/gst/Pages/gst_ci.aspx*

Table 2 shows run down of some Asian nations executed VAT/GST worldwide under the plan no refinement is made amongst products and ventures for collecting of assessment. This imply merchandise and administration pull in a similar rate of duty yet in India has distinctive assessment rate at 5%, 12% and 18 percent. In this paper our targets are, to investigation of expense rate of horticultural divisions under GST, distinction between existing duty rate and GST impose rate and most imperative to examine effect of GST on farming segment.

PROCEDURE

The Researchers utilized an exploratory research system in light of past writing from individual diaries, yearly reports, daily papers and magazines covering wide accumulation of scholarly writing on Goods and Service Tax. As indicated by the destinations of the examination, the exploration configuration is of enlightening in nature. Accessible auxiliary information was widely utilized for the examination.

WRITING REVIEW

Chadha *et al.* (2009) have broke down that GST would prompt effective portion of elements of creation. The general value level would go down. It is normal that the genuine comes back to the components of creation would go up. Their outcomes demonstrated picks up in genuine comes back to arrive extending somewhere in the range of 0.42 and 0.82 for each penny. Wage rate increases changed somewhere in the range of 0.68 and 1.33 for every penny. The genuine comes back to capital would pick up some place, somewhere in the range of 0.37 and 0.74 for every penny. In whole, usage of a far reaching GST in India is relied upon to prompt proficient allotment of components of generation in this way prompting picks up in GDP and fares.

Satish Chander, Director General, FAI said that compost items are probably going to experience the ill effects of higher occurrence of charges with execution of GST. Thusly, it is unequivocally felt that there is a requirement for the administration to give careful consideration to manure area, keeping in see its immediate linkage with ranchers and horticulture. Any new duty administration ought not straight forwardly or in a round about way increment the cost of composts to the ranchers, particularly when government keeps on giving sponsorship on manure specifically or by implication. At first sight, the legislature should in this way; either permits zero or concessional rate of GST on composts.

Shaik *et al.* (2015) have same view about GST, they said that GST goes about as partner in the aggregate pick up for industry, exchange, farming and normal customers and in addition for the Central Government and the State Government and along these lines at last accommodating being developed of Indian economy. It was additionally revealed that GST will prompt give business benefits, which were stayed immaculate by the VAT framework. Jaiprakash had same view that GST at Central and State levels are required to give more help to agribusiness, industry and shoppers. He likewise demonstrated that exchange and industry have urging reactions to GST. Along these lines GST offers us the best alternative to expand our expense base and we ought not miss this chances to present it when the conditions are very ideal and economy is getting a charge out of enduring development with just mellow expansion.

Nirmal Khurana, Chairman of the ITA's said that tea is a result of mass utilization; it ought to have an extraordinary rate under the GST administration. GST rate on tea ought to be kept on a standard with the present duty rate of 5–6 per penny. The present concessional charge rate of 0.5/1per penny for teas sold through sell-offs is permitted to proceed under the GST administration, otherwise, tea will wind up costlier. Generally speaking GST is useful for the improvement of Indian economy too it will be particularly useful in enhancing the GDP of the nation in excess of two percent say by Chaurasia *et al.* (2016) in their examination.

Effect of GST on Agricultural Sector

There are sure sustenance things like rice, sugar, salt, wheat, flour which are exempted from CENVAT. Under the state VAT, oats and grains are saddled at the rate of 4%. Rural items experience a great deal of permitting and various roundabout taxes (VAT, extract obligation, benefit charge) under the present expense laws. State VAT is right now material to all the horticultural merchandise at each state; it goes through preceding last utilization. In spite of the fact that there are sure exclusions accessible from state VAT for certain natural sustenance items like meat, eggs, organic products, vegetables etc. GST is fundamental to enhance the straight forwardness, dependability, timetable of store network system. A superior production network instrument would guarantee a decrease in wastage and cost for the ranchers/retailers. GST would likewise help in lessening the cost of overwhelming apparatus required for creating farming products. Under the model GST law, dairy cultivating, poultry cultivating, and stock reproducing are kept out of the meaning of horticulture. In this manner these will be assessable under the GST. Manures an essential component of agribusiness was already burdened at 6% (1% Excise + 5% VAT). In the GST administration, the assessment on manures has been expanded to 12%. A similar effect is on Tractors. Wavier on the produce of Tractors is expelled and GST of 12% has been forced. This is valuable as now the makers will have the capacity to assert Input Tax Credit.

India's drain creation in 2015–16 was 160.35 million ton, expanded from 146.31mt out of 2014–15. Currently, just 2% VAT is charged on drain and certain drain items yet under GST the rate of new drain is NIL and skimmed drain is kept under 5% section and consolidated drain will be saddled at the rate of 18%. Tea is likely a standout amongst the most urgent things in an Indian family unit. The cost of tea may likewise increment because of the duty rate of 5% under GST rate from the present normal VAT rate of 4–5% with Assam and West Bengal except for 0.5 and 1%. GST is vital for making a way in regards to the effective execution of NAM. A large portion of the aberrant duties collected on farming items, would be subsumed under GST. GST would give every dealer, the info kudos for the duty paid on each esteem expansion. This will make a straight forward, bother free store network which would prompt free development of agri-wares crosswise over India. A large portion of the farming wares are transitory in nature. An enhanced store network instrument because of GST would decrease the time taken for between state transportation. The advantage of diminishment in time would be passed on to the agriculturists/retailers. A few states in India like Maharashtra, Punjab, Gujarat, Haryana gain more than Rs 1000 crore from charging CST/OCTROI/Purchase Tax. GST would subsume all the above assessments. Consequently these states should be adjusted for the loss of income. We will clarify the effect of GST on horticultural area point savvy.

1. The execution of GST is required to support the farming business sector as tax collection under a subsumed single rate would influence the development of horticultural items to problem free as the items would have the capacity to achieve places through trucks betterly. Interstate exchanging of a specific item regularly is subjected to different assessments, authorization, permit required for various states at each purpose of their exchange. This had regularly made obstacle in exchanging of items the nation over for some dealers before. So executing GST would be the initial move towards changing the advertising of farming items and making a smooth exchange of merchandise.
2. GST would make the agro-hardware reasonable to the little and peripheral ranchers in India which was past their scope because of high extract obligation on the apparatus. Rural items were constantly subject to assorted variety in the tax collection rates so a solitary rate of merchandise and administration expense would profit the national agrarian market and help the agriculturists and merchants to offer their items in any piece of the nation and get the best cost for their item.
3. The GST rate ought to give consistency in expense of handled and natural sustenance things so prepared nourishment comes extremely close to every one of the purchasers. The piece for GST rate of handled sustenance ought to be diverse for various wage gathering to make the advantage of such nourishment accessible for every one of the customers. At present, there is no assessment to secure drain from agriculturists. We just pay 2 for every penny focal VAT on special of drain powder to an organization. At the point when GST gets executed, the expense can be 12.5 per penny or 15 per penny or 18 per penny. There will be a straight cost climb in drain and drain item costs. India positions first in drain creation covering around 18.5 per penny of the world generation. Its yearly creation for the year 2015–2016 added up to 155.49 million ton and records an expansion consistently, and drain being an essential need in numerous families, an increment in the cost would not be promptly invited by the shoppers.
4. GST is fundamental to upgrade the execution of inventory network component as far as straight forwardness; unwavering quality and now and again which is turn will guarantee lessening in waste and cost of horticultural generation.
5. Service expense will likewise be exempted in different administrations identified with horticultural deliver.

6. The execution of GST is required to encourage the usage of National Agricultural Market by virtue of subsuming a wide range of charges/ cess on showcasing of horticultural create and also it would ease interstate development of agrarian items which would enhance promoting productivity, encourage improvement of virtual markets through distribution centers and decrease overhead advertising cost.
7. GST is good to go to build the costs of most agrarian information sources, similar to seeds, pesticides, and homestead gear coming about into increment in the cost of rural creation.
8. The prices of Fertilisers (NPK) goes down (Table No. 3) due to the low level of GST rate comparing to the previous existing tax rate. It is shows a positive sign for the agricultural farmer which plays an important role to enhance the agricultural production and productivity.
9. Drip sprinkler water system hardware which as of now draws in a VAT rate of 5% will be saddled at 18% under GST. Concurrent assessment rate on pesticides sprayers has gone up from 6% to 18% and electric engines from 7% to 12%. Following tables will indicates different expense rate under VAT and GST.

Table 3: GST rates of agricultural goods and services.

Sl. no.	*Items (cheaper goods)*	*Existing rate (2)*	*GST rate (3)*	*Revised GST rate (4)*	*Difference in rate (Col 2–Col 4)*
1	Seeds, (cotton seed mustard seed etc.)	0	0	0	0
2	Hand pump and its parts	12.5	12	2.5	+ 10
3	Tractors	12.5	12	6	+ 6.5
4	Fertilizer	12	5	2.5	+ 9.5
5	Agricultural implements (spades, shovel, pick etc)	0	0	0	0

Source: *http://www.gstcouncil.gov.in/cgst-rates-goods.*

Table 4: GST rates of agricultural goods and services.

Sl. no.	*Items*	*Existing rate (2)*	*GST rate (3)*	*Revised GST rate (4)*	*Difference in rate (Col 2-Col4)*
1	Tractor Tire and Rim	12.5	18	18	–5.5
2	Other Tractor parts	12.5	18	2.5	–5.5
3	Harvester, Earth grader parts	0	12	12	–12
4	Pesticides	5.5	18	9	–3.5

Source: *http://www.gstcouncil.gov.in/cgst-rates-goods*

In both tables (Table 3) and (Table 4) the column number (4), is the difference between Existing rate and Revised GST rate. In the above table, the Plus sign indicates the positive impact on above-mentioned items such as Hand pump and its parts, Tractor, and fertilizers in the last column. But in below table (Table 4), the negative sign simply shows the negative impact on below-listed items such as Tractor Tire and Rim, Other Tractor parts, Harvestor or Earth Grader parts and pesticides.

CONCLUSIONS

It can be said from the above discussion that GST is expected to have both positive and negative impact on the farm sector. In case of branded milk, Tea and Fertilizer it is expected to show a negative impact. These are the most popular commodities in India. In case of milk there is no tax to procure milk from farmer, when GST will be implemented it leads to increase the milk prices and this would not be welcomed by consumers. GST will make tax system more transparent as single tax system is available to whole country. Agricultural products were subjected to diversity of taxation rates; as single rate of goods and service tax would help the farmers and also to traders because they can sell their produce in any part of the country. GST is also helpful in avoiding Tax evasion, improved Tax collection and compliances. It reduces the cost of goods and services to some extent and creates a supportive environment for the facilitation of international trade, thereby helping in revenue generation leading to the increase in the GDP of the country. Similarly, it will also be helpful in lowering the Tax burden on the various segments of the economy. Industries, dealers, retailers and the agriculture sector as a whole will benefit from GST.

An increase in the cost of few agricultural products is anticipated due to the rise in inflation index for a brief period. Though, implementation of GST is going to over all benefit a lot, the farmers/ distributors in the long run as there will a single unified national agriculture market. GST would ensure that farmers in India who contribute the most to GDP, will be able to sell their produce for the best available price.

REFERENCES

Abdul Aziz Awang (2011). Cukai Barang dan Perkhidmatan (Goods and Services Tax).

Alappatt, M. (2015). Forthcoming Procedure of Goods and Service Tax (GST) in, 2 (December 2014), pp. 210–213.

Chadha, R., Tandon, A., Ashwani, Mohan G. and Mishra, P. (2009). Moving to goods and services tax in India: Impacton India's growth and international trade (NCAER Working Paper No. 103).

Chaurasia, P., Singh, S. and Sen, P.K. (2016). Role of good and service tax in the growth of Indian economy. *International Journal of Science Technology and Management*, 5(2): 152–157.

Curtis, J.L. (2010). Implications of the Introduction of the Goods and Services Tax for Families in Canada. *Canadian Public Policy / Analyse De Politiques*, 4(36): 503–520.

David Lai (2013). GST. *The Edge*, pp. 22–25.

Fatt, C.K. and Ling, L.M. (2006). Towards Goods and Services Tax in Malaysia: A Preliminary Study. *Global Business & Economics Anthology*, pp. 75–86.

Gupta, N. (2014). Goods and Services Tax: Its implementation on Indian economy, *International Research Journal of Commerce, Arts and Science (CASIRJ)*, 5(3): 126–133.

Modi, A. (2009). Report of the Task Force on Goods & Services Tax. New Delhi, Thirteenth Finance Commission.

Patel, J.K. (2011). Goods and Service Tax - An Introductory Study. *Golden Research Thoughts*, 1(7): 1–3.

Rao, M.G. (2009). Feasibility of Introducing GST in April 2010. *Economic and Political Weekly,* 29(44): 10–13.

Rao, M.G. (2009). Goods and Services Tax: Some Progress towards Clarity. *Economic and Political Weekly*, 40(51): 8–1.

Rao, R.K. (2004). Impact of VAT on Central and State Finances. *Economic and Political Weekly,* 39(26): 2773–2777.

Refaqat, S. (2005). Redistributive Impact of GST Tax Reform: Pakistan, 1990–2001. *The Pakistan Development Review,* 44(4): 841–862.

Roberts, A. and Rose, J. (1995). Selling the Goods and Services Tax: Government Advertising and Public Discourse in Canada. *JSTOR*, 28(2): 311–330.

Ruggeri, G.C. and Bluck, K. (1990). On the Incidence of the Manufacturers' Sales Tax and the Goods and Services Tax. *Canadian Public Policy / Analyse De Politiques*, 16(4): 359–373.

Shaik, S., Sameera, A.S. and Firoz, C.S. (2015). Does goods and services tax (GST) leads to Indian economic development? *Journal of Business and Management,* 17(12): 1–5.

10

Demand and Supply of Power Energy in J&K State

Tariq Ahmad Bhat[1*], Khursheed Hussain Dar[1] and Nighat Mukhtar[1]

ABSTRACT

Electricity is vital for sustained economic growth of a nation. An increase in demand for power implies growth of the economy leading to modernization, industrialization and improvement in basic amenities into a better quality of life. The present study was conducted in Jammu and Kashmir to know the demand and supply power in the state, which has huge potential of power generation due to its vast water resources. It was found that state has huge power potential, but only 20% of that has been utilised so far. With the result state is facing huge power deficits both in winter and summer season.

Key words: Power, Potential, Consumption, Deficit, Demand, Supply, Economy.

INTRODUCTION

Electricity is an essential source of commercial energy. It is vital for sustained economic growth. An increase in demand for power implies growth of the economy leading to modernization, industrialization and improvement in basic amenities culminating into a better quality of life of people. The State is currently focused on generation through big hydro power project. Potential of micro Hydel power and Solar are increasingly being tapped. Grid electricity penetration in remote hilly areas of J&K is techno-economically unviable by virtue of geographical disadvantages and scattered household pattern. Moreover, the power sector of the State is already facing

[1] Vikram University of Ujjain, Ujjain, Madhya Pradesh.

**Corresponding author:* E-mail: tariq0920@gmail.com

difficulties like slow rate of capacity addition, poor power evacuation facility, high AT&C losses and mismatch in load profile. Power utilization mix is not commensurate with the State's climatic conditions. Promotion and utilization of renewable energy is the most feasible solution which would also promote low carbon growth and can meet the decentralized energy requirement of the remote locations.

The state of Jammu and Kashmir is endowed with significant hydel potential which, when exploited fully, will provide a strong impetus for the growth of its economy. Development of this potential would need huge resources, technical expertise, administrative reforms, congenial environment, proper regulation and management, besides competitive marketing, policy formation and private participation. Optimal exploitation of available hydel resources in the State would not only meet the internal demand but will also supply power to the Northern grid to boost the overall development of the State.

The rich water resources of J&K offer immense potential for commercial hydropower generation. The potential is as high as 14,000 MW of hydro power but only about 10% of this has been exploited so far. The reasons are the restrictions imposed by the Indus Water Treaty, the high capital costs which reduce the viability of the projects, the difficult terrain and scarcity of resources.

Out of total power demand of 17,323 million units, power generation from the State owned power houses is only 2,562.723 million units. Bulk of electricity consumption in the State is by the domestic sector. With modernization and increased urbanization, per capita energy consumption of the State has increased from 849.98 kWh in 2010–11 to 882.82 kWh in 2011–12. The energy demand has gradually increased during last five years at an annual rate of 5 to 6%. According to the sixteenth All India Power Survey, the power requirement of the State is expected to reach 19,500 million units during 2020–21.

MATERIAL AND METHODS

The present study makes use of secondary data from different state government publications, Reports, records and internet. The Study is all about demand and supply of power energy in Jammu and Kashmir State. Simple growth technique was used to find out the comparison over the years.

OBJECTIVES

1. To know the demand, supply and per capita power energy in the state.

2. To highlight the state's revenue generation, power deficit and transmission loss over the years.

RESULTS AND DISCUSSION

J&K is one of the energy-starved states within India and the inadequacy of the existing power capacity power has been affecting the pace of development in all sectors of the economy. The state has a unique position in the power generation and power market within northern India. Historically the principal energy source in J&K has been hydroelectricity and still constitutes around 68% of the total energy mix. Its rivers, which are the main source of power generation, have the maximum flow during the summer season (April-October) and thus have a potential to meet the pressing energy demands. However, during the rest of the year, *i.e.,* in the winter season, the water level drops to one third of the annual average and the demand increases due to the extra usage of electricity for heating and lighting purpose and thus resulting in purchase of large quantities of power from adjacent states. This has placed the state finances in a deficit situation.

Power Development in Jammu and Kashmir has a long and distinguished history. 9MW Mohra Hydro-electric Plant, among the first of its kind in the subcontinent, was developed as early as 1905. The estimated hydro power potential of the state is 20,000 Megawatts (MW), of which about 16475 MW have been identified. This comprises 11283 MW in Chenab basin, 3084 MW in Jhelum basin 500 MW in Ravi Basin and 1608 MW in Indus basin. Out of the identified potential, only 3263.46 MW *i.e.,* 19.80 % (of identified potential) has been exploited so far, consisting of 1211.96 MW in State Sector from 21 power projects, 2009 MW in Central Sector from 7 projects and 42.5 MW in private sector from 4 projects. These projects are techno-economically viable, besides being eco-friendly and socially beneficial. Jammu and Kashmir has a total power generation capacity of 2,648.46 MW under central and State sector. The State is heavily relying on power purchase from the NEWNE grid and thermal power generation units and gas and diesel based power units during winters when its own hydro power generation reduces and power demand rises. The State is facing power crisis owing to untapped renewable energy, high rate of AT&C losses including pilferage.

The demand for power energy has gradually increased during 2011–12 to 2016–17 by 6.72%. While as the energy availability has increased by 41.25% during the same period. Still there is huge gap between demand and supply of power energy in the state. The state has power deficit about 2820.14 MUs in 2016–17 as shown in Table 1. To bridge the gap between demand and supply, the department has enforced the power cuts. These cuts are of the order of 8 hours in summer and 10 hours in winter. Even after the cuts, the restricted demand was around 15667.44 MUs in 2016–17, which necessitated banking of power during summer with other state utilities and using of the same during winter.

Table 1: Demand and supply of power in Jammu and Kashmir (in MUs).

Year	*Energy requirement*	*Restricted energy availability*	*Energy deficit*	*Energy deficit (%)*
2011–12	17323.00	11091.26	6207.59	35.83
2012–13	17669.46	12120.02	5549.43	31.40
2013–14	18022.83	12666.59	5356.38	29.72
2014–15	18000.00	13701.00	4299.00	23.88
2015–16	18200.00	14226.05	3973.95	21.83
2016–17	18487.59	15667.44	2820.14	15.25
Growth rate	6.72	41.25		

Source: J&K Economic Survey 2016–17.

During peak season (winter season) there is scarcity of power both in terms of total energy availability and actual demand for it. Table 2 state there is huge peak power deficit in the state of Jammu and Kashmir is about 22 MW during 2016–17. Due to this gap state is forced to purchase from Northern Grid and return in summer season.

Table 2: Demand and supply of power in Jammu and Kashmir (in MW).

Year	*Peak demand*	*Peak supply*	*Peak deficit*	*Peak deficit*
2011–12	2500	1788.9	711.1	28.44
2012–13	2550	1717.0	733	28.75
2013–14	2600	1991	609	23.42
2014–15	2650	2043	607	22.90
2015–16	2740	2158	582	21.24
2016–17	2750	2140	610	22.18

Source: J&K Economic Survey 2016–17.

Jammu and Kashmir State has huge power generation potential but due to one or the other reason these could not harnessed yet. Table 3 indicates that states own power generation share *vis-à-vis* central in 2011–12 was 23.10% and has increased merger to 24.13% in 2016–17. This clearly states that government is not taking any positive step to harness this potential which state actually has.

Table 3: States power sources and generation capacity (MU).

Sources	*2011–12*	*2012–13*	*2013–14*	*2014–15*	*2015–16*	*2016–17*
From states own source	2562.49	2519.94	2337.23	2470.76	2519.70	3809.24
Free power	1045.08	1056.10	1089.21	1330.63	1391.70	1323.76
Total	3687.57	3576.04	3426.44	3801.39	3911.40	5133.00
Purchased from Cen. Govt	7403.68	7764.14	9240.14	11230.55	10314.65	10534.44
% Share of Total Availability	23.10	20.02	18.45	18.03	17.71	24.31

Source: J&K Economic Survey 2016–17.

It can't be denied the fact that state govt could not met its target as for as revenue is concerned. Table 4 clearly indicates that govt has targeted to earn 3860.61 crores during 2016–17 but manage to get only 1877.72 crores during the same year. Which leads to gap of 1982.64 crores in 2016–17 which is actually deficit of the government, and this deficit has shown increasing trend from 2011–12 to 2016–17, which actually increased 467.01% during the reference period in Table 4. The reason of increased deficit or low rate of realised revenue is due to power thrift by the consumers, which becomes a big challenge for the state government. The state government's actual expenditure on power sector was 4452.01 crores and has increased to 6224.23 crores during 2011–12 to 2016–17 as shown in Table 4. However during this period, realised revenue increased from 1200.16 crores to 1877.72 crores during the same period as shown in Table 5.

Table 4: Revenue targeted/ realised revenue (Rs. in crores).

Year	*Revenue targeted*	*Realised revenue*	*Gap*
2011–12	1549.82	1200.16	349.66
2012–13	2011.47	1693.51	317.96
2013–14	2200.00	1714.26	485.74
2014–15	2390.00	1736.27	653.73
2015–16	3357.55	1937.34	1420.21
2016–17	3860.36	1877.72	1982.64
Growth Rate	149.08	56.45	467.01

Source: J&K Economic Survey 2016–17.

Table 5: Power purchases from all sources (Rs. in crores).

Year	*Total expenditure*	*Percentage*
2011–12	4452.01	—
2012–13	4790.50	7.60
2013–14	5137.53	7.24
2014–15	5929.69	15.41
2015–16	6004.23	1.25
2016–17	6224.23	3.66

Source: J&K Economic Survey 2016–17.

The Transmission and Distribution of power is looked after by Power Development Department in the State of J&K. Effective and Efficient Transmission and Distribution is as vital as the generation of power. The need of power in the State is growing, so does the generation. In 2011–12 transmission and distribution loss was 6824.25 MU and has increased in 2016–17 to 8070.59 MU at the rate of 5.56% per year as shown in Table 6. State of Jammu and Kashmir is ranked as one in terms of transmission and distribution losses among the northern states of India. However, one may ask that this huge loss may be due to topographical features of the state.

The answer is that Jammu and Kashmir State has same topographic features like that of Himachal Pradesh. Where this transmission loss is minimum as compared to J&K state. The main reasons for such high losses are technical as well as commercial. The high technical losses are due to existing outdated distribution network. To minimize losses, the system needs up-gradation and improvements. Commercial losses include theft, unaccounted and uncontrolled consumption of power beyond agreement load, unregistered consumers, lesser contract demand etc.

Table 6: Year wise details of transmission and distribution losses (unit: MU).

Year	*Transmission and distribution loss*	*Percentage*
2011–12	6824.25	0
2012–13	6957.14	1.94
2013–14	6912	–0.64
2014–15	7565.12	9.44
2015–16	7645.41	1.06
2016–17	8070.59	5.56

***Source*:** J&K Economic Survey 2016–17.

Per capita consumption in J&K State has shown steady growth and is presently around 1089 units (Table 7) which are nearly at par with national average. Due to extreme climatic conditions in most parts of the state the per capita consumption is low. The issue needs to be addressed by increased generation for which the state has framed ambitious plans to add 9000 MW during next decade.

Table 7: Year wise details of per capita consumption of energy in J&K.

Year	*Consumption of energy (KWHr)*	*Percentage*
2011–12	868.39	0
2012–13	927.86	6.84
2013–14	952.34	2.63
2014–15	1010.72	6.13
2015–16	1064.62	5.33
2016–17	1089.41	2.32

***Source*:** J&K Economic Survey 2016–17.

CONCLUSIONS

Jammu and Kashmir is one of the energy-starved states within India and the inadequacy of the existing power capacity power has been affecting the pace of development in all sectors of the economy. The demand of power energy continuously goes on increasing day by day. Therefore huge portion of the money is utilized in purchase of power from various sources outside the state. However, if the states power potential is fully exploited, the state would be in a position to meet its own demand and may have enough power surpluses that can sell to Central government and neighbouring states by earning huge amount of money. Need of the hour is not only to utilize the power potential which state has but also to reduce the transmission and distribution loss of power, by enhancing and up-gradation the system.

REFERENCES

Economic Survey of Jammu and Kashmir 2016–17.

Haq UI. (2014). 'Economic analysis of hydro power generation in the state of Jammu and Kashmir, India', *European academic research*.

JKPDD, Annual Report 2013, Jammu and Kashmir Power Development Department.

Lohan, S.K., Dixit, J., Modasir, S. and Ishaq, M. (2012). 'Resource potential and scope of utilization of renewable energy in Jammu and Kashmir, India'. *Renewable Energy*, Vol.(39).

Nazakat, R. and Nengroo, A. (2012). 'Impact of Indus water treaty on Jammu and Kashmir State: With special reference to hydro power potential'. *Journal of Resent Sdvances in Agriculture.*

Verma, M. (2014). Daily 'Much touched hydel policy fails to take off Projects evoke poor response in Jammu and Kashmir'. Excelsior News Paper report.

http:// www.jkspdc.nic.in.

http://jkspdc.nic.in/

http: / /www.unido.org/fileadmin/import/5239.

11

Connectivity and Economic Development: Introspecting the Indo-Myanmar Border Trade and Connectivity

SAMPURNA GOSWAMI[1*]

ABSTRACT

The Indo-Myanmar border acts as a bridge connecting the two significant regions, South Asia and South East Asia. In the era of Globalization where regionalism as a concept emerged, the Indo-Myanmar border can in no way be ignored in terms of regional integration following the Neo-Functional theoretical framework that essentially deals with regional security, overall regional growth and economic interdependence. India's "Act East Policy"- a renovation of the earlier "Look East Policy" adopted in 1991 has considered Myanmar as the gateway to South East Asia. Taking into account the fact that Myanmar is a part of the golden triangle, this border is not only vulnerable in terms of illegal drug trafficking, but also recognized for the immense amount of illegal arms that is fabricated in China and infiltrated through the Moreh-Tamu border in Manipur, and the Rhi-Zokhawthar Border in Mizoram. The insurgency problem along the boundary line has brought both India and Myanmar to solve the issue unitedily. Apart from these factors the India-Myanmar border in general and infrastructural projects like the Asian Highway, the Kaladan Multimodal Transport project in particular has not only helped in connecting India and South Asia with the ASEAN nations but has also provided India's 'not so developed' North East a market for economic development. Level of border trade taking place at markets along Indo-Myanmar border is low but significant. Border Trade is immensely linked with the third world economies like China which actually supply goods. Opening of border Trade has benefited the local people in terms of employment, infrastructural development and also improved other

[1] Department of International Relations, Jadavpur University, Kolkata, West Bengal.

**Corresponding author:* E-mail: mailto.sampurna@rediffmail.com

relationships between India and Myanmar. Myanmar is critical for India not only as a border trade partner but also for India's Act East Policy (LEP) which is an instrument designed for developing strategic and economic relations with East and South East Asian countries. Thus, the focus of my paper is to make an analysis of the two border trade zones, Moreh-Tamu and Rhi-Zokhawthar, and to examine the possibilities of regional integration within the theoretical framework of Neo-Functionalism. The paper will also focus on the successes, failures and the future of the Indo-Myanmar border trade along with connectivity and security.

***Key words*:** Regionalism, Indo-Myanmar Border, Neo functionalism, Act east policy, Moreh-Tamu, Rhi-*Zokhawthar*.

INTRODUCTION

With the waves of Globalization that gradually began to encompass the entire world after the immediate fall of the Soviet Union in 1991, scholars from various parts of the world reached a consensus that the waves of Globalization shall essentially melt down the borders that compartmentalized the world until then. But did the borders actually melt down? Did the notion of national boundaries actually wither away? It is true that globalization have enabled a free flow of goods and services across the national borders but it is also true that it essentially restricts the free flow of people. Thus, even in the globalized world, borders do have an immense role to play in securing a nation's territory, sovereignty and people. Proliferation of borders and their development have drawn scholars to examine what happens at the borders and because of borders to a nation state and also the difference between other geopolitical borders like the borders of the regions, cities and supra national politics (Donnan, 2012).

Coming on to the borders in India, the total length of India's territorial borders is 15,106.70 km. India borders with countries like Pakistan and Afghanistan in the North West, China, Nepal and Bhutan in the North, Myanmar in the North East, Bangladesh in the East and also share a maritime boundary with Sri Lanka in the South. If we look at the Northern Frontier of India, it comprises of the mighty Himalayas and the Himalayas have been considered to be a boon for India in regards to its security and as pointed out by Professor Jayantanuja Bandyopadhyay that the Himalayan frontier is of great geopolitical significance not only that it separates the mainland India from the rest of Asia but it is also significant from the military aspect as the eight passes along the Border are the points which are to be strongly defended by the army and these passes also provides connectivity both in terms of economy and transportation (Bandyopadhay, 2003).

Taking into consideration the strategic location of India, the Indian Subcontinent as a whole have become immensely important in the international scenario as it along with her neighbours have developed into a potential region known as South Asia. This region essentially includes countries like Pakistan, Afganistan, Nepal, Bhutan, Bangladesh, Sri Lanka and Maldives. The present world order is often described as a world of regions. Now, what are regions, how are they formed and the related questions shall be answered in the following sections of this paper.

Apart from the nations stated above that constitute the South Asian Region, India also shares its borders with Myanmar which is considered to be a nation of South East Asia. However, Barry Buzan who sketched the Regional Security complex theory pointed out that Burma being politically isolated can be considered as a "*Buffer Zone*" between South Asia and South East Asia. Drawing from this, then it can be claimed that, although Burma is not a part of South Asia it essentially is a bridge between the two important regions and may be that is why, India since 1991, through its "Look East Policy" in general and through the Border Trade Agreement in 1994 in particular, started to engage with Myanmar considering it to be a gateway to South East Asia. Today, India is not only an active participant of the India-ASEAN East Asia Summit or ASEAN-India Free Trade Agreement but is also involved with Myanmar in various sub regional arrangements such as BIMSTEC[1], BCIM[2], Mekong Ganga Cooperation[3], etc.

This paper thus, will critically examine the prospects and the problems of the India-Myanmar Border mainly the Moreh-Tamu Border and the Rhi-Zokhawthar Border. The potentialities of the regional integration following the Neo-Functional Theory will be introspected. The North Eastern part of India that borders Myanmar is essentially an area that negates to remain confined within the South Asian Geopolitical scenario and tends to sway towards the South East Asia and Asia Pacific (Lahiri, 2017) and thus, needs an in depth understanding of the present situations and future possibilities that will enhance India's engagement and development in a new regional setup.

UNDERSTANDING 'REGIONALISM' THROUGH THE THEORIES OF REGIONAL INTEGRATION

The process of Regionalization emerged as an effective force since the end of the cold war. However, with the spread of globalization, regionalism has gradually become a means to setup regional economic and security complexes. The discourse on regionalism began with the analysis of the European integration and this was the time when scholars were more interested in studying the regions as new power structures in the world. With the waves of regionalization spreading across the globe, it was found that the conflict prone middle eastern countries were also interested in meeting in the regional forums to discuss the possibilities of future regional cooperation (Schulz, 2001). A region does not have any specific definition in the discourse of International Relations. However, scholars have reached a consensus regarding the elements that are mandatory in describing a particular entity as a region. A region should be a geographically continuous territory that includes land as well as water bodies. It should have three basic features and those are patterned interactions, common characteristics and shared interests.

The increasing scope, fluidity and non-conformity of the new regions was often known as the wave of "New Regionalism". Schulz essentially argued that regionalism is a heterogeneous, pluralistic and multi-dimensional but nevertheless global (Schulz, 2001). Schulz also argued that the world order, today is a tripolar one that centres around EU, NAFTA and Asia Pacific. The regional institutions by themselves are not enough for understanding the regional dynamics and thus it is necessary to understand regionalization through the various theories of regional integration. The principle theories include Neo-realism, Neo-functionalism, Institutionalism etc. However, this paper shall essentially focus on Neo-functional theory to explain the problems and prospects of the Indo-Myanmar border in a regional context.

Developed by Ernst B. Haas and Leon Lindberg, the theory of Neo-functionlism tries to explain and understand the process of European Integration. Lindberg tried to argue that political socialization, interest articulation and aggregation, political communication and decision output are some of the chief categories of political integration (Lindberg, 1970). The foundation of Neo-functionalism is pluralism and a pluralistic thought. Ernst B. Haas on the other hand tried to draw a kind of connection between economic cooperation and political integration. Thus, the Neo-functional theory essentially tries to portray that economic cooperation among nations can often lead to political integration thereby resulting in the formation of regions. This can be somehow used in understanding EU that began as European Economic Community and later developed into a region. If we also take a deeper look at other successful regions like the Asia Pacific we can understand that in most cases economic cooperation is a fundamental factor that have led to the creation of these regions. Neo-functionalists believe that the process of integration is dependent upon elite groups, political parties and also the decision making phenomenon. Thus, Neo-functionalists lay great emphasis on the foreign policy as a factor in creating regions.

Following the Neo-functional approach, India's "Look East Policy" now known as the "Act East policy" therefore had a major role to play in the formation of the sub-regional groupings for greater engagement with Myanmar. It is important to note here, that India can engage with Myanmar through sub-regional groupings (smaller regions within one or more regions). "Asian Regionalism" is characterized by the three regional powers *vis-a-vis* India, China and Russia and their relations with other smaller Asian states (Reinhardt & Senz, 2014). If we talk about economic cooperation then it is immensely important to understand a country's Foreign Economic Policies, its trading relations with other countries and the degree of border trade with its neighbours. India's eastern part in general and the North East in particular have a potential to be developed as a region because to the north is China and Bhutan, to the East is Bangladesh and Myanmar, no other part in India have such a geo-strategic position (Lahiri, 2017). North East, today calls for deeper engagement with neighbours as it's backwardness and the role played by some of the neighbours have helped to sustain insurgency problem in North East (Patgiri, 2016). Thus, there are three basic questions that comes up. First, what is the degree of border trade between India and Myanmar? Secondly, what is the present scenario regarding the security concerns and connectivity issues along the Indo-Myanmar border? Finally, to what extent the present scenario at the border can justify India's objective of achieving greater engagement with Myanmar and subsequent development of its economy through multilateral and regional integration with East and South East Asian Nations?

India-Myanmar Border

India has a 1,642 km long border with Myanmar. The four North Eastern states namely Arunachal Pradesh, Nagaland, Manipur and Mizoram shares their borders with Myanmar. Burma was a continuation of the mainland India in the pre-British period and was only divided during the British rule. As it has been the case with most of the African nations, the Indo-Border as demarcated by the British took into account the political considerations but essentially left out the entho-cultural considerations thereby dividing numerous ethnic tribes who inhabited in the land along the border.

India has a long ethnic and cultural connections with Myanmar. Being the birthplace of Lord Buddha, India has remained a land of pilgrimage for the Burmese. India borders the Chin and the Saggine divisions in Myanmar (Thakur, 2014). If we look at the geography then the terrain is essentially hilly, the purvanchal or the sub Himalayan range has made the Indo-Myanmar Border a rugged terrain. One of the major problem across the India-Myanmar Border is the presence of numerous ethnic militant groups who are essentially exploiting the the cultural and ethnic ties of the population. Some of the most important insurgency groups are the National Socialist council of Nagaland-Khaplang (NSCN K), National Socialist Council of Nagaland-Isak Muviah (NSCN IM), United National Liberation Front (UNLF), United Liberation Front of Assam (ULFA) and People's Liberation Army (PLA).

Moreh-Tamu and Rhi-Zhokhwatar Border Outpost; A Comparative Analysis Moreh-Tamu[4]

Connectivity: Moreh is a small border town located in the Chandel District of Manipur. This particular town shares its border with a small town known as Tamu located in the Sagine division of Myanmar.

Moreh is an international border town on the National Highway 39 also known as the Asian Highway-1. It is important to understand that this roadway is one of the major road linkages between India and Myanmar. Moreh is situated 110 km away from the capital city of Manipur, that is Imphal. This means that it should take approximately 3–4 hours to reach Moreh from Imphal. However suspicion of the Indian para-military forces, poor road condition and under developed infrastructures often posses difficulty in smooth transportation.

Another major problem is the use of underdeveloped techniques of checking and inactiveness on the part of the military, in the security check posts that essentially delays the movement of the traffic. What is also important in this context is that India has to take into account that this particular road is an integral part of international road linkage and therefore should be improved from all aspects including security perspectives. The deployment of AFSPA (Armed Forces Special Power Act) in Manipur is the reason behind this kind of a strict security system however underdeveloped techniques of checking can question the degree of security at times.

The first check post is at Bongyang, this check post is under the 20 Assam Rifles Force. It is embarrassing to mention that male military personnels open ladies' bags to check, which in itself is a major cause of harrasment. The second check post is located in the Tengnoupal; a subdivision headquarters of the Chandel District. This check post is under the 26th sector of the 24 Assam Rifles Force. Here the checking mechanism is quiet slow as they permit only one car at a time. This reduces the pace of the traffic movement. Just after this comes the Lokchao Bridge. The bridge is a single way narrow bridge, only one car can pass at a time. Travellers face huge problems at times when this bridge is repaired and renovated. In such situations it may take more than one and a half hours or even two hours to cross the bridge. Traffic coming from Moreh or from Imphal stands in a line to cross this bridge often leading to lots of commotions and traffic jams.

After crossing the Lokchao Bridge the traffic movement is much smoother as the road now is quiet well maintained. This road crossing the Chandel District of Manipur reaches Moreh having the last security check post as Kundengthabi. Traffic gets stuck at this particular point, one vehicle is checked at a time which makes the movement very slow. It is highly recommended for the Government of India to essentially look into this matter. Baggage scanners or even better technologies can be used as this will not only be convenient for the travellers and the army but will also bring about transparency and cleanliness in the checking process. Kundengthabi check post is the gateway to Moreh.

Moreh shows some peculiar and exotic features. Being a very important town commercially as well as from diplomatic aspects, this town does not have any proper hotels and restaurants. Local population especially the women folk provides minimal facilities of boarding and lodging as well as fooding for those who visit this town. Manipur is known to be a dry state but being an integral part of Manipur, Moreh shows a different picture, people have a very free and open access to liquors which are mostly Chinese. Moreh being a border town where people from the other side, that is Myanmar; have daily access do not show a positive picture of India not only because of the reasons mentioned above but also because the town is extremely dirty. The Land Custom's Station (LCS) or the army people do not even maintain their own compounds.

The only requirement to cross this bridge is an immigration letter from the customs house. Moreh is connected to Tamu *via* the Indo-Myanmar Friendship Bridge. In contrast to that of India, the Myanmarese army do not open the bags of each and every person. They only check the immigration letter. Most astonishingly Tamu being a very small town in the Sagine division of Myanmar, is extremely clean, well maintained and decorated. The road from Tamu reaches Mandalay as a part of the Asian Highway 1, the road in Myanmar have been constructed by the Government of China. Unlike Moreh, Tamu have small eateries as well as big restaurants. There are big hotels and shops where almost everything is available. One fact needs mentioning that Indians are unable to visit the interiors of Tamu as the Indian insurgent groups sheltered in Myanmar prohibits such movement. But on the whole Tamu shows a much better picture of Myanmar than what is shown by Moreh in that sense.

Border trade and commerce: Before analyzing the degree of border trade that takes place along the Moreh -Tamu section, it is important to understand, as to what is border trade. Border trade can be defined as, any transaction that crosses the national border along the International boundary is a border trade (Khundrakpam, 2016). Ministry of the Development of North East Region defines Border Trade as "over-land trade" by way of "exchange of commodities" from a bi-laterally agreed list by people living along both sides of the international border (Ministry of Development of North Eastern Region, Government of India, 2017). The Moreh-Tamu border trade outpost was formally opened on 12th April 1995. Moreh was considered as a transit town in regards to Indo-Myanmar Border Trade Agreement. According to this particular agreement ethnic locals are allowed free movement on both sides of the border but only upto 40 kms for 12 hours a day. These movements are not regulated by the Director General of Foreign

Trade (DGFT). However in 2010 both the governments of India and Myanmar have reduced the free movement upto 16 kms only. Exchanges are done, both in forms of currency exchange and barter system (Ministry of Development of North Eastern Region, Government of India, 2017).

There is a market place near Gate No. 2 on the Indian side. However, most of the Indian people go to Tamu for their commercial transactions, while few come from Myanmar for their economic exchanges to Moreh. This shows that Myanmar is having better gains than India in this context. Shopkeepers readily accept Rupees from Indians and this is helping Myanmar to increase their foreign reserves. The Tamu market at gate number 2 provides a huge variety of products, ranging from vegetables to electronic goods however, most of these products were Chinese, on the contrary the Indian market at Moreh does not leave an array of choices for the consumers, presenting only rice, pulses and garments before them. This is one of the major reasons behind people's preference to go to Tamu for trading purposes. It is extremely necessary for India to develop Moreh as an important commercial town. Economic development, through border trade is quite evident in Tamu compared to Moreh and if India wants to make some valuable gains from its Act East Policy and it should obviously develop Free Trade Agreements (FTAs) and potential markets in the regional setup (Lahiri, 2017). A distinctive feature regarding border trade is the gradual increase in Tamils, Marwaris and Punjabis as major stake holders in the border trade in Moreh. The border trade in this particular area was highly dominated by the Nagas, Kukis and Meiteis even before the border trade agreement was signed.

Rhi-Zokhawtar[5]

Connectivity: The second most important road linkage between India and Myanmar starts from Aizwal in Mizoram, runs through the Champhai district up to Zhowkhatar and enters Rhikhawdar in Myanmar through a friendship bridge across the Tiaou River which marks the border between the two countries. This road is also known as the Rhi-Tidim Road.

The distance of Champhai, which is the border district, from Aizwal is 186 kms. This road is again undoubtedly a mountainous one. The section of the road from Aizwal to Seling is pretty broad. However it gets narrower in certain areas. It takes two hours to reach Seling. After crossing Seling, the road becomes extremely narrow and this continues up to Champhai. The next important town after Seling on this road is Saitung. The best thing about this particular roadway is that there are small villages and town at an interval of every two to three hours. All these villages have shops, eateries and most importantly passengers and travellers get the opportunity to freshen up as most of the roadside hotels provide washroom facilities. This is something absolutely different from that of the Imphal-Moreh-Tamu Road.

The entry to Champhai district is marked by a vibrant and big town Khawzawl. In Khawzawl there is an Assam Riffles Post, some missionary schools, some offices and quite a few shops. From Khawzawl it takes about 3 hours to reach Champhai. At the entry to the Champhai district town there is a check post under the District Police. This is a major contrast to Moreh, which clearly shows that the army or the paramilitary is not very active in this part of the International Border. The road from Champhai to Zokhawthar is 26 kms. According to the Local officials the World Bank have given funds for the development of the road. One thing needs a special mention, that is the entire road from Aizwal to Zokhawthar is maintained by Border Road Organization (BRO). This road ends in the Indo-Myanmar Bridge across the Tiao river and enters Rhi village where the road condition is extremely poor. Infrastructure on the whole is underdeveloped. There is again a Land Customs Station (LCS) near the bridge. Contrary to the Moreh-Tamu outpost, the Rhi-Zokhawthar section is not that busy. Polpulation is scanty with no lodging facilities for travellers. Ethnic local are allowed free movement. There is a village market in Khawmawi (Myanmar) where the mizo people generally go for their daily business. Roads on the Myanmar side is underdeveloped however, the roads are being constructed in cooperation with Border Roads Organization (BRO-India). Compared to Moreh-Tamu Section, this particular section is not at all vibrant in terms of trade, infrastructure and market.

Border trade and commerce: It is quite evident that border trade or commerce in this particular section of the India-Myanmar border is negligible. The basic reason behind this unfavourable Balance of Trade can be many but general observations revealed that lack of infrastructure, poverty, lack of promotion on the part of the government, community cohesion amongst the Mizo people, have made trade and commerce an unpopular game in the area. Although the India-Myanmar Border Trade Agreement of 1994 lays down that border trade between India and Myanmar should be conducted through both the border posts in Manipur and Mizoram but the outpost in Mizoram shows poor results. It was noted that informal trade was more than formal trade and the items of informal trade were mainly beetle nuts and agro products. Two important pictures that came up in this particular area was the presence of huge number of medicine shops in Zokhawthar. Rajeev Bhattacharya, a Guwahati based renowned journalist pointed out that either the rare availability of doctors and healthcare facilities in Rhikhawdar have raised the demands of medicine shops in Zowkhawtar or the demand may emerge due to the steady consumption of drugs amongst the village population (Bhattacharya, 2015). And the other, was the fact that most of the food and snacks products sold in Zokhawthar and Champai were mainly Myanmarese and Bangladeshi. Most of the toys, candies and essential goods sold in small shops in Rikhawdar were goods manufactured in China. Thus, the presence of Chinese in Myanmar's economy is evident both in Rikhawdar and Moreh.

As per the Indo-Myanmar Border Trade Agreement of 1994 that operationalized in 1995, 22 items are supposed to be traded as notified by the Public notice No. 289 (PN(/92–97 dated 10thapril, 1995. 18 commodities notified by Public Notice No. 106 (RE-2008)/2004–2009 dated 7th November, 2008 and 22 new commodities were notified through Public Notice No. 30(RE-20012)/2009–2014 dated 16th November, 2012 (Khundrakpam, 2016). Therefore toltal 62 items are tradeable through the Moreh-Tamu and Rhi-*Zokhawthar* Border. India's import from Myanmar includes agricultural products mainly beans, pulses and timber and India's major exports to Myanmar includes pharmaceuticals, iron and steel, electric machineries, rubber articles, plastics etc (Ministry of External Affairs, Government of India, 2016). Until 2013, the total trade between India and Myanmar had seen considerable fluctuations. During the year 2010, there was a decrease in the total trade between India and Myanmar but since 2011 there has been a consistent rise in the total trade (See figure 1). However, what needs to be noted, is the fact, that India's exports to Myanmar have remained less compared to India's imports. (See Table 1 and Fig. 1). However, evidences reveal that informal trade along both these border outpost have shown considerable rise rather than the formal trade. For the formal trade and commercial purposes, transactions are done in currency format. Myanmar accepts Indian Rupees and India accepts Myanmar Kyat. There is a United Bank of India in Moreh and a Myanmar Economic Bank in Tamu that exchanges the currencies. However in case of Rhi-*Zokhawthar* such banking system was not found. Amongst informal trade items, narcotics and illegal arms proliferation have been a major sourch of income from trade although; in this type of trade the insurgent groups are engaged who tends to use the poor ethnic local for trading these items. Narco trade and drugs trade is a two way process (Singh, 2009) in these sectors. Chemicals like Ephedrin used in production of synthetic drugs are illegally traded from India. Illegal arms mainly AK 47 riffles are sold in parts in the Arms Market in Shilong but is trafficked through the Moreh-Tamu Border post. On the other hand it was reported with the District Police at Champei that M-Series riffles manufactured in Cambodia (by a Chinese company) are being infiltrated through *Zokhawthar* by local stakeholders. This type of phony trade is posing a major threat along the India Myanmar border.

Table 1: India-Myanmar bilateral trade (in million US $).

Year	*2009–2010*	*2010–2011*	*2011–2012*	*2012–2013*
India's exports to Myanmar	207.97 (6.17%)	320.62 (54.17%)	545.38 (70.1%)	544.53 (–0.16)
India's import from Myanmar	1,289.80 (38.84%)	1,289.80 (38.84%)	1,324.82 (30.18%)	1,404.76 (6.03%)
Total trade	1,497.77 (30.17%)	1,338.29 (–10.65%)	1,870.20 (39.75%)	1,949.28 (4.23%)

Source: *https://www.mea.gov.in/Portal/ForeignRelation/India-Myanmar_Relations.* pdf Data according to CSO, Government of Myanmar, (accessed on 16th November, 2017)

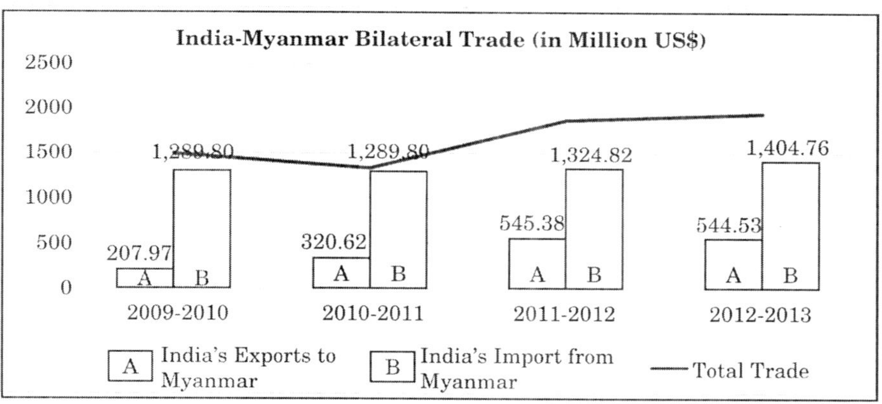

Fig. 1: Graphical representation of India-Myanmar bilateral trade (in million US $). *Source*: *https://www.mea.gov.in/Portal/ForeignRelation/India-Myanmar_Relations.pdf*, Data according to CSO, Government of Myanmar, (accessed on 16th November, 2017)

***Security concerns along the border*:** With the concept of regionalism spreading across the world, regional security besides economic cooperation have become a new catch phrase. With the Treaty of Peace signed at Westphalia in 1648 that ended the Thirty Year's War and brought into light the concepts of sovereignty and territorial integrity, countries, in a globalized world, do take into consideration both these concepts and also tend to achieve regional peace, security and economic cooperation. To achieve regional peace it is important that the International boundaries are essentially peaceful because a peaceful border tends to create a peaceful region. India's International boundaries have never remained at peace. Apart from the other conflictuous boundaries of Pakistan, Bangladesh and Nepal, India-Myanmar Border is extremely disturbed and insecured. The major in securities along the India-Myanmar Border are: First, the presence of numerous insurgent groups who are funded by China and trained by Pakistan. These insurgents groups are using safe territories of Myanmar along the border and are carrying out anti Indian activities. Secondly, the infiltration of huge amount of drugs. It is quiet a well known fact that Myanmar is a part of the famous Golden Triangle and it is also astonishing to note that drug trade is a two way process in the border. Huge amount of Cough Syrups and tonics containing Ephedrin is illegally traded to Myanmar from India and in return Synthetic Drugs are manufactured. Earlier Kuki and Naga militant groups wanted to control Moreh because Moreh have more than 10 un-metalled roads that lead to Imphal which helps in smooth smuggling of contrabands. Drug pedaling is associated with these militant groups because it is an effective way of making quick money (Kumar, 2016). Effects of drug intake amongst the youth residing along the borders is evident from the steep rise in HIV positive cases amongst the population. Today Manipur is ranked 3rd amongst the states of India having highest number of HIV cases (Singh, 2009). Thirdly, the illegal arms proliferation. Both Moreh and *Zokhawthar* have shown evidences that huge amount of illegal arms are regularly infiltrating through the borders. Local residents in Moreh claimed that AK-47 riffles manufactured in China are brought into India by local stake holders. These people do not take the NH39 route which is checked by the Indian Military but they are taking the forest roads. On the contrary, it was found in a personal interview with the District Commissioner and the Superintendent of Police in Champai, that poor village people, especially the kids and the women go to the other side and get hold of M-Series Riffles manufactured in Cambodia, and carry them to India in baskets along with beetle nuts and such other agricultural products. Personal interviews also revealed that Moreh-Tamu outpost is dominated by the insurgent groups who often manages to get help and funding from China and they are the ones who are engaged with the illegal arms trade. The NIA in 2011 confirmed, after interrogating Anthony Shimary (NSCN-IM), that the North-East insurgent groups are procuring arms from China (Chatterjee, 2015). On the contrary, in Mizoram, insurgency problem is missing, infiltration of Chinese stakeholders is also missing because of the strong community cohesion amongst the Mizo people. However, there are few brokers or mafias who are engaged in arms proliferation and they tend to sway the youth into such trading. The sources also revealed that the arms available at Moreh is manufactured by 'Norinco' the largest arms manufacturing company in China. On the other hand, those coming through *Zokhawthar* are manufactured in Cambodia but in support of Chinese investment. Another major problem along the border, especially in Moreh, is the Law and Order problem. What is important is to note that the increasing number of Tamils have created a community crisis. The problem is between the Kukis and the Tamils and the Kukis and the Meitis. Thus, taking into consideration the above security threats along with the poor infrastructure especially poor defence mechanism, inactiveness on the part of the Land Customs stations, poor banking facilities and the ethnic factors, it can be concluded that the Indo-Myanmar border is vulnerable in terms of security.

CONCLUSIONS

Neo-functionalists tend to explain that regional integration have three basic causal factors: First, is the economic integration amongst the nation states, secondly, to build institutions that will enable to resolve disputes and thirdly, supranational market rules that will essentially replace the national regulations. Neo-functionalists also sketches that, integration in one sector can cause a "Spill Over Effect", that will eventually enable integration in other sectors too. Now taking into consideration this particular theoretical approach and after a rigorous research on the India-Myanmar Border it is very difficult to reach to a positive conclusion. It is true that border trade in this particular area is extremely low but is significant, on the other hand, the economy of this region is essentially connected with China, which in itself is highly significant. Therefore, economic integration is no more confined within India and Myanmar but is essentially bringing in countries like China and Bangladesh. In this context, it was realized much earlier by the policy makers that India's Look East Policy cannot only be directed towards the South East Asian economies because the geo-strategic location of India's North East will bring into picture, countries like Bangladesh, China, Bhutan and Nepal. This in itself shows that India-Myanmar border is extremely important strategically as two regions are intersecting along this border. Thus, the adoption of Sub-Regional Groupings like BIMSTEC, BCIM and such others, are valid and very well conceived ideas of achieving greater regional integration.

But for a successful region, it is important that the borders are secured, there is a thriving border trade and there is a free movement of people engaged in the border trade. However, it is necessary that such a movement is regulated to prohibit illegal activities and the border towns are vibrant in terms of infrastructure and basic facilities. The survey of the *Moreh-Tamu* and Rhi-*Zokhawthar* border outposts revealed that these two borders do not meet any of the criterias mentioned above. The apparent presence and the influence of China in Myanmar are often taking a difficult posture and is also a reason of apprehension for India. The growth in the illegal arms proliferation, the infiltration of amrs fabricated in China and the steep rise in drugs trade in posing a major threat along the border and the area adjoining the border. It is also worth mentioning that the arms proliferation along the borders is enabling the numerous insurgent groups, active in North East, to get hold of arms and ammunitions at a cheaper rate. This persistent theatre is not only hampering the cross border trade but is also hampering the notion of regional intergration.

Many scholars today also argue that the process of fencing along the India-Myanmar Border that started after Than Shwe and Dr. Manmohan Singh decided that both the countries shall jointly work to prevent insurgency, has ignited the fire of protest amongst the ethnic locals. Scholars are also of the opinion that this very protest shall essentially halt the fencing procedure and thereby provide a greater opportunity for the insurgents to carry out their activities. It should also be noted that the transactions done in the illegal trading involves huge amount of black money and fake currencies. This is one of the most imperative reasons as to why, the border trade is not adding much to the Indian Economy.

Thus what is the future? How can such issues be resolved? Can such Cross Border Infrastructural Development bring about a sustained economic growth and a vibrant market for the North East? Such issues can be resolved by connecting the entire North East with the mainland India. The proposed rail link from Imphal to Moreh should take a faster pace. Secondly, its high time for the policy makers to realize, that considering the geo-strategic factors, Moreh and Zokhawthar can easily be developed as important economic centres. Infrastructural and logistic development in both these towns should be such that it attracts both locals as well as other business communities to invest and carry out healthy cross border trade. Many experts have also come up with the opinion of a Regional Trade Agreement that would facilitate cross border trade along with a more comprehensive strategy of addressing the security issues. One basic way of resolving the conundrum is by making North East an economic hub and a market that will provide the local people a better way of exploring themselves and earning their living. A very positive development since 2011 is the democratization in Myanmar. This in turn have helped Myanmar to take up some comprehensive political and economic reforms, hence, it is now much more easier for India to develop the infrastructural projects like the India-Myanmar-Thailand Trilateral Highway and the India-Myanmar-Bangladesh Oil and Gas Pipeline. Such projects will not only be a game changer for the North East but will also be important for India's objective of regional integration and maybe one of the best way to cope up with China and Chinese policy of encircling India. Therefore, it is impotant that there is a balanced development on both sides of the border because only that can bring a better opportunity for both the countries to make some absolute economic gains from enhanced regional integration.

NOTES

[1] It was originally launched as Bangladesh, India, Myanmar, Sri Lanka, Thailand Economic cooperation but was changed in 1997 o Bay of Bengal Initiative for Multi-Sectoral technical and Economic Cooperation. It acts as a link between South and South East Asia with 13 priority sectors led by the member nations. BIMSTEC is constanly working for regional integration, economic growth, technological cooperation and trade liberalization.

[2] It is popularly known as the Kunming Initiative which is an economic corridor linking Kolkata in India and Kunming in China two fastest growing economies through Bangladesh and Myanmar, two least developed economies. Basically its main objective is to traverse areas of underdevelopment especially the North East of India and the South western part of China through transnational connectivity, economic integration and cross border cooperation.

[3] This is one of the decisive sub-regional initiative of Indo-ASEAN cooperation that was formally launched in 2000 comprising of India, Thailand, Vietnam, Cambodia, Laos and Myanmar. It has a five member group which works on tourism, education, culture, communication and on plan of action.

[4] The information, given in this section, apart from those cited, is purely based on the authors personal experiences in a field trip organized by the Jadavpur Association of International relations (JAIR) and supported by Maulana Abul Kalam Azad Institute of Asian Studies (MAKAIAS) from (9th January - 13th January, 2015), Moreh-Tamu.

[5] The information, given in this section, apart from those cited, is purely based on the authors personal experiences in a field trip organized by the Jadavpur Association of International Relations (JAIR) and supported by Maulana Abul

Kalam Azad Institute of Asian Studies (MAKAIAS) from (21st June - 25th June, 2015) Rhi-Zokhawthar.

REFERENCES

Bandyopadhay Jayantanuja (2003). *The Making of India's Foreign Policy*. New Delhi: Allied Publishers Private Limited.

Bhattacharya Rajeev (2015). "Border Trade in Rhi-Zokhawthar: Wide Gap between Goals and Realities." *JAIR Journal of International Relations*, pp. 67–69.

Chandran Suba and Bhavna Singh (2015). India, China and Sub-regional Connectivity in South Asia. New Delhi. Sage Publications.

Chatterjee Gadadhar (2015). "North East Insurgencies: An Introspection." *JAIR Journal of International Relations*, pp.73–75.

Das, Gurudas and Thomas C. Joshua (2016). *Look East to Act East Policy: Implications for India's North East*. New Delhi. Routledge.

Donnan Hastings and Thomas Wilson (2012). *A Companion to Border Studies*. New Jersey: Wiley Blackwell.

Khundrakpam Padmavati (2016). *Experiences of Manipur and Indo-Myanmar Border Trade: A Relook*. New Delhi: Akansha Publication.

Kumar Saurabh (2016). *Analyzing the Security Issues Originating from the Myanmar Border. http://idrw.org/analysing_security_issues_originating_myanmar_border/*

Lahiri Imankalyan (2017). *Peace, Development and Community, The Look East Imagination of India with Special Reference to North East India*. New Delhi: KW Publishers Private Limited.

Lindberg Leon (1970). "Political Integration as a Multi-Diamensional Phenomenon requring Multi-variate Analysis." International Organization, pp. 649–731.

Ministry of Development of North Eastern Region. Government of India. Border Trade. *http://mdoner.gov.in/content/border-trade* (accessed on February 16, 2017).

Ministry of External Affairs. Government of India. India-Myanmar Relations. *http://www.mea.gov.in/Portal/ForeignRelations/Myanmar_Feb_2016.pdf* (accessed on February 16, 2017).

Nepram Binalakshmi (2002). South Asia's fractured frontiere; Armed Conflicts, Narcotics and Small Arms Proliferation in India's North east. New Delhi, Mittal Publications.

Patgiri Rubul and Hazarika Obja Borah (2016). "Locating North East in India's Neighborhood Policy; Transnational Solutions to a problem of Periphery." *Indian Quarterly; A Journal of International Affairs*, pp. 234–246.

Reinhardt Dieter and Senz Anja (2014). "Closer Cooperation in the BCIM Region-A New Success story of Asian Regionalism?" *Connecting India, China and South East Asia. http://econpapers.repee.org/scripts/redir.pdf* (accessed on February 14, 2017).

Schulz Michael, Soderbaun Frederick and Ojendal Joakim (2001). *Regionalization in a Globalizing World; A Comparative Perspectives on Forms, Actors and Processes*. London: Zed Books.

Singh Kishan Thingnam (2009). *Look East Policy in India's North East; Polemics and Perspectives*. New Delhi: Concept Publishing Company.

Thakur Sanjay (2014). "Indo-Myanmar Border Linkages". *Centre for Land Warfare Studies. http://www.claws.in/* (accessed on February 15, 2017).

12

Mudra: A Tool for Inclusive Growth in Jammu and Kashmir

AABID AHMAD KOKA[1*]

ABSTRACT

Finance is very effective tool in enhancing economic opportunity and fighting poverty. To remove the financial difficulties faced by micro and small business units the government of India launched a scheme on 8th April 2015 called Micro Unit Development and Refinance Agency or MUDRA. The present study is an attempt to know about the product offerings of the MUDRA and its performance in Jammu and Kashmir. For the study secondary data has been used. The study finds that the finance to micro units is given in three schemes Shishu, Kishore and Tarun which shelters loans up to Rs 50 thousand, above Rs 50 thousand up to Rs 5 lakh and above Rs 5 lakh up to Rs 10 lakh respectively. MUDRA is performing well in Jammu and Kashmir. In financial year 2015–16 the total amount sanctioned was Rs.1185.13 Crore and the amount disbursed was Rs. 1152.15 Crore which increased to Rs 1845.37 Crore and Rs. 1663.51 Crore in the financial year 2016–17 respectively. In the coming years MUDRA will definitely prove to be a tool for inclusive growth in Jammu and Kashmir if it continues to perform well. If it is implemented properly at the poor people, it may work as a game changing financial inclusion initiative of Government of India because Jammu and Kashmir is a hilly state. To establish a large industry here is a difficult task. It is better to rely on the micro units. For the creation of these units MUDRA is a perfect tool.

Key words: Finance, MUDRA, Jammu and Kashmir, Financial inclusion, Inclusive growth.

[1] Jiwaji University, Gwalior, Madhya Pradesh.

**Corresponding author:* E-mail: aabideco18@gmail.com

INTRODUCTION

Finance is very effective tool in enhancing economic opportunity and fighting poverty. Financial Inclusion is a much cherished policy in India and our economic policy has always been driven by an underlying intent of a sustainable and inclusive growth[1]. To remove the financial difficulties faced by micro and small business units the government of India launched a scheme on 8th April 2015 called Micro Unit Development and Refinance Agency or MUDRA[2]. The formation of the agency was initially announced in the 2015 union budget in February 2015. MUDRA is a public sector financial institution in India which provide loans at low rates to micro financial institutions and non-banking financial institutions which then provide credit to micro, small and medium enterprises (MSMEs). The money lenders exploit the small entrepreneurs of India so far, but MUDRA will instill a new self-confidence in them that the country is ready to support them in their efforts that are contributing so strongly to the task of nation building. MUDRA is still not a fully-fledged bank and is in its initial stages. It will provide its services to small entrepreneurs outside the service area of regular banks, by using last mile agents[3]. A vast part of the non-corporate sector operates as unregistered enterprises. They do not maintain proper Books of Accounts and are not formally covered under taxation areas. Therefore, the banks find it difficult to lend them. Majority of this sector does not access outside sources of finance. PMMY aims to bank the unbanked. The objective of PMMY is to support the entrepreneurs of the micro class via Micro Units Development and Refinance Agency (MUDRA) Bank[4].

REVIEW OF SOME PREVIOUS STUDY

Mehar, L. (2014)[5] has showed that the financial inclusion in India has increased in the last few years with new innovations like mobile banking, ultra small branches etc.

Verma S. (2015)[6] has explained that the design of MUDRA scheme will not only caters to the financial problems of MSMEs but also give moral support to a lot of young population to become an entrepreneur.

Rudrawar, M.A. and Uttarwar, V.R. (2016)[7] has explained that PMMY can bring a desired transformation. If it will be applied properly at the bottom level, it may act as a game changing idea and boost the Indian economy. It should include less documentation and easily accessible. In coming few years, MUDRA will play a crucial role for the development of entrepreneurship, increase in GDP and development of employment.

Roy, A.K. (2016)[8] has displayed that the small businesses are the foundation of economic development. A major number of initiatives have been taken in the past few years in the right direction.

Venkatesh, J. and Kumari, L. (2017)[9] has showed that besides the schemes that are being introduced for the overall growth and development of the MSME sector, initiatives have been launched which focus solely on entrepreneurs. The schemes will contribute to the well-being of the individuals engaged in small scale industries which will positively affect the progress of the whole economy.

Rupa, R. (2017)[10] has showed that the MUDRA scheme is very much successful in Tamil Nadu. It is found that the MFIs have contributed substantially to increase the number of accounts financed under the PMMY.

RESEARCH METHODOLOGY

The study is based on secondary data. The data and information for the study is gathered from sources like journals, newspapers, magazines, various websites including website of MUDRA Yojana.

OBJECTIVES OF THE STUDY

- To study the Product offerings of MUDRA.
- To study the performance of MUDRA in India.
- To analyze the performance of MUDRA in Jammu and Kashmir.

DISCUSSION

Any Indian Citizen who has a wage producing plan from small scale business exercises in exchanging, assembling and preparing and whose advance pre requisite is under Rs.10 lakh can approach advances under PMMY. Loan rate is regulated by Reserve Bank of India (RBI) time to time. Non corporate Small Business Sector (NCSBS) occupied with benefit division, miniaturized scale fabricating units, natural products and vegetable distributing, support and repairing, handiworks and working nourishment administrations and so on are benefited under the plan. The idea of MUDRA Bank is not just based on meeting the credit and financial needs of small enterprises. Rather than just providing credit, it is based on the "Credit Plus" approach under which access to credit will be combined with various enterprises development and welfare related services. MUDRA Bank is providing much needed financial access to NCSBSs, promote growth of small businesses, help boost the country's GDP and create job in the coming times[11]. Fig. 1 represents the offerings of MUDRA bank Product.

MUDRA Product Offerings

The funding supports from MUDRA are of four types:

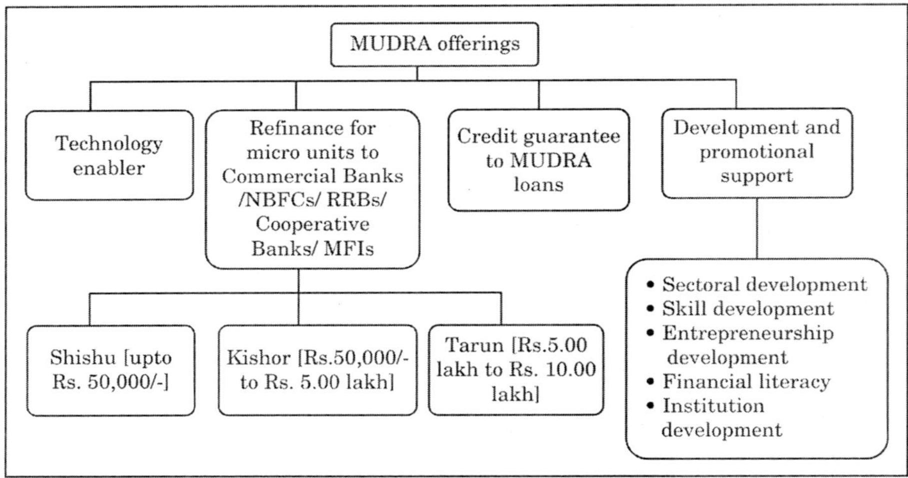

Fig. 1: MUDRA Offerings. ***Source*:** mudra.org.in/offerings

A. *Micro credit schemes*

Micro Credit Scheme is offered mainly through Micro Finance Institutions (MFIs), which deliver the credit up to Rs.1 lakh, for various micro enterprise activities. Although, the mode of delivery may be through groups like SHGs/ JLGs, the loans are given to the individuals for specific income generating micro enterprise activity. The MFIs for availing financial support need to enroll with MUDRA by complying with some of the requirements as notified by MUDRA, from time to time.

B. *Refinance schemes for banks*

Different banks like Commercial Banks, Regional Rural Banks and Scheduled Cooperative Banks are eligible to avail of refinance support from MUDRA for financing micro enterprise activities. The refinance is available for term loan and working capital loans, up to an amount of 10 lakh per unit. The eligible banks, which have enrolled with MUDRA by complying with the requirements as notified, can avail of refinance from MUDRA for the loan issued under Shishu, Kishor and Tarun categories.

C. *Women enterprise programs*

In order to encourage women entrepreneurs the financing banks / MFIs may consider extending additional facilities, including interest reduction on their loan. At present, MUDRA extends a reduction of 25 bps in its interest rates to MFIs / NBFCs, who are providing loans to women entrepreneurs.

D. *Securitization of loan portfolio*

MUDRA also supports Banks / NBFCs / MFIs for raising funds for financing micro enterprises by participating in securitization of their loan assets against micro enterprise portfolio, by providing second loss default guarantee, for credit enhancement and also participating in investment of Pass through Certificate (PTCs) either as senior or junior investor[12].

The loan to the MSMEs under MUDRA will be disbursed under following three schemes:

1. ***Shishu:*** This is targeted towards startups and sanctioned loan amount will be up to Rs. 50 thousands. The idea is to provide enough financial support to cover the expenses for business set up.
2. ***Kishore*:** This is targeted towards already existing businesses that lack exposure. The sanctioned loan amount will be between Rs. 50 thousands and Rs. 5 lakh. This scheme will help businesses to gain exposure by expanding their supply segment, which will in turn help to reach out to more customers.
3. ***Tarun*:** This is for those businesses which have grown to a certain level and have enough exposure but need help to take business to a new level. The sanctioned loan amount will be between Rs. 5 lakh and Rs. 10 lakh.

Performance of MUDRA in India

Table 1 and Chart 1 shows the performance of MUDRA in India. It can be seen from the table that in financial year 2015–16 the total amount sanctioned was Rs. 137449.27 Crore and the amount disbursed was Rs. 132954.73 Crore which increased to Rs. 180528.54 Crore and Rs. 175312.13 Crore in the financial year 2016–17 respectively. In 2017–18 the loan sanctioned was Rs. 253677.10 Crore and loan disbursed was Rs. 246437.40 Crore. In 2018–19 till date the figures are also satisfactory. It can be said that the MUDRA is doing well according to its objectives. Chart no 1 also show the performance of MUDRA in India.

Table 1: Performance of MUDRA in India.

Financial year	*No. of loans sanctioned*	*Amount sanctioned (Rs. Crore)*	*Amount disbursed (Rs. Crore)*
2015–16	34880924	137449.27	132954.73
2016–17	39701047	180528.54	175312.13
2017–18	48130593	253677.10	246437.40
2018–19 up to06 July 2018	8928996	47758.63	43928.66

Source: PMMY report

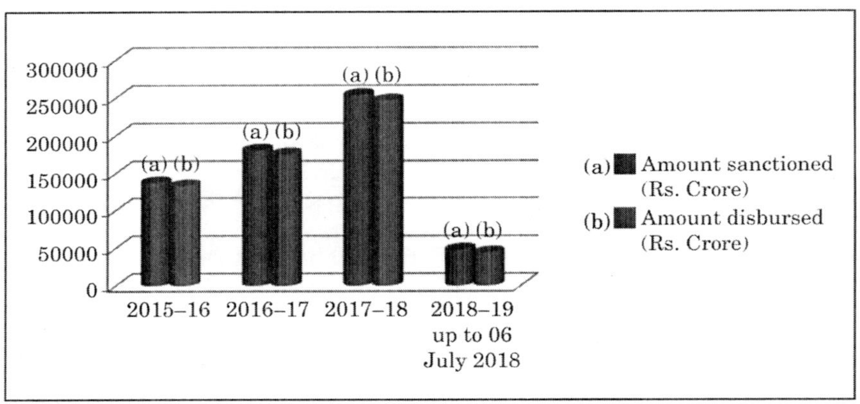

Chart 1: Performance of MUDRA in India. *Source:* Derived from Table 1

Performance of MUDRA in Jammu and Kashmir

The state of Jammu and Kashmir is the northern most state of India. It is located between latitudes 32°172 north and 36°582 north longitude 73°262 east and 80°302 east. Its boundaries touch the neighboring countries of Tibet in the east, China and Afghanistan in the north and Pakistan in the west. To its south lie Punjab and Himachal Pradesh states of India. With its borders sealed on the east, the north and west, the state of Jammu and Kashmir is accessible only from the south. It is through its south that the state has road, railway and air links with the rest of the country. Such a position gives the state an appearance of a bottle lying on its side with its mouth facing south. Geographical position of the Jammu and Kashmir state can be divided into four Zones. First, there is the sub-monate and semi-monate plain most of which is known as Kandi or dry belt. This mingles into second geographical division of hills including the well-known Shivalik Range. It is backed by the 3rd zone of the high mountains mainly constituting the Kashmir Valley, Pir Panjal and its offshoots. This includes Doda, Poonch, Rajouri and parts of Kathua and Udhampur districts. The fourth geographical division comprises Tibetan Tract of Ladakh, Kargil, Gilgit and Skardu (the latter two are now held by Pakistan) consisting of middle run of the Indus river.

As per details from census 2011, Jammu and Kashmir has a total population 12541302 out of which male and female were 6640662 and 5900640 respectively. The population of J&K forms 1.04% of India population. Of the total population of J&K around 72.62% live in villages of rural areas.

It can be reveled from the Tables 2, 3, 4 and 5 that the amount sanctioned under Kishore is the highest in all the three financial years and the Tarun has the second highest amount sanctioned and Shishu is at the third place. MUDRA is performing well as can be seen from the Table 5 that in financial year 2015–16 the total amount sanctioned was Rs. 1185.13 Crore and the

Table 2. Performance of MUDRA in Jammu and Kashmir in 2015 (amount in Rs. crores).

Shishu			*Kishore*			*Tarun*		
No. of sanctions	***Amount sanctioned***	***Amount disbursed***	***No. of sanctions***	***Amount sanctioned***	***Amount disbursed***	***No. of sanctions***	***Amount sanctioned***	***Amount disbursed***
19057	64.07	62.32	34388	760.31	738.18	4529	360.75	351.65

Source: PMMY report 2015–16

Table 3: Performance of MUDRA in Jammu and Kashmir in 2016–17 (amount in Rs. crores).

Shishu			*Kishore*			*Tarun*		
No. of sanctions	***Amount sanctioned***	***Amount disbursed***	***No. of sanctions***	***Amount sanctioned***	***Amount disbursed***	***No. of sanctions***	***Amount sanctioned***	***Amount disbursed***
23589	79.88	72.14	59232	1237.30	1114.22	6891	528.19	477.15

Source: PMMY report 2016–17

Table 4: Performance of MUDRA in Jammu and Kashmir in 2017–18 (amount in Rs. crores).

Shishu			*Kishore*			*Tarun*		
No. of sanctions	***Amount sanctioned***	***Amount disbursed***	***No. of sanctions***	***Amount sanctioned***	***Amount disbursed***	***No. of sanctions***	***Amount sanctioned***	***Amount disbursed***
19532	69.04	67.74	73095	1725.60	1678.84	10498	792.15	768.26

Source: PMMY report 2017–18

Table 5: Performance of MUDRA in Jammu and Kashmir in 2018–19 (provisional) (amount in Rs. crores).

Shishu			*Kishore*			*Tarun*		
No. of sanctions	***Amount sanctioned***	***Amount disbursed***	***No. of sanctions***	***Amount sanctioned***	***Amount disbursed***	***No. of sanctions***	***Amount sanctioned***	***Amount disbursed***
4781	18.01	17.54	20054	502.72	484.21	3520	268.94	256.16

Source: PMMY report 2018–19 up to 06 July 2018

Table 6: Overall Performance of MUDRA in Jammu and Kashmir.

Financial year	*Loans sanctioned*	*Amount sanctioned (Rs. crore)*	*Amount disbursed (Rs. crore)*
2015–16	57974	1185.13	1152.15
2016–17	89712	1845.37	1663.51
2017–18	103125	2586.80	2514.84
2018–19 up to 06 July 2018	28355	789.67	757.92

Source: PMMY report

amount disbursed was Rs. 1152.15 Crore which increased to Rs. 1845.37 Crore and Rs. 1663.51 Crore in the financial year 2016–17 respectively. In 2017–18 the loan sanctioned was Rs. 2586.80 Crore and the loan disbursed was Rs. 2514.84 Crore. In 2018–19 the figures so far are also satisfactory. There is an increasing trend in the overall performance of the MUDRA from its ordaining. Chart 2 represents the performance of MUDRA in Jammu and Kahmir.

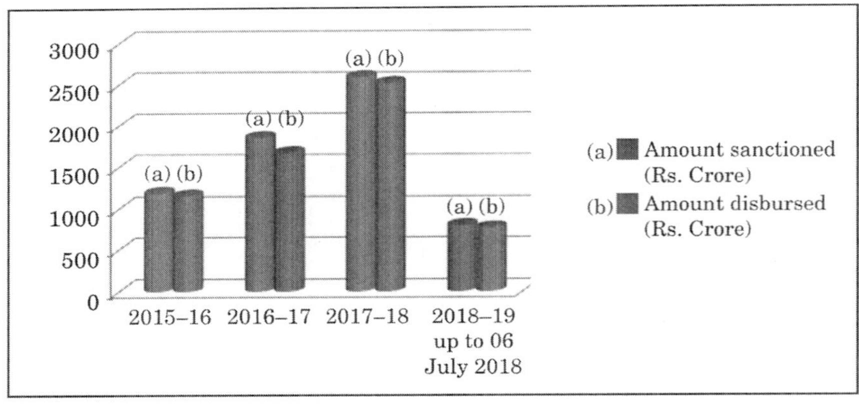

Chart 2: Performance of MUDRA in Jammu and Kashmir. ***Source:*** Derived from Table 6

CONCLUSIONS

The small businesses form the foundation of the economic development needs to be strengthened and supported. A large number of schemes have been taken in the past few years are a step in the right direction. MUDRA Yojana is the most recent scheme to boost up the small and micro business units in India. MUDRA has been formed with the primary objective of developing the micro enterprise sector in the country by extending various supports including financial support in the form of refinancing, so as to achieve the goal of "funding the unfunded". The GOI Press release of 2 March 2015 has laid down the roles and responsibilities of MUDRA.

Subsequently, GOI has also decided that MUDRA will provide refinance support, monitor the PMMY data by managing the web portal, facilitate offering guarantees for loans granted under PMMY and take up other activities assigned to it from time to time. We have concluded from the study that due to PMMY there is a bigger change in the area of micro finance. This scheme will promote competition to give credit support to this weaker section, low income group and this unfunded population. If it is implemented properly at the poor people, it may work as a game changing financial inclusion initiative of Government of India. In Jammu and Kashmir MUDRA is also performing well according to its objectives. In the coming years MUDRA will definitely prove to be a tool for inclusive growth in Jammu and Kashmir if it continues to perform. As stated earlier Jammu and Kashmir is a hilly state. To establish a large industry here is a difficult task. It is better to rely on the micro units. For the creation of these units MUDRA is a perfect tool.

REFERENCES

[1] Godha, A. and Nama, D. (2017). Pradhan Mantri Mudra Yojana: A New Financial Inclusion Initiative. *International Journal of Engineering Technology, Management and Applied Sciences,* 5(3): 200–204.

[2] Kumar, S. (2017). Impact of Mudra Yojana on Financial Inclusion.

[3] Sonia (2017). Mudra Yojana - A Strategic Tool for Small Business Financing. *International Journal of Enhanced Research in Management & Computer Applications,* 6(8), 23–27.

[4] Shahid, M. and Irshad, M. (2016). A Descriptive Study on Pradhan Manthri Mudra Yojana (PMMY). *International Journal of Latest Trends in Engineering and Technology,* pp. 121–125.

[5] Mehar, L. (2014). Financial Inclusion in India.

[6] Verma, S. (2015). Mudra Bank to Fund small Businesses.

[7] Rudrawar, M.A. and Uttarwar, V.R. (2016). An Evaluatory Study of MUDRA Scheme. *International Journal of Multifaceted and Multilingual Studies,* 3(6).

[8] Roy, A.K. (2016). Mudra Yojana - A Strategic tool for Small Business Financing. *International Journal of Advance Research in Computer Science and Management Studies,* 4(1): 68–72.

[9] Venkatesh, J. and Kumari, L. (2017). Performance of MUDRA bank: A study on financial assistance to MSME sector.

[10] Rupa, R. (2017). Progress of MUDRA with the special reference of Tamil Nadu.

[11] Jain, V. (2016). Mudra Bank: A Step towards Financial Inclusion, Review of Research. *International Multidisciplinary Journal,* 5(4): 1–4.

[12] Shahid, M. and Irshad, M. (2016). A Descriptive Study on Pradhan Manthri Mudra Yojana (PMMY). *International Journal of Latest Trends in Engineering and Technology,* pp. 121–125.

Websites

1. www.mudra.org
2. *https://en.m.wikipedia.org/wiki/mudra.*
3. www.conferenceworld.in

13

GDP Growth Rate of Public Expenditure on Education in India

REJIMON P.M.[1*]

ABSTRACT

A better-educated workforce enhances a nation's stock of human capital, which is crucial for increased productivity and economic development from an economic point, education is associated with high rates of return, both private and social. Especially now, during financial and economic crisis, more effort must be put into higher education to help young people avoid unemployment. Moreover, the demand for education during crises tends to increase. When making decisions on whether to participate in workforce or in education, individuals decide to invest more in education when unemployment rates are higher. Moreover, education is an important tool not only for tackling the present economic crisis, but also for developing a more sustainable, adaptive and creative society. At the UNESCO World Conference on Higher Education in July 2009, it was stated that: "At no time in history has it been more important to invest in higher education as a major force in building an inclusive and diverse knowledge society and to advance research, innovation and creativity" (UNESCO, 2009). Present paper analyses the trend in government expenditure on education since Independence.

Key words: Human capital, GDP, Public expenditure, Education.

[1] Department of Economics, University of Calicut, Kerala.
**Corresponding author:* E-mail: pmrejimon@gmail.com

INTRODUCTION

During the 2017–18 budget speech finance minister Arun Jaitley announced plans to invest significantly in higher education. The keen observation of the budget shows that there is a 10 percent increase happened in higher education investment when compared to previous year. IIT's and NIT's received 25 percent of budgetary expenses, but it increased to one third during 2017–18 budgets. 2018–19 Budget shows a 16.42 percent increase in total education expenditure from revenue account of the centre government. At the same time accidently we had gone through a slogan "Educate, Agitate, Organize" of students from IISER. They highlighted the sudden increase in the required CPI for inspire scholarship from 6 to 7 across all batches, halved the number of scholarships from 2016–17 onwards and increase of tuition fees by three to four fold. Moreover, they raised slogans against the crunch in fund for research. This contradiction made an interest in investigating in a more detailed manner the condition of public expenditure on education. The article aimed to analyze the actual trend in public expenditure on education in different plan periods and place the fact in the context of India's present human development condition. Along with this, the article tries to analyze the trend in central government budgetary expenses on education especially in higher education during 2012–18 periods.

PURPOSE OF PUBLIC SPENDING ON EDUCATION

Traditional economic theory by and large viewed capital in physical terms only. Based on aggregate production function data economists during the late 1950's, found that the standard measures of simple labour and physical capital were incapable of explaining adequately the rapid post-War growth (Viswanath *et al.,* 2009). Endogenous growth theory highlighted the importance of education and the term 'human capital' is considered to be an important variable responsible for economic growth and development. Human capital is formed from investment in skills and education. A study of the joint development of government expenditures and economic growth in 23 OECD countries conducted by Lamartina and Zaghini (2007) showed that there is a structural positive correlation between public spending and per capita GDP. Thus an increase in government's spending on human capital development is expected to culminate in an increase of per capita output (Stephen & Oluranti, 2011). It is found that the rates of return to investment in human capital are well above those on physical capital in a large number of countries and it is highest in the case of primary education (Psacharopoulos, (1972 & 1994). All these studies typically look at the direct effect of educational expenditure on growth. However, if education outcomes affect growth, and educational expenditure affects education outcomes, then expenditure also has an indirect effect on growth. By using recent US data it is found that a 10% increase in per-pupil spending each year for 12 grades of public school was found to lead to 0.27 more completed years of education,

7.25% higher wages and 3.67 percentage point reduction in the annual incidence of adult poverty (Jackson, Johnson & Persico, 2017). In this context it is relevant to analyze the pattern of public spending on education in India.

Public Expenditure on Education in India After Independence

From the above discussion it is clear that expenditure incurred for education is considered to be an important variable for the socio economic development of a nation. Hence this session analyses the public expenditure on education after independence. As it is a well known fact that the first national policy on education is announced by then Prime Minister Indira Gandhi in the year 1968. NPE 1968 called for increasing education spending to six percentage of the national income by 1985. In this context, it is relevant to analyze the trend in public expenditure on education after independence.

The public expenditure on education shows a continuously increasing trend after the first National Policy on Education up to 1989–90. After 1990, the increase of expenditure on education was sluggish (Figs. 1 & 2). While analyzing the education expenditure during five plan periods, fourth five year plan onwards, the education expenditure improves drastically. But still it is far below the Kothari commission target of six percentage of GDP. While analyzing the trend, it is interesting to note that the highest public expenditure on education by education department was in 89–90 period. After that the growth was stagnant, both in the case education expenditure by education department and other departments. In 1999–2000, again the education expenses as a percentage of GDP (public expenditure on education by education department and other departments together) become 4.19. It is interesting to note that after 1971 onwards, other departments are also spending money on education other than education department. It may be

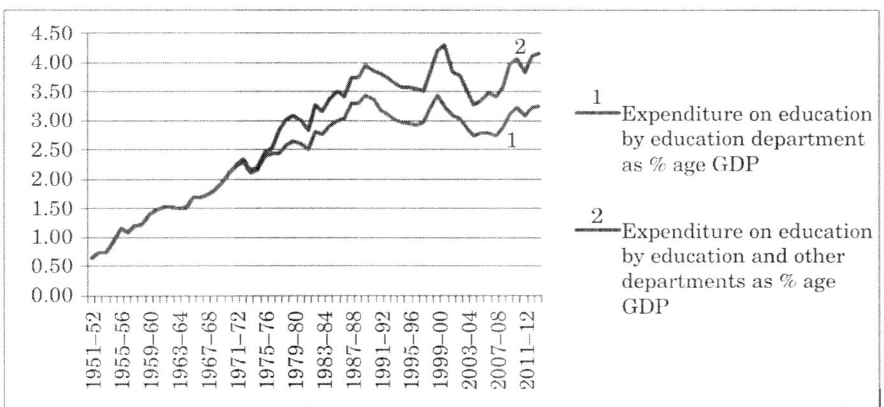

Fig. 1: Yearly trend in public expenditure on education (1951–2012). ***Source:*** Compiled from various years of MHRD data.

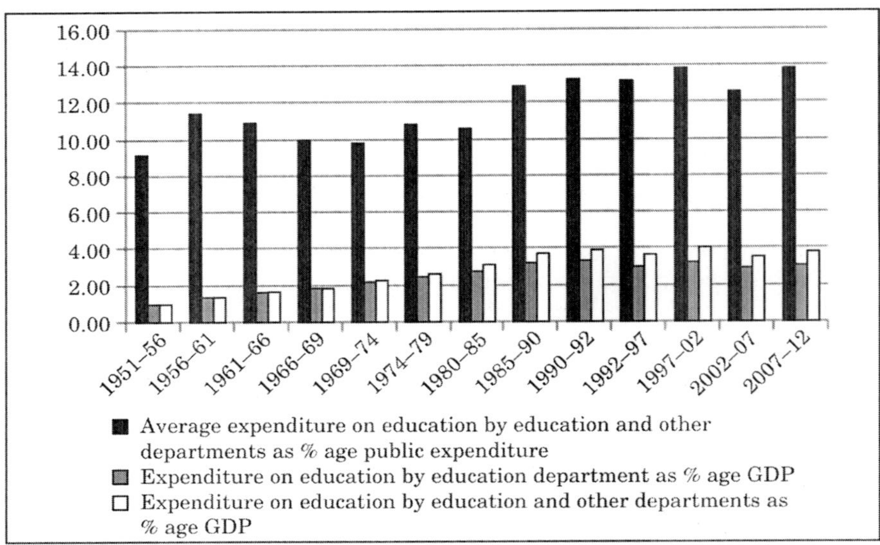

Fig. 2: Public expenditure on education in different plan periods in India. ***Source:*** Compiled from MHRD data

due to the recommendations of first National education policy which called for a "radical restructuring" and equalize educational opportunities in order to achieve national integration and greater cultural and economic development. The increase in education expenses by other departments like, department of tribal development, rural development clearly indicate change in nations priority in education and human capital after the first national education policy.

Table 1 provides the average public expenditure on education in various plan periods. It is really interesting to see that during the first plan period, the average public spending as a percentage of GDP was only less than one (0.84) percentage. It increased to an average of 3.76 during 11th plan period. Public expenditure on education was only less than 10 percentage of total government spending in the first plan period increases to 13.83 percent in the 11th plan period.

Moreover, it is seen that up to third five year plan, public expenditure on education is only through education department alone, but fourth five year plan onwards; education expenditure is incurred not only by education department, but by other departments also. Up to seventh five year plan, education expenditure as a percentage of GDP shows an increasing trend, but after that the growth was sluggish or negative. This clearly indicates that after the adoption of new economic policy in 1991, the growth of public spending on education got stagnated. This may be due to the importance of privatization, liberalization and globalization which give importance to private sector in education spending.

Table 1: Public expenditure on education in different plan periods in India.

Year	*Average expenditure on education by education and other departments as percentage of public expenditure*	*Expenditure on education by education department as a percentage of GDP*	*Expenditure on education by education and other departments as a percentage of GDP*
1951–56	9.13	0.84	0.84
1956–61	11.34	1.28	1.28
1961–66	10.90	1.55	1.55
1966–69	9.83	1.74	1.74
1969–74	9.82	2.12	2.15
1974–79	10.81	2.40	2.60
1980–85	10.58	2.69	3.10
1985–90	12.85	3.21	3.66
1990–92	13.26	3.28	3.82
1992–97	13.14	2.99	3.60
1997–02	13.80	3.19	3.92
2002–07	12.55	2.85	3.47
2007–12	13.83	3.01	3.76

Source: Calculated from the MHRD data down loaded from; _http://mhrd.gov.in/sites/upload_files/mhrd/files/statistics/PubExpdt-2013.pdf

In this context, it should be seen that total public expenditure in 1951 was only 8.08 percent of GDP that increased to 31.15 percentage of GDP in 1983–84. From Fig. 3, it is seen that public expenditure as a percentage of GDP increased sharply from 1951 to 1983–84 and then stagnant afterwards. It was lying in between 25 to 30 percentage of GDP all the years. But in a country where the world's largest population of illiterates lives (287 million, 37 percent of total illiterates of the world), 6.60 lakh children is out-of-

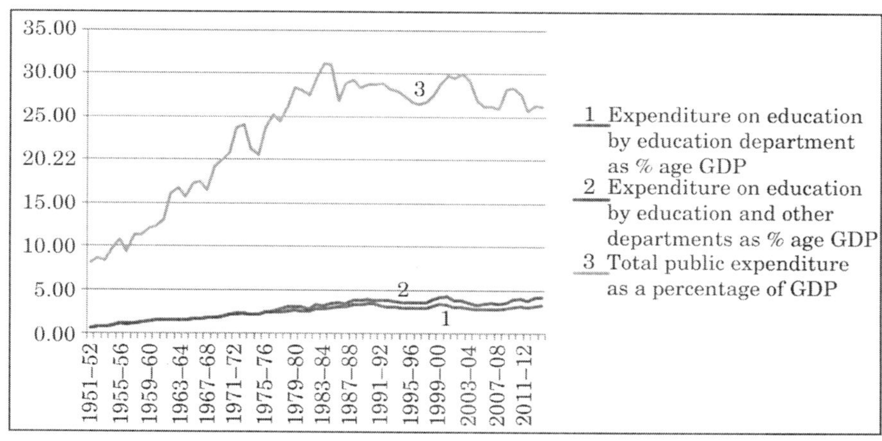

Fig. 3: Trend in total public expenditure as a percentage of GDP. ***Source:*** Compiled from MHRD data

school, ranked 123rd out of 135 countries in female literacy rate, spent only less than four percentage of its total GDP for education when total public expenditure is more than 26 percentage is something which should be noted.

Figs. 3 to 7 reveals that the average public expenditure on education will increase only a negligible amount and which is not adequate for creating the qualitative human capital formation. The percentage increase in growth rate of public expenditure and education is going opposite direction especially after the globalization period.

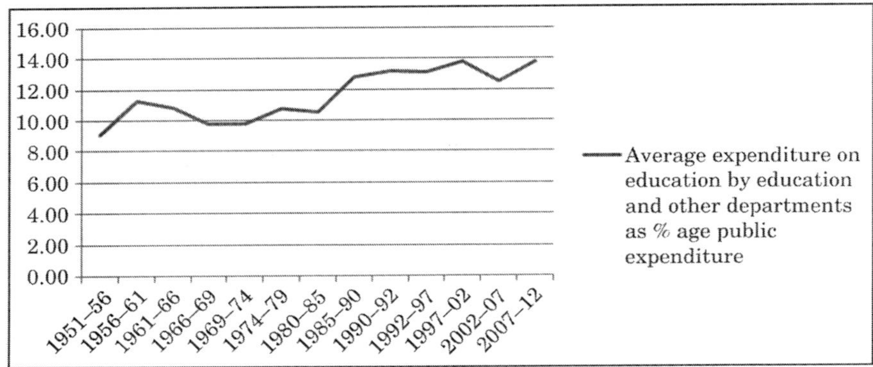

Fig. 4: Average expenditure on education by education and other Depts. as percentage of public expenditure. ***Source:*** Calculated from the MHRD data down loaded from http://mhrd.gov.in/sites/upload_files/mhrd/files/statistics/PubExpdt-2013.pdf

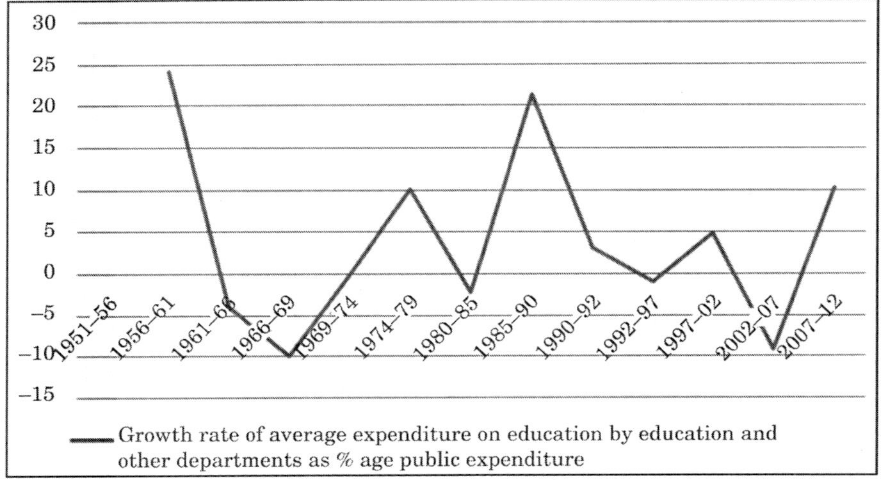

Fig. 5: Growth rate of average expenditure on education by education and other Depts. as percentage of public expenditure. ***Source:*** Calculated from the MHRD data down loaded from http://mhrd.gov.in/sites/upload_files/mhrd/files/statistics/PubExpdt-2013.pdf

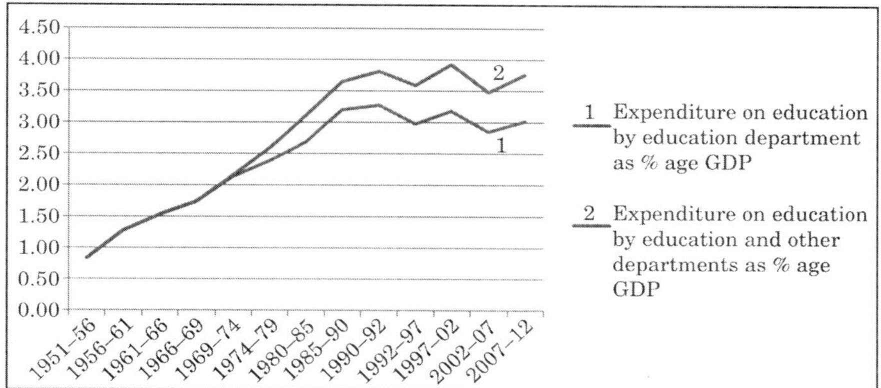

Fig. 6: Expenditure on education by education department as percentage of GDP and expenditure on education and other department as percentage of GDP. ***Source:*** Calculated from the MHRD data down loaded from http://mhrd.gov.in/sites/upload_files/mhrd/files/statistics/PubExpdt-2013.pdf

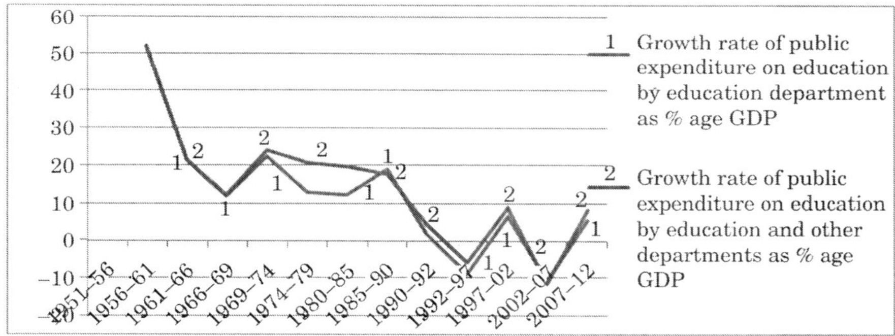

Fig. 7: Growth rate of public expenditure on education by education by education department as percentage of GDP and growth rate public expenditure on education and other department as percentage of GDP. ***Source:*** Calculated from the MHRD data down loaded from http://mhrd.gov.in/sites/upload_files/mhrd/files/statistics/PubExpdt-2013.pdf

HOW INDIA STACKS *VS.* GLOBAL AVERAGES

In this context is relevant to mention the fact that according to World Economic Forum's Global Human capital index, India has been placed at a low 103th rank out of 130 countries. It is the lowest among BRICS economies. The WEF said India is ranked lower than its BRICS peers, with Russian Federation placed as high as 16th place, followed by China at 34th, Brazil at 77th and South Africa at 87th place. Data shows that Brazil and South Africa, trying to improve their position in the case of Human capital through improving their expenditure on education but India cannot expect a better future because still India spent shamefully low in education. As per the

BRICS Joint Statistical Publication for 2015, India had spent the least amongst the peer nations on education. India has decreased its spending on education from 4.19 percent of GDP in 1999 to around 3.71 percent as per 2018–19 budget estimate, undermining the work done in getting more children into school, and its prospects for improving its poor quality of education. The Kothari Education Commission had recommended an allocation of 6 percent of GDP on education, which has never been achieved.

"Most of the developed world, having a more mature education system than India and higher levels of GDP are even today spending around 4.5 to 6 percent of GDP on education sector, realizing the benefit the education sector has on society, but in India, despite the massive demand-supply gap in the quality of education, still has not been able to reach those levels," Rohin Kapoor says.

EDUCATION STATUS OF INDIA BOTH QUANTITATIVE AND QUALITATIVE

In the above discussion it is clear that India's education expenditure lagged behind most of its competent countries, while its actual demand is much higher than the rest of the countries. Table 2 provides the education status of India during different time periods along with comparison of other BRICS countries. India's position should be connected with its education expenditure which we discussed earlier session. It is only through increasing public expenditure on education India can solve the pathetic status when compared to other countries. Figs. 6 and 7 clearly shows that there is a positive correlation exists between five year average public expenditure as a

Table 2: Status of education in India.

Years India	*Expected years of schooling*	*Mean years of schooling*
1990	7.6	3.0
1995	8.2	3.5
2000	8.3	4.4
2005	9.7	4.8
2010	10.8	5.4
2011	11.3	5.3
2012	11.5	5.6
2013	11.6	5.8
2014	11.6	6.1
India (2015)	11.7	6.3
Brazil (2015)	15.2	7.8
Russia (2015)	15	12
China (2015)	13.5	7.6
South Africa (2015)	13	0.3

Source: HDI Report 2016

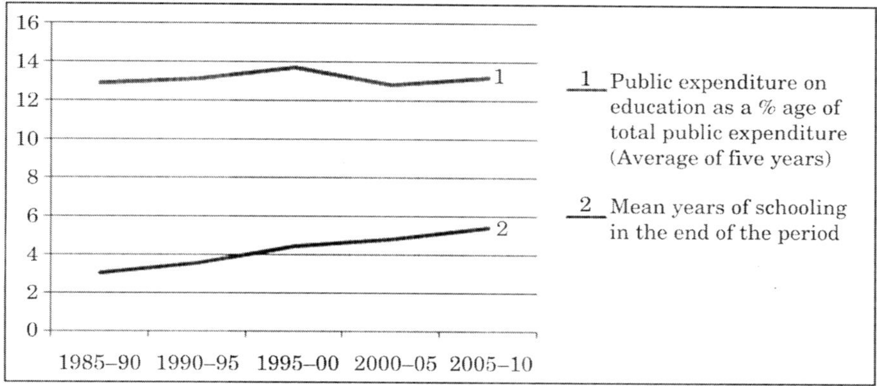

Fig. 8: Public expenditure on education as percentage on education as a percentage of total public expenditure and mean year of schooling. ***Source:*** Public expenditure on education data are from MHRD and mean years of Schooling is from HDR 2006.

percentage of total public expenditure and the average years of schooling in the end year. Average public spending as a percentage of total public spending was 12.85 during 1985–90 periods, and the average mean years of schooling for the year 1990 are 3. The average percentage of public spending on education increased for the five year period 1995–2000 to 13.11, the mean years of schooling also increased to 3.5. Though there is no such theory to correctly explains the relationship between public expenditure on education and adult literacy rate without much lag, it can be argued that the plan orientation may have influenced the persons not to drop out from higher education or to re-enter in education institutions which may create a direct relationship between government spending and mean years of schooling.

The average years of schooling and literacy rates are quantitative measures of education, but the qualitative aspect also India lagged behind. In the PISA test for the international test for educational attainment 2009 result was something which India should open its eye in the area of quality of our education system. Indian students placed 72nd rank out of 74 countries participated in the international student's achievement test conducted by OECD. The ASER survey result also highlighted the relevance of improving the standard of our education system. It is seen that the Percentage of students who enrolled in Vth std. could not read IInd level test increased from 46.3 in 2010 to 53.2 in 2012. And the percentage of students in this category who was not able to do simple to digit subtraction increased from 29.1 to 46.5 during 2010 to 2012 period. In the case of division, that number is more alarming, it was 63.8 in 2010 increased to 75.2 in 2012. Moreover, the Percentage of students enrolled in third std. could not read a first level test was 54.4 in 2010 went up to 6.3 in 202. The case of government schools the situation is more pathetic (Tables 3 & 4). In connection with enrolling the schooling, especially after the 1995, the average public expenditure on

Table 3: Quality of education in India, data from ASER survey 2012 report.

Year	*Percentage of students who enrolled V could not read Std. IInd level*	*Percentage of students enrolled in V std could not do simple two digit subtraction problem*	*Percentage of students enrolled in V std could not do simple two digit division problem*	*Percentage of children enrolled in std III who cannot read a STD I level test (Govt. school)*
2010	46.3	29.1	63.8	54.4 (57.6)
2011	51.8	39	72.4	59.7 (64.8)
2012	53.2	46.5	75.2	61.3 (67.7)

Source: ASER Report 2012 downloaded from http://img.asercentre.org/docs/Publications/ASER%20Reports/ASER_2012/nationalfinding.pdf on 7-6-2018

Table 4: India's participation in PISA 2009 + cycle: Results from Himachal Pradesh and Tamil Nadu.

	Mean	*S.E.*
Himachal Pradesh	317	4
Tamil Nadu	337	5.5
OECD average	493	0.5
Shanghai-China	556	2.4

Source: Education in India: India's participation in PISA 2009 + cycle Results

education is declining and is more affected by the rural area. Fig. 8 shows this down trodden trend of the public expenditure.

From this analysis it is seen that in the case of quantitative and qualitative aspects India's position is very poor, and this part can be solved only through increasing government education expenditure. As it is found that though data is not available, private sector's education spending is increasing (from the increased enrollment of students in private schools and the increase in number of private colleges clearly shows that private spending in education is increasing along with the evidence from expenditure data of NSSO) the role of government is still very high. As per UNESCO data, India has one of the lowest public expenditure rates on education per student, especially compared to other Asian countries like China. India spends $264 per student per year compared to $1,800 spent by China. The World Bank report on its worldwide survey of public spending on education stated that India spent a meager 11 percent of public expenditure on education, compared to 20 percent in China.

CENTRAL GOVERNMENT SPENDING ON EDUCATION DURING 2012–18 PERIODS

The Economic Survey carries a tacit acknowledgment of the unimpressive investment in social infrastructure. "Being a developing economy, there is not enough fiscal space to increase the expenditure on critical social infrastructure like education and health in India. However, given the limited resources, the Government has consistently prioritized, strengthening the educational and health profile of the population," the survey states. But data shows otherwise. From Figs. 9 and 10, it is evident that central government expenditure on education is showing a declining tendency during 2012–18 period.

Central government expenditure on education as a percentage of GDP was 0.66 in 2002–13 actual while that is only 0.49 in 2016–17 actual. It

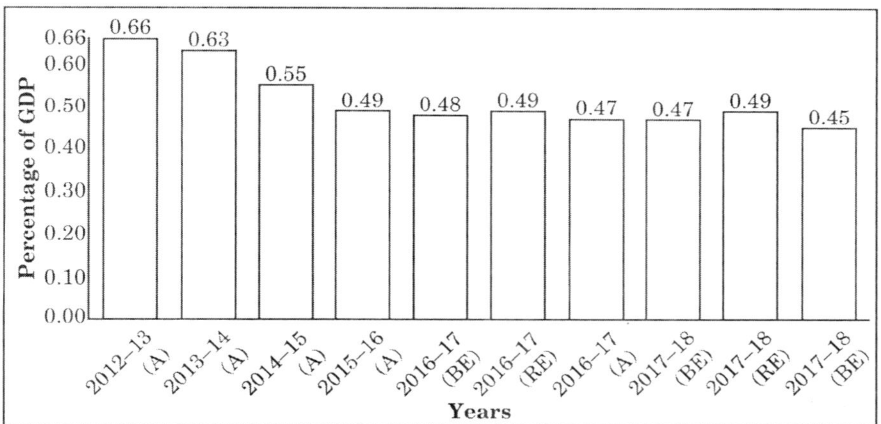

Fig. 9: Union Govt. spending on education as percentage of union budget. ***Source:*** https://union 2018. open budgets india.org/en/sectors/education/union-govt-spending-education-gdp

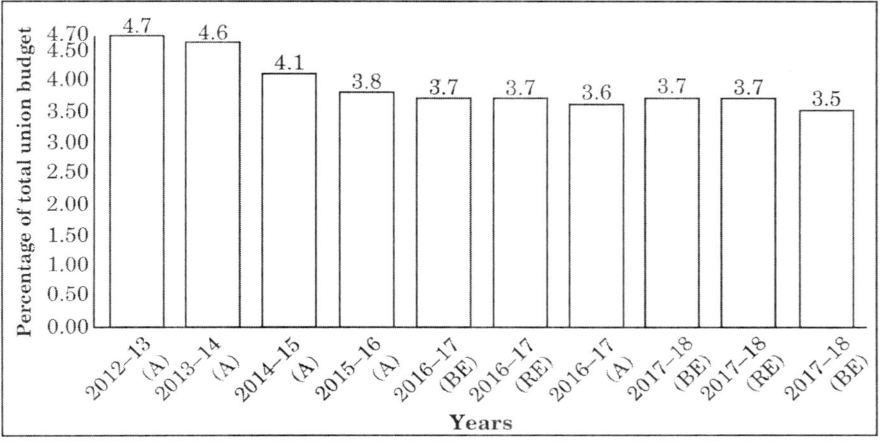

Fig. 10: Union Govt. spending on education as percentage of union budget. ***Source:*** https://union2018.openbudgetsindia.org/en/sectors/education/union-govt-spending-education-gdp/

Table 5: Central Government budget expenditure on higher education (Rs. crores).

Ministry/ Department	*Head of expenditure*	*2016–17 Actual*	*2017–18 BE*	*2017–18 RE*	*2018–19 BE*
Higher education	Support to IIT's	4973.98	7171	1100	680
Higher education	UGC	4471.92	4691.94	4922.74	3022.23
Higher education	Grants in aid to state Govts.	2825.41	1745	1715.6	960
Higher education	Support to NIT's	2751.3	3280	3484.4	2919.4
Higher education	Improvement of salary of University/College teachers	1427.97	700	670.6	950
Higher education	RUSA	1416.06	1300	1300	200
Higher education	Scholarship for colleges and University Students	240.49	320	294	40
Higher education	e-shodh sindhu	235	240	240	180

Source: https://union2018.openbudgetsindia.org/en/sectors/education/union-govt-spending-education-gdp/

further fell down to 0.47 in 2018–19 budget estimate. Likewise, central government expenditure on education as a percentage of total central government expenditure was 4.7 in 2012–13 actual, while that was only 3.6 in 2016–17 and it fell again fall down o 3.5 in 2018–19 budget estimates. Table 5 provides an answer for the question of why the fellowships and funds are cut in the national important institutions like IISER. It shows almost all the sectors, the spending has declined in the higher education sector. Student's fellowships, aid to state governments, RUSA, UGC, and even e-shodh also shows a reduction in fund during 2016–18 period. His definitely reflects the research and development and there by improvement in human capital development. In majority of higher education funds funded by central government faced a decline during 2012–18 period.

CONCLUSIONS

Governments today increasingly face the limitation to raise means owing to the fiscal pressures, increased demand for access to education, rising costs, expectations for improvement in infrastructure, increasing the resources, enhancing, quality and competing prioritized demands on the government treasury. For a developing country like India, it is difficult to assume that government alone would be able to achieve the mammoth task of assuring access to education for the masses. Higher efficiencies can be achieved by the allocation of the funds on the criterion of 'performance based funding'. Increased accountability should be accompanied by increased autonomy to raise funds at the institutional level, with wisdom to assure the opportunity of access to quality education for anyone willing to pursue the same.

The government through necessary regulatory changes should incentivize philanthropic and alumni contributions by allowing tax rebates on incurring such expenditures by individuals. Income generated through consultancies, research and development and providing training workshops in the area of expertise should be appreciated and encouraged. Considering the present and future demand for higher education in India, it cannot be denied that financing remains a serious challenge. To achieve this mammoth task, all possible sources of funding will have to be explored to assure a qualitative and equitable access to higher education.

REFERENCES

Afonso, A. and Aubyn, M. (2005). Non-parametric approaches to education and health efficiency in OECD countries. Universidad del CEMA, Buenos Aires, Argentina. *Journal of Applied Economics*, VIII(002): 227–246.

Bergstrom, T., Blume, L. and Varian, H. (1986). On the private provision of public goods. *Journal of Public Economics*, 29(1): 5–49.

Bhattacharya, I. and Sharma, K. (2007). India in the knowledge economy – An electronic paradigm. *International Journal of Educational Management*, 21(6): 543–568.

Bush Jeb (2012). The Blended and Virtual, Learning Frontier Special Report, A Research Report from the center for digital education and converge.

Chandra, S. and Patkar, V. (2007). ICTS: A catalyst for enriching the learning process and library services in India. *The International Information & Library Review*, 39(1): 1–11.

Cholin, V.S. (2005). Study of the application of information technology for effective access to resources in Indian university libraries. *The International Information & Library Review*, 37(3): 189–197.

Cross, M. and Adam, F. (2007). ICT Policies and Strategies in Higher Education in South Africa: National and Institutional Pathways. *Higher Education Policy*, 20(1): 73–95.

Economic Survey (2016), Ministry of Finance, Govt. of India.

Economic Survey (2017), Ministry of Finance, Govt. of India.

Economic Survey (2018), Ministry of Finance, Govt. of India.

Kozma, R. (2005). National Policies that Connect ICT-Based Education Reform to Economic and Social Development. *Human Technology*, 1(2): 117–156.

Levin, J., Glass and Meister, G. (1984). Cost-effectiveness of four education interventions. Stanford, CA: Institute for Research of Education Finance and Governance.

Lim, C.P. and Chai, C.S. (2004). An activity-theoretical approach to research of ICT integration in Singapore schools: Orienting activities and learner autonomy. Computers & Education, 43(3): 215–236.

Lockheed, M. and Marlaine, E. (1989). The Measurement of Educational Efficiency and Effectiveness. *In:* Paper presented at the Annual Meeting of the American Educational Research, New Orleans, LA.

Makris, M. (2009). Private provision of discrete public goods. *Games and Economic Behaviour,* 67(1): 292–299. http://www.sciencedirect.com/science/article/pii/S0899825608002030 [10.12.2011].

Mandl, U., Dierx, A. and Ilzkovitz, F. (2008). The effectiveness and efficiency of public spending. Economic paper, p. 301, European Communities.

Mehta, S. and Kalra, M. (2006). Information and Communication Technologies: A bridge for social equity and sustainable development in India. *The International Information & Library Review*, 38(3): 147–160.

Plomp, T., Pelgrum, W.J. and Law, N. (2007). SITES2006 — International comparative survey of pedagogical practices and ICT in education. *Education and Information Technologies*, 12(2): 83–92.

Richards, Jack C. (2006). Communicative Language Teaching Today, Cambridge University Press 32 avenue of the Americas, New York, NY 10013–2473, USA, pp. 10–14.

Samuelson, P.A. (1954). The Pure Theory of Public Expenditure. *The Review of Economics and Statistics*, 36(4): 387–389. The MIT Press, *http://www.jstor.org/stable/1925895* [17.12.2011]

Sanyal, B.C. (2001). New functions of higher education and ICT to achieve education for all. Paper prepared for the Expert Roundtable on University and Technology-for-Literacy and Education Partnership in Developing Countries, International Institute for Educational Planning, UNESCO, Paris.

Sharma, R. (2003). Barriers in Using Technology for Education in Developing Countries. IEEE 0-7803-7724-9103.

Techhogger, Digitization of Indian Education (2013).

UNESCO (2002). Open and Distance Learning Trends, Policy and Strategy Considerations, UNESCO.

UNESCO (2009). World Conference on Higher Education: The New Dynamics of Higher Education and Research for Societal Change and Development.

14

A Study of Growth and Present Status of Higher Education in Haryana (India)

SURAJ WALIA[1*]

ABSTRACT

Haryana, which was carved out of the erstwhile Punjab in 1966, had come into existence as a deprived and underdeveloped state. The efforts of the people of the State and the Government have led to a stage, where Haryana has the distinction of having the third highest per capita income after Goa and Sikkim. Over the period of time, Haryana has made tremendous progress in overall education including higher education. And it hardly needs any justification that higher education is an engine of economic growth as well as human development in any economy including Haryana. The present study is a humble attempt to investigate the growth and present status of higher education in Haryana. And concludes that no-doubt significant growth has been taken place in higher education since 1966 but there is a rationale of proper balance between quantity and quality of higher education in Haryana. To improve quality of higher education, public expenditure should not only be enhanced by state government but need to change from targeted approach to result orientation with manpower planning. To make Haryana a human resource development (HRD) hub, we need to be humble in slow and steady progress in all HRD activities including higher education which calls for recognizing them as the infrastructural activities and required to be undertaken as essential services.

Key words: Higher education, Quantity *vs*. Quality and Haryana economy.

[1] Department of Economics, R.K.S.D. (PG) College, Kaithal, Haryana.
**Corresponding author:* E-mail: surajwalia.2010@rediffmail.com

1. INTRODUCTION

It hardly needs any justification that higher education is an engine of economic growth as well as human development which improves physical quality of life index (PQLI) in any economy including Haryana. It contributes to national development through dissemination of specialized knowledge and skills. Haryana, which was carved out of the erstwhile Punjab in 1966, had come into existence as a deprived and underdeveloped state. The efforts of the people of the State and the Government have led to a stage, where Haryana has the distinction of having the third highest per capita income after Goa and Sikkim. It lies in northern part of India and is boarded by Indian states of Chandigarh, Delhi, Punjab, Himachal Pradesh, Rajasthan and Uttar Pradesh. It is comparatively small state having an area of 44212 sq. km. According to the latest census 2011, the population of Haryana is 25353081 out of which 51.54 per cent are males and 48.46 per cent are females. Education in general and higher education in particular is the pillar on which rests the edifice of human resource of any region including Haryana. At the threshold of the new millennium, the Government of Haryana has sought to address the challenges thrown up by the changing environment and the problems being faced by the state in terms of key HRD indicators by bringing education at the central stage of its development agenda. Investment in education leads to the formation of human capital, comparable to physical capital and social capital, and that makes a significant contribution to economic growth (Dickens *et al.,* 2006; Loening, 2004; Gylfason & Zoega, 2003; Barro, 2001). The major contribution to the issue on the relationship between education in general and higher education in particular and economic growth was first made by Adam Smith, followed by Marshall, Schultz, Bowman and others (Tilak, 2005). In this regard, many studies have been made from time to time all over the world, by Becker, Denison, Dholakia, Harbison and Myers, Mukerji and Krishna Rao, Psacharopoulos, Schultz, Solow, Tilak and Todaro.

Keeping in view, the present study is a humble attempt to analyse the growth and present status higher education in Haryana. Section II describes the objectives of study and data source. Section III and IV dedicated to the growth and present status of higher education scenario in Haryana respectively and Section V highlights the conclusions with policy implications to develop the Haryana a knowledge economy.

2. OBJECTIVES OF THE STUDY AND DATA SOURCES

The present paper is a humble attempt to analyse the growth and present status of higher education in Haryana. The specific objectives of the study can be enumerated as:

- To examine the growth of higher education facilities in Haryana.

- To analyse the present status or trend of higher education in Haryana.
- To draw policy implications to develop the State as a knowledge economy.

To fulfil the abovementioned objectives, the present study is of analytical in nature and exclusively based on secondary data, which has been collected from various issues of Statistical Abstract of Haryana, Economic Survey of Haryana, Census of India, Census of Haryana and All India Survey of Higher Education (AISHE). The study considers the time period from the year 1966 onwards to analyse the growth of higher education in Haryana.

To analyse the present status of higher education, time period 2006 onwards has been taken due to non-availability of data and data from All India Survey of Higher Education (AISHE) has been taken. To examine the growth and present status of higher education in Haryana, the available data have been processed and presented in form of suitable tables and graphs.

3. GROWTH OF HIGHER EDUCATION IN HARYANA

Higher education has significant role in supporting knowledge driven economic growth strategies. Over the period of time, Haryana has made tremendous progress in overall education including higher education. The period between the 1975 and 1985 can be characterized by as one of the substantial growth period of education system of Haryana. During this period the number of institutions and students rose rapidly, creating budgetary pressures and resource crunch that dominant and worry the present day government. Around 1999–2000 when the government of Haryana attempted to restructure the higher education sector of the state merging some of programmes depending on the availability of students and staff with in the colleges and widening the rural education base by starting more colleges in rural areas, the entire higher education landscape of Haryana changed dramatically. Education is a systematic process through which a child or an adult acquire knowledge, experience, skill and sound attitude. It makes an individual civilized, refined, cultured and educated. The goal of education is to make an individual perfect and every society gives importance to education because it is panacea for all evils. It is the key to solve the various problems in life (Parankimalil, 2012).

Literacy rate is one of the basic indicators to know the level of development achieved by any economy including Haryana. Literacy forms an important input in overall development of individuals enabling them to comprehend their social, political and cultural environment better and respond to it appropriately. Higher levels of education and literacy lead to an improvement of economic and social conditions of any economy including Haryana. The following Table 1 provides an insight the overall literacy rate includes male and female literacy rate of India and Haryana recorded under census 2001 and 2011.

It is clear from the above Table 1 that according to census 2001, overall literacy rate in Haryana was 67.91 percent, out of which male literacy rate was recorded as 78.49 percent and female literacy rate as 55.73 percent which was comparatively higher than the national average because overall literacy rate in India was 65.38 percent, out of which male literacy rate was recorded as 75.26 percent and female literacy rate as 54.16 percent. According to latest census 2011, overall literacy rate in Haryana was 76.6 percent, out of which male literacy rate was recorded as 85.4 percent and female literacy rate as 66.8 percent and overall literacy rate in India was 74.04 percent, out of which male literacy rate was recorded as 82.14 percent and female literacy rate as 65.46 percent. The comparison of 2001 census and 2011 census shows an improvement has made in Haryana overall literacy rate by 8.7 percent and an improvement has made in India overall literacy rate by 8.66 percent which clearly indicates that level of literacy in Haryana is improving is at par level of literacy in India and literacy rate of Haryana is comparatively higher than the national average which is a positive symbol for the State.

Table 1: Male-female and rural-urban literacy rate in India/ Haryana according to census 2001 and 2011 (%).

Year	***India***		***Haryana***	
	2001	***2011***	***2001***	***2011***
Total	65.38	74.04	67.91	76.6
Male	75.26	82.14	78.49	85.4
Female	54.16	65.46	55.73	66.8
Rural	58.74	67.77	63.19	71.42
Male	70.7	77.15	75.37	81.55
Female	46.13	57.93	49.27	60.02
Urban	79.92	84.11	79.16	83.14
Male	86.27	88.76	85.83	88.63
Female	72.86	79.11	71.34	76.9

Source: Census of India and Haryana.

After analyzing the literacy rate, the following Fig. 1 presents the higher educational infrastructure in terms of number of recognized institutions (colleges and universities) in State of Haryana from 1966–67 onwards. From figure, it is clear that there has been appreciable growth of higher education institutions since 1966–67. Number of universities and colleges has grown up from 1 to 43 and 40 to 238 respectively from 1966–67 to 2015–16 which clearly indicates that over the period of time, significant growth of higher educational institutions have been taken place in Haryana due to the sincere efforts of the State Governments.

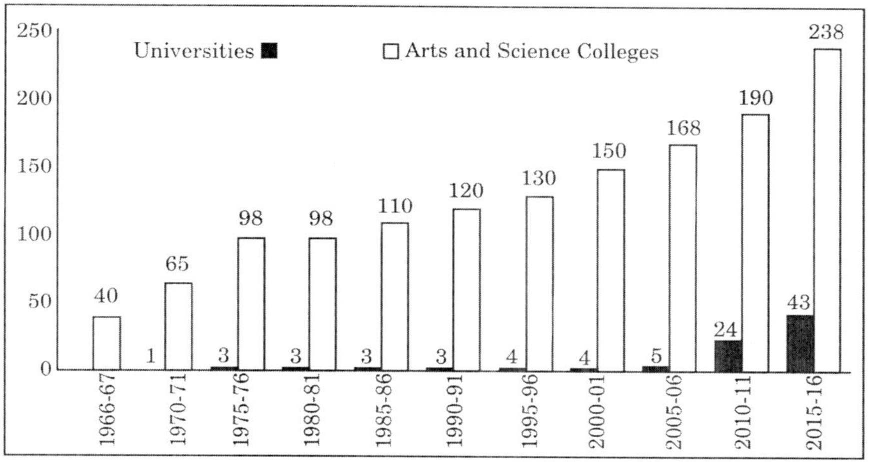

Fig. 1: Number of universities and colleges (arts & science) in Haryana. ***Source:*** Various issues of statistical abstract of Haryana

In Haryana, educational institutions are binary in nature means that either these institutions are Government funded or private funded. Now it's important to see the how many colleges are managed by Government and how many are aided and unaided colleges. The following Table 2 highlights the classification of arts and science colleges in Haryana from 1966–67 onwards.

Table 2: Classification of Arts and Science Colleges by Management.

Year	*Government*		*Aided*		*Un-aided*	
	General	*Women*	*General*	*Women*	*General*	*Women*
1966–67	8	2	23	7	–	–
1970–71	10	1	40	14	–	–
1975–76	12	1	64	21	–	–
1980–81	23	1	52	22	–	–
1985–86	32	1	51	26	–	–
1990–91	39	2	50	29	–	–
1995–96	39	3	50	38	–	–
2000–01	48	7	47	33	7	8
2005–06	49	11	48	33	11	16
2010–11	60	16	48	34	12	20
2012–13	65	21	48	35	18	21

Source: Various Issues of Statistical Abstract of Haryana.

In 1966–67 there were 10 government colleges in which 8 were general and 2 were women colleges. Over the period of time, the number has increased to 86 out of which 65 are general and 21 are women colleges. In 1966–67 aided colleges were 30 in which 23 were general and 7 were women colleges. The number of aided colleges have increased to 83 (48 general and 35 women) in 2012–13. Unaided colleges were 15, out of which 7 were general and 8 were women in 2000–01. It has increased to 39 out of which 18 are general and 21 are women in 2012–13. Details of colleges according to management wise in all the districts of Haryana are shown from the Table 2. To make correct assessment of higher education in Haryana, it is very essential to know the enrolments of boys and girls in higher education institutions (arts, science and home science colleges).

The below Fig. 2 reveals the picture of students enrolled in arts, science and home science colleges. In 1966–67 there were 27332 numbers of students were enrolled out of which 21603 (79.03 percent) were boys and 5729 (21.7 percent) were girls. Girl's enrolment was just 21.7 percent of total enrolment. This number has increased to 332363 in 2012–13, in which 171534 (51.63 percent) are boys and 160829 (48.38 percent) are girls. Girls are 48.39 percent of total enrolment. Girl's enrolment was highest in 2011–12 *i.e.,* 56.14 percent. It has fallen down recently. To examine the position of district-wise enrolment in higher education, following Table 3 is presented which shows the district wise number of students enrolled in recognized colleges (Arts, Science and Home Science) of Haryana according to latest data 2015–16.

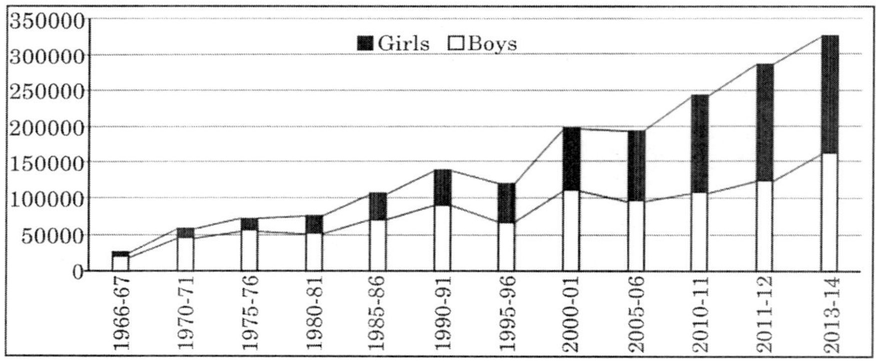

Fig. 2: Number of total students in arts, science and home science colleges in Haryana.
Source: Various Issues of Statistical Abstract of Haryana

Table 3 reveals that in 2015–16, maximum students (36343) are enrolled in Rohtak district which is followed by district Bhiwani. Out of total in overall districts, except few districts, girl's enrolment in higher education is more than boy's enrolment. And in Schedule caste (SC) category, Bhiwani district is on first number in total SC's enrolment which is followed by district Hisar. Very less enrolment in total and SC category can be observed from Nuh district.

Expansion of education including higher education both quantitative and qualitative in any state is entirely depends upon extent of Government spending. Public expenditure is very much justified in education including

Table 3: District-wise growth of enrolments in recognized colleges (arts, science and home science) for general education in Haryana (2015–16).

District	***Total students including schedule caste***			***Schedule caste (SC) students***		
	Total	***Boys***	***Girls***	***Total***	***Boys***	***Girls***
Ambala	17898	8523	9645	3898	1880	2018
Panchkula	8494	4771	3723	1622	898	724
Yamunanagar	21008	8080	12928	4297	1201	3096
Kurukshetra	10282	4113	6169	1684	873	811
Kaithal	13435	5739	7696	1728	941	787
Karnal	18022	9156	8866	3064	1638	1426
Panipat	17862	8550	9312	1756	946	810
Sonipat	15674	3669	12005	1972	767	1205
Rohtak	36343	20462	15881	4581	2425	2156
Jhajjar	10540	4325	6215	1733	749	984
Faridabad	21169	10449	10720	2914	1590	1324
Palwal	6622	2665	3957	1024	445	579
Gurugram	20669	9322	11337	3331	1589	1742
Nuh	2879	2236	643	336	205	131
Rewari	16824	7067	9757	3101	1258	1843
Mahendergarh	22669	11110	11559	4226	1949	2277
Bhiwani	27048	12293	14755	5492	2680	2812
Jind	19758	9905	9853	3254	1963	1291
Hisar	25578	11927	13651	4764	2423	2341
Fatehabad	7747	3625	4122	2044	1108	936
Sirsa	11738	6157	5581	2296	1153	1143

Source: Statistical Abstract of Haryana 2015–16

higher education to achieve sustainable inclusive growth and development. One of another indicator to judge the growth of higher education in Haryana *viz.* expenditure on education in general and higher education in particular. Expenditure on education and higher education in Haryana is shown from the following Fig. 3.

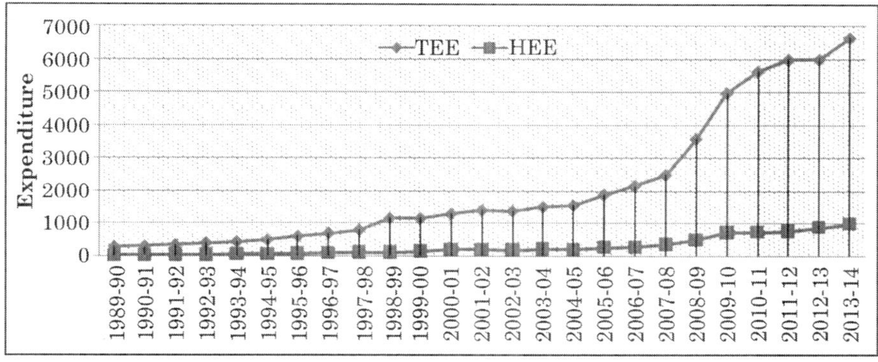

Fig. 3: Expenditure on Higher Education (HEE) out of Total Education Expenditure (TEE) in state of Haryana. ***Source:*** Various Issues of Statistical Abstract of Haryana

In 1989–90 total expenditure incurred on education was Rs. 288.63 crores. Out of which Rs. 53.29 crores was spent on higher education. This was 18.46 percent of total expenditure incurred on education. And in 2013–14 expenditure on education rose to Rs. 6650.03 crores out of which Rs. 1001.85 crores was spent on higher education. It is 15.06 per cent of total expenditure.

Another following Fig. 4 presents the picture of government expenditure incurred on total education including higher education out of GSDP of Haryana. It is clear from the figure that GSDP has increased in the span of 25 years from 1989–90 to 2013–14 considerably. But expenditure on education is not increasing in such a manner in Haryana economy. Fig. 4 reveals that spending on total education out of GSDP is 1.65 percent which is not sufficient to full fill the growing requirements of higher education and produce quality human resource in Haryana.

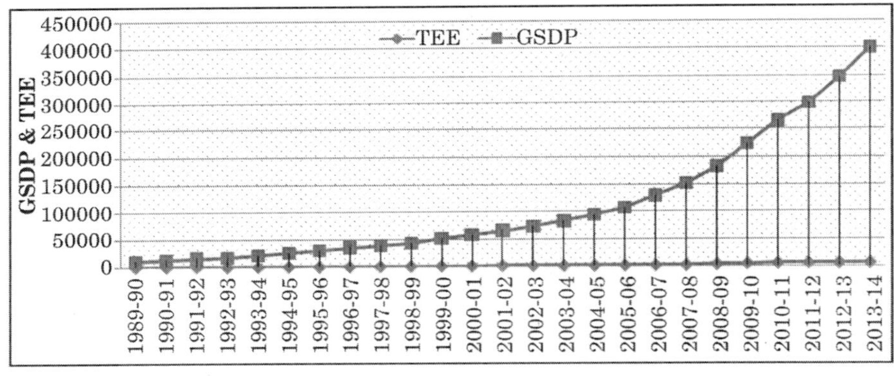

Fig. 4: Expenditure on Total Education (TEE) including higher education out of GSDP in Haryana. ***Source:*** Various Issues of Statistical Abstract of Haryana.

4. PRESENT STATUS OF HIGHER EDUCATION IN HARYANA

After discussing the growth of higher education in Haryana in terms of literacy rates, number of higher education institutions, enrolments (both male and female), expenditure on education and higher education in Haryana. Now we will discuss the present status/trend of higher education in Haryana. The following Table 4 represents the types of universities in Haryana since 2006–07.

It is clear from the above Table 4 that total number of universities in Haryana is 25 in 2012–13 out of which 1 is central university, 10 state universities, 8 private universities, 5 deemed universities and 1 is institute of national importance. To see the actual growth of higher education, it is very essential to know the present situation of enrolments (both males and females) in higher education institutions. The following Table 5 presents

Table 4: Type of universities in Haryana since 2006–07.

Type of Universities	*2006–07*	*2007–08*	*2008–09*	*2009–10*	*2010–11*	*2011–12*	*2012–13*
Central Universities	0	0	0	1	1	1	1
Institute of National Importance	0	1	1	1	1	1	1
State Universities	5	6	6	7	10	10	10
Private Universities	0	0	0	0	2	3	8
Deemed Universities	3	3	3	3	7	7	5
Grand Total	8	10	10	12	21	22	25

Source: Various reports of All India Survey of Higher Education.

Table 5: Enrolment of students according to various social categories in Haryana since 2006–07.

Years	*All*			*Schedule caste*			*Other backward caste*		
	Male	*Female*	*Total*	*Male*	*Female*	*Total*	*Male*	*Female*	*Total*
2006–07	202426	151058	353484	25181	11804	36985	NA	NA	NA
2007–08	260684	181970	442654	37749	24054	61803	NA	NA	NA
2008–09	344582	231682	576264	33489	18423	51912	NA	NA	NA
2009–10	352696	241199	593895	39752	23067	62819	NA	NA	NA
2010–11	458239	305283	763522	53733	32196	85929	87388	56979	144367
2011–12	491321	397488	888809	69239	51777	121016	NA	NA	NA
2012–13	504040	408453	912493	69302	51464	120766	100983	89742	190725

Source: Various reports of All India Survey of Higher Education.

the trend of enrolments according to the various social categories since 2006–07. It can be easily observed from the Table 5 that enrolment in all categories has increased tremendously in Haryana over the period of time.

The following another Table 6 presents the picture of students enrolments in various courses such as Ph.D. /M.Phil, P.G., U.G. etc in Haryana. It is clear from the table that enrolment of students in all the courses has increased in a considerable manner.

Table 6: Enrolment of students at various levels in Haryana.

Courses	*2006–07*			*2010–11*			*2012–13*		
	Male	*Female*	*Total*	*Male*	*Female*	*Total*	*Male*	*Female*	*Total*
Ph.D. /M.Phil.	1101	824	1925	1479	1821	3300	1464	1601	3065
P.G. Degree	8018	9570	17588	44635	49767	94402	36276	49978	86254
U.G. Degree	128451	99792	228243	343731	239957	583688	390109	338553	728662
P.G. diploma	NA	NA	NA	1040	838	1878	2390	991	3381
Post School Diploma	2651	2163	4814	67354*	12900*	80254*	73801*	17330*	91131*
Grand Total	140221	112349	252570	458239	305283	763522	504040	408453	912493

Source: Various reports of All India Survey of Higher Education Note: *Includes enrolment in Diploma, Certificate and Integrated Courses.

To see the status of higher education in any state/country including Haryana, Gross Enrolment Ratio (GER) is most important indicator which is shown from the following Table 7.

Table 7: Gross Enrolment Ratio (GER) in higher education in Haryana.

Year	***Haryana***						***India***					
	All			***Schedule caste***			***All***			***Schedule caste***		
	Male	***Female***	***Total***	***Male***	***Female***	***Total***	***Male***	***Female***	***Total***	***Male***	***Female***	***Total***
2006–07	13.05	12.57	12.84	8.39	5.18	7	14.53	10.2	12.39	11.52	6.96	9.35
2007–08	16.1	13.3	14.8	12	9.2	10.8	15.2	10.7	13.1	13.2	8.6	11
2008–09	21	16.5	18.9	10.5	6.9	8.9	15.8	11.4	13.7	12.5	8.3	10.5
2009–10	21.2	16.8	19.1	12.3	8.4	10.5	17.1	12.7	15	13	9	11.1
2010–11	27.2	20.7	24.1	16.5	11.5	14.2	20.8	17.9	19.4	14.6	12.3	13.5
2011–12	28.4	27.3	27.9	18.8	16.9	17.9	21.6	18.9	20.4	15.4	13.5	14.5
2012–13	29.1	28.1	28.7	18.8	16.8	17.9	22.3	19.8	21.1	16.0	14.2	15.1

Source: Various reports of All India Survey of Higher Education.

Gross enrolment ratio determines the number of students enrolled in education at different levels. Data include details on gender wise gross enrolment ratio in higher education for categories SC in India and Haryana in Table 7. It can be observed from the table that GER of both male and females are improving over the period of time in both Haryana and India. In 2006–07, GER was 12.84 and 7 percent in all and schedule caste category respectively in Haryana. And GER grew to 28.7 and 17.9 percent in all and schedule caste category respectively in Haryana in 2012–13. And GER of females is also increased more than double from the period 2006–07 to 2012–13.

Gender Parity Index (GPI) is also another important indicator to analyse the ratio of girls to boys in any type of education including higher education. GPI in higher education is calculated for 18–23 years of age group. The ratio of the female to male in higher education measures progress towards gender equity and the level of learning opportunities available for women in relation to those available to men. GPI also serves as a significant indicator of the empowerment of women in society. It can be easily observed from the following Table 8 that GPI varies from 0.96 to 0.92 and 0.61 to 0.89 in Haryana and India respectively from 2006–07 to 2012–13. Greater gender parity exists in Haryana in year 2010–11 because the value of GPI was 0.76. But the value of GPI is highest that is 0.98 in 2011–12 which indicates that lesser gender parity exist in Haryana. Similarly greater gender parity exists in 2006–07 in India because the value of GPI was 0.61 and over the period of time, gender parity reduces in India because value of GPI increases from 0.61 in 2006–07 to 0.89 in 2012–13.

Table 8: Gender parity index since 2006–07.

Year	*Haryana*		*India*	
	All Categories	*Schedule caste*	*All categories*	*Schedule caste*
2006–07	0.96	0.62	0.61	0.60
2007–08	0.83	0.77	0.70	0.65
2008–09	0.79	0.66	0.72	0.66
2009–10	0.79	0.68	0.74	0.69
2010–11	0.76	0.70	0.86	0.84
2011–12	0.98	0.91	0.88	0.88
2012–13	0.92	0.85	0.89	0.89

Source: Various reports of All India Survey of Higher Education.

To present the comparative picture of India and Haryana on the basis of few indicators such as average enrolment per college, availability of college per lakh population and total number of colleges, following Table 9 is presented. Various college indicators during last six years in India and Haryana are presented through the following Table 9.

Table 9: Various college indicators during last six years.

Year	*Average enrolment per college*		*College per lakh population*		*Number of college*	
	India	*Haryana*	*India*	*Haryana*	*India*	*Haryana*
2010–11	700	766	23	33	32974	1054
2011–12	703	785	25	33	34852	1061
2012–13	715	730	25	34	35525	1072
2013–14	742	698	26	34	36634	1098
2014–15	731	683	27	35	38498	1113
2015–16	721	646	28	35	39071	1113

Source: All India Survey of Higher Education (AISHE) Report 2015–16.

Table presents the data on three college indicators such as average enrolment per college, college per lakh population and number of colleges in India and Haryana. Average enrolment per college has increased from 2010–11 to 2015–16 in India but in Haryana average enrolment per college has declined. This may be due to the expansion of number of colleges in Haryana over the period of time. Similarly, college per lakh population has also increasing trend in both India and Haryana. And number of colleges also has increased from 1054 in 2010–11 to 1113 in 2015–16 in Haryana and 32974 in 2010–11 to 39071 in 2015–16. Therefore analysis reveals that Haryana is performing well in terms of higher education.

5. CONCLUSIONS WITH POLICY IMPLICATIONS

In sum up, there is the sizeable increase in higher education in Haryana over the period of time, which is the outcome of sincere efforts of the Government in the form of expenditure on education in general and higher education in particular. From the analysis of growth rate, it becomes clear that growth rate of higher education in terms of institutions, enrolments and expenditure on education in general and higher education in particular has taken place in Haryana significantly. On the other hand, higher educational facilities are inclusive in nature means that enrolments of women in higher education, enrolments of schedule caste, minority communities have increased in a significant manner. Therefore, in brief, all types of higher education have grown over time in a right manner but there is a rationale of proper balance between quantity and quality of higher education in Haryana. To improve quality of higher education, public expenditure should not only be enhanced by Government but need to change from targeted approach to result orientation with manpower planning. In order to become Haryana as a knowledge economy, Government has to qualitatively strengthen education in general and higher education with research and development in particular. For this, we have to design the higher education with relevance to the present as well as future.

To make Haryana a human resource development (HRD) hub, we need to be humble in slow and steady progress in all HRD activities including higher education which calls for recognizing them as the infrastructural activities and required to be undertaken as essential services. The expenditure on such activities should no more be treated under social services sector and calls for separate head to be treated as investment. The implications for the policy making can be drawn from the study that Haryana policy makers should pay attention to higher education human resources and make policies to increase the higher education expenditure to build and attract outstanding higher educational infrastructure. To build excellent higher educational institutions with quality infrastructure, enrolment rates of both male and females in higher education will increase. The expenditure on education including higher education is still much below the accepted international standards, near 4 percent of the GDP as against the accepted and declared goal of 6 to 7 percent of GDP, which is required for 100 per cent literacy. Government should follow 'Eastern Strategy' as was done by Japan during 1868–1911, Europe in 1913's, China in 1970's etc. These countries spend nearly 40 to 50 percent of their budgets is on human development and human capital. Not only the Government, but the corporate sector, NGO's, the philanthropists and others capable to do so should come forward on a massive scale for the development of educational infrastructure in any economy including Haryana.

SUGGESTED READINGS

Chandra Abhijeet (2010). Does Government Expenditure on Education Promote Economic Growth? An Econometric Analysis. Jamia Millia Islamia (Central University), New Delhi, MPRA Paper No. 25480.

Goel, M.M. and Walia Suraj (2011). "Education and Economic Growth in Haryana (India): Using Granger Causality Approach" in international journal. *Journal of South Asian Studies*, 17(1).

Goel, M.M. and Walia Suraj (2011). "Higher Education: An Engine of Economic Growth in Post Reform India" Panjab University, Chandigarh. *Research Journal Social Sciences*, 19(3).

Goel, M.M. (2012 Second Edition). *'Economics of Human Resource Development in India'* VK Publications, New Delhi. ISBN:978-93-5058-014-1

Goel, M.M. and Walia, Suraj (2015). "Indian Higher Education: Trends, Growth & Challenges". *International Journal, Voice of Research*, 3(4): 33–38.

Goel, M.M. and Walia Suraj (2017). "Higher Education and Economic Growth in Haryana: An Application of Cointegration and Vector Error Correction Model (VECM) Approach". *Multi-Disciplinary International Research Journal, Asian Resonance*, VI(III).

Mekdad Yousra, Dahmani Aziz and Louaj Monir (2014). Public Spending on Education and Economic Growth in Algeria: Causality Test. *International Journal of Business and Management,* II(3).

Pradhan, R.P. (2009). Education and Economic Growth in India: Using Error Correction Modelling (ECM). *International Research Journal of Finance and Economics*, Issue 23. ISSN 1450–2887.

Ray Sarbapriya (2013). Does Education Spending of Government Really Accelerate Economic Growth in India? Sciknow Publications Ltd. *Financial and Quantitative Analysis*, 1(1): 1–7.

Reports of All India Survey of Higher Education (AISHE).

Solanki Melina (2013). Relationship between Education and GDP growth: A Bi-variate causality analysis for Greece. *International Journal of Economic Practices and Theories*, 3(2): 133–139.

Statistical Abstract of India (Various issues).

Statistical Abstract of Haryana (Various issues).

University Grant Commission (UGC) Reports.

Walia Suraj (2010). "Analysis of Education Infrastructure in Haryana", Unpublished M.Phil. Dissertation (with Prof. M.M. Goel), Kurukshetra University, Kurukshetra.

Walia Suraj (2015). *"Higher Education in India: Progress and Emerging Issues". The Indian Economic Journal (Journal of the Indian Economic Association)* special issue.

Walia Suraj (2015). *"Higher Education: Issues and Challenges"* published in National Magazine, *"Economy India"* in February 2015 Issue.

Walia Suraj (2016). "Educational Infrastructure & Economic Growth: An Analysis of Higher Education in Haryana" in edited book by V.K. Global Publication Pvt. Ltd. ISBN 978-93-5058-587-0

Walia Suraj and Walia, K. Ritu (2013). "A Study of Linkage between Education and Poverty in India". *Indian Journal of Applied Research*, 3(12).

Walia Suraj and Walia, K. Ritu (2014). "Education and Entrepreneurship Development in India: An Analysis" in edited book by Twenty First Century Publications, Patiala. ISBN 978-81-89463-68-7.

Walia, Suraj and Walia, K. Ritu (2016). "The Linkage between Higher Education and Skill Development in India: An Analysis" published in *National Seminar E-proceedings* (Organized by R.K.S.D. College, Kaithal) published. ISBN 978-93-5254-810-1

15

Women Leadership: A Unique Horizon in Management

MADHURIMA BASU[1*] AND KUMKUM MUKHERJEE[1]

ABSTRACT

The topic of leadership is of worldwide interest. Leadership is an integral part of every organization. The success or failure of an organization is dependent on the efficiency of the leaders across the various levels. Leadership is a process in which leaders and followers interact in a dynamic manner in a specific situation or in an environment. Leadership influences the behaviour of the followers. Effective leadership always makes a difference and it may be enhanced through greater awareness of the vital factors in shaping the leaders. Women though under-represented at the organizational leadership positions are gradually finding their way to the top positions. Changes are visible at the macro-organizational level and societal levels that in a way is contributing to greater gender equality in leadership; for instance changing organizational culture, women's career development, mentoring opportunities for women, and rise in the number of women in strategic positions is leading to the increase in the presence of women in eminent leadership roles. Elliot and Stead (2008) found in their study a web of four inter-related factors which connects women leaders to their community that in a way play a fundamental role in their lives. The four inter-related factors are upbringing, environment, focus, network and alliances. The present paper is an attempt to study the significance of the inter-related factors in shaping women leaders as proposed by Elliot and Stead (2008), of a particular woman executive working in a department under the central government of India; which might have contributed to her present leadership style. An in depth interview was taken of the women executive to understand her life philosophy and her world outlook. Additionally, her subordinates were also interviewed

[1] Indian Institute of Social Welfare and Business Management (IISWBM), Kolkata, West Bengal.

Corresponding author: E-mail: madhuapri@gmail.com

extensively to understand the impact of her leadership style on their job performance level. It was found from the interview data of the women executive that factors such as her upbringing years, environment, focus along with network and alliances has left a strong impact on her leadership style; which seems to corroborate to the findings of Elliot and Stead's (2008) study. The interview data of the subordinates seems to suggest the women executive's exhibited leadership style has enhanced their job output level. This seems to have made a positive impact on the job performance level of the subordinates.

Key words: Leadership, Women leaders, Leadership styles, Life experiences.

INTRODUCTION

The concept of leadership is both intriguing and complex. Leadership is the ability to influence a group of individual followers to abide by one's guidance or comply with one's decision. The process of leadership prevails within the context of a specific group of followers; therefore leadership and followership may be considered to be interdependent. Organizational leadership is one of the pivotal factors for enhancing organizational performance. The success or failure of an organization is dependent on the leadership efficiency across the levels. Leadership is a process by which an individual influences others to accomplish an objective and directs the organization in a manner that makes it more cohesive and coherent (Hasan & Othman, 2013). Traditionally in the Indian society it was considered men will go out to earn, while women folk were supposed to provide moral support to their male counterparts. With the gradual progress of social evolution and changing mind set across the various strata of the society, women have started getting a lot more space in the male dominated professions. The modern day women have show cased exceptional passion, grit and determination both in their personal life and work situation, excelling their male counterparts. Women's attitudes are predominantly influenced by their family background. Women develop skills such as that of a good planner and organizer, people management and hospitality coming naturally to them. Some of the inherent traits women develop are innovation, compassion, loyalty and resilience. In the last decade there has been a significant increase in the number of women in leadership positions at the organizational level (Basu & Mukherjee, 2018). The successive changes are visible at the macro-organizational level and societal levels that in a way is contributing to greater gender equality in leadership positions; for instance changing organizational culture, women's career development, mentoring opportunities for women, and rise in the number of women in strategic positions is leading to the increase in the presence of women in eminent leadership roles. At the societal level structural changes are visible which include more equitable distribution of child rearing and domestic duties (Northouse, 2014). Women have the innate characteristics of nurturing talents, listening skills, collaboration along with partnership harmony which are the most sorted for leadership qualities in today's corporate world (Menon & Sukumaran, 2015). Scholars have taken note of the fact that the increasing number of women and racial minority directors on boards have led to a growing attention towards social responsibilities, charitable giving and community connections (Stanwick & Stanwick, 1998; Williams, 2003). Gender diversity at the top management position is the need of the hour. Women leadership styles are different from the traditional and men centric leadership styles which were usually specified with personal traits and situational context in across diverse types of organizations (Kim, 2016). Evidencing the fact that the change will happen with the positive approaches from the various industries and society at large, the number of women leaders in India too are on the rise.

REVIEW OF LITERATURE

Leadership

'The topic of leadership continues to preoccupy us in every sphere of life. Whether it is questioning our own capacities for leadership; considering leadership in our family systems; looking at leadership at work; or assessing leadership in the political sphere, the desire to experience 'leadership' in some shape or form is invariably present. Because we are so dependent on leaders and vulnerable to the results of their leadership exploits, it is quite natural that we should want to understand what leadership is all about and which criteria, skills and talents make a good leader' (Beeral, 2015). Leadership is the ability of an individual to influence, motivate and to facilitate a group of followers to contribute towards enhancing the organizational effectiveness (House, Hanges, Javidan, Dorfman & Gupta, 2004). A leader's behaviour influences on the psychological reactions of the individual followers and group of followers' at large. The psychological responses comprises of followers attitudes, feelings, perception, motivation levels and degree of expectations. More specifically the factors include followers' satisfaction with the administration, general job satisfaction, commitment towards the organization, job stress, role clarity, motivation and group cohesion (Howell & Costley, 2008; Basu & Mukherjee, 2018). The crucial parameter for effective leadership is effective communication which built through trust and confidence in the top management (Lamb & McKee, 2004). According to Jago (1982) a good leader is a product of self-study, training, education and experience. Therefore, it may be said a good leader is made not born. There are certain qualities which are perceived as the prime prerequisites for effective leadership. Some of them are 'self-reliant, independent, assertive, risk taker, dominant, ambitious, and self-sufficient' (Hasan & Othman, 2013). The outcome of effective leadership and followership gets reflected in the accomplishments of the organizational goals.

Women Leadership

Over the last few decades there has been a significant increase in the number of women joining the diverse organizational sectors around the globe. The eventual elevation of women to the top posts in the organizational management has paved the way for research in the field of women leadership. Women leaders tend to be the practitioners of participative or collaborative decision making. At the present time there are not many women leaders in at the top management posts (Hasan & Othman, 2013). Various studies on women leadership suggests talented and confident women leaders have a number of characteristics in common that distinguishes them from the conventional male leadership style. Hasan and Othman (2013) figured out some of the characteristics of women leadership in their study. As suggested by Hasan and Othman (2013), first of all women leaders tend to have high value on relationships and evaluate the success of their organizations based on the worth of the relationship they share with them. Secondly, women leaders place high value on direct communication (Hasan & Othman, 2013). Thirdly, as put forward by Hasan and Othman (2013) women leaders are open to diversity, having been the minority in the top leadership positions they seem to understand it well what kind of options fresh eyes could bring forth. Fourthly, women leaders seem to be unwilling to compartmentalize their lives and as a result experiences from their personal life get reflected in their professional life (Hasan & Othman, 2013). Women leaders prefers to lead from the centre rather than from the top. Women leaders when exposed to the string of rejection have the propensity to learn from the adverse situations. Women leaders exhibit an all-inclusive, team building leadership style to deal with the diverse situations and ultimately take decisions. Women leaders prefer to ignore rules and take risks. Women across the globe are emerging as leaders across the diverse sectors. The growing ability of women to reach the decision-making positions has enabled them to become notable minority rather than merely a symbolic few; they still do not enjoy adequate representation in the upper echelons of management. The factors that shape the path of advancement for women leaders may be categorized into three levels; societal, familial and individual (Moor, Cohen & Beeri, 2015). On the societal layer, organizational changes that enforce mechanisms for facilitating optimal balance between family and career for both the genders have shown to empower women to make better advancement in the ranks of the organization (Eagly & Carli, 2007; Eagly & Karau, 2002; Cheung & Halpern, 2010; Kark & Eagly, 2010; Moor, Cohen & Beeri, 2015). Past studies have shown that emotional or instrumental support at the home environment lead to greater progress for the female folk in the workplace (Ezzedeen & Grossnickle-Ritchey, 2008; King, Mattimore, King & Adams, 1995; Salas, Deitrick, Mahady, Gertner & Sabino, 2011). Growing up in a gender neutral social environment seems to contribute immensely to the development of androgynous personality of women which contributes to their gradual advancement to the positions of power in public domain (Ragins, 1998; Singh Vinnicombe, 2004). According to Kim (2016), women leaders are no less than their male counterparts when it comes to exhibiting leadership qualities like transformational skills and emotional intelligence. The ability to transform along side show casing emotional intelligence is a much required prerequisite to deal with the cultural diversity and drastic social changes taking place globally (Kim, 2016). Gender diversity in the top management is considered to be analogous to investing in the fields of research and development (Miller & Triana, 2009). The blend of the diverse behavioural characteristics exhibited by women leaders seems to be an added advantage for the organizations around the globe.

Inter-Related Factors in Shaping Women Leaders (Elliot & Stead, 2008)

Elliot and Stead (2008) carried out a study to have a better understanding of the relevance of the diverse sociological components in shaping the women leaders. The four inter-related factors which contribute in developing leadership skillsthat emerged from their study are upbringing, environment, focus, network and alliances.

Upbringing

Upbringing plays a foundational role in the path to acquire leadership skills and it also plays a vital role in the continuous development of the women leaders. In the words of Elliot and Stead (2008) 'this is a very broad theme, that includes the woman's childhood, how they were raised their place within the family and their early experiences as an adult both at home, in their community and their workplace'. The components of upbringing acts as the outliners of leadership skills.

Environment

Environment plays a pivotal role in an individual's life. The components of environment as taken for consideration in Elliot and Stead's study (2008) are social, political, historical and cultural landscape prevalent in the society during the growing up years of the women leaders.

Focus

Focus is the key to achievement. The passion borne out of experience that entails the focus to be sustained particularly when reward or success is hard won (Elliot & Stead, 2008). Focus may be described as being determined to achieve the goals and at the same time having the clarity regarding the path to be opted for to accomplish the predetermined goals.

Network and Alliances

Network and alliances are the most instrumental parameter linking the upbringing, environment and focus. Elliot and Stead (2008) is of the opinion that network and alliances is actually the overlapping arenas of personal and professional networks. Personal network for alliances comprises of family members and friends who have genuine concern at heart for the women leaders. Professional networks include 'people well known in the women's chosen field and are more fluid in nature, shifting to reflect the woman's current position' (Elliot & Stead, 2008).

OBJECTIVES

Elliot and Stead (2008) conducted a study on women leadership to understand the contributions of the various sociological dimensions in shaping women in the lead. They found in their study a web of four inter-related factors which connects women leaders to their community that in a way play a fundamental role in their lives. The four inter-related factors as proposed by Elliot and Stead (2008) are upbringing, environment, focus, network and alliances. The present paper is an attempt to evaluate the significance of the inter-related factors in shaping women leaders as put forward by Elliot and Stead (2008), of a particular woman executive working in a department under the central government of India; which might have contributed to her present leadership style. Additionally, her subordinates were also interviewed extensively to understand the impact of her leadership style on their job performance level.

METHODOLOGY

The present study follows qualitative methodology. To further the research design it is based on case study research methodology (Errikson & Kovalainan, 2014). The present paper follows single subject case study framework (Thomas, 2011). The data for the present study was collected through standardized structured interview guidelines.

FINDINGS AND DISCUSSION

Profile of the Woman Executive

Upbringing: The woman executive for the present study was born into an illustrious family of engineers and scientists. The lady is extremely well educated. She has earned her M.Phil degree in the field of economics. The lady acknowledged she had a strong influence of her family members during her growing up years. The woman made a special mention of her mother, 'I wanted to make everything happen emulating my mother and drawing inspiration from her who was educated up to secondary school level but the respect and love she commanded across the various sections of the society was mind boggling. It was her perseverance to learn every aspect of life from domestic chores to legal matters interspersed with social work in form of entertaining senior citizens, who were uncared for, and teaching music to young and the old alike, having started her life in a village'. The lady proudly admitted it is only because of her mother's influence she has learnt to take up challenges in life amidst strife and tribulations; according to the lady this motto of her life has led her to her present status in the society. The lady stated she has inherited the boldness factor in her personality from her mother and grandmother. The emergent view from the interview data of the woman executive seems to finds support to the 'upbringing' parameter in shaping women leaders as proposed by Elliot and Stead (2008).

***Environment*:** The lady during the course of the interview shared with the researcher how her surrounding environment played a pivotal role in her life. The lady expressed she had causally applied for the clerical cadre at the organization she is presently working with. She clearly specified to the researcher during the course of the interview that though she had no fascination to join the clerical cadre. The lady narrated she had an offer for the post of an officer at a leading government organization. The city where she was scheduled to be posted was prone to frequent social political unrest at that time. So, it was on her grandfather's insistence she joined her present organization at the clerical cadre. The executive gladly said although she is a highly educated individual she never had any remorse for working as a clerk during the initial phase of her career. It may also be noted here the lady belongs to a highly educated family background. The narrative account of the executive's career choice seems to substantiate the 'environment' factor as one of the dimension for shaping women leaders as suggested by Elliot and Stead (2008).

***Focus*:** The lady described herself to the researcher as a dedicated optimist who believes in the motto 'you should bring your people along with you' and 'keep on motivating others through thick and thin.' The very description of her self-perception of herself seems to suggest the lady is determined to overcome every obstacle and achieve goals. The woman said 'I always believed that all people are born alike but the difference lies in making their life meaningful through sincere dedication and hard work'. The lady affirmed to the fact that it was only because of her sheer determination that presently she is working as a top management official in the organization. The officer commented on her career graph in the following way, 'I started my career only as a clerk in this organization despite having an M.Phil degree, as there were domestic compulsions to remain with the family. The day I joined the organization, I had made up my mind to reach the level of the highest officer in the organization, but with a difference, of being the best officer. Today, I feel proud to have achieved status in life in the official circles, simultaneously engaging into humanitarian acts help to the destitute without compromising my family responsibilities'. The narrative account as stated by the lady seems to authenticate the'focus' parameter as proposed by Elliot and Stead's (2008) study.

Network and Alliances: The woman executive admitted she has imbibed the passion, commitment and visionary outlook of her family members while sharing her thoughts with the researcher on personal network. The lady has been conferred with several awards by the top management for making noteworthy contributions towards excelling organizational growth. She has also led various teams dealing with challenging projects and has successfully completed them. The lady professed it is only due to her amicable interpersonal relationship with her superiors, colleagues and subordinates that she can easily complete even the most difficult assignment/s without compromising on her work ethics. Post marriage the lady acknowledged her parents-in-laws; husband and children became her additional support system. Thus, it resulted into striking the perfect balance between the personal and professional life. The different descriptive accounts as shared by the executive related to the interconnections of her personal and professional life seems to corroborate to the 'network and alliance' dimension as suggested by Elliot and Stead (2008).

SUBORDINATES' NARRATIVES

The interview data of the subordinates working under the woman executive seems to suggest that majority of them perceives her to be a leader in the truest sense. One of the subordinate stated that the lady always motivates and provides guidance to her team. Another subordinate shared with the researcher that the lady executive's helpful attitude and sense of equality for all her team members inspires them to perform better. Most of the subordinates' in complete agreement admitted it is due to the lady's determined nature, honest approach, nurturing skills, communication skills and exceptional ability to bind the team members together as a unit that has played a significant role in shaping their professional skills. Therefore, the interview data of the subordinates seems to suggest the woman executive's exhibited leadership behaviour has enhanced their job output level. This seems to have made a positive impact on the job performance level of the subordinates.

CONCLUSIONS

Leadership as an area of research has garnered interest among researchers throughout ages. One of the most important factors contributing to organizational growth is the prevalent organizational leadership. Over the decades, the organizational environment has evolved around the globe.

Diversity in the organizational management is one of the key essential for the long term survival of every organization. There is a steady rise in the number of women joining the work force which stands in contrast with the workplace dynamics in the yesteryears. Women leaders are emerging to be skilled leaders leading organizations worldwide. The emerging findings from the interview data of the women executive seems to suggest that her upbringing years, environment, focus along with network and alliances has left a strong impact on her exhibited leadership style at the workplace. Therefore, the findings of the present study in context to the various sociological dimensions of the women executive seems to corroborate to the web of four inter-related factors as put forward by Elliot and Stead (2008). Additionally, the descriptive narratives of the subordinates seem to suggest the woman executive's leadership style has enhanced their overall job output level. This seems to have made a positive impact on the job performance level of the subordinates. Extensive studies exploring the impact of the various sociological factors on women leaders will help the researchers to have a better understanding in the area of women leadership.

REFERENCES

Basu, M. and Mukherjee, K. (2018). Women Leadership: An Effective Perspective. *In*: Ahmed Alam, P., Kundu, K. and Baksi, A.K. [*eds*.]. Exploring New Horizons in Management & Business Practices, Kolkata: Aliah University Press.

Beerel, A.C. (2009). *Leadership and Change Management*, London: SAGE.

Cheung, F.M. and Halpern, D.F. (2010). Women at the top: Powerful leaders define success as work + family in a culture of gender. *American Psychologist*, 65(3): 182–193.

Eagly, A.H. and Carli, L.L. (2007). Women and the labyrinth of leadership. *Harvard Business Review*, 4: 62–71.

Eagly, A.H. and Karau, S.J. (2002). Role congruity theory of prejudice toward female leaders. *Psychological Review*, 109(3): 573–598.

Elliott, C. and Stead, V. (2008). Learning from Leading Women's Experience: Towards a Sociological Understanding. *Leadership*, 4(2): 159–180.

Eriksson, P. and Kovalainen, A. (2016). *Qualitative Methods in Business Research*, London: Sage.

Ezzedeen, S.R. and Ritchey, K.G. (2008). The Man behind the Woman. *Journal of Family Issues*, 29(9): 1107–1135.

Hasan, A. and Othman, A. (2013). When it Comes to Leadership, Does Gender Matter? *Oman Chapter of Arabian Journal of Business and Management Review*, 2(10): 71–78.

House, R.J., Hanges, P.J., Javidan, M., Dorfman, P.W. and Gupta, V. (2004). *Culture, Leadership, and Organizations: The Globe study of 62 societies*. London: Sage.

Howell, J.P. and Costley, D.L. (2008). *Understanding Behaviors for Effective Leadership*. New Delhi: Prentice Hall of India.

Jago, A.G. (1982). Leadership: Perspectives in Theory and Research. *Management Science*, 28(3): 315–336.

Kark, R. and Eagly, A.H. (2010). Gender and leadership: Negotiating the labyrinth. *In*: Chrisler, J. (*ed*.), *Handbook of Gender Research in Psychology*, pp. 443–368, New York: Springer.

Kim, Y. (2016). Women's Leadership in School Administration: A Review Recasting the Literature. *The Social Sciences*, 11(23): 5776–5785.

King, L.A., Mattimore, L.K., King, D.W. and Adams, G.A. (1995). Family Support Inventory for Workers: A new measure of perceived social support from family members. *Journal of Organizational Behavior*, 16(3): 235–258.

Lamb, L.F. and McKee, K.B. (2004). Applied Public Relations: Cases in Stakeholder Management. Mahwah, New Jersey: Lawrence Erlbaum Associates.

Menon, R.U. and Sukumaran, V.P. (2015). Women Leadership in Indian Banking Industry -An Overview. *International Journal of Research in Management*, 5(1): 95–102.

Miller, T. and Del Carmen Triana, M. (2009). Demographic Diversity in the Boardroom: Mediators of the Board Diversity-Firm Performance Relationship. *Journal of Management Studies*, 46(5): 755–786.

Moor, A., Cohen, A. and Beeri, A. (2015). *In*: Quest of Excellence, Not Power: Woman's Path to Positions of Influence and Leadership. *Advancing Women in Leadership*, 35: 1–11.

Northouse, P.G. (2014). *Leadership: Theory and Practice,* (6th Edition), London: Sage.

Ragins, B.R. (1998). Gender gap in the executive suite: CEOs and female executives report on breaking the glass ceiling. *Academy of Management Perspectives*, 12(1): 28–42.

Salas-Lopez, D., Deitrick, L.M., Mahady, E.T., Gertner, E.J. and Sabino, J.N. (2011). Women leaders-challenges, successes and other insights from the top. *Journal of Leadership Studies*, 5(2): 34–42.

Singh, V. and Vinnicombe, S. (2004). Why So Few Women Directors in Top UK Boardrooms? Evidence and Theoretical Explanations. *Corporate Governance*, 12(4): 479–488.

Stanwick, P.A. and Stanwick, S.D. (1998). The Relationship between Corporate Social Performance and Organizational Size, Financial Performance and Environmental Performance: An Empirical Examination. *Journal of Business Ethics*, 17(1): 195–204.

Thomas, G. (2010). *How to do your case study*, London: Sage.

Williams, R.J. (2003). Women on corporate boards of directors and their influence on corporate philanthropy. *Journal of Business Ethics*, 17(1): 1–10.

16

Nutritional Situation of Women in Rural India

SAROJ KUMAR YADAV[1*]

ABSTRACT

Adequate nutrition is the cornerstone of health for everybody especially women. Inadequate nutrition not only has bad effect on the health of the women but their children also. Children of malnourished women have poor cognitive skills, delayed growth and development, inability to learn, are more prone to diseases and have stunted growth. Apart from this they are at greater risk of falling ill and dying. The woman spends a centrifugal role in the nutritional status of the children. Therefore in Rural India, the extent of the problem of malnourishment in women is seen in relation to the child's nourishment or malnourishment and the condition at birth. The aim of this study is to analysis the relative health situation of women among states in Rural India and to see in which states the relative health status of women is better and in which it is bad. To analysis the above objectives we have used three indicators- Life expectancy at birth, Maternal Mortality Ratio (MMR) and the situation of women affected with CED. The index is expressed as the distance to be traveled by a state to reach the best possible situation as a proportion of the total distance between the best and the worst states. The Index of all the indicators are calculated separately and there average is taken out. Thus this average is the composite Index of Female Adult Health in rural India. From the analysis it is found that in rural India, the condition of health of women in the states like Chhattisgarh, Madhya Pradesh, Jharkhand, Uttar Pradesh, Assam, Gujarat, Rajasthan, Bihar and Orissa is worst. Among these states, the condition of women is worst Because of the bad situation of all the three indicators, the health infrastructure in these states like maximum number of women affected with anaemia, more number of unvaccinated children, lack of pure drinking water and rural infrastructure and means of livelihood being less as compared to other states

[1] Department of Economics, University of Allahabad, UP (211002).
**Corresponding author*: E-mail: srj2015@gmail.com

and therefore there is a need to take immediate steps to improve it. For this with the initiation of new programmes, the past and existing programmes should be examined again and their limit and their feasibility should be ascertained.

Key words: Life expectancy, CED, MMR, Adult health index.

1. INTRODUCTION

Adequate nutrition is the corner stone of health for everybody especially women. Inadequate nutrition not only has bad effect on the health of the women but their children also. Children of malnourished women have poor cognitive skills, delayed growth and development, inability to learn, are more prone to diseases and have stunted growth. Apart from this they are at greater risk of falling ill and dying. The woman spends a centrifugal role in the nutritional status of the children. Therefore in Rural India, the extent of the problem of malnourishment in women is seen in relation to the child's nourishment or malnourishment and the condition at birth. This can be seen with the help of Fig. 1.

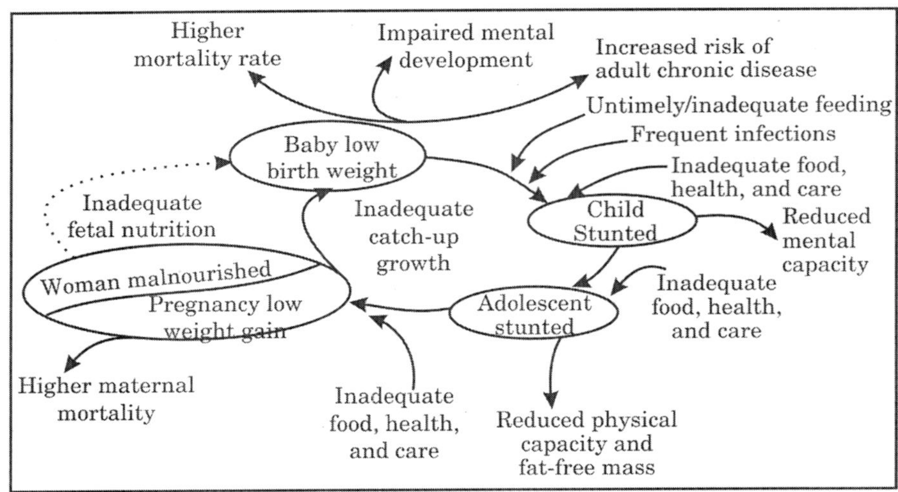

Fig. 1: Poor nutrition throughout the life cycle. ***Source:*** Adapted from the ACC/SCN-appointed Commission on the Nutrition Challenges of the 21st Century.

The problem of under nourishment in women is not only due to lack of adequate and diversified food but due to other factors also such as early marriages, conception at small age, education, empowerment of decision making and domestic violence. These factors affects directly or indirectly the nutritional status of women. There are many policies for these issues in rural India but their implementation is weak. It is necessary to give importance to the role of women's nutrition for reducing under nourishment in children with right to healthy life.

1.1. Objectives

The aim of this study is to analysis the relative health situation of women among states in Rural India and to see in which states the relative health status of women is better and in which it is bad.

1.2. Methodology

To analysis the above objectives we have used three indicators - Life expectancy at birth, Maternal Mortality Ratio (MMR) and the situation of women affected with CED. The index is expressed as the distance to be traveled by a state to reach the best possible situation as a proportion of the total distance between the best and the worst states. The Index of all the indicators are calculated separately and there average is taken out. Thus this average is the composite Index of Female Adult Health in rural India. The calculation of Index of the indicators is done as follows:

IMMR = Index of Maternal Mortality Ratio

$$IMMR = (X_{ij} - X_{imn})/(X_{imx} - X_{imn})$$

ICED = Index of Chronic Energy Deficiency

$$ICED = (X_{ij} - X_{imn})/(X_{imx} - X_{imn})$$

ILE = Index of Life expectancy at Birth

$$ILE = (X_{imx} - X_{ij})/(X_{imx} - X_{imn})$$

IAH = Index of adult health

$$IAH = (ILE + IMMR + ICED)/N$$

Where

X_{ij} : i^{th} Adult Health Indicator in j^{th} state

X_{imx} : i^{th} Adult Health Indicator in the state with highest value of the indicator

X_{imn} : i^{th} Adult Health Indicator in the state with lowest value of the indicator

N : Number of indicators

The value of the index is between 0 and 1. In which 0 signifies the best situation and 1 the worst situation. According to this index, the states are given ranks according to their health status.

Using the Natural break (that follow the pattern of the data to decide the class intervals) of Are-View GIS software, the figures of mixed index are used to divide the 17 states into five categories according to the health status of women in these states and analysis is done to find the states in which the women's health is better and in which states it is bad and it is shown also with the help of diagram.

1.3. Iron

The deficiency of iron caused due to its decreased absorption by a body for a very long time results in anaemia. Anaemia is caused due to deficiency of Iron and Vitamin B12. Haemoglobin is essential for transporting oxygen from lungs to different parts of the body. Low level of haemoglobin in the blood level results in anaemia. Deficiency of Iron lowers the capacity of the person to work and hence lowers his productivity. Anaemia in mothers hinders the growth of child in the uterus, causes birth of low weight baby, increase in prenatal mortality, high maternal mortality and premature deliveries. Deficiency of iron during infancy and childhood causes apathy, tiredness, inactivity and poor cognitive skills in children. The most important problem of iron deficiency is the weakening of immune system of a person thereby making him more prone to infections.

Moreover According to the analysis of figures of NFHS- IV(2014–16) it is clear that in rural India, Children between the age of 6 months to 59 months have anaemia. The states that have maximum anaemic children are from Haryana, Jharkhand, Madhya Pradesh, Gujarat, Bihar, Karnataka, Uttar Pradesh, Rajasthan and Andhra Pradesh where more than 60% children (between 60–72%) suffer from anaemia. This percentage is more than 59.4% of all the children affected by anaemia in the country. The Percentage of women suffering from anemia in these states including West Bengal and excluding Karnataka is between 50–67%. Contrary to this, the states with less number of children suffering from anaemia are Kerala and Assam with 35.7% and 36.5% respectively and percentage of women suffering from anaemia is less in Assam, Karnataka and Maharashtra, which is 46–47% and in other states the percentage is less or more than the national average of 54.2%.

On Comparing the figures of NFHS-IV and NFHS-III it is clear that in all the states between the year 2005–06 and 2015–16 there is an increase in the percentage of rural women suffering from anaemia who are mainly from Haryana, Kerala, Punjab, Tamil Nadu and Uttar Pradesh. Kerala has the highest increase in the percentage of anaemic women whereas in all other states the percentage has lowered (Table 1.1).

Table 1.1: Women adult health indicator in rural India.

		1	*2*	*3*	*4*	*5*
Sl. no.	*State/ India*	*Life expectancy of female at birth in rural India (2010–14)*	*Maternal mortality ratio in India (U+R) (2010–12)*	*Women whose body mass index below 18.5 in rural India (%)*	*Children age 6–59 months who are anemic (%) in rural India*	*All women age 15–49 years who are anemic (%) in rural India*
	India	68.43	178	26.7	59.4	54.2
1	A.P.	69.33	110	20.3	60.8	61.1
2	Assam	64.61	328	27	36.5	46.3
3	Bihar	68.10	219	31.8	64	60.5
4	Chhattisgarh	65.54	230	29.6	41.2	48.2
5	Gujarat	70.01	122	34.3	64.6	57.5
6	Haryana	70.82	146	18.2	72.9	63.9
7	Jharkhand	65.76	219	35.4	71.5	67.3
8	Karnataka	69.61	144	24.3	63.4	46.2
9	Kerala	78.10	66	10.2	35.7	54.2
10	M.P.	64.96	230	31.8	69.9	53.8
11	Maharashtra	72.43	87	30	54	47.8
12	Orissa	66.50	235	28.7	45.7	51.8
13	Punjab	72.45	155	13.5	57.2	54.4
14	Rajasthan	69.70	255	29.9	61.6	49
15	Tamil Nadu	71.33	90	18.5	52.5	56.8
16	Uttar Pradesh	64.65	292	28.1	62.7	52.4
17	West Bengal	70.82	117	24.6	53.7	64.4

Source: Col.1 www.indiastate.com; Col. 2, Special Bulletin on Maternal Mortality in India 2010–12, SRS office of Registrar General of India; Col. 3, 4, 5, NFHS-4 (2015–16)

1.4. Life Expectancy

Life expectancy refers to the statistical measure of the average number of years a new born is expected to live under current mortality conditions. Adequate food absorption can be seen as the level of nutrition in children and adults. The level of adult health can be measured with the help of indicators like life expectancy, intake of calories, mortality rate or Chronic Energy Deficiency. Among all the indicators life expectancy is most important because the long lasting result of food security can be seen by the improvement of life expectancy of the population.

The increase of life expectancy in rural India is the indication of improvement in food security. Although life expectancy is low in many states and to achieve the high level of life expectancy standard of living should be improved, nutritional deficiencies should be removed and better medical facilities should be provided.

In the year 2013, In India according to the Health and Family welfare statistics, in rural India between the year 2010–2014, life expectancy of women at birth is 68.43 whereas Kerala has the highest life expectancy among all states followed by Punjab, Maharashtra, Tamil Nadu, Haryana, West Bengal and Gujarat having life expectancy of 72.45 yrs, 72.43 yrs, 72.43 yrs, 71.33 yrs, 70.82 yrs, 70.82 yrs and 70.01 which is higher than the life expectancy at National Level whereas the lowest life expectancy in rural India is of Assam of 64.61 yrs followed by Uttar Pradesh and Madhya Pradesh with 64.65 yrs, 64.96 yrs (Table 1.1 & Map 1).

Life expectancy is not the result of consumption of nutritious food for few days but its long term intake. It is also dependant on other factors such as level of education, Knowledge of nutrition and care of health by past generations. Consumption of good food for healthy and long life is one of its aspect. Absorption and assimilation of food is dependent on balanced diet and situation of health. Therefore for long life, balanced diet and consumption of calories is important aspect but not adequate guarantee because where life expectancy is high level of education is also high. Likewise, apart from calorie intake other factors are also responsible for high life expectancy.

1.5. Maternal Mortality Ratio

Maternal Mortality Ratio (MMR) is the number of maternal deaths caused due to complication during delivery per 1,00,000 live births. As per Sample Registration System (SRS), the maternal mortality rate of India is 178, whereas among states, Assam has the highest ratio of 328 followed by Uttar Pradesh, Rajasthan, Orissa, Madhya Pradesh, Chhattisgarh, Jharkhand and Bihar with 292, 255, 230, 230 and 219. Whereas the lowest Maternal Mortality ratio is of Assam followed by Maharashtra, Tamil Nadu, Andhra Pradesh and West Bengal which is less than the national average (Table 1.1 & Map 2).

1.6. Chronic Energy Deficiency (CED)

In Adults Chronic Energy Deficiency is the result of long term undernourishment and malnutrition which can be seen through Body Mass Index (BMI). BMI is used to find out the ideal weight limit of a person. It is calculated by dividing the weight of a person in kilograms by the height of a person in metre square. When BMI is less than 18.5 then the person is said to be suffering from malnutrition and is underweight. The person is said to have ideal weight when the BMI is between 18.5 and 24.9. Whereas when BMI is between 25 and 29.9, the person is said to be overweight and the person having BMI of more than 30 is said to be obese. Therefore BMI is an ideal tool to measure the nutritional status of an individual and malnutrition and obesity have their own side effects on the health of the person.

In rural India, in every state, the percentage of adul two men suffering from chronic energy deficiency is used as an indicator for the Adult Health

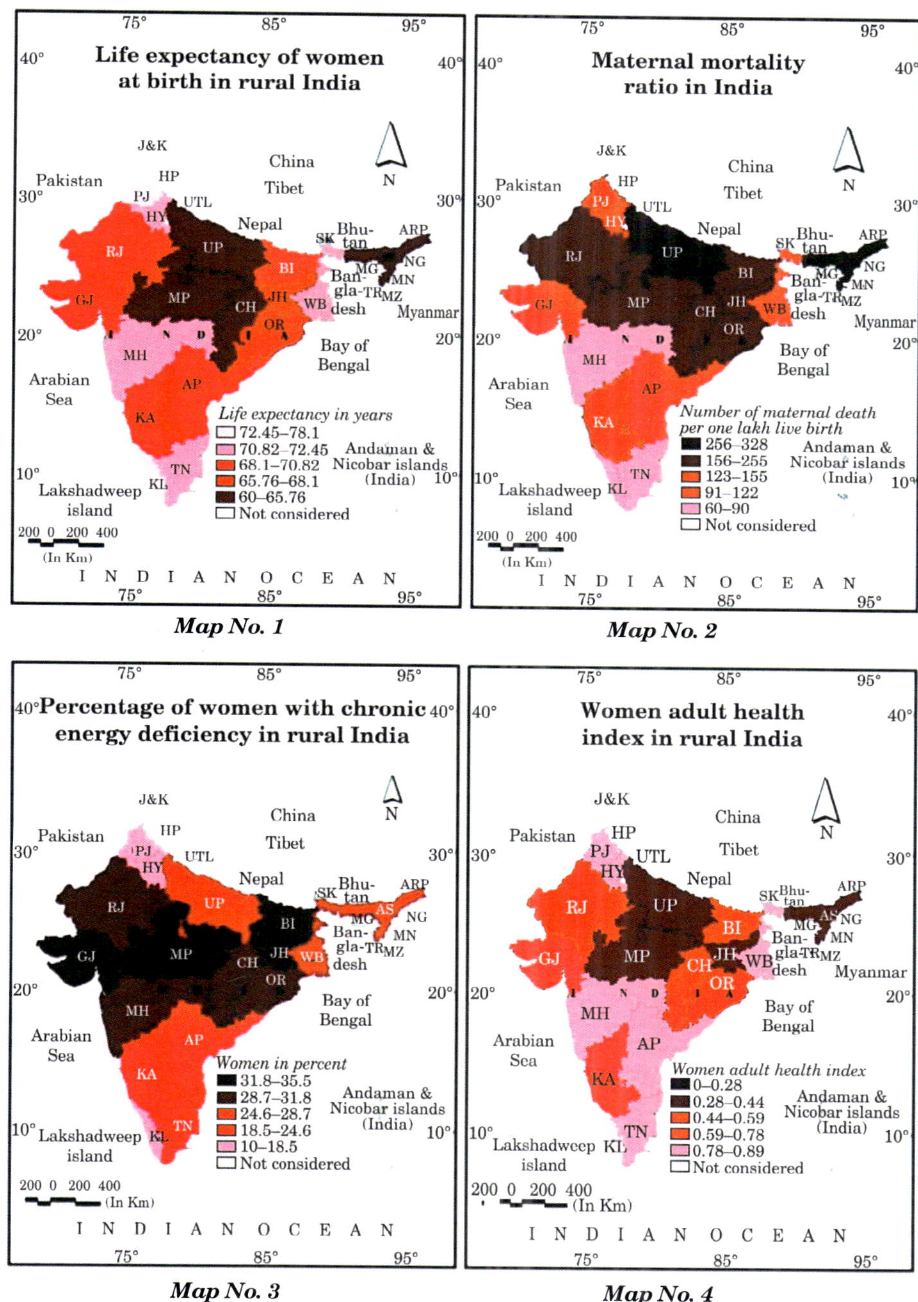

Map No. 1 to 3: Mapping Index of Women Adult Health Indicator in Rural India. ***Source:*** Calculated by Author (Based on Table 1.1)

Map No. 4: Mapping Index of Women Adult Health Index in Rural India. ***Source:*** Calculated by Author (Based on Table 1.2)

Index of a woman. From the analysis of percentage of women suffering from CED, in rural India, it is found that the highest percentage of women suffering from CED is in Jharkhand with 35.4% followed by Gujarat (34.3%), Bihar (31.8%), Madhya Pradesh (312.8%), Maharashtra (30%), Rajasthan (29.9%) and Chhattisgarh (29.6%). The states least affected by CED are Kerala (10.2%), Punjab (13.6%), Haryana (18.2%), Tamil Nadu (118.5%), Andhra Pradesh (20.3%) and Karnataka (24.3%). In other states the percentage lies between 24 and 29 (Table 1.1 & Map 3).

Apart from these in rural India there is a negative relation between the percentage of women affected from Chronic Energy deficiency and Rural Infrastructure Index. Therefore the states in which rural infrastructure is low percentage of adult women suffering from CED is more. Moreover the states in which there is a diversification in production and consumption, the percentage of women affected with CED is also less.

1.7. Women Adult Health Index in Rural India

The effect of Intake of calorie, protein and micronutrients can be seen on the health and nutrition level of an individual. Therefore the calculation of adult health index is done on three factors *i.e.,* Life expectancy of women, percentage of women affected with CED and Maternal Mortality Ratio (MMR) which shows the result of long term level of health. This index gives the comparative view of present health status of rural adult women among the states which are divided through Natural break of Arc view according to the status of states into 5 topographies (Table 1.2 & Map 4).

1.7.1. *Extremely low health status of women*

According to the analysis of Adult Health Index it is clear that in Rural India the condition of women is worst in 5 states *i.e.,* Chhattisgarh, Madhya Pradesh, Jharkhand, Uttar Pradesh and Assam whose class interval lies between 0.78 and 0.89. Among these 5 states, the condition of women is worst in Assam and Uttar Pradesh. Because of the bad situation of all the three indicators in these states, the health infrastructure in these states like maximum number of women affected with anaemia, more number of unvaccinated children, lack of pure drinking water and rural infrastructure and means of livelihood being less as compared to other states. According to the figures by Yojana Aayog in 2011–12 rural poverty in these states lies between 30–45%, families dependant on labour is more, lack of drinking water facility in the premises of the household results in waste of time and labour in fetching the water from long distances. According to the Drinking water, sanitation, hygiene and housing condition in India 2011–12 of NSSO, the average time spent by rural people per day in arranging for drinking water is 35 minutes. According to these reasons the health condition of women in these states is bad.

Table 1.2: Women adult health index (Actual value – Minimum value / Range) in rural India.

		1	*2*	*3*	*4*	*5*
Sl. no.	***State/ India***	***Index of life expectancy at birth in Rural India***	***Index of maternal mortality ratio in India (U+R)***	***Women whose BMI is below < 18.5 (%)***	***Adult health index***	***Rank***
1	Andhra Pradesh	0.650	0.17	0.40	0.41	13
2	Assam	1.000	1.00	0.67	0.89	1
3	Bihar	0.741	0.58	0.86	0.73	7
4	Chhattisgarh	0.931	0.63	0.77	0.78	5
5	Gujarat	0.600	0.21	0.96	0.59	9
6	Haryana	0.540	0.31	0.32	0.39	14
7	Jharkhand	0.915	0.58	1.00	0.83	3
8	Karnataka	0.629	0.30	0.56	0.50	10
9	Kerala	0.000	0.00	0.00	0.00	17
10	Madhya Pradesh	0.974	0.63	0.86	0.82	4
11	Maharashtra	0.420	0.08	0.79	0.43	12
12	Orissa	0.860	0.65	0.73	0.75	6
13	Punjab	0.419	0.34	0.13	0.30	16
14	Rajasthan	0.623	0.72	0.78	0.71	8
15	Tamil Nadu	0.502	0.09	0.33	0.31	15
16	Uttar Pradesh	0.997	0.86	0.71	0.86	2
17	West Bengal	0.540	0.19	0.57	0.44	11

Mapping index	***Mapping Typology***	***States***
0.78–0.89	1. Extremely low health status of women	CH, MP, JH, UP, AS
0.59–0.78	2. Very low health status of women	GJ, RJ, BI, OR
0.44–0.59	3. Low health status of women	WB, KA
0.28–0.44	4. Moderate health status of women	PJ, TN, HY, AP, MH
0–0.28	5. High health status of women	KL

Source: Calculated by Author

1.7.2. *Very low health status of women*

This typology whose class interval is between 0.59 to 0.78 consist of four states like Gujarat, Rajasthan, Bihar and Orissa. These states like the above mentioned states are kept in this group because of the following reasons *i.e.,* lack of health facilities and livelihood. Likewise the percentage of children unimmunized in the three states except Orissa is 39%, the percentage of women affected with anaemia is 48% and families dependent on labour income is between 25–39 percent. Although the condition of livelihood is good in Gujarat its impact is not seen on the health of women.

1.7.3. *Low health status of women*

In rural India, the adult health index of rural women lies in this group whose class interval lies between 0.44 and 0.59. Only two states fall in this group namely West Bengal and Karnataka. These states lie in this group because the health facilities and condition of livelihood is better as compared to other states.

1.7.4. *Moderate health status of women*

This typology whose class interval lies between 0.28 and 0.44 consist of five states namely Punjab, Tamil Nadu, Haryana, Andhra Pradesh and Maharashtra. The condition of health of rural women in these states is average *i.e.,* neither good nor bad because Punjab and Haryana are rich states with variety of food and easy access to livelihood the condition of health in these states is good. Whereas Tamil Nadu and Andhra Pradesh due to less poverty and better medical facilities belongs to this group although the number of families dependent on labour income are more in these states.

1.7.5. *High health status of women*

Only Kerala comes under this typology. In this state the women have best health condition, there are better health facilities and rural infrastructure, Public Distribution system is efficient and the transference of income from gulf countries is high which is the cause of the state's prosperity and because of these reasons Kerala falls in this group. Although the percentage of families dependent on labour income is 37.30 percent and Production of food is much less than the consumption.

2. CONCLUSIONS AND SUGGESTIONS

From the above analysis it is found that in rural India, the condition of health of women in the states of first two groups is bad and therefore there is a need to take immediate steps to improve it. For this with the initiation of new programmes, the past and existing programmes should be examined again and their limit and their feasibility should be ascertained. The following measures should also be taken to improve the health condition of women.

Besides educating rural people regarding the intake of micronutrients, facilities for educating women should be provided which will help in the long term improvement of their health condition because with this the age of marriage and conception will increase and they will have better physical growth. Besides Rural adolescent girls should be educated about pregnancy and nutritional needs during adolescence and nutrients intake for lactating mothers. Awareness regarding health and intake of nutrition should be created in them. This will help the future generation to ascertain the quality of life.

SUGGESTED READINGS

Bhatia, B.D., Tyagi, N.K. and Sur, A.M. (1988). "Nutritional indicators during pregnancy". *India Paed.*, 25(10): 952–59.

Dewan Manju (2008). "*Malnutrition in Women*". *Stud. Home Comm. Sci.*, 2(1): 7–10.

Gopalan, C. (1994). "Low birth weight: Significance and implications. Nutrition in Children, Developing Country Concerns "(New Delhi: Imprint).

Ransom Elizabeth, I. and Elder Leslie, K. (2003). "Nutrition of Women and Adolescent Girls: Why It Matters". This article is online downloaded from the Following website: http://www.prb.org/Publications/Articles/2003/Nutritionof WomenandAdolescentGirlsWhyItMatters.aspx

Rao Shobha (2001). "Nutritional status of the Indian population". *J. Biosci.,* 26(4).

Vir Sheila, C. and Malik Richa (2015). "Nutrition Situation of Women in India: Current Status, Implications on Child Undernutrition and Challenges Ahead". *Statistics and Applications* {ISSN 2454-7395(online)} (New Series), 13(1 & 2): 71–84.

17

Evidence of J-Curve Phenomenon in India Using Bounds Test Approach

JIGISHA SINGH[1*]

ABSTRACT

This paper empirically tries to investigate the short run and long run elasticity and absorption approaches on trade balance in India by taking quarterly data from 2000:01 to 2017:04. It utilizes ARDL bounds test approach to ascertain the long run association and short run dynamics between the trade balance, exchange rate, national income and money supply. There is some evidence that depreciation eventually improves trade balance. Moreover, there is presence of J-curve in India with lag.

***Key words*:** Trade balance, ARDL, Bounds test, J-curve.

INTRODUCTION

Depreciation has crucial impact on country's trade balance and is important for successful implementation of trade policy. The foreign trade policy changes were at center of structural reform measures India took in early nineties. In current economic climate, where countries' currency is losing its value, it becomes important to study the effect of depreciation on nation's macroeconomic aggregates. The paper tries to explore whether exchange rate depreciation improves trade balance, and whether appreciation worsens it.

Conventional theory says that, due to depreciation a country's import must fall because now it is expensive for home nationals to buy from abroad and exports should rise because now it is cheaper for foreign nationals. Thus, the net effect of these changes should result in positive trade balance.

[1] Aligarh Muslim University, Aligarh, UP (202001).
**Corresponding author*: E-mail: jigishasingh1993@gmail.com

The relationship between trade balance and exchange rate is much debated one. Much of the debate arises from the role of real exchange rate in effecting trade balance (Miles, 1979). Concludes that adjustment to depreciation is purely a monetary phenomenon involving only a portfolio adjustment and has no effect on trade balance. Still other researchers have argued that depreciation in fact impact trade balance though differ in timing and size of impact.

This paper explores the long run as well as short run relation between exchange rate and trade balance using the Marshall Lerner and J-curve phenomena. The J-curve is a path introduced by (Magee, 1973) that a nation's trade balance may follow over time following a depreciation of its currency. Many nations' trade balances have a tendency to worsen before improving. Tracing the path over time on a graph often resembles the shape of the letter J, hence the name J-curve. The Marshall-Lerner condition states that if the absolute value of nation's import and export elasticities add up to one or higher it is expected that depreciation will move trade balance towards surplus. However, if this condition is not met then it is possible to observe the J-curve path (Bahmani-Oskooee, 1985).

Diverse literature exists which explores whether depreciation of nation's currency leads to improvement in trade balance or not. The literature ranges from developed countries such as the US, Canada and Japan to a number of emerging Asian and European market economies as well as some developing African countries.

LITERATURE REVIEW

Review of some selected theoretical and empirical contributions on various aspects of exchange rate is presented here.

Kutan (2011) uses monthly data from 11 East Europen emerging economies to test the J-curve hypothesis. They conclude that Bulgaria, Croatia and Russia empirically supports J-curve phenomenon.

Onafowora (2003) tests Marshall Lerner conditions using vector error correction framework for 3 ASEAN countries *viz* Thailand, Malaysia and Indonesia. He finds that though Indonesia and Malaysia follow the J-curve hypothesis, Thailand is consistent with the S-curve pattern.

Yang (2004) using annual data from 1974 to 1994 and employing Cointegration and causality tests concludes that although with depreciation trade balance improves but no evidence of negative short run effect is seen.

This paper adds to the above empirical evidence by examining whether and how exchange rate affects trade balance in India in the long and short run. The period that is explored is from 2000 to 2017, when India, after structural and stabilization reforms in the 1990s, opened up and adopted more outward looking policies. However this period has broader relevance as it encompasses a large inflow of capital, substantial real exchange rate appreciation and ensuing current account deficit both in India.

DATA DESCRIPTION AND METHODOLOGY

Quarterly time series data from 2000:01 to 2017:04 is employed in this paper. The period so chosen is relevant for our study because this period witnessed a trade surplus after initial economic reforms in India. Data on trade of goods has been sourced from International Monetary Fund's "International Financial Statistics". Data on other variables such as GDP, exchange rate and money supply as taken from Reserve Bank of India. For money supply RBI's M3 has been used as a proxy variable. Variable trade balance used in analysis is calculated as ratio of exports to imports. Exchange rate is the rate of exchange between India and US. The data is seasonally adjusted and is in dollar terms to maintain uniformity in the analysis.

It is evident from Fig. 1 that trade balance depicts a puzzling picture, a sharp increase followed by steep fall. Overall the trade balance has been unfavorable and shows a declining trend. Exchange rate has been sharply increasing with a steep dip during the sub-prime financial crisis. GDP of

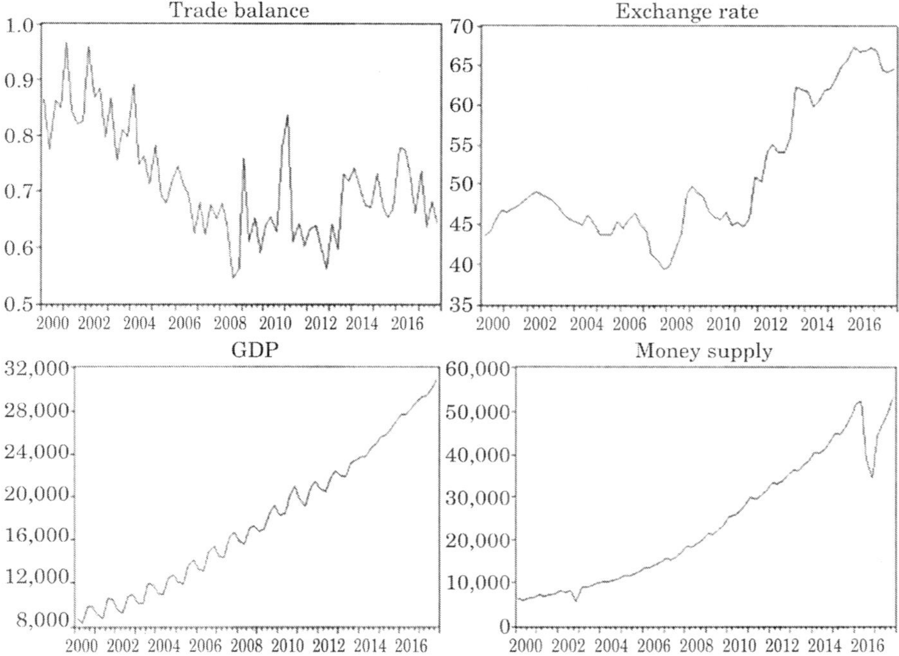

Fig. 1: Showing time series used in empirical analysis. ***Source:*** Author's Compilations

country is showing an upward increasing trend. A dip in money supply is witnessed beginning 2002:03 which ends at 2003:01. This behavior of money supply was because of large inflows from abroad which led to absorption of excess liquidity *via* policy operations which had a negative impact on monetary base. Again a sharp decline in money supply can be seen at end of sample period which was because of demonetization of currency.

We use the log-linear model to estimate the relation between chosen variables. Moreover, some literature suggests that the log-linear form is superior to the linear when it comes to applied work. Thus, a model has been developed by combining the core elements of absorption and monetary approaches to investigate the relationship between trade and its determinants. The model developed for the study is as follows:

$$\ln TB_t = a_1 + a_2 \ln ER_t + a_3 \ln GDP_t + a_4 \ln MS_t + e_t$$

where, lnTB = log of Trade Balance

lnER = Log of Exchange Rate

lnGDP = Log of GDP

lnMS = Log of Money Supply

et = Error Term

and ln stands for natural log

From the correlation matrix of the above variables we can decipher that exchange rate and trade balance have negative but non-significant relationship. On the other hand, exchange rate has positive and highly significant relation with GDP and money supply. Trade balance has negative correlation with GDP and money supply as well. Whereas money supply and GDP are positively correlated with strong correlation coefficient.

Correlation and Covariance Matrix

Covariance Correlation	*TB*	*ER*	*GDP*	*MS*
TB	0.0091			
ER	–0.10	68.71		
	–0.13	1		
GDP	–324.87	44492.48	41705613	
	–0.5257	0.831139	1	
MS	–657.46	1026348	92162687	2.13E+08
	–0.47	0.847423	0.976	1

Source: Author's Compilation

To explore the regression model Auto Regressive Distributed Lag (ARDL) or bounds test approach as introduced by Persaran *et al.* (2001) is employed. Bounds test approach is superior to other multivariate co-integration techniques such as developed by Johansen and Juselius (1990) because it allows the co-integration relationship to be estimated by OLS after the lag order of the model is identified and different variables can be assigned different lag-lengths as they enter the model. Secondly, ARDL model incorporates mixture of I(0) and I(1) series in same regression model. Thirdly, it involves regressing a single-equation set-up which makes it easier to implement and interpret the results and is efficient for small sample sizes.

Following Pesaran *et al.* (2001) we apply bounds test procedure by modeling the following equation:

$$\Delta\ln TB_t = \alpha_0 + \Sigma\alpha_i\Delta\ln TB_{t-i} + \Sigma\beta_j\Delta\ln ER_{t-j} + \Sigma\gamma_k\Delta\ln GDP_{t-k} + \Sigma\theta_l\Delta\ln MS_{t-l} + \Psi_0\ln TB_{t-1} + \Psi_1\ln ER_{t-1} + \Psi_2\ln GDP_{t-1} + \Psi_3\ln MS_{t-1} + e_t \text{ - - - - - - - - - -} \quad (1)$$

where, e_t is random error term and is assumed to be serially independent.

We perform "F-test" of the hypothesis

$$H_0: \Psi_0 = \Psi_1 = \Psi_2 = \Psi_3 = 0$$

Against the alternative hypothesis

$$H_1 = \Psi_0 \# \Psi_1 \# \Psi_2 \# \Psi_3 \# 0$$

The guideline for rejection of null hypothesis is that F-statistic is greater than upper-bound. If this persists, we conclude that there exists a dynamic long-run relationship between the variables. On the other hand, if computed F-statistic falls below lower bound than we interpret that the variables are I(0) *i.e.*, no Cointegration. If the F-statistic falls between the critical lower and upper bounds, the test is inconclusive. The critical values of bounds are obtained from Persaran and Chin (2001 p.)

Once we have successfully concluded that Co-integration exists between variables, we estimate long run model for TB_t as

$$\ln TB_{t =} \delta_0 + \delta_1\ln ER_t + \delta 2\ln GDP_t + \delta 3\ln MS_t + v_t \quad (2)$$

and the error correction model

$$\Delta\ln TB_t = \alpha_0 + \Sigma\alpha_i\Delta\ln TB_{t-i} + \Sigma\beta_j\Delta\ln ER_{t-j} + \Sigma\gamma_k\Delta\ln GDP_{t-k} + \Sigma\theta_l\Delta\ln MS_{t-l} + \theta z_{t-1}$$

$$\text{Where } z_t = (\ln TB_{t-1} - \delta_0 - \delta_1\ln ER_{t-1} - \delta 2\ln GDP_{t-1} - \delta 3\ln MS_{t-1}) \quad (3)$$

ESTIMATION AND RESULTS

To begin with the ARDL model we start with checking whether the series are I(0) or I(1) because the model is not stable if any of the series are I(2). To check for the stationarity of series we use Augmented Dickey Fuller test (Dickey & Fuller, 1979) and Dickey-Fuller Generalised Least Squares (DF-GLS) de-trending test as introduced by Elliot *et al.* (1996). DF-GLS test is used because it solves the problem of over rejection of null hypothesis by ADF test. When there is a presence of variables which are integrated of order two, it results in spurious results, we cannot interpret the values of F statistics provided by Pesaran *et al.* (2001).The results of Unit Root Tests are given in Table 1 and Table 2. ADF and DF-GLS test when applied to lnTB, lnER, lnGDP, lnMS at levels the results denotes the acceptance of null hypothesis that all the series have unit root.

Table 1: Unit test results at levels.

Variable	*ADF*	*DF-GLS*
	t-statistic	*t-statistic*
lnTB	–2.36	–1.54
lnER	–0.32	0.24
lnGDP	–0.56	0.42
lnMS	–1.13	1.04

Source: Author's Compilation

Table 2: Unit root test results at first difference.

Variable	*ADF*	*DF-GLS*
	t-statistic	*t-statistic*
lnTB	–3.43	–0.84
lnER	–6.41	–6.40
lnGDP	–3.75	–0.30
lnMS	–11.44	–10.20

Source: Author's Compilation

From Table 2 we can infer that when ADF and DF-GLS tests are applied to the first difference of the data series, we reject the null hypothesis of non-stationarity for all the variables used in this study. Thus, all the variables are integrated of order one.

Critical values for ADF and DF-GLS at 5% level are –2.90 and –1.94 respectively.

The estimation of ARDL model (equation1) is reported in Table 3. The results of the ARDL bound testing approach for co-integration shows that the value of computed F-statistic is 4.34 which is greater than the upper bound of critical values at 5 percent significance level as computed by Pesaran *et al.* (2001, p. 300). Following the bounds test we conclude that, we cannot reject the null hypothesis of no co-integration among the chosen variables and there in fact exists a dynamic association among the variables in the model.

Table 3: Estimated ARDL model based on equation 1.

Dependent Variable: ΔlnTB			
Variables	***Coefficient***	***T-Statistic***	***p-value***
$\Delta lnTB_{t-1}$	0.16	0.72	0.46
$\Delta lnTB_{t-2}$	0.21	1.02	0.31
$\Delta lnTB_{t-3}$	0.17	0.98	0.33
$\Delta lnTB_{t-4}$	–0.008	–0.006	0.95
$\Delta lnER_{t-1}$	–0.509	–1.33	0.18
$\Delta lnER_{t-2}$	–0.059	–0.16	0.87
$\Delta lnER_{t-3}$	(–0.564)***	–1.59	0.11
$\Delta lnER_{t-4}$	(–0.0997)*	–2.73	0.00
$\Delta lnGDP_{t-1}$	–0.130	–0.18	0.85
$\Delta lnGDP_{t-2}$	0.877	1.23	0.22
$\Delta lnGDP_{t-3}$	–0.583	–0.84	0.40
$\Delta lnGDP_{t-4}$	0.127	0.19	0.84
$\Delta lnMS_{t-1}$	–0.101	–0.53	0.59
$\Delta lnMS_{t-2}$	0.02	0.13	0.89
$\Delta lnMS_{t-3}$	0.00	0.001	0.99
$\Delta lnMS_{t-4}$	0.02	0.13	0.89
TB_{t-1}	(–0.916)*	–3.72	0.005
ER_{t-1}	(0.72)*	3.86	0.00
GDP_{t-1}	(–0.56)***	–1.71	0.09
MS_{t-1}	0.096	0.56	0.57

R^2= 0.665; AdjustedR^2=0.520; F-Statistic = 4.576 [0.000]*; *(**)*** denotes 1% (5%)10% significance level; ***Source:*** Author's Compilation

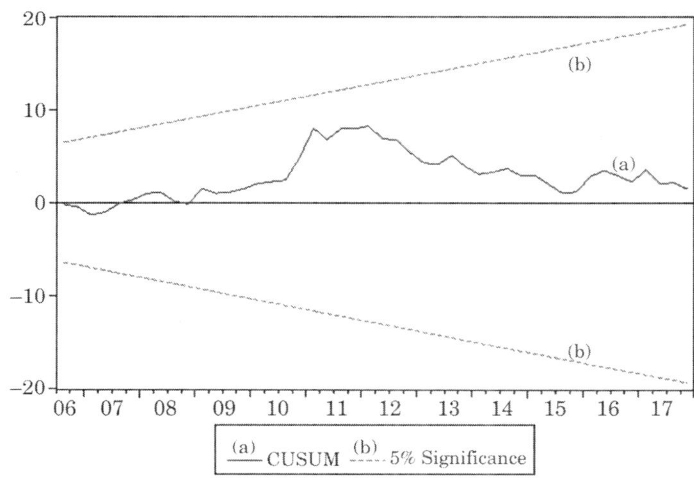

Fig. 2: Plot of cumulative sum of recursive residuals. ***Source:*** Author's Compilation

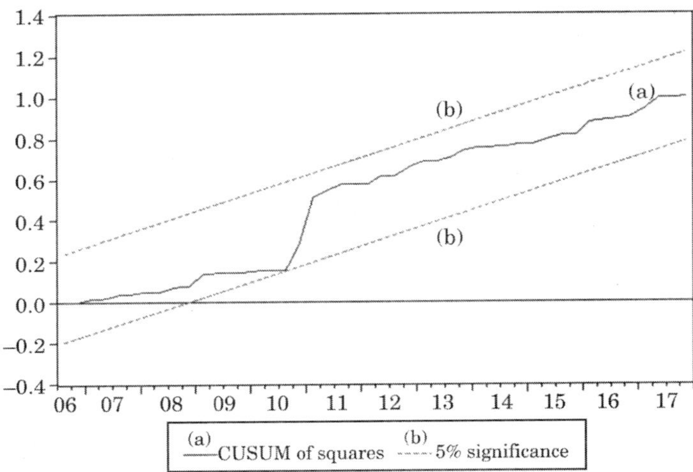

Fig. 3: Plot of cumulative sum of squares of recursive residuals. ***Source:*** Author's Compilation

The model thus estimated shows no sign of serial correlation. The stability of model is checked by CUSUM and CUSUMsq test and the results are shown in Fig. 2 and Fig. 3 respectively. The plots of both the CUSUM and the CUSUMsq lie within the boundaries of 5 percent significance band. So we can conclude that our model is stable.

Now once we have established co-integration between variables we can go for long run relation between them by estimating equation(3). The results of estimation are given in Table 4.

Table 4: Short run dynamics from error correction model.

Variable	***Coefficient***	***t-statistic***	***p-value***
$\Delta \ln TB_{t-1}$	0.20	0.92	0.36
$\Delta \ln TB_{t-2}$	0.25	1.24	0.21
$\Delta \ln TB_{t-3}$	0.20	1.16	0.24
$\Delta \ln TB_{t-4}$	–0.00	–0.03	0.97
$\Delta \ln ER_{t-1}$	–0.37	–0.99	0.32
$\Delta \ln ER_{t-2}$	–0.037	0.10	0.91
$\Delta \ln ER_{t-3}$	–0.44	–1.26	0.21
$\Delta \ln ER_{t-4}$	–0.82	–2.33	0.02
$\Delta \ln GDP_{t-1}$	–0.38	–0.58	0.55
$\Delta \ln GDP_{t-2}$	0.72	1.12	0.26
$\Delta \ln GDP_{t-3}$	–0.76	–1.14	0.25
$\Delta \ln GDP_{t-4}$	0.06	0.09	0.92
$\Delta \ln MS_{t-1}$	–0.06	–0.48	0.62
$\Delta \ln MS_{t-2}$	0.02	0.20	0.83
$\Delta \ln MS_{t-3}$	–0.03	–0.24	0.80
$\Delta \ln MS_{t-4}$	–0.01	–0.14	0.88
ecm_{t-1}	–0.9093	–3.72	0.00

Source: Author's Compilation

The coefficient of error-correction term is –90.93 and the p-value is 0.00. Therefore, the speed of adjustment towards long run equilibrium is 90.93% Wald test is also employed to test the robustness of long-run relationships among the variables. And we reject the null hypothesis of no causality. Further again the model was tested for serial correlation and stability. It was found that the model has no serial correlation and the polt of CUSUM and CUSUMsq lies within the 5% significance boundaries.

Although the coefficient of error correction term confirms high rate of convergence to equilibrium and causality runs from trade balance to exchange rate, GDP and money supply, the coefficients of model are not significant except exchange rate with last quarter.

The trade balance exhibits negative relation with GDP in first quarter which is consistent with the theory. This means that when nation's GDP increase it leads to fall in trade balance *i.e.,* increase in imports is greater than exports. The negative relation between exchange rate and trade balance means the Marshall Lerner conditions are not met and import and export elasticities do not add up to 1. The exchange rate is a statistically significant determinant of the trade balance following the depreciation of the Indian currency but with lags. This means that an effect of exchange rate can be seen on trade balance after fourth lag. The coefficients of exchange rate are negative evidence of J-curve phenomena for India.

CONCLUSIONS

This study examines the role of exchange rate, national GDP and money supply in determining movements of the trade balance in India. Combining elasticity and absorption approach a regression model is formed to analyze each of the models for the period of 2000:01 to 2017:04. Our results revealed the existence of long-run relationship among trade balance, exchange rate, income and money supply through ARDL bounds testing and ADF and DF-GLS tests were employed to investigate the order of integration of the running model. In long span of time, there exists a relation between trade balance, exchange rate, nation's money supply and income with robust results. Depreciation of exchange rate deteriorates the trade balance and improvements in trade policies are required to deal away with the trade deficit in future. Money supply had a weak negative relation with trade balance which was surprising. The results of this study also suggest that the Marshall-Lerner conditions are not met for India. Further the impact of the depreciation lingers for three additional periods in the future. This means that currency depreciation would be an appropriate tool to reduce trade deficit.

REFERENCES

Akbostan, E. (2002). "Dynamics of the Trade Balance: The Turkish J-curve. *ERC Working Papers*.

Backus, D.K. (1994). Dynamics of the Trade Balance and the Terms of Trade: The J-Curve. *American Economic Review*, pp. 84–103.

Bahmani-Oskooe, M. (1998). "Co-integration Approach to Estimate the Long-Trade Elasticities in LDCs. *International Economic Journal*, pp. 89–96.

Bahmani-Oskooee, M. (1985). "Devaluation and the J Curve: Some Evidence from LDCs". *The Review of Economics and Statistics*.

Bahmani-Oskooee, M.A. (2004). "ARDL Approach to Test the Productivity Bias Hypothesis". *Review of Development Economics*.

Bahmani-Oskooee (1992). "More Evidence on the J-Curve from LDCs" . *Journal Policy Modeling*, pp. 641–653.

Elliot, G.R. (1996). Efficient Tests for an Autoregressive Unit Root. *Econometrica*.

Engle, R.F. and Granger, C.J. (1987). Co-integration and Error Correction: Representation, Estimation and Testing. *Econometrica,* 55(2): 251–276.

Ferda (2007). "The bilateral J-curve: Turkey versus her 13 Trading Partners". MPRA Paper no. 3564.

Himarios (1989). "Devaluation Improve the Trade Balance and the Balance of Payments". *Canadian Journal of Economics*, pp. 806–823.

Johansen, S.J. (1990). Maximum Likeliwood Estimation and Inference on Cointegration-With Application to the Demand for Money. *Oxford Bulletin of Economics*, pp. 169–210.

Kutan, M.B.O. (2011). The J-curve in the emerging economies of Eastern Europe. *Applied Economics*.

Magee, S.P. (1973). Currency Contracts, Pass through and Devaluation, University of Chicago.

Meade, J.E. (1951). "The Balance of Payments". Oxford.

Onafowora, O. (2003). "Exchange Rate and Trade Balance in East Asia: Is there a J-curve. *Economics Bulletien*.

Pesaran, M.S. (2001). Bounds Testing Approaches to the Analysis of Level Relationships. *Journal of Applied Econometrics*, pp. 289–326.

Rose, A.A. (1989). Is There a J-Curve? " *Journal of Monetary Economics*.

S.S., A. (1959). "Effects of a Devaluation: A Simplified Synthesis of Elasticity and Absorption Approaches. *American Economic Review*, pp. 21–42.

Yang, J.A. (2004). Estimation of J-curve in China. East West Centre Working Papers.

18

FDI in Retail in India: An Attempt to Deepen India-US Economic Ties

MOHD. FAISHAL[1*]

ABSTRACT

The preeminent fortitude behind this research paper is to examine the affirmative chances of making strong relationship between India and United States of America through the gateway of foreign direct investment in retail sector. Choice-oriented consumers are contributing in the growth of Indian retail sector which is providing optimal factors for the intense development of Indian economy. If US retail companies get this opportunity to build up their empire in India, both countries would be benefitted economically as Indian consumers would be capacitated with modernization whereas US companies would be acquiring large number of consumers, it will deepen US-India economic relationship. This study intends at presenting some areas in retail sector which needs improvement particularly supply chain management and skill development and through giving invitation to US companies, we can make those improvements possible. Assessment of challenges in Indian retail sector has been done and findings indicate though Indian government has opened the door of opportunity for US companies but still there is a hindrance with the name of FDI in defense, some localization policies and intellectual properties issues are stumbling stone for US companies on the way of their arrival in India.

***Key words*:** Economic relationship, Indian retail sector, Indian economy, Foreign direct investment, Development.

[1] Aligarh Muslim University, Aligarh, UP (202001).
**Corresponding author*: E-mail: faisal0740@gmail.com

INTRODUCTION

Economic relationship has been established between India and the United States of America with bilateral ties that involve direct investment and trade. Since the doors to direct foreign investment has been opened up by Indian government in 2012 for foreign companies, it is become an aspiration for the US retail companies to invest in Indian retail market. "The singular act of opening the multi-brand retail sector to foreign direct investment will significantly benefit the Indian consumers by spurring the modernization of India's vast agri-retail market place" (U.S. India Business Council). US retail companies are contemplating a prosperous retail market in India due to business friendly norms by the Indian government and availability of enormous choice-oriented consumers with middle-class background. They are providing numerous opportunities for Indian consumers including availability of new fashion and series of retail stores in semi-urban retail markets in India.

It is evaluated that low percentage of economic risk with Indian retail market allures US companies to invest in this sector. Indian retail markets consist of organized and unorganized retail companies. Since India is the third-largest consumer-based market sector in the world, economist shave already marked that retail industry is playing a pivotal role in strengthen Indian economy. It has been proved that "Walmart" company is "Global Blimp Company" in the world market; hence India is also going to be benefitted by FDI in retail sector in case Multi-brand gets approved. With the advancement in technology, efficiency of human resource sector will improve and ultimately the economic relationship will also deepen. "India is one of the most attractive retail markets in the world, given its size and growth rate, and our investment is an opportunity to partner with the company that is leading the transformation of e-commerce in the market" (McMillon-President of WallMart). This topic has a multi-pronged approach along with different opinions and debates.

1. U.S. India Business Council was formed in 1975 as an organization to encourage investment from private sectors from both countries.

HISTORICAL BACKGROUND OF INDIA AND THE US ECONOMIC RELATIONSHIP

The history of US-Indian relations has always been topic of discussion. In the last few years, significant efforts have been made to integrate the country into the global economic matrix. This new sense of pragmatism that pervades India's economic sector stimulates the national security dialogue as well. Gary Bertsch, Seema Gahlaut and Anupam Srivastava (2003), pointed that as modern India searches for its changing place in the community of nations, it presents unique challenges as well as opportunities to the world's largest democracy, the United States. India has completed a decade of economic growth at twice the pace of the previous half century. Its politics have shifted from the dominance of a single party to a pattern of coalitions. The end of the Cold War changed the character of its close ties with the US and is emerging as its most important extra regional relationship.

Before the connect with Europeans, America and India had robust production and trade economies, even if they did not meet the definition of modern capitalism. For instance Charles Harrington outlines two eras (pre-1491 and twentieth and early twenty first century tribal economies) and finds much of value in both. Similarly Joseph Scott Gladstone recounts pre-contact and historical trade patterns among a variety of Indian groups. He looks at trends in more recent post-contact history that have tended to undermine Indian trade and business. Post-contact economic movement in native communities has traditionally been largely top-down, motivated by government policies and officials. Srivastava also considers the costs and benefits challenging India as it evaluates the international missile non-proliferation efforts and the costs and benefits to the United States and the Missile Technology Control Regime (MTCR), as they seek to engage India. He proposes a number of recommendations to India and US in the civilian and military sections. These recommendations lay the ground work for Indo-US engagement, and economic and security cooperation, in the space and missile issue area.

Gahlaut states that the present period is suitable for initiating non-symbolic public dialogue in both the countries. With the end of the Cold War, some new factors have been considered in the policy environment. These include the changing priorities of the post-independence generation in India and the recent successes of economic liberalization in India. Indira Gandhi had informed the Indian Parliament that the "Atomic Energy Commission is studying conditions under which peaceful nuclear explosions can be carried out underground without causing environmental hazards and this could be of economic benefit to India. In the past despite several instances of overlapping security interests, US-Indian relations have had divergent worldviews that led both countries not to develop the type of relations that United States had with other major democracies.

As pointed by Amit Gupta (2005), the initial uncertainties between the two nations after the independence stemmed because of India's adoption of a socialist economy and its reluctance to entrust the western coalition subsequently resulted in cold war. The association momentarily flourished throughout and instantly after the Korean War with India. As member of the United Nations (UN) armistice commission, it soon ran stranded with the twin crises of 1956-Hungary and Suez. Relations between the two countries again briefly flourished after the Sino Indian war of 1962 when the United States transferred conventional weapons to India. At the economic level, India became a major recipient of US assistance. The US provided significant amounts of food aid to India in the 1960s first to tide over the country during the Bihar famine and later to start an agricultural Green Revolution in the country.

Anjali Sahay (2009) pointed that, "Initially the United States emerged as the global leader of the twentieth century in various affairs, both ideological and military, especially after the Second World War in 1945". India's political and economic history after independence in 1947 was turbulent and chaotic, facing internal challenges of post colonialism, poverty, backwardness, growth, and diversity. After the Second World War both inherited their share of prejudices and viewed each other with suspicion. India had seen that US was obsessed with anticommunism and on the other hand US viewed India as firmly placed in the socialist camp with Nehru, who was showing obvious affinities for the Soviet Union, in particular for socialism. But despite Washington's unsympathetic views on India's economic policies and in particular the debt crisis in the 1980s, the United States managed to maintain a relationship of sorts with India, providing economic assistance in times of need.

The end of the Cold War and globalization coupled with India's economic reforms and liberalization led to one of the most "strategic partnerships" that of India and United States. Even though they had immense diverse aims, doctrines, ideologies and schemas, both countries remained firm advocates of democracy and the free market economy. The United States is currently India's largest trading partner and India is one of the largest investment sites for US based multinational corporations. An era of increased economic interdependence and greater foreign trade coupled with the revolution in information technology and communications. This has eventually spurred on the movement of people across countries and continents. A different kind of relationship between the two countries has thus emerged with the movement of people from India to the United States and it has increased by four folds since 1990s. Thus it becomes important to classify significant political and economic events central to both countries to gain a better perception on the migration linkage.

Many new chapters have been added in Indian-US economic relationship until today. A trade agreement on agricultural sector has been approved by both countries in 2005 and this agreement got revived many times. This has developed a strong foundation between both countries in the sector of economic development. This agreement involves bilateral knowledge advancement initiatives and capacity building program through establishing research institutions. Apart from this agricultural agreement, free trade agreement is also in the pipeline. Different opinions have been accumulated on free trade agreement. "For too long, ambitious for the US-India economic relationship have not matched the soaring strategic rhetoric" (Raymond & Vickery, 2018). While US-India economic meet, US ambassador quoted, "I want to see a US-India FTA...a strategic view of our economic relationship could eventually lead to a road map for a US-India Free Trade Agreement,".

This would result in relationship getting stronger if free trade agreement gets approved unanimously by both countries but unfortunately several debates are still giving a clear demonstration of disapproval.

FDI IN RETAIL SECTOR IN INDIA: A DOOR OF OPPORTUNITIES FOR US

Foreign Direct Investment or FDI is an investment or a contribution made by an enterprise or firm in one country for business related interest in another country. When an investor sets up business operations or gets a foreign business asset then FDI takes place. In India FDI is regulated by Foreign Exchange Management Act, 2000 governed under Reserve Bank of India (RBI). A person can invest in India through under Automatic Route that does not demand from RBI.

The most obvious development in FDI is the global economic landscape. FDI provides a win-win situation both to the host as well as home country. FDI is assumed to uplift output, technology, employment and skill levels in other sectors and regions of economy. India is receiving FDI inflows from a number of sources but large percentage of FDI inflows is vested with few major countries. Retail trade is one that cuts off smaller portions from large lumps of goods. The Retail sector of India is vast and has huge potential for growth and development, as the majority of its constituents are un-organized.

Federation of Indian Chambers of Commerce and Industry (FICCI) has notified in a report that after the arrival of FDI, advancement and improvement in Indian Retail Sector is observed. Following are the areas that have been marked in which there is a large scope of advancement.

- Advancement in Supply Chain Management
- Investment in Technology
- Manpower and Skill Development
- Tourism Development
- Advancement in Agriculture
- Efficiency in Small Scale Industries.

All these areas would positively influence in establishing US companies and India will also get an advantage of improvising infrastructure along with human resource. This exchange of knowledge and technology will boost both countries' relationship and may explore more sectors to be collaborated. This collaboration would lead towards a strong relationship where both countries will get equal opportunity of economic development.

"The retail world is undergoing a fast paced revolution, one which is being driven by consumers and fuelled by tech advancements. The pace of this revolution is remarkable with no sign of slowing down, provided all stakeholders embrace this change simultaneously." (JLL)

Retail investors will keep an eye on the report by "Global Retail Development Ranking" for having a clue on the emerging markets that will lead them towards optimal growth in investment. This global ranking includes 25 macroeconomic and retail specific variables to assess the performance of developing countries. This is an affirmative fact that now India leads among 30 developing countries in retail sector. India obtained top rank in Global Retail Development Ranking, 2017. There were three key factors, mentioned in report which are driving Indian retail market towards concrete growth.

- Rapidly expanding economy (Indian retail industry is contributing high in GDP and capacitating its population with employment which is ultimately strengthening India's economy)
- Relaxation of FDI rules (100% FDI is allowed in B2B commerce, online retail sector is booming)
- Consumption (India has 2nd largest population which promotes high consumption as well as creates large markets)

This reports had an positive data which was giving a clear demonstration towards the fact that "India's retail sector has been growing at an annual rate of 20%". This report also published that e-commerce is playing an important role in growing potential of retail sector as it has become easier also to operate e-businesses with ease of doing business as well as with the availability of easy mode of payment.

A comparative analysis between the performance of India and China in retail sector can be done. India was holding 20th rank in "Global Retail Development Ranking", 2014 and China was at 2nd rank but now India has outdone China and has been emerged as a largest country for retail industry. China is seeing a growth in retail market due to its population and its attractive size of retail markets, but due to FDI rules and inarguable efforts by the Indian government it is grown to achieve this top rank and success.

"Because of the increased use of social media on smart phones and social media's involvement in retail sales, "social selling" has become red hot. Anyone hoping to improve their online sales success must take advantage of emerging trends" (Eddie Machaalani, Co-founder of Big commerece).

With the advancements of mobile networks, consumers are getting attracted towards online business in India. Since 4G network has been launched in India, it has become easier to reach to the targeted audience. E-Commerce is holding its feet in Indian retail markets which are increasing by leaps and bounds. Several of government policies have contributed positively towards the establishment of online business in India like - Digital

India, Make in India, Digital Wallets and other initiatives. The most important factor is the ease in digital payments which has resulted in less or completely no hindrance in the way online business.

M-commerce is also a part of online business which allows running a business completely through smart phone. Variety of smart phones ranges has become popular among all generations in India which ultimately fosters an environment for doing online business. All these online businesses have contributed in the development of retail sector in India.

FDI is benefitting USA in a tremendous way as India is acquiring goods and services in huge amount from it.

For example: Lay's is a brand name of potato chip company that was founded in the U.S. in 1932. It is also called Frito-Lays. These chips are manufactured by USA and exported to many other countries as well as in India. The chips present in the wrapper are of 10 to 20g but the expense of it is Rs. 20 for the small one and Rs. 40 for the large one. The actual cost of potatoes for 1.2 kilo or two and a half pounds or 8–10 potatoes is very less. This brand is providing a lot of profit to the USA. However, by promoting this which is a junk food brand it is causing lot of ill-effects on children's health.

There are many more retail goods which India is getting imported that are of sheer wastage for the country, like Mac Donald's, KFC's, Dominos and endless more goods.

Liberty Shoes has been operating or managing for more than 60 years and has established its presence around everywhere. Currently with an annual turnover exceeding Rs. 5 billion (US$ 80.3 million), the company is amongst the top five manufacturers of leather footwear industry in the world, producing more than 50,000 pairs a day using a capacity of more than 0.3 million square feet of leather per month. This statistics itself illustrations the profit gain of US brand across the globe and majorly in India.

Challenges of FDI in the Retail Sector of India

"The industrial policy 1991 had crafted a trajectory of change whereby every sectors of Indian economy at one point of time or the other would be embraced by liberalization, privatization and globalization. FDI in multi-brand retailing and lifting the current cap of 51% on single brand retail is in that sense a steady progression of that trajectory" (Agrawal, 2011). The retail segment in India has undergone extensive makeover in the past 10 years. Traditionally, Indian retail sector has been characterized by the existence of a large number of small-unorganized retailers. However, in the past decade there has been growth of organized retailing, which encouraged large private sectors players to invest in this sector. The majority of the foreign players have penetrated India through diverse paths such as test marketing, franchising, wholesale cash-and-carry operation. With the higher GDP growth, increased liberalization and consumerism of the manufacturing sector, India is being portrayed as an attractive target for foreign direct investment (FDI) in retailing. However, at present, this is one of the few sectors, which is closed to FDI.

Within the country there has been major protest from trading associations and other stakeholders against allowing FDI in retailing. Arpita, Mukherjee and Nitisha Patel (2005) analyzed in their studies- The current retail development in India and inspected the growth across different segments of retailing. They also evaluated the impact of allowing FDI in retailing. The recent few years has witnessed a large number of big players like Reliance, Tata, Pantaloon, Birla etc jumping into retailing. The Government's decision to allow foreign investors to open single brand retail stores would result multiple affects and stimulate growth in mall culture. Single brand retail has received 51% FDI investment permit and would enhance the investment situation of the country. This in turn will lead to tough competition in Indian retail sector and thus the need for pioneering marketing strategies will arise.

Girish K. Nair and Harish K. Nair (2011) of A T Kearney, the renowned global management consultancy, reported that India has been lately identified as the second most attractive retail destination globally from among thirty emergent markets. With a input of 14% to the national GDP and utilizing 7% of the entire personnel in the country, the retail industry is undeniably one of the supports of the Indian economy.

The importance of internet retailing is growing all over the world. A few of internet retailers, such as rediff.com and e-bay are providing vendors a proposal to advertise their product online, however they do not take the responsibility for delivering the product to the buyer. They offer only virtual shopping space to the vendors. On the other hand, online retailers such as amazon.com and walmart.com maintain their own warehouses to stock products and do take responsibility for delivering products to the buyers. With the rapid growth of the Internet and globalization of market, the retail sector has become an increasingly competitive and dynamic in nature. Business and marketing activities are also affected by the infusion of Internet technologies and are revolutionizing constantly in all aspects of marketing. The retail industry is in the midst of a revolution.

As quoted by Manfred Krafft, Murali K. Mantrala (2009) despite the current developments in retailing and its enormous contribution to the economy, retailing continues to be one of the least evolved industries. The growth of organized retailing has been much slower as compared to the rest of the world. Over a phase of 10 years, the share of organized retailing in total retailing has developed from 10 percent to 40 cent in Brazil and 20 percent in China, while in India it is only 2 percent (between 1995–2005). India has not imposed the minimum capital requirement condition in any sector and hence it is not being imposed in retailing as well. FDI should not be restricted to certain product types (*i.e.*, branded products) or store formats (large department stores). Rents are a challenge for retailers, as cost of acquiring retail space in India is increasing. A study indicates that rentals in established malls, in top metropolitan areas have jumped by 20–30% in the last 6 months.

Multiparty coalition governments have become increasingly common in India because of which the decision making is become difficult. For example the decision to allow FDI in retail initially looked uncomplicated but became complex as a consequence of the political situations. Such decisions are largely influenced by the political emotions of the constituencies of the diverse political parties. Until a single party forms a government at the Center, there are likely to be delays in taking few critical decisions. There are also some of the regulatory issues that international players may find it difficult to tackle and some issues that are not in common to the domestic and the foreign players. For example, the Land and Property laws specify that only Indians have the right to own land and property in India and this may act as an inhibiting factor for foreign retailers. Also, the tax structure of India is not favorable to the foreign players. According to the industry sources, the corporate tax rate for domestic companies is 36.59%, whereas it is 42.82% for foreign companies.

Currently the labor laws are slanted more towards protecting the jobs of store workers, which is in contrary to the requirement of running modern formats. Adjustments to store operation timing and labor laws would help both the foreign and domestic retailers. In order to encourage global retailers to come to operate in India, the government may need to modify some laws and regulations. Technology plays a major role in retail developments in India. In a country where almost 97% of retailing is in the hands of small independent retailers, it can be expected that retailers are going to have some operational inefficiency. The impact of the entry of foreign retailers on employment is controversial. While some studies show that they have led to increase in employment, there are few more studies that show they have led to unemployment by forcing the local players out of business. Entry of large low-cost retailers leads to lower prices. Global retailers carefully plan their international operations, even before entering a new market they should do a feasibility study and design the best strategy for market entry.

FDI in Defense and US Perspective: A New Vision For Economic Relationship

"Significant tariff and non-tariff barriers, subsidies, localization policies, restriction on investment and intellectual property concerns that limit market access and impede US exporters and businesses from entering the Indian market." (National Review Journal) FDI in defense would lead to more opportunities for strong economic relationship. However with respect to defense area, major multinational companies are unwilling for invest in India as a result of government's ambiguous policy. India is seeking a positive response in investment with respect to manufacturing of military weapons and transports along with aircraft. However the multinational companies are unwilling for this "Technology Transfer".

However defense is an area in India where further scope for improvement in economic relationship of both countries is required.

How US and India is Going to Benefit From FDI

FDI is replacing trade as the principal provider of goods and services across the borders. Most of the direct investment in the United States comes from other highly developed nations. Theodore H. Moran, Lindsay Oldenski (2013), noted that the top three are all European countries, with Japan ranking fourth. China is the 18th largest source of FDI in the United States. Many qualms about the effects of foreign multinationals entering United Nations are based on pragmatic questions about the characteristics of foreign investors and their performance. This holds true for questions about employment, wages, trade and the types of activities that foreign firms choose to look for in United States in comparison to US companies. As per the studies, of David Marchick (2006) evidences are presented that foreign owned firm which is operating in the United States actually performed better on a number of measures than US owned firms.

Americans have for long been uncertain towards foreign direct investment (FDI) in the US. The US tax system is predominantly business unfriendly for foreign companies which takes into account the United States as a site for business (Hufbauel & Wong, 2011). At 39 percent, the combined US tax rate is 11 percent points higher than the unweighed average of contending countries. However, it is not just the statutory taxes that make the US unfriendly to businesses. There is huge demand for software services where the employees are outsourced to America to work with the American clients; however they are times when they are sent back to native land from the United States. As observed by K.S. Mehra (2000), US is the main trading partner of India; as nearly twenty percent of Indian exports in the eighties were directed to the U.S. Similarly, nearly forty percent of (FDI) is coming from the U.S. It has been observed that US will remain the largest trading partner in the medium and long run even after the recent enforcement of NAFTA.

The USA accounts for about forty percent of the world production and consumption of communication services. India needs more telecom services and in the recent past has adopted new policies regarding both basic and value added services. India has a large diversity of attractions to offer with respect to tourism however, there is a scope for improvising. Official tourism promotion agencies, travel agents, tour operators and airlines should be motivated to develop effective functional tie-ups with their American counterparts to increase the flow of US tourists into India. As for foreign direct investment, the fiscal and FERA laws in India have been considerable liberalized and India has become attractive to the US investors. Though US is the most important source of FDI in India and the share of FDI from the US is increasing after liberalization, some reservations still persist among the US investors. Indian firms regard the US as a good source of technology and technology transfer. India is now looking for technology which will be internationally competitive.

US have been the largest source of imported technology for India, and it continues to be so in the post-liberalization period. Relative to other developing countries, the US affiliates spend highest on R&D in India. It is believed that FDI will stay in India in the event of a currency crisis, and it is believed that FDI is bolted down as it involves investment in physical plants and equipment which is hard to get cleared off. Foreigners believe and trust their markets; and organizations do not feel the need to be physically present to earn returns. That is why economists in US have been getting anxious about the rise in the share of FDI in total flows.

Munir Hassan (2006), states that India and the US the world's largest democracies have realized that in the present globalised administration, both the nations cannot remain in segregation. Ever since the launch of India's liberalized regime, there has been a massive enhancement in Indo-US economic relations especially on trade and investment (FDI) horizons. Both the countries are enriching their economic relations on all horizons. Trade is rising; FDI is on the increase and more people are travelling. Indian exports to the USA in the last 10 years have increased by 234.2 percent, while imports from the US went up by 47.3 percent; US exports to India are up by 50 percent and India's exports by 15% for the first 3 months. The US wants to trade with India, and trade is expected to increase sharply in other directions too. Indo-US trade is growing sharply and the US commitment to develop deep economic and commercial ties with India has never been stronger. Being India's top trading partner, the US accounts for nearly a fifth of India's merchandise export and a tenth of India's non oil imports. However it accounts for a tiny share in the US global merchandise trade.

Due to advanced exports to US and lesser imports from US, the balance of Indo-US trade has continued to linger in India's favor, given enormous inequality in per capita incomes between the two countries. In addition to large US corporate, it appears that small and medium firms in the US possess considerable potential for transfer of technology to India. It is therefore necessary to strengthen contacts between Indian firms and the small and medium firms in the US. To sum up, there is a large potential for expanding the Indo-US economic relations. To realize the potential, government to government dialogue as well as growing contacts and business relationships between Indian and US business are essential. The rate of return in the manufacturing sector in India on US FDI is high enough to attract US FDI. Trade associated with US FDI is a very important activity for any host country because MNC's have marketing network which can create exports for the host countries. Keeping in mind the persisting trends, India and the US have an urgent need to develop sound and new policies for trade in dual use items, which would protect national security and anti-proliferation objectives.

CONCLUSIONS

Many research papers, comparative studies and debates have taken place over this topic that trade is one of the strongest pillars which holds the powerful relationship of India and US. This has definitely is said to have transformed India-US relationship. Though this relationship entails disputes and concerns at strategic level, they are growing partner at economic level. Gradual improvement in the relationship between the countries is observed as there are reports which indicate positive talks between Prime Ministers of both the nations. "On the economic side, the two sides had very productive discussions. The economic changes in both countries are creating new demands and once you have the high level comfort between India and the U.S., the other partner is well placed to meet those demands" (S. Jaishankar).

REFERENCES

"Aam bania is more powerful than the aam aadmi" (2011). The Times of India.

"Backlash grows over reform of Indian retail" (2011). The Financial Express.

Bertsch Gary, Gahlaut Seema and Srivastava Anupam (2013). "Engaging India: U.S. Strategic Relations with the World's Largest Democracy", Routledge, p. 312.

Borensztein, E., Gregori, J. De and Lee, J.W. (2010). How Does Foreign Direct Investment affect Economic Growth? *Journal of International Economics*, 45(1): 115–135.

"Commerce Minister Anand Sharma speaks to NDTV on FDI", NDTV (2011).

"Discussion Paper on Foreign Direct Investment (FDI) in Multi-Brand Trading" (PDF) (2001). Indian Venture Capital and Private Equity Association.

"FDI in retail, India debate: Parliament of India (2012)".

"For India's Consumers, Pepsi Is the Real Thing" (2010). *Bloomberg Business Week*.

Global Insights. "The Economic Impact of WalMart" (PDF).

Grant Tavia (2011). "The Wal-Mart effect: Food inflation tame in Canada". The Globe and Mail, Toronto.

Gupta Amit (2005). "The U.S.-India Relationship: Strategic Partnership or Complementary Interests?" Diane Publishing, pp. 5–15.

Gupta, S.L. (2007). Retail Management: An Indian Perspective Text and Cases, Wisdom Publications, Print

"Indian retail kings around the world", Rediff., (2011).

Pradhan Swapna (2009). Retailing Management, New Delhi, Tata McGraw Hill Companies, Print

"Revolt escalates against Indian retail reform" (2011). The Financial Express.

Sahay Anjali (2009). "Indian Diaspora in the United States: Brain Drain or Gain?" Lexington Books, pp. 57–65.

"Walmart Fact Sheets", Walmart (2011).

"Walmart Asia to make India an export hub". Business Standard (2010).

"Whole Foods annual report, FY 2010" (PDF). Whole Foods, (2011).

19

Foreign Direct Investment Inflows and Macroeconomic Variables in India: Approach from Time Series Analysis

ISHFAQ HAMID[1], PABITRA KUMAR JENA[1] AND AQIB MUJTABA[1]

ABSTRACT

This study is based on two objectives, the first one is to investigate the determinants of foreign direct investment (FDI) inflows into India at the macro level on the basis of monthly data and the second one is to cognize the structural paths between FDI inflows and Macroeconomic Variables in India. Stepwise linear regression method is used for finding out the determinants of FDI inflows. Whereas structural Equation Modelling (SEM) has been used to find out the structural paths between FDI inflows and Macroeconomic Variables in India. The study finds that on the basis of monthly data five variables (export, saving with commercial banks, money supply, exchange rate and inflation rate) stand out as significant determinants for FDI Inflows into our country after globalization. The study also finds that 19 significant paths are possible between FDI inflows and different Macroeconomic variables. India should plan for boosting exports as it would lead to better FDI inflows. Because there are some FDI which are export oriented. India should control more rises in WPI because it discourages foreign investor to invest in India. Since it is an important determinant for deciding FDI inflows, India should have a tight policy to control this variable. Further, the paper goes on to discuss some of the policy suggestion for better inflows of FDI in India.

Key words: Foreign direct investment, Human capital, Macro Economic Variables and Structural equation modeling.

JEL Classification: F21, E24, E29 and C30

[1] Shri Mata Vaishno Devi University, Katra, Jammu and Kashmir (182320).
Corresponding author: E-mail: bhatishfaq260@gmail.com

1. INTRODUCTION

India is being eyed upon as one of the largest economies in terms of market size by several developed countries including some developing economies too. It has been ranked among the top 10 attractive destinations for Foreign Direct Investment (FDI) inflows. The main objective behind the introduction of several rounds of FDI reforms is to invite global players for opening up their subsidiaries in the country and cause for massive foreign capital inflows. Therefore the trend analysis of FDI data also supplements this idea by showing 266% growth of FDI since 1991 (129 million USD) to 2014 (34.4 billion USD). Not only the magnitude of FDI increases but also it affects various macroeconomic variables like national income in aggregate and in per capita, its growth rate, capital formation, industrial set-up, money supply, inflation rate, volume and direction of trade exchange rates and foreign exchange reserve. Empirical findings also suggest that FDI inflows plays a major role in promoting national welfare by enhancing competitiveness, technological advancements, and increment in human capital. The benefits of FDI include serving as a source of capital, employment generation, facilitating access to foreign markets, and generating both technological and efficiency spillover to local firms. It is expected that by providing access to foreign markets, transferring technology and generally building capacity in the host country firms, FDI will inevitably improve the integration of the host country into the global economy and foster growth (Kathuria, 2000).

The Neo-Classical Growth Model, as well as endogenous growth models, provide the foundation for most of the empirical works on the relationship between FDI and economic growth. On one hand, trade liberalization may lead to macroeconomic instability by making terms of trade unfavorable and on the other hand, it may help in the process of economic growth when a country utilizes its abundant factor of production in an efficient manner. There is a pool of empirical and theoretical literature which explains the role of FDI in economic growth. A positive relationship between these two factors is conventionally supported by some empirical studies, though there are still conflicting views on heterogeneous impacts of FDI in economic growth. Another interesting aspect related to FDI and economic growth is the causality between these two factors. It is important to determine the direction of causality between these two variables because it can provide a government with guidelines for their future economic policy making. However, this causality is still controversial and ambiguous since it varies across countries. There is no uniform pattern of the impact of FDI on promoting economic growth.

The impact of FDI can be analyzed by either microeconomic or macroeconomic perspectives. By and large, the existing studies have looked at the FDI-GDP growth nexus, but their results have been far from conclusive. While some researchers reported that direction of causality is from FDI inflow to economic growth, some others showed the direction of causality is from economic growth to FDI inflow and yet others concluded that there is bidirectional causality between FDI inflow and economic growth whereas some researcher showed that there is no causality between FDI inflow and economic growth. Not only economic growth but also other macroeconomic variables do affect the FDI inflows and are also being affected by the same. Therefore there is a need to investigate a structural path relationship between FDI inflows and Macroeconomic Variables.

The rest of the paper is organized as follows. The next section introduces a brief review of the theoretical and empirical literature. Section 3 highlights the need and significance of the present study. The estimation strategy, data, and variable constructions, an econometric methodology is illustrated in section 4. Section 5 and 6 is devoted to the analyses of the determinants of FDI inflows into India after globalization and structural paths between FDI inflows and macroeconomic variables in India. Finally, section 7 concludes the paper with some strong policy recommendations.

2. A BRIEF LITERATURE REVIEW

It is seen from the literature review that major determinants of FDI inflows at macro level which can be measured are Gross Domestic Product at Factor Cost (GDPFC), Growth Rate of Gross Domestic Product (GRGDPFC), Gross Domestic Capital Formation (GDCF), Gross Domestic Saving (GDS), Per Capita Income (PCI), Wholesale Price Index (WPI), Real Effective Exchange Rate (REER), Index of Industrial Production (IIP), Index of Infrastructure Condition (IIC), Foreign Institutional Investment (FII), Money Supply (MS), Export (EX), Import(IM), Trade Balance (TB) and Openness of the economy (OPEN). Several authors have dealt with these facts.

Apart from the above determinants, there are also some qualitative factors which cannot be measured in quantitative terms at macro level governing FDI inflows into India. They are; absorption capacity of the host country, skill level of labour force, tastes and preferences, level of technology, availability of natural resources of the host country, availability of information regarding market, environment condition of the host country, political condition of host country, tax policy, trade policy, legal structure and level of corruption (Ang (2008); Asiedu (2008); Sahoo (2006); Root & Ahmed (2002); Cheng & Kwan (2000)). Going by UNCTAD classification (WIR, 2002), tax policy, trade policy, privatization policy, macroeconomic policy are policy determining variables; investment incentives are the business determining variables; market size, market growth, and market structure are market-related economic determinants; raw materials, labour cost, and technology are resources related economic determinants; transport and communication costs and labour productivity are efficiency related economic determinants (Moosa, 2006). In this study, economic variables have been examined carefully for identifying determinants of FDI inflows in India by taking both annual and monthly data. In this context, such analysis will be useful to prescribe better policy initiatives for the creation of a conducive environment for multi-national enterprises to undertake FDI inflows.

A number of studies have been attempted by researchers over the years to find out true determinants of FDI inflow but no consensus view has emerged in the sense that there is a set of widely accepted explanatory variables that can be regarded as the true determinants of FDI inflow. In a limited sense, some commonality is seen in a few cases. Some of them are compiled together in the Table 1.

Table 1: Empirical literature review of selected macroeconomic variables and FDI inflows.

Variables	*Authors*
GDP	(Remco & Beugelsdijk (2009); Ang (2008); Kolsted & Villanger (2008); Asiedu (2008); Malik, & Pentecost (2007); Sahoo (2006); Moosa & Cardak (2006); Gast (2005); Faeth (2005); Balasubramanyam & Mahambare (2003); Root & Ahmed (2002); Gopinath (1998); Wang & Swain (1995); Chen (1992); Tsai (1991); Kravis & Lipsey (1982).
Per capita income	Root and Ahmed (2002); Wang and Swain (1995).
Labour cost	Asiedu (2008); Sahoo (2006); Son *et al.* (2002); Lucas (1998); Chen (1992); Tsai (1991); Kravis and Lipsey (1982).
Trade openness	Ang (2008); Asiedu (2008); Sahoo (2006); Kobrin (2005); Son *et al.* (2002).
Distance	Halid (2009); Remco and Beugelsdijk (2009); Gast (2005).
Infrastructure	Ang (2008); Asiedu (2008); Sahoo (2006); Root and Ahmed (2002); Cheng and Kwan (2000).
Level of human capital	Holger and Nunnenkamp (2009); Kobrin (2005); Cheng and Kwan.
Export	Lin (2009); Moosa and Cardak (2006); Kravis and Lipsey, (1982).
Import	Shahmoradi and Thimmaiah (2010); Kravis and Lipsey (1982).
Exchange rate	Balasubramanyam and Mahambare (2003); Edwards (1990); Blonigen and Feenstra (1996); Tuman and Emmert (1999).
Foreign exchange reserve	Gopinath (1998).
Inflation	Schnieder and Frey (1985); Bajo-Rubio and Sosvillo-Rivero (1994); Yang *et al.* (2000); Srinivasa (2011).
Tax rate	Swenson (1994); Billington (1999); Porcano and Price (1996); Wei (2000); Schoeman *et al.* (2000); Hines (1996).
Government incentives	Tsai (1991); Chen (1992); Ihrig (2000).
Socio political conditions	Root and Ahmed (2002); Kolsted and Villanger (2008); Asiedu (2008); Malik and Pentecost (2007); Balasubramanyam and Mahambare (2003); Schneider and Frey (1985).

Source: The 45 years of foreign direct investment research: Approaches, advances and analytical areas by Justin Pauland Gurmeet Singh.

3. NEED AND SIGNIFICANCE OF THE STUDY

Over the years, a large number of studies have been carried out by researchers to identify true determinants of FDI inflows but no consensus view has emerged in the sense that there is a set of widely accepted explanatory variables that can be regarded as the true determinants of FDI inflows. It is clear that determinants of FDI inflows are not the same in different countries, in different periods and in different industries. Hence, a detailed study is needed for the Indian economy to know the determinants of FDI inflows into India in the post-liberalization period. It becomes important to examine whether determinants of FDI inflows into India will remain the same or any other new determinants would emerge. Such findings may provide useful insights to the policymakers for formulating the policy that will strengthen the FDI inflows into India and speed up economic growth. But the number of studies available regarding structural path between FDI inflows and Macroeconomic Variables in India are only the handful. Even though a few studies are available on determinants and structural paths between FDI inflows and Macroeconomic Variables in India but they seem to be dated in the present context. Therefore a rigorous analysis is needed that will bridge the gap in empirical literature applying structural path analysis between FDI inflows and Macroeconomic Variables.

The specific objectives of the study are: (1) to examine determinants of FDI inflows into India after Globalization and (2) to develop a comprehensive model for the structural path between FDI inflows and Macroeconomic variables.

4. METHODOLOGY AND DATA SOURCES

The study has taken the help of step-wise regression method to find out a compressive model for deciding determinants of FDI inflows into India using monthly data. This method is based on a forward step-wise regression technique. The regression is carried out in two steps. In the first step, it has taken all the variables in the model. In the second step, it has dropped insignificant variables to fit a model which will include only the significant variables. The study used Variance Inflated Factor (VIF) and Tolerance Level (TOL) for checking multi collinearity in the given data. The study also used Structural Equation Modeling (SEM) for understanding structural paths between FDI inflows and Macroeconomic Variables in India. The study used monthly data from August 1994 to May 2015. The present study uses FDI data published by the Reserve Bank of India (RBI). The data on macroeconomic variables have been collected from the Handbook of Statistics on the Indian Economy (HSIE) published by RBI. The present study has taken the help of India FDI Fact Sheet published by Department of Industrial Policy and Promotion (DIPP) under Ministry of Commerce and Industry.

5. DETERMINANTS OF FDI INFLOWS INTO INDIA AFTER GLOBALISATION

This section tries to specify a comprehensive model on the basis of the chosen variables. The functional form for the determination of FDI inflow of the Indian economy at the macro level using monthly data can be written as

$$\text{FDII} = \text{F (WPI, FER, EX, IIP, FII, SB, MS, REER)} \qquad (1.1)$$

More specifically, we can write

$$\text{Log FDII} = \alpha + \beta_1 \text{WPI} + \beta_2 \text{Log FER} + \beta_3 \text{Log EX} + \beta_4 \text{Log IIP} + \beta_5 \text{Log FII} + \beta_6 \text{Log SB} + \beta_7 \text{Log MS} + \beta_8 \text{Log REER} + .e \qquad (1.2)$$

Where FDII, WPI, FER, EX, IIP, FII, SB, MS, and REER are the foreign direct inflows into India, wholesale price index, foreign exchange reserve, export, index of industrial production, foreign institutional investment, saving with commercial banks, money supply and real effective exchange rate respectively. The error term '.e' in the above equation is assumed to satisfy all the assumptions of the classical regression analysis. It is an unexplained variable apart from all said above variables.

The general model of the current study is given below in the following equation.

$$\text{FDII} = 26.789 - 0.018\,(\text{WPI}) + .001\,(\text{FER}) + 1.347\,(\text{EX}) + 0.003\,(\text{IIP}) - .050\,(\text{FII}) + 5.034\,(\text{SB}) + 4.163\,(\text{MS}) + .007\,(\text{REER}) \qquad (1.3)$$

In Table 2 step-wise regressions has been used for determining most important determinants of FDI inflow after Globalization.

Table 2: Model summary of stepwise regression.

Model	*R*	*R square*	*Adjusted R square*	*Std. error of the estimate*	*Durbin-Watson*
1	.901[a]	.811	.804	.496	
2	.901[b]	.811	.805	.495	
3	.901[c]	.811	.806	.494	
4	.900[d]	.810	.806	.494	1.998

a. Predictors: (Constant), REER, FII, MS, FER, IIP, EX, WPI, SB; b. Predictors: (Constant), REER, FII, MS, IIP, EX, WPI, SB; c. Predictors: (Constant), REER, MS, IIP, EX, WPI, SB; d. Predictors: (Constant), REER, MS, EX, WPI, SB; e. Dependent variable: FDII; *Source*: Author's own compilation

From the above step wise regression model following four models can be formulated:

Model One

$$FDII = 26.798 + .003\ (IIP) - .018\ (WPI) + .001\ (FER) + 1.347\ (EX). - 050\ (FII) + 5.034\ (SB) + 4.163\ (MS) + 0.007\ (REER) \quad (1.4)$$

Model Two

$$FDII = 25.799 + .003\ (IIP) - .018\ (WPI) + 1.349\ (EX) - - .049\ (FII) + 5.034\ (SB) + 4.167\ (MS) + 0.007\ (REER) \quad (1.5)$$

Model Three

$$FDII = 26.422 + .003\ (IIP) - .018\ (WPI) + 1.363\ (EX) + 5.060\ (SB) + 4.181\ (MS) + 0.007\ (REER) \quad (1.6)$$

Model Four

$$FDII = 27.326 - .021\ (WPI) + 1.453\ (EX) + 5.174\ (SB) + 4.328\ (MS) + 0.008\ (REER) \quad (1.7)$$

From the above four models (1.4–1.7), model 1.7 is a most suitable model because in this model all the variables are significant. If we consider multi collinearity aspect here VIF is very minimum (close to 1) for all variables which imply an absence of multicollinearity. For further, confirmation of multicollinearity it has been seen that Tolerance Level (TOL) are also close to 1 which means there is absence of multicollinearity in the current study.

Out of total eight variables, six variables (IIP, FER, EX, SB, MS and REER) have positive impact of FDI inflows whereas two variables (WPI and FII) have negative impact Again, out of these six variables which have positive impact, two variables (IIP and FER) have insignificant result. Therefore four variables (EX, SB, MS and REER) have a significant positive impact on FDI inflows. So we should make these variables more robust for more FDI inflows into India.

6. STRUCTURAL PATHS BETWEEN FDI INFLOWS AND MACROECONOMIC VARIABLES IN INDIA

This section tries to explore various paths or structure of FDI inflows into India economy by using Structural Equation Modeling (SEM) method. In this section, SEM has been explored using very simple diagrams. The structure can be like the following diagram.

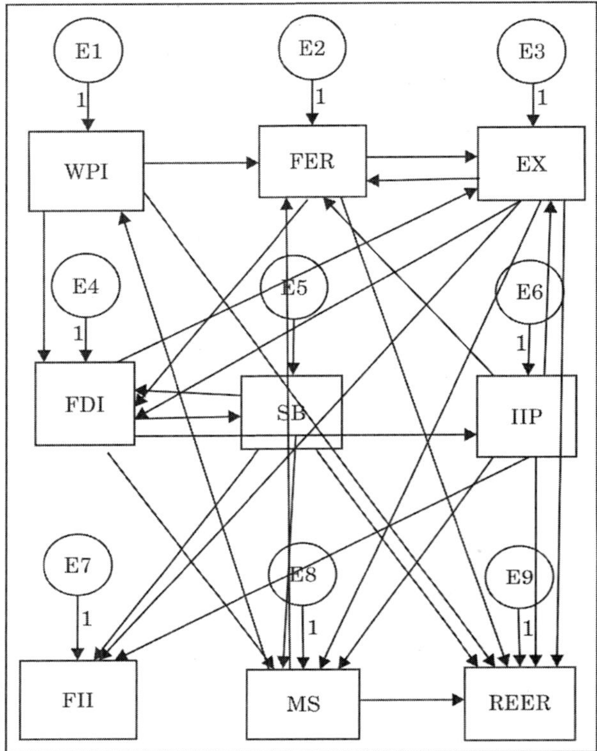

Fig. 1: Proposed Structcural Equation Model for Path Determination. ***Source*:** Author's own compilation. ***Data collected from:*** Reserve Bank of India (RBI), FDI fact sheet published by Department of Industrial Policy and Promotion (DIPP), Handbook of statistics on the Indian Economy (HSIE) Published by RBI.

This model proposes a complex test of many simultaneous regression models indicated by the arrows. The independent variables are to the left (where the arrows begin) and the dependent variables are the where the arrows end.

The proposed model contains WPI, FER, EX, FDI, SB, IIP, FII, MS and REER as observed variables. This model also used E1, E2, E3, E4, E5, E6, E7, E8 and E9 unobserved variables.

Regression Results

The Table 3 shows regression Results of proposed structural Equation Model:-

Asterisk (*) and (**) denote statistically significant at 1% and 5% levels respectively. In Table 3, there are 28 paths seen in the proposed model.

Table 3: Regression results of the proposed model.

	Path		*Estimate*	*S.E.*	*C.R.*	*P-value*	*Decision*
FDI	←	WPI	–1752.23	1046.64	–1.67	0.094	Not significant
FDI	←	EX	3.24	1.87	1.73	0.083	Not significant
FDI	←	SB	96152.76	58257.41	1.65	0.099	Not significant
MS	←	FDI	0.000	0.000	5.75*	0.000	Significant
MS	←	SB	1.042	0.029	35.74*	0.000	Significant
EX	←	FER	–4162.20	638.08	–6.52*	0.000	Significant
REER	←	EX	0.003	0.001	2.70*	0.007	Significant
REER	←	MS	–180.73	22.39	–8.06*	0.000	Significant
WPI	←	MS	31.69	9.14	3.46*	0.000	Significant
FER	←	MS	0.71	0.28	2.51**	0.012	Significant
FER	←	EX	0.000	0.000	2.52**	0.011	Significant
IIP	←	FDI	0.007	0.113	0.066	0.947	Not significant
EX	←	IIP	107.67	9.20	11.70*	0.000	Significant
FII	←	IIP	56.70	23.57	2.41**	0.016	Significant
REER	←	IIP	0.521	0.113	4.63*	0.000	Significant
REER	←	SB	112.40	32.50	3.46*	0.000	Significant
FER	←	IIP	–0.009	0.003	–3.19*	0.001	Significant
MS	←	EX	0.000	0.000	–4.29*	0.000	Significant
REER	←	FER	15.23	7.67	1.99**	0.047	Significant
FER	←	WPI	0.017	0.006	2.81*	0.005	Significant
FII	←	EX	–0.560	0.143	–3.92*	0.000	Significant
EX	←	FDI	0.330	0.195	1.69***	0.091	Not significant
SB	←	FDI	0.002	0.005	0.377	0.706	Not significant
SB	←	EX	0.003	0.005	0.600	0.548	Not significant
MS	←	IIP	–0.001	0.000	–2.61**	0.009	Significant
REER	←	WPI	–0.688	0.393	–1.749	0.080	Not significant
FII	←	SB	–2240.43	1055.34	–2.12**	0.034	Significant
FDI	←	FER	–25432.88	15946.16	–1.59	0.111	Not significant

Source: Author's own compilation

Out of that 9 are insignificant and 19 are significant. This means there are 19 simultaneous equations possible in this model.

Goodness of Fit Results

This proposed model is a good model because it confirmed all goodness of fit assessment test criteria of structural equation model namely CMIN/DF, GFI, AGFI, NFI, RFI, IFI, TLI, CFI and RMSEA. Threshold value of CMIN/DF, GFI, AGFI, NFI, RFI, IFI, TLI, CFI, and RMSEA are 3, 0.90, 0.90, 0.90, 0.90, 0.90, 0.90, 0.90 and 0.08 (Bagozzi & Yi, 1988).

In Table 4, the value of CMIN/DF in default model is 2.206 which show that proposed SEM is a good model because the threshold value of CMIN/DF is 0.3

Table 4: Model fit summary.

Model	*NPAR*	*CMIN*	*DF*	*P*	*CMIN/DF*
Default model	55	24.27	11	0.012	2.20
Saturated model	66	.000	0		
Independence model	11	5148.60	55	0.000	93.61

Source: Author's own compilation

In Table 5 the value of GFI in default model is 0.979 which shows that proposed SEM is a good model because the threshold value of GFI is 0.90. Similarly, AGFI also touching 0.9 which confirming one of the assessment criteria of the good model.

Table 5: AGFI and GFI results

Model	*RMR*	*GFI*	*AGFI*	*PGFI*
Default model	38580.03	0.979	0.876	0.163
Saturated model	0.000	1.000		
Independence model	7730521.17	0.162	–0.006	0.135

Source: Author's own compilation

In Table 6 the value of NFI, RFI, IFI, TLI and CFI in default model are 0.99, 97, 99, 0.98 and 0.98 which shows that proposed SEM is a good model because threshold value of NFI, RFI, IFI, TLI and CFI is 0.90.

Table 6: NFI and CFI results

Model	*NFI Delta1*	*RF Irho1*	*IFI Delta2*	*TL Irho2*	*CFI*
Default model	0.995	0.976	0.997	0.987	0.997
Saturated model	1.000		1.000		1.000
Independence model	0.000	0.000	0.000	0.000	0.000

Source: Author's own compilation

In Table 7, the value of RMSEA in default model is 0.077 which shows that the proposed SEM is a good model because the threshold value of RMSEA is 0.08. Thus from analysis, it is clear that our purposed model, in general, is a good model for explaining the simultaneous relationship of FDI with WPI, FER, EX, IM, FII, REER, GDS, IIP, TB and MS.It is observed

Table 7: RMSEA results

Model	*RMSEA*	*LO 90*	*HI 90*	*PCLOSE*
Default model	0.077	0.035	0.119	0.125
Independence model	0.679	0.663	0.694	0.000

Source: Author's own compilation

that 28 paths seen in the proposed model. Out of that, 9 are insignificant and 19 are significant. This means, there are 19 significant paths possible between FDI and different macroeconomic variables. This seems to be the first attempt ever made in the literature to find out different paths of FDI inflows with other macroeconomic variables thus unique in nature.

7. CONCLUDING AND POLICY SUGGESTIONS

This paper provides evidence that 19 significant structural paths among different macroeconomic variables are significantly contribute for more FDI inflows into India. This study also finds that macroeconomic variable impacts positively and significantly on FDI inflows in India when we control for the effects of macroeconomic variables. Apart from determinants of FDI inflows into India, this study had observed that structural paths among different macroeconomic variables are very much important from policy view point. So government should think how to strengthen the macroeconomic variables for attracting more FDI inflows. It Shoud make suitable monetary and fiscal policy for better FDI inflows. Its foreign policy should also be beneficial for foreign companies to invest in India. India's place in FDI potential Index is in the first quartile whereas in FDI attraction index, its place is in the second quartile. It shows that India needs to be more attractive as a destination for FDI inflows at a global level. On the basis of the above result it may Suggested that India should plan for boosting exports as it would lead to better FDI inflows. Because there are some FDI which are export oriented. India should increase its industrial export to other countries as it is attracts more export oriented FDI inflows. Likewise saving with the commercial bank in India should grow continuously. More saving would also generate opportunities for foreigners to invest in India this is a new evidence emerged from the study which shows that more saving with commercial bank in India would attract more FDI inflows into India. Further, the money supply should increase in India. This indicates more money supply leads to more investment in infrastructure, research and development, human capital formation and procurement of sophisticated technologies which causes more FDI inflow into India. There should be balance exchange rate between countries for more FDI inflows. Since variable (WPI) has the negative and significant impact on FDI inflows India should try to control WPI for more FDI inflows. Further, India should control more rises in WPI as it discourages foreign investor to invest in India. Since it is an important determinant for deciding FDI inflows India should have a tight policy to control this variable.

REFERENCES

Agrawal, P. (2000). Policy Regimes and Industrial Competitiveness: A Comparative Study of South Asia and India. Macmillan Press Limited, London.

Aitken, B. (1997). Spillovers, Foreign Investment and Export Behavior. *Journal of International Economics*, 43: 103–132.

Aitken, E.H. (1999). Do Domestic Firms Benefit from Direct Foreign Investment? *American Economic Review,* 89(3): 605–618.

Ang, J.B. (2008). Determinants of Foreign Direct Investment in Malaysia. *Journal of Policy Modeling*, 30: 185–189.

Asiedu, E. (2002). On the Determinants of Foreign Direct Investment to Developing Countries: Is Africa Different. *World Development*, 30(1): 107–119.

Balasubramanyam, N.V. and Mahambare, V. (2003). FDI in India. *Transnational Corporations*, 12(2): 44–72.

Banga, R. (2004). Impact of Japanese and US FDI on Productivity Growth: A Firm Level Analysis. *Economic and Political Weekly*, pp. 454–460.

Bergman, A. (2006). FDI and Spillover Effects in the Indian Pharmaceutical Industry. *RIS Discussion Papers*, 113: 1–51.

Blomstrom, M. (1986). Foreign Investment and Productivity Efficiency: The case of Mexico. *Journal of Industrial Economics,* 15: 97–110.

Brander, J.A. and Spencer B.J. (1987). Foreign Direct Investment with Unemployment and Endogenous Taxes and Tariffs. *Journal of International Economics*, 22: 257–279.

Buckley, P. and Casson M. (1976). The Future of the Multinational Enterprises, Macmillan Press Limited, London.

Buckley, P.J. (1995). Foreign Direct Investment and Multinational Enterprises. Macmillan Press Limited, London.

Carkovic, L. (2002). How Does Foreign Direct Investment Affect Economic Growth? *Journal of International Economics,* 45: 115–135.

Chakraborty, C. and Basu, P. (2002). Foreign Direct Investment and Growth in India: A Co-integration Approach. *Applied Economics,* 34(9): 1061–1073.

Chakraborty, C. and Peter, N. (2007). Economic Reforms, FDI and Economic Growth in India: A Sector Level Analysis. *World Development*, 36(7): 1192–1212.

Chen, C.H. (1996). Regional Determinants of Foreign Direct Investment in Mainland China. *Journal of Economics Studies*, 23: 18–30.

Chen, T.J. (1992). Determinants of Taiwan's Direct Foreign Investment, The case of a Newly Industrializing Countries. *Journal of Development Economics*, 39: 397–407.

Cheng, L.K. and Kwan, Y.K. (2000). What is the Determinants of the Location of Foreign Direct Investment? The Chinese Experience. *Journal of International Economics*, 51: 379–400.

Choe, J.I. (2003). Do Foreign Direct Investment and Gross Domestic Investment Promote Economic Growth? *Review of Development Economics*, 7(1): 44–57.

Coelli, T. (1996). A Guide to DEAP Version 2.1, *A Data Envelopment Analysis.*

De Mello, L. (1999). Foreign Direct Investment-Led Growth: Evidence from Time Series and Panel Data. *Oxford Economic Papers,* 51: 133–151.

Dua, P. and Rasid, A.I. (1998). FDI and Economic Activity in India. *Indian Economic Review,* 33(2): 153–168.

Dunning, J.H. (1988). The Eclectic Paradigm of International Production: A Restatement and Some Possible Extensions. *Journal of International Business Studies*, 19: 1–31.

Faeth, I. (2005). Determinants of FDI in Australia: Which theory can explain it best? Research Paper No-946, University of Melbourne, pp. 1–27.

FDI Statistics (2008). Department of Industrial Policy and Promotion, Ministry of Competence and Industry, Government of India, New Delhi.

Gachino, G. (2007). Foreign Direct Investment and Firm Level productivity: A Panel Data Analysis. UNU Working Paper No. 16, pp. 1–45.

Gast, M. (2005). Determinants of Foreign Direct Investmentof OECD Countries 1991–2001. European Association of Agricultural Economists working paper, pp. 1–15.

Gopinath, T. (1998). Foreign Direct Investment in India: Policy Issues, Trends and Prospects. *Reserve Bank of India Occasional Papers*, 18: 453–470.

Gorg, H. and Greenaway, D. (2004). Much about nothing? Do domestic firms really benefit from foreign direct investment? *The World Bank Research Observer*, 19(2): 171–197.

Gorg, H. and Nunnenkamp, P. (2009). Determinants of FDI inflow in case of China: An Empirical Analysis. *European Management Journal*, 27: 336–345.

Haddad, M. and Harrison, A. (1993). Are There Positive Spillovers from Direct Foreign Investment? Evidence from Panel Data for Morocco. *Journal of Development Economics*, 42: 51–74.

Hegde, D.S. and Jena, P.K. (2011). On the causality between FDI and Economic Growth. *The Asian Economic Review*, 53(3): 515–532.

Hejazi, W. (2009). Does China Receive More Regional FDI than Gravity Would Suggest? *European Management Journal*, 27: 327–335.

Henley, J.S. (2004). Chasing the dragon: Accounting for the under-performance of India by comparison with China in attracting foreign direct investment. *Journal of International Development*, 16(7): 1039–1052.

Hymer, S.H. (1976). The International Operation of National Firms: A study of Direct Foreign Investment, MIT Press, Cambridge.

Iyer, C.G. (2009). Foreign Firms and Inter- Industry Spillovers in Indian Manufacturing: Evidence from 1989 to 2004. *Margin-Journal of Applied Economic Research*, 14: 297–317.

Kathuria, V. (2001). Foreign Firms, Technology Transfer and Knowledge Spillovers to Indian Manufacturing Firms: A Stochastic Frontier Analysis. *Applied Economics*, 33: 625–642.

Keller, W. and Yeaple, S. (2003). Multinational Enterprises, International Trade and Productivity Growth: Firm Level Evidence from the United States, NBER Working paper No. 9504, pp. 234–256.

Khan, M. and Kim, Y.H. (1999). Foreign Direct Investment in Pakistan: Policy Issues and Operational Implications. ERCD Report Series No. 66, pp. 212–219.

Kokko, A. (1996). Productivity Spillovers from Competition between Local Firms and Foreign Affiliates. *Journal of International Development*, 8: 517–530.

Kravis, I.B. and Lipsey, R.E. (1982). The Location of Overseas Production and Production for Export by U.S. Multinational Firms. *Journal of International Economics*, 12: 201–223.

Lin, F. (2009). The determinants of Foreign Direct Investment in China: The case of Taiwanese firms in the IT industry. *Journal of Business Research*, 112: 107–112.

Lucas, R.E.B. (1993). On the Determinants of Direct Foreign Investment: Evidence from East and Southeast Asia. *World Development*, 21: 391–406.

Moosa, I.A. and Cardak, B.A. (2006). The Determinants of Foreign Direct Investment: An Extreme Bounds Analysis. *Journal of Multinational Financial Management*, 16: 119–211.

Narula, R. and Dunning, R. (2000). Industrial Development, Globalization and Multinational Enterprises: Realities for Developing Countries. *Oxford Development Studies*, 28(2): 141–167.

RBI Bulletin (2008). Foreign Investment Flows Report, Reserve Bank of India, Government of India, New Delhi, pp. 905–907.

Sasidharan, S. (2006). Foreign Direct Investment and Technology Spillovers: Evidence from the Indian Manufacturing Sector.UNU Working Paper No. 10, pp. 1–33.

Schneider, F. and Frey, B.S. (1985). Economic and Political Determinants of Foreign Direct Investment. *World Development*, 13: 161–175.

Siddharthan, N.S. and Lal, K. (2004). Liberalisation, MNE and Productivity of Indian Enterprises. *Economic and Political Weekly*, pp. 448–451.

Sun, Q., Tong and Yu, Q. (2002). Determinants of Foreign Direct Investment across China". *Journal of International Money and Finance*", 21: 79–113.

Tsai, P. (1991). Determinants of Foreign Direct Investment in Taiwan: An Alternative Approach with Time-Series Data. *World Development*, 19: 275–285.

Zhang, K.H. (2001). Does Foreign Direct Investment Promote Economic Growth? Evidence from East and Latin America. *Contemporary Economic Policy*, 19(2): 175–185.

20

Impact of FDI on Economic Growth in India: A Time Series Analysis

KANCHAN KUMARI SHARMA[1*]

ABSTRACT

Foreing Direct Investment has been an important source of economic growth for India, bringing in capital, technology, and management knowledge needed for economic growth. The study has been carried out to find out the linkage between Foreign Direct Investment and Economic Growth in terms of GDP for India over the period 1991 to 2017; using the Granger Causality test, Unit Root test and Co-integration test. The results show that there exists a long-run relationship between the variables and the direction of causality is bi-directional.

***Key words*:** Granger causality, Co-integration, Unit root, Foreign direct investment, Gross domestic product.

1. INTRODUCTION

Foreign Direct Investment (FDI) refers to an investment directly into production in a country by a company located in another country, either by buying a company located in another country, either by buying a company in target country or by expanding operations of an existing business in that country. FDI is one of the measures of growing economic globalization. Investment has always been an issue for the developing country such as India. The world has been globalizing and all the countries are liberalizing their policies for welcoming investment from countries which are abundant in capital resources (Singh, 2016). The ultimate goal of development is to reduce poverty and improve standard of living. For this to happen, sustainable

[1] Department of Economics, Arunachal University of Studies, Namsai, Arunachal Pradesh 792103.

**Corresponding author*: E-mail: kksdholla@gmail.com

economic growth and investment in people are necessary. However given the prevalence of resource constraint, developing countries like India cannot achieve this goal by itself. There is a need that the developing countries should seek support from donors in the form of aid for financing project and programmes in needy areas.

FDI in India has played an important role in the development of the Indian economy during recession. FDI in India has enabled India to achieve a certain degree of financial growth and stability in a number of ways. This money has allowed India to focus of the areas that may have needed economic attention and address various problems that continue to challenge the country. The factors that attracted investment in India are stable economic policies, availability of cheap and quality human resources and opportunities of new unexplored markets (Singh, 2016). Mostly FDI are flowing in service sector and manufacturing sector recorded very low investments. Romer (1986) and Sala-i-Martin (1996) claim that FDI brings technology to the target country as well. FDI has helped India to attain a financial stability and economic growth with the help of investment in different sectors. FDI has boosted the economic life of India. After liberalization of trade policies in India, there has been a positive GDP growth rate in Indian economy. FDI helps the developing countries by generating revenues in the form of tax and incomes, financial stability to the government, development of infrastructure, backward and forward linkages to the domestic firms for the requirements of raw materials, tools, business infrastructure and act as support for financial system.

2. LITERATURE REVIEW

In developing countries, it is believed that FDI definitely contributes to economic growth. At the firm level several studies provide evidence of technology spillovers and enhanced firm productivity (Zhou & Tse, 2002). At the macro level, FDI positively contributes to higher GDP per capita, industrial productivity (Zhao & Zhang, 2010) and higher positive externalities (Wang, 2010). Furthermore, based on the neoclassical growth model, FDI promotes economic growth *via* expanding the quantity of total investment and in the Endogenous growth model, FDI stimulates growth by producing technological and knowledge spillovers from the developed world to the host economies. This means that through FDI, a host country gains new inputs, technology, skills/knowledge, organizational and managerial practices, enhanced R&D and access to markets (Balasubramanyam, Salisu & Sapsford, 1996; De Mello, 1997; Noorbakhsh, Paloni & Youssef, 2001). Zhang (1999) investigates the causal impact FDI on growth in 10 East Asian economies and find that FDI appears to enhance growth in the long run for mainland China, Hongkong, Indonesia, Japan and Taiwan and in the short run for Singapore. Apart from the positive impacts FDI has some negative effects in a host economy. For instance, it might place more pressure on domestic firms if it is not export based. In addition, FDI might also cause natural resource depletion and pollution (Acharya, 2009; Yang, Yang & Xu, 2008) if a host government does not have sufficient capacity to manage their resources efficiently. Again some literatures on the impact of FDI reveal the crowding out effects on domestic investments (Adams, 2009). However, some empirical studies do not support the growth impact of FDI. For instance, Kholdy (1995) carries out Granger Causality test using data from 10 East Asian economies to examine the growth impact of FDI. Findings of the study do not confirm the causation between FDI and productivity. Findlay in his research work postulated that FDI increases the rate of technological progress in the host country through a 'contagion' effect from the more advanced technology, management practices etc. used by the forign firms. De Gregorio showed in a panel data of 12 Latin American countries, which FDI is about three times more efficient than domestic investment using time series data at the industry level for US firms during the early 1970s. Noorzoy (1980) concluded that a positive relationship prevailed between investment at home and abroad. On the other hand more recent studies have shown a negative relationship to exist between FDI and home country investment.

The above discussion shows that a common conclusion on the growth impact of FDI cannot be reached. This means that findings on the impact of FDI on growth are still debatable.

3. OBJECTIVES

The main objective of this research work is to investigate the relationship between FDI and Economic Growth in India.

4. DATA SOURCE AND METHODOLOGY

This study uses yearly data over the period 1991 to 2017. Data for both the macroeconomic variables has been collected from the database of World Bank website.

The present study employs the time series data analysis technique to study the relationship between the FDI and GDP. In a time series analysis, the results might provide a spurious if result if the data series are non-stationary. The most popular and widely used test for stationarity is the unit root test. The presence of unit root indicates that the data series is non-stationary. The Augmented Dickey-Fuller (ADF) is performed to check the stationarity of the series.

For this study, SPSS and E-views Microsoft package has been applied. OLS was run using SPSS Microsoft regression package with GDP as dependent variable and FDI as independent variable. Then the calculated F value is compared to the critical value or the level of significance. If the calculated F value is greater than the critical F value at a choosen level of significance, the null hypothesis is rejected, otherwise accepted.

Similarly Granger Causality test was run using E-views Microsoft package. Then the calculated F value is compared to the critical value or the level of significance. If the calculated F value is greater than the critical F value at a choosen level of significance, then the null hypothesis is rejected; otherwise accepted.

Unit Root Test: The objective of the unit root test is to empirically examine whether a series contains a unit root or not. If the series contains a unit root, this means that the series is non-stationary. Otherwise, the series will be considered as stationary.

Co-integration Test: Co-integration test is used to find out the long-term relation between the variables.

Ordinary Least Square Method: Here we will assume the hypothesis that there is no relationship between FDI and Economic Growth in terms of GDP. To confirm about our hypothesis let us consider, linear regression Equation

$$GDP_i = \alpha_i + \beta_i FDI_{i+} \Sigma_i \tag{1}$$

Where, GDP_i and FDI_i shows the Gross Domestic Product annual growth rate and Foreign Direct Investment at a particular time respectively while Σ_i represents the error term; α_i and β_i represent the slope and coefficient of regression. The coefficient of regression, β_i indicates how a unit change in the independent variable (FDI) affects the dependent variable (GDP). The error term is incorporated in the equation to cater for the other factors that may influence GDP. The validity or strength of the OLS method depends on the accuracy of assumptions. In this study, the Gauss-Markov are used. The procedures involves specifying the dependent and the independent variables; in this case GDP is the dependent variable and FDI is the independent variable.

Granger Causality Test: FDI and GDP are in fact, interlinked and co-related through various channel. There is no theoretical or empirical evidence that could conclusively indicate sequencing from either direction. For this reason, the Granger Causality Test was carried out on FDI and GDP.

Following Seabra and Flach, Granger Test is implemented by running the following regression:

$$GDP = \Upsilon_O + \sum_{i=1}^{k+d} \alpha 1iGDP_{\ t-1} + \sum_{j=1}^{k+d} \beta 1jFDI_{\ t-1} + \mathcal{E}_{1t} \tag{2}$$

$$FDI = \Upsilon_O + \sum_{i=1}^{k+d} \alpha 2iFDI_{t-1} + \sum_{j=1}^{k+d} \beta 2jGDP_{t-1} + \mathcal{E}_{2t} \quad (3)$$

Where, GDP and FDI are respectively, the Gross Domestic Product and Foreign Direct Investment at current US $. k is the optimal lag order, d is the maximal order of integration of the variables in the system and Σ_1 and Σ_2 are the error term. Using the maximal order of integration and (d_{max}=1) and optimal lag (k=1,2,3) in eq. 2 and 3:

$$GDP_t = \Upsilon_O + \sum_{i=1}^{k+d} \alpha 1iGDP_{t-1} + \sum_{j=1}^{k+d} \beta 1jFDI_{t-1} + \mathcal{E}_{1t} \quad (4)$$

$$FDI_t = \Upsilon_O + \sum_{i=1}^{k+d} \alpha 2iFDI_{t-1} + \sum_{j=1}^{k+d} \beta 2jGDP_{t-1} + \mathcal{E}_{2t} \quad (5)$$

5. EMPIRICAL RESULTS AND DISCUSSION

The descriptive statistics for both the variables under study, *viz*, Foreign Direct Investment (FDI) and Gross Domestic Product (GDP) are presented in Table 5.1. The descriptive statistics as evidenced in Table 5.1 reveals approximate normality in the data distribution of each variable in terms of skewness and Kurtosis. The FDI has a larger standard deviation as compared to the standard deviation of GDP, which supports the general institution that FDI is highly volatile. The value for kurtosis in each variable is below the benchmark for normal distribution of 3 which confirms near normality. The coefficient of skewness for both the variables is low and positive which indicates positively skewed distribution.

Table 5.1: Descriptive statistics of variables.

	FDI	*GDP*
Mean	16608805137.00	1199326.349
Median	5429250989.85	699688852930.27
Maximum	44458571545.79	2597491162897.67
Minimum	73536738.38	266502281094.117
Std. deviation	16520944451.42	735797888505.38
Skewness	0.5067	0.67
Kurtosis	1.603	2.01
Jasque-Bera	3.350	3.10
Probability	0.187	0.211
Sum	4.48E+11	2.75E+13
Sum square deviation	7.10E+21	1.41E+25
Observations	2.7	27

Source: Author' Estimation

In Ordinary Least Square method we reject the hypothesis that there is no relationship between the variables and the results of OLS are summarized in Table 5.2. Similarly the results of Unit Root test, Co-Integration test and Granger Causality test are discussed below.

Table 5.2: Ordinary least square.

GDP	*Coefficient*	*Std. Err.*	*T*	*P>%t%*
FDI	40.93	3.51	11.66	0.000
Constant	3.40e+11	8.15	4.17	0.000

Observation = 27, F-Statistics = 3.28, R-Squared = 0.84

H_0: There is no relationship between the variables, H_1: There is relationship between the variables.

The null hypothesis is rejected as the calculated F-Statitic value is greater than the critical F value. The OLS method indicates that there is positive relationship between FDI and GDP.

To check the stationarity of the underlying data series, we follow the standard procedure of unit root test by employing the Augmented Dickey-Fuller (ADF) test. The results are presented in Table 5.3. On the basis of these tests, both the series are found to be non-stationary at level with intercept. However, after taking the first difference these series are found to be stationary at 1, 5 and 10 percent level. Thus the test indicate that both the series are individually integrated of order I(1).

Table 5.3: Result of augmented Dickey Fuller unit root test.

Variables	*Trend*				*Trend and Intercept*		*None*	
			t-Statistic	*Prob**	*t-Statistic*	*Prob**	*t-Statistic*	*Prob**
FDI	Augmented Dickey-Fuller test statistic		–0.701	0.82	–2.49	0.32	0.35	0.77
	Test critical values	1 % Level	–3.71		–4.35		–2.65	
		5 % Level	–2.98		–3.59		–1.95	
		10 % Level	–2.62		–3.23		–1.60	
GDP	Augmented Dickey-Fuller test statistic		2.94	1.00	–0.69	0.96	6.05	1.00
	Test critical values	1 % Level	–3.711		–4.35		–2.65	
		5 % Level	–2.98		–3.59		–1.95	
		10 % Level	–2.62		–3.23		–1.60	

Source: Author's Estimation

The presence and the number of co-integrating relationships among the underlying variables are tested through the Johansen procedure. Specifically, trace statistic and maximum eigenvalue are used to test for the number of co-integrating vectors. The result of both trace statistic and the maximum eigen test statistic are presented in Table 5.4 A and Table 5.4 B. Both the trace statistic and maximum eigenvalue statistics identify one co-integrating vector. The result show that long-run equilibrium relationship exists between the FDI and GDP.

Table 5.4 A: Result of Johansen's Co-integration test unrestricted Co-integration rank test (Trace).

Hypothesized no. of CE(s)	*Eigen value*	*Trace statitic*	*0.05 critical value*	*Prob.***
None	0.4419	18.25	12.32	0.0045
At most 1	0.1365	3.67	4.12	0.0657

Trace Test indicates 1 cointegrating eqn(s) at the 0.05 level; *denotes rejectrion of the hypothesis at the 0.05 level; ** denotes MacKinnon-Haug-Michelis (1999) p-values

Table 5.4 B: Result of Johansen's Co-integration test unrestricted Co-integration rank test (Maximum Eigen value).

Hypothesized no. of CE(s)	*Eigen value*	*Trace statitic*	*0.05 critical value*	*Prob.***
None	0.4419	14.58	11.22	0.012
At most 1	0.1365	3.67	4.12	0.065

Max-eigen value Test indicates 1 cointegrating eqn(s) at the 0.05 level; *denotes rejections of the hypothesis at the 0.05 level; **denotes MacKinnon-Haug-Michelis (1999) p-values

Now, the pair-wise Granger Causality test is performed between all possible pairs of variables to determine the direction of causality. The rejected hypothesis is reported in Table 5.5. The results show that the FDI granger causes GDP and GDP granger causes FDI.

Table 5.5: Result of Granger causality test.

Null hypothesis	*Obs.*	*F-statistic*	*Prob.*	*Decision*
GDP does not Granger Causes FDI	25	7.14	0.004	Reject
FDI does not Granger Causes GDP	25	2.11	0.14	Reject

Source: Author's Estimation

6. CONCLUSIONS

This study examined the inter-linkage between FDI and GDP using Johansen's Co-integration and Granger Causality framework. The study used the yearly time series data for the period 1991–2017 which has been collected from the World Bank database. We can conclude the analysis by saying that the FDI formed significant long run relationship with GDP. The findings from Granger Causality indicate a bi-directional relationship between FDI and GDP both in short run and long run. The present study confirms the beliefs that FDI continues to affect the Indian GDP.

7. REFERENCES

Acharyya, J. (2009). "FDI, Growth and the Environment: Evidences from India on CO_2 Emission during the last two decades". *Journal of Economic Development,* 34: 43–58.

Adams, S. (2009). "Foreign Direct Investment and Economic Growth in Sub-Saharan Africa". *Journal of Policy Modeling,* 31: 939–949.

Antwi, S. and Zhao, X. (2013). "Impact of Foreign Direct Investment and Economic Growth in Ghana: A Cointegration Analysis". *International Journal of Business and Social Research (IJBSR),* 3(1).

Balasubramanyam, V.N., Salisu, M. and Sapsford, D. (1996). "Foreign Direct Investment and Growth in EP and in Countries". *The Economic Journal,* 106: 92–105.

De Gregoria, J. (1992). "Economic Growth in Latin America". *Journal of Development Economics,* 39(1): 59–84.

De Mello L.R., Jr. (1997). "Foreign Direct Investment in Developing Countries and growth: A Selective Survey". *Journal of Development Studies,* 34: 1–34.

Findlay, R. (1978). "Relative Backwardness, Direct Foreign Investment and the Transfer of Technology: A Simple Dynamic Model". *Quarterly Journal of Economics,* 96: 1–16.

Gorg and Greenway, D. (2004). *World Bank Research Observed*, 19: 171–197.

Kholdy, S. (1995). "Causality between Foreign Direct Investment and Pillover Efficiency". *Applied Economics*, 27: 745–749.

Kundan, P.M. (2010). "A Time Series Analysis of Foreign Direct Invsetment and Economic Growth: A Case Study of Nepal". *International Journal of Business and Management,* 5(2).

Noorbakshsh, F., Paloni, A. and Yousef, A. (2001). "Human Capital and FDI Inflows to Developing Countries: New Empirical Evidences". World Development, 29: 593–1610.

Noorzoy, M.S. (1980). "Flows Direct Investment and their Effect on US Domestic Investment". *Economic Letter*, 5: 311–317.

Singh, G. (2014). "Time Series Analysis of Foreign Direct Investment and Economic Growth: A Study in India", Research Gate.

Tshepo, M. (2014). "The Impact of Direct Investment on Economic Growth and Employment in South Africa: A Time Series Analysis". *Mediterranean Journal of Social Sciences,* 5(25).

Wang, Y. (2010). "FDI and Productivity Growth: The Role of Inter-industry Linkages". *Canadian Journal of Economics,* 43: 1243–1272.

Yang, W.P., Yang, Y. and Xu, J. (2008). "The Impact of Foreign Trade and FDI on Environment Pollution ". *China-USA Business Review*, 7: 1–11.

Zhang, K.H. (1999). "Foreign Direct Investment and Economic Growth: Evidences from ten East Asian Economies". *International Economics.*

Zhao, Z. and Zhang, K.H. (2010). "FDI and Industrial Productivity in China: Evidences from Panel Data in 2001–06". *Review of Development Economics,* 14: 656–65.

Zhou, D., Li, S. and Tre, D.K. (2002). "The Impact of FDI on Productivity of Domestic Firms: The Case of China". *International Business Review*, pp. 465–484.

21

Understanding Socio-Economic Dilemmas of Peri Urban India: A Case Study

MOHAMMAD ARIF[1]*

ABSTRACT

An important development in the urban settlement during the last few decades has been the rapid expansion of population and built-up area into the administratively different suburbs and areas surrounding the large towns and cities. These areas suffer from the negative consequences of unplanned urban growth, associated land use changes, rapid social change, and degradation of natural resources. Burdwan city is situated along the greater Kolkata metropolitan area and Asansol industrial area corridor. As a result, this city has experienced problems which are socio-economic segregation, and cultural gaps as well as uncontrolled land markets and the spread of informal development. Present study examines the empirical findings of socio-economic transformation as a part of peripheral urbanization. For better analysis, livelihood asset index (LAI) is analysed. Asset Index is analysed by considering four capitals i.e., physical, human, financial and human with 19 index components. Villages located nearby city have high index whereas far distance villages have low index. This chapter also analysed different kinds of synthesis in economic environment in peri urban area. Finally, it is concluded that as livelihood asset increases, the quality of life also increases in the peri-urban villages of Burdwan area.

Key words: Asset index, Burdwan, Environment, Peri urban.

[1]Department of Arts, KLEF University, Vijayawada, Andhra Pradesh 522502.
**Corresponding author:* E-mail: arifaligs@gmail.com

INTRODUCTION

An important development in the urban settlement during the last few decades has been the rapid expansion of population and built-up area into the administratively different suburbs and areas surrounding the large towns and cities. Many geographical changes at the urban periphery are associated with the transfer of land from rural to urban utilities. Significant research has been carried out on Indian cities in recent times with regard to their emerging dynamics and resulting development patterns. As Di Gaetano and Klemanski (1999) stated that on one hand, peri-urban areas have become an assemblage of many economic activities and have brought multidimensional changes in the lives of the middle class by providing a salubrious residence. On the other hand, these areas suffer from the negative consequences of unplanned urban growth, associated land use changes, rapid social change, and degradation of natural resources. Earlier urban and regional studies, especially in West Bengal, focused on either rural or urban area as delineated by definite administrative boundaries. Thus, the dynamics of the interface area remained less explored. The phenomenon of 'rural' dynamics in 'urban' regions, and, correspondingly, 'urban' activity in 'rural' spaces has led to the emergence of 'neither completely urban nor rural' areas in the region. These areas have a tremendous influence on the future of regional development, particularly in the less developed nations. This haphazardly developed zone is always in a state of a chaos-constantly changing pattern of land occupancy, small farm sizes, intensive production of crops, mobile population of low and moderate density, and incomplete provision of public utility services, all of these results in giving it a dynamic impression.

The formation and development of a peri-urban area is the result of an interaction between rural areas and the city. Peri-urbanization, irrespective of context, is characterized by a transformation of economic activities from agriculture-based livelihoods into non-farming occupations. Based on a study of *in-situ* urbanization in China, Dong (2004) finds that rural areas are no longer associated with agrarian livelihoods. There are several significant factors fostering the transformation of rural to an urban economy that includes the relocation of manufacturing and service industries to the peripheral areas of the city because of a lowland rent that in turn incentivizes people to leave the city and reside in suburban areas. Then decline in employment, particularly for those who live in relatively remote regions, has forced the young population to migrate out and engage in non-farm work in the peripheries. Last the desire of the urban middle-class to seek a better quality of life by residing in a healthy, salubrious, and verdant milieu in the peripheral zones.

Peri-urbanization research shows that each peri-urban area has particular features that leads a play of different dynamics which warrants a specific planning strategy based on the context. Among many, the major contributing issues are diversified environment, economic structure, social tier and government institutions that implement development policy (Peter & Pfeiffer, 2013). It is pertinent that a new thinking of urban development planning and strategy comes up to face challenges in this area so that socially and environmentally unsustainable development could be impeded and uprooted. In between all these, the most important factor is the way local governments are prepared for this transitional zone and deal with city's out skirts through a situated urban growth management strategy.

Peri-urban areas as the interface between urban and rural regions are currently experiencing enormous changes due to the extension of urban activities. The rapid growth of newly built environment and the apparent transformations of socio economic structure reveal how these areas become contested regions. It is recognized that peripheral areas have many advantages to accommodate the agglomeration of urban functions. As a result, the rapid pace of in-migration has been reshaping land-use patterns, economic structures, traditional culture, and neighbourhood life (Agergaard & Gough, 2009).

Burdwan city is situated along the Kolkata-Asansol corridor. As a result, this city has experienced remarkable growth in last few decades both horizontally and vertically. With the passage of time, peripheral urbanization started occurring at the outskirts of the city. It has formed the part of urban agglomeration and now faces great challenges in terms of urban development and land management. So it is the most active frontier of urban development in Burdwan. This is a space where paddy cultivation, squatter settlements, and newly gated enclaves reside together in proximity. The rural-urban transitions conspicuous in almost all the new settlements have reached unprecedented levels, with the intensity of problems and challenges certain to increase in the future. The emerging problems are socio-spatial segregation, socio-economic and cultural gaps as well as uncontrolled land markets and the spread of informal development.

STUDY AREA

Peri-urban area of Burdwan city extends over 170 square kilometres with a geographical extent between 23° 10′ to 23° 20′ north Latitude and between 87°46′ to 87°58′ east Longitude. This area is connected to Durgapur industrial complex in the north-west, greater Kolkata metropolitan area in the South-east, Katwa, Kalna, Siuri, Arambagh in other directions by road and rail networks. The total area is lies within 10 kilometres from the center of the Burdwan city.

The study area includes 1,58504 persons in 57 villages of 7 gram panchayats (village council) in two community development blocks (C.D. Block) *i.e.,* Burdwan I and Burdwan II. Within Burdwan I block, there are 34 villages in 126 square kilometres area and 23 villages in 44 square kilometres area in the Burdwan II block (Table 1). Being the administrative centre of the entire district, a wide range of government institutions are located in this city and mostly concentrated in the collectorate and Court compound area. Besides, the block offices of Burdwan I and II block are located in Kamnara and Pamra, respectively. These villages are located in the peri-urban area. Fig. 1 depicts the peri-urban area of Burdwan city in West Bengal state.

Table 1: Administrative framework of study area in context of state.

	West Bengal	*Bardhaman district*	*Study area*	*Percentage of share in district*
Total population	91276115	7717563	158504	2.05
Urban population	29093002	3078299	73540	2.38
Rural population	62183113	4639264	84964	1.83
No. of households	20309872	1725511	38089	
Area (in sq.km.)	88752	7024	170	2.42
Density of population (persons per sq. km.)	1028	1099	1265	

Source: Census of India, 2011

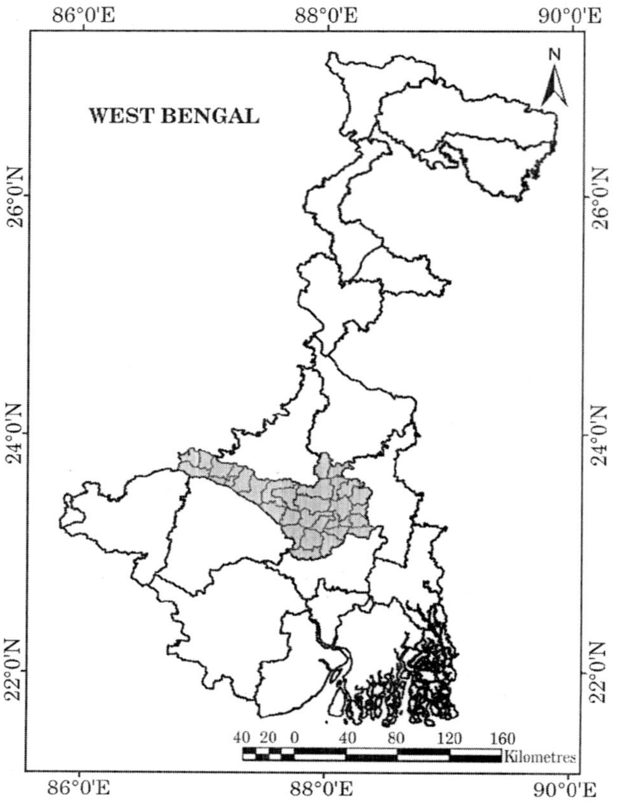

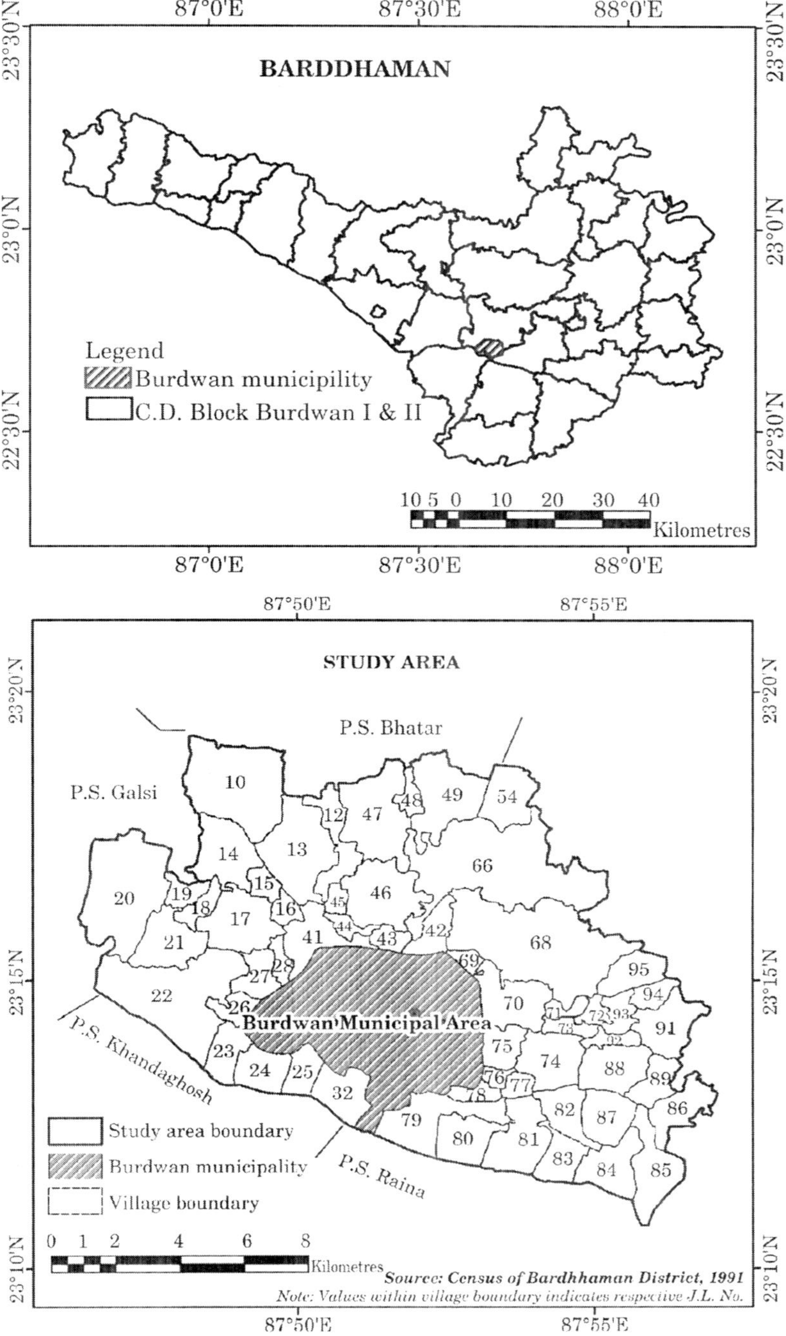

Fig. 1: Location map of the Peri-urban area in Burdwan city. ***Source:*** Census of Barddhaman district, 1991

OBJECTIVES

This paper aims to explain the empirical findings with respect to socio-economic transformations taking place as a consequence of development processes in the peri-urban areas of Burdwan city. It is divided into two major sections. The first part examines the synthesis of economic change in which specific circumstances and new opportunities lead the resident people to involve in the non-farming sector. The next section will discuss the transformations taking place in a social environment of the peri-urban area.

DATABASE AND METHODOLOGY

The present study requires a detail information regarding socio-economic transformation in the peri-urban area of Burdwan city. To meet this end, a wide range of data were collected from different sources especially for getting a reconnaissance idea of the study area and the land use changes over time. Besides, a large array of primary information was also procured from the field survey of the sample areas. Data of 250 households are collected through stratified random sampling. About 16 villages are surveyed out of 57 villages on the basis of three categories of population density and distance from city center. As it is considered that density gradually decreases as we move out from the city centre. Hence to get the variety, we have set a logic to survey of villages considering both the distance from the city and density of population. So we have three categories of villages. These are least distant and high density, average distance and medium density, low density and most distance from the city center. Based on previously mentioned indices sample villages are selected to analyze the socio-economic transformation in the peri-urban area of Burdwan city.

DISCUSSION

The sample household in the peri-urban area creates growth of new residential colonies within the village, which dramatically alters the demographic and sociological profile. Village population does not increase in a similar fashion everywhere. It is divided into two distinct socio spatial categories. The old village settlement continues to exist with its original residents along side the migrant population settled in new residential colonies. The migrant people belong to a different caste, linguistic and regional groups. Therefore, these village populations are largely heterogeneous.

1. Synthesis in the Social Environment

Social transformation in the peri-urban area is very much important as this zone is interlacing both urban and rural ways of living. As economic status of an area determines its social status (Pandey, 2010) occupational diversification and land sale in the peri-urban has brought changes not only in the economic but also in the social life of the population in the peri-urban. People engaged in the tertiary sector have more probability to social mobility, and so on and so forth. The combined impact of land use changes, occupation diversification, and increase in income level and better education facilities in the peri-urban area has transformed the social life also.

1.1. *Improving living standards*

The sample survey finds that the sample households in the peri-urban area have certainly benefited from urban proximity. They take advantage of the city's economic developments, as a result, there are significant improvements in the peri-urban household's quality of life. Most of the improvement in the peri-urban is because of the inflow of money by village land transactions. Farming as an occupation is progressively decreasing in importance and the way of life in the village is increasingly getting urbanized (Ramachandran, 1992). As a result, villagers tend to invest their money and time on different livelihood assets. The houses in the village site also get a facelift. Brick kilns replace mud walls and tiles, and other modern building materials are used to renovate the dilapidating houses. There have been a betterment of household assets, electricity connections, and sources of drinking water in the peri-urban area.

A respondent when interviewed about the poor infrastructure of their village, said:

> *"We suffer from the chronic scarcity of water supply. During summer water level is so low that we do not even get drinking water. So we appeal to you to look into the matter".*
>
> (Suman, Interview, Belkhas village, 07/08/2017)

1.2. *Livelihood asset index*

The present discussion is largely based on an analysis made on the footsteps of DFID's Sustainable Livelihood Framework (SLF). It is modified to fit into the present study and is characterized by multidimensional, integrated and rational approach targeted to understand the livelihood of households that ranges from rich with greater access to resources to poor with lesser access to resources (Ashley & Carney 1999). A household (HH) is a clearly distinguishable social unit under the management of a household head (HHH) (Morse *et al.*, 2000). The HH shares a commonality in being answerable to an HHH and shares a common kitchen. To evaluate the livelihood asset index, some capital assets are used for broad analysis. Capital assets are critical markers of livelihood conditions available in the peri-urban households of Burdwan city. Four main types of livelihood assets are considered here-physical, human, financial and social assets-each of which is administered using context-specific indicators. The analysis consists of 12 quantitative indicators at village-level that were used for measuring the status of four livelihood capital assets. The four capital assets in the framework are major elements to analyse dynamic processes of socio-economic transformation in peri-urban area. Assets are not only resources that people use; they are also what give people the capability to act (Banu & Fazal, 2017). These capital assets are illustrated as below:

Physical capital refers to the basic material infrastructures needed for any household to have a decent life (Hulme & McKay, 2007). However, in the present study, the physical capital assets focus on the village-level infrastructural facilities like the type of housing material, access to blacktop road, availability of market, and drinking facility. Human capital includes the level of literacy, type of fuels used for cooking, the percentage of the non-agricultural population and family size of the HH. It can be measured both quantitatively and qualitatively. Financial capital refers to monetary resources that are available to the households in peri-urban villages. It includes per capita income and type of employment. An examination of HH assets as a means of assessing wealth information is often used in some cases. Social capital assets are important aspects of any society. Money borrowing and assistance from relatives is considered as an indicator for measuring social capital. It can be assumed how much affluent household in peri-urban area with this indicator. The measurement of livelihood assets is based on a balanced weighted average approach where each index components contributes equally to the overall index. So this way asset index is summarized as:

Livelihood asset index = Sum of physical, human, financial and social capital

The index is constructed after adding up the scores of different variables for a particular observation. In this analysis, each index value is standardized between 0 and 1. For livelihood Asset Index higher score means better conditions. After analyzing all the capitals, it is found that Gopalnagar village has the highest livelihood asset index followed by Nari village (Fig. 2). The given figure illustrates the asset index.

From Table 2, it is found that Gopalnagar, Jotram and Nari villages have higher livelihood asset index. These villages are located nearby to the municipal boundary. Most of the villagers are highly educated and have good income.

1.3. *Incarnation of new social class*

The social relationships between the new migrant residents and old village

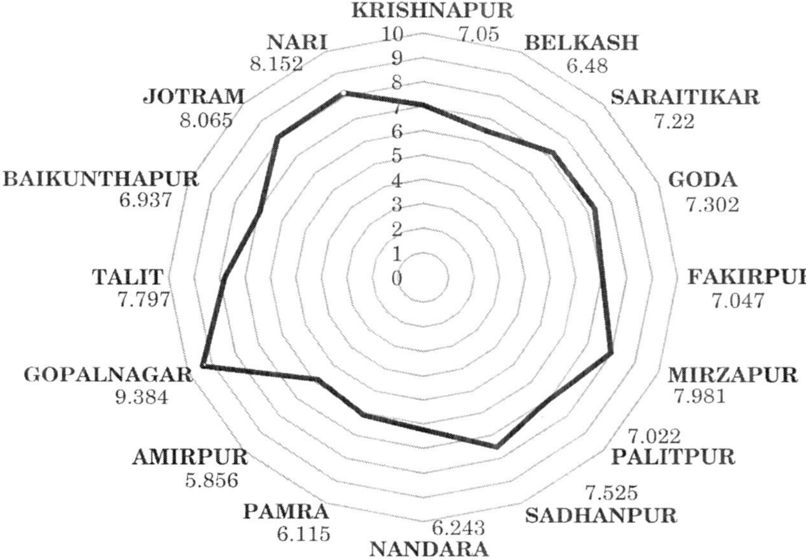

Fig. 2: Livelihood asset index chart of sampled villages. ***Source:*** Based on Sample survey (2017)

Table 2: Livelihood asset index score in sampled villages.

Sl. no.	*Name of village*	*Livelihood asset index*
1	Krishnapur	7.05
2	Belkash	6.48
3	Saraitikar	7.22
4	Goda	7.302
5	Fakirpur	7.047
6	Mirzapur	7.981
7	Palitpur	7.022
8	Sadhanpur	7.525
9	Nandara	6.243
10	Pamra	6.115
11	Amirpur	5.856
12	Gopalnagar	9.384
13	Talit	7.797
14	Baikunthapur	6.937
15	Jotram	8.065
16	Nari	8.152

Source: Based on Sample survey (2017)

residents are fragile and superficial. The two social classes have different values and have very different perceptions of the city. In most of the villages, the poorer sections of the original population provide certain services such as domestic work and other menial jobs. The dominant caste in the village often feels hostile to the new residents. Another important matter that is observed is that in each village there are three types of locality based on caste and religion. These are Bamunpara (higher caste Hindu area), Muchipara (lower caste Hindu area) and Muslimpara (Muslim community area). People are living in their own social areas demarcated based on caste and religion. However better development in public amenities seen in higher caste Hindu area. It is observed that tertiary workers are mainly involved in government jobs and remain aloof from the village people. They mainly interact within their own fraternity. However, migrant workers who come for low paid menial jobs only afford to live in squatter settlements located near factories, on the roadsides, near drains and other unhealthy places. There is a dialectic relationship between land and slum-land as slum and slum as land (Mishra, 2018). As most of the low paid workers living in slum area in peri urban villages. Because slum land is relatively low price area. Informal workers can afford this place so easily. These areas are multi activity household to urban monetized economy to generate higher incomes required for sustenance.

1.4. *Exalted public amenities*

The process of urbanization has its impact on the surrounding villages in the peri-urban area in many different ways. The sample survey finds that households have certainly benefitted from urban proximity as they take advantage of the city's economic development. Overall, the city's infrastructure and facilities have helped in the development of peri-urban villages.

1.4.1. *Road*

Burdwan city and its surrounding peri-urban villages have improved accessibility especially in terms of road transport. A large number of people could come to the city for different purposes due to the good accessibility provided by the roads. The improvement in roads has significantly helped the expansion as well as the development of the peri-urban area. In this area, the total length of the bitumen road is 39 km and the concrete road is about 85 km (data collected from panchayat office). Most of the people come to the city by cycle and bus, while some also come by bike or electric car (Table 3). About 89 percent people come to city by cycle whereas 45 percent villagers came by motor cycle (Fig. 3). The survey shows that most of the household's daily commute to the city is for education, marketing, and employment. Nevertheless, many villages still have poor transport infrastructure.

Table 3: Means of transport for city visit.

Means of transport for city visit	*Percent of sampled village*
Cycle	89.6
Bike	45.2
Car	2.8
Electric car	66
Bus	80.4
Others	16.4

Source: Based on Sample survey (2017)

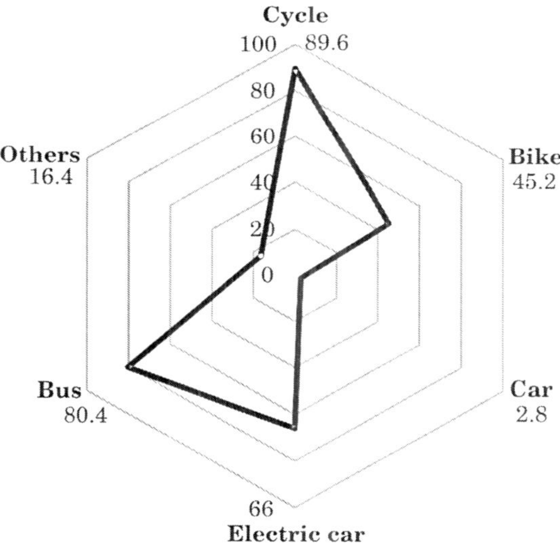

Fig. 3: Means of transport for city visit. ***Source:*** Based on Sample survey (2017)

1.4.2. *Education*

Burdwan city has a huge bearing on the education of the peri-urban area. Though there is not much variation with regard to literacy, there are conspicuous variations in the level of education among the peri-urban villages. Sample survey finds that about 28.8 percent have received primary education. About 50 percent people have a secondary level of education. A significant number of people send their children to government or private schools.

1.4.3. *Electricity*

Most of the households have electricity connection. Sampled villages receive almost 20 hours of uninterrupted electricity per day. Most of the households have an electric fan, tubelight, and mobile phones.

It should be noted that public amenities and development varies from village to village. Higher caste people get more amenities from the government or its agencies *vis-à-vis* the lower caste. Therefore it is pertinent to develop all the pockets of the villages more a more inclusive growth.

With the change in land use in the area, new economic activities prosper at the cost of core city economic health, which attracts population from nearby areas. These migrating populations change their earlier occupations so as to attune it to the nature of work in the receiving area. However, the transformation in economic activity in the peri-urban area is the result of the coexistence of urban (mainly secondary and tertiary activities) and rural (mainly primary or natural resource-based) activities.

2. Synthesis in the Economic Environment

The households in the peri-urban area of Burdwan city take advantage of the proximity to the city; the urban-based economic activities (consisting of secondary and rapidly expanding tertiary sector) draw a large number of workers. Majority of these workers are less and intermediately educated and thus do not possess sufficient skill and expertise. Therefore, they engage in menial jobs mostly in the informal sector. About 59 percent people in this sector work close to his or her habitation. Another 25 percent people in this sector come to the city for his or her employment (Table 4). The remaining numbers of villagers work in the neighboring villages. Significantly, women from these villages have a sizeable presence in work participation. It is observed that from large distant villages many numbers of low caste people come to the city or peri-urban villages for work.

Table 4: Place of work for household persons.

Type and place of work	*Percent of sampled village*
Own area	59
In city area	25
Peri-urban area	11
Outside peri-urban area	5

Source: Based on Sample survey (2017)

2.1. *Occupational change*

A large percentage of working population in non-agricultural activities is characteristic feature of urban area and used as level of urbanization. It is in this context that distribution of working population on the basis of economic activity in peri-urban area assumes importance. An increasing concentration of working population in the secondary and tertiary sectors of economic activities can be regarded as level of urbanization (Gopi, 1978).

In Burdwan city, people coming from the peri-urban area dominate the informal commercial sector. Among them, some are daily wage earners, while others are self-employed in the city as vendors, hawkers, petty traders and so on. However, it is observed that the lower caste population initiate into low paid works. Another striking feature observed in the peri-urban area is the declining preference for agriculture as a livelihood option. This leads to a large-scale occupational transformation in this area. The supplementary reason for this transformation is the decreasing land for farming activity that leaves a small farmer with no choice but to opt for urban-based livelihood. A broad analysis of the sample data show that 15.6 percent workers are engaged in a primary activity, 2 percent in the secondary activity and 82.4 percent in the tertiary sector. It is observed that inner peri-urban villagers are engaged in secondary and tertiary sector activities. Most of the dwellers are either self-employed or work in private or government sectors. However, outer peri-urban villages are mostly engaged in cultivation or be self-employed. The high percentage of workers in the tertiary sector indicates the growing impact of the urban economy on the peri-urban zone. In total, sample villages have shown that about 31.25 and 14.25 percent people are engaged in the government sector and private sector, respectively, whereas about 59 percent people are self-employed. However, non-farm activities are dominated by small-scale industry and in parallel, home-based enterprises are rapidly growing. They have become the most appealing non-agricultural economic sector, employing not only a large number of local young villagers but also pulling young people from neighboring districts, either as permanent residents or as seasonal migrants. However migrants from Bihar and Jharkhand are backbone of informal sector of peri-urban economy.

2.2. *Decrease in work participation rate*

Work Participation Rate (WPR) refers to the percentage of main and marginal workers to total population. The Occupational characteristic of an area is highlighted by work participation. The working population and work participation rate highlights the occupational distribution of a region. The temporal analysis of total workers in the peri-urban area of Burdwan city shows a substantial increase in the last decade. In the present study, total WPR has been considered including agriculture, industry and other services. Major changes between 1991–2011 are that WPR increases in the villages nearest to the riverine area (Fig. 4). It may be considered this is due to agricultural intensification. In some cases, WPR found to be slightly increased or remain the same. It might be attributed from that there is no such industrial development. Hence major labour mobility has occurred to construction and other informal sectors. Finally decreasing WPR might be considered a direct result of urbanization. An analysis of the census pertaining to this shows some trends-

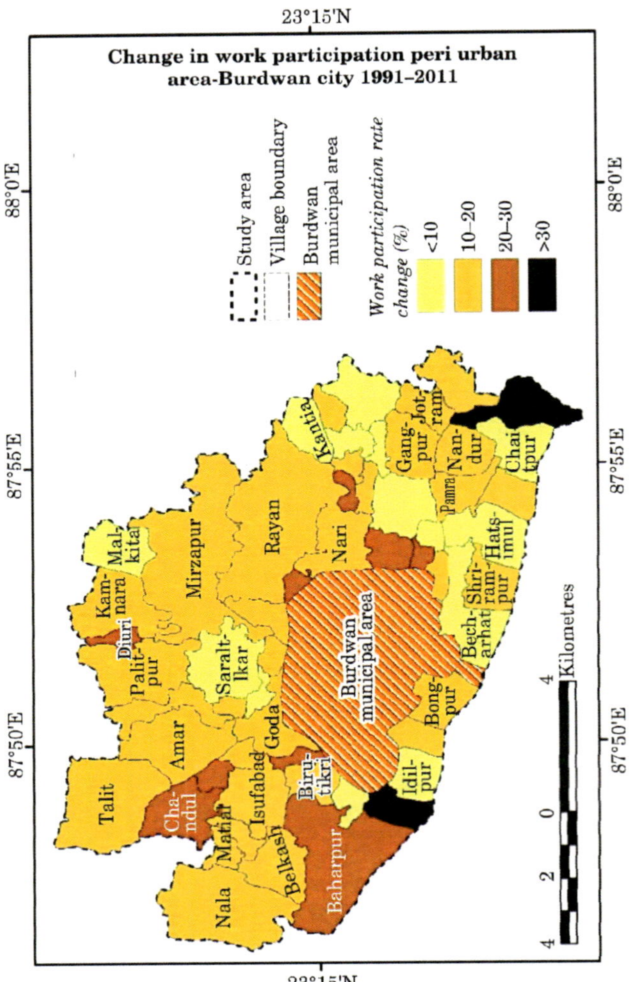

Fig. 4: Change in work participation from the year 1991 to 2011. ***Source:*** Census of India 1991 and 2011

- Over the time period increase in Women WPR, contributes to the overall increase in WPR in the study villages.
- The process of urbanisation and expansion of Bardhaman Municipality urban area pulls a large number of people for to urban informal section from its surrounding villages. These people in 1991 census were mostly engaged in agricultural and allied sectors, where seasonality of work is very high. As a result, there is a huge increase in WPR within this period.
- Increase in demand of daily vegetables in Burdwan Municipality has also encouraged many to grow vegetables for meeting the need. It has consequently swelled up WPR.

2.3. *Better and regular wages*

Analysis of the data shows that there are great variations in the income level among the population in the peri-urban area. It ranges between 8000 rupees per capita (monthly) and 32000 rupees and above per capita (monthly). To depict the distribution of average monthly per capita income in the sample areas, data is grouped into five income classes. The lowest class is prepared on the basis of Ministry of Labour and Employment wage structure to unskilled and skilled laborers. The peri-urban area provides opportunities to all kind of workers, like unskilled, semi-skilled and skilled workers in the secondary sector and highly skilled workers in the tertiary sector. The analysis shows that the highest percentage of households in the peri-urban area fall in the two income classes 'Rupees 8000 and 8000–16000'. The reason for the lowest per capita income is a relatively higher percentage of diverse households in all of the sample villages. The income varies with the diversification of economic activities, which is highest in the high density and least distant villages (Table 5). Following table clearly depicts that about 11.2 percent people have a high income in the peri-urban villages.

Table 5: Family income of sampled households.

Total family income	*Percent of sampled village*
<8001	23.6
8001–16000	31.6
16001–24000	22
24001–32000	12
>32000	11.2

Source: Based on Sample survey (2017)

2.4. *Manifold economic activities*

Distribution of occupation type is not uniform all over the peri-urban villages (Fellmann *et al.*, 2007). The zone near the Burdwan city has higher urban influence and prototypical urban land use than the areas farther away from the city, which influences the occupation structure. The study finds that informal work, petty trading, and low-level services have diverse nature in the sampled villages. Sample survey examined that income diversification with different sectors is very much common with the combination of farming and non-farming activity. The main occupation in the primary sector is cultivation. Villages located in the most distant and low-density areas have a higher percentage of medium and large holdings. In addition, the availability of other activities is low; hence, a large number of people are still cultivators. Besides, many people have also engaged in livestock ranching, and milk-producing in these villages. In the secondary sector, the occupation group of skilled workers has the least percentage of workers. Sample village analysis with regard to occupation structure shows that the village Palitpur has the highest percentage of factory workers who accommodate themselves within the industrial complex. Mirzapur village holds the second position in the proportion of factory workers. Another occupation, in the secondary sector, is the laborers engaged in construction and allied activities. In tertiary class is the various kinds of shops that have sprung in the area to meet the demand. Village Mirzapur and Gopalnagar that has the highest percentage of graduates, postgraduates,and technically qualified population, tops in the percentage of workers in the service sector. Naturally, these villages observe high-level income (Rupees 24000 and above per month) population. Analysis of the survey shows that Service class occupation is the dominant occupation in the peri-urban. However, the pattern of diversification as observed in the peri-urban area is crucial to maintaining different sources of livelihood.

3. Inferential Analysis of Sample Villages

In this chapter, a detailed analysis of the collected data is attempted. Hypotheses are also tested based on the findings of the study, interpretation, and results. For the better result, inferential statistics like Chi-square test is used to verify the hypotheses as stated below.

Chi-Square test (χ^2) is used to verify the hypotheses stated here.

***Alternative hypothesis* (H_1):** Peri-urban areas are dynamic. They undergo rapid change in physical, social and economic infrastructure.

***Null hypothesis* (H_0):** The physical, social and economic infrastructure changes are not taking place in the peri-urban area of Burdwan city.

The tabulated $\chi^2_{0.02}$ for 2 *d.f.* = 9.21. Since the calculated value is higher than tabulated value, the null hypothesis is rejected at 1% level of significance (Table 6). The percentage of LPG usage shows a significant improvement in livelihood in the peri-urban area. Hence, it can be concluded that the social transformation is taking place in the peri-urban villages.

Table 6: Chi square test for social changes as type of fuel used for cooking.

Type of fuel	*Percent of sampled village*	*Chi square value*
Wood-cow dung	50.4	32.83
Kerosene	13.2	
Liquid Petroleum Gas	64.4	

Source: Based on Sample survey (2017)

The tabulated $\chi^2_{0.02}$ for 2 *d.f.* = 9.21. Since the calculated value is lower than the tabulated value, the null hypothesis is accepted at 1% level of significance (Table 7). The percentage of RCC Roof status shows that not much improvement has taken place in the peri-urban residences.

Table 7: Chi square test for physical changes as type of house materials.

Type of house materials	*Percent of sampled village*	*Chi square value*
Mud Brick Thatched	26	3.92
Brick–Cement Non RCC Roof	32	
Brick–Cement with RCC Roof	42	

Source: Based on Sample survey (2017)

Table 8: Chi square test for economic changes as monthly income range.

Total family income	*Percent of sampled village*	*Chi square value*
<8001	23.6	16.69
8001–16000	31.6	
16001–24000	22	
24001–32000	12	
>32000	11.2	

Source: Based on Sample survey (2017)

The tabulated $\chi^2_{0.04}$ for 4 *d.f.* = 13.277. Since the calculated value is higher than the tabulated value, the null hypothesis is rejected at 1% level of significance (Table 8). Hence, it can be established that economic changes are taking place in the peri-urban area.

Table 9: Chi square test for economic changes as types of employment in households.

Type of employment	*Percent of sampled village*	*Chi square value*
Temporary worker	21.5	36.63
Self-employed	59	
Private sector worker	14.25	
Govt. employee	31.25	

Source: Based on Sample survey (2017)

The tabulated $\chi^2_{0.03}$ for 3 *d.f.* = 11.345. Since the calculated value is higher than the tabulated value, the null hypothesis is rejected at 1% level of significance (Table 9). The percentage of private and government workers shows an increasing tendency in the peri-urban area.

Table 10: Chi square test for social change in quality of life.

Educational status	*Percent of sampled village*	*Chi square value*
Illiterate	21.6	49.98
Primary	28.8	
Secondary	24	
Higher secondary	12.8	
Graduation and Above	12.8	

Source: Based on Sample survey (2017)

The tabulated $\chi^2_{0.04}$ for 4 *d.f.* = 13.277. Since the calculated value is higher than the tabulated value, the null hypothesis is rejected at 1% level of significance (Table 10). Hence, it can be concluded that the educational level has increased in the peri-urban area.

Data collected through field survey has been examined, analysed and outcomes are specified in this chapter. It has found that physical, social and economic environment has been improved in last decade.

CONCLUSIONS

This study has examined the spatial and socio-economic transformation of the peri-urban Burdwan. The pull factor of urban infrastructure and good employment opportunities attract migrants from the surrounding villages. The study finds that there are clear signs of socio-economic transformation in the peri-urban area of Burdwan city. This zone is characterized by the coexistence of both primary, secondary, and tertiary activities. The easy access to market and the monetized urban economy is of great advantage for these peri-urban producers and providers. Thus better economy, larger market, greater advantage and higher wages have led peri-urban households to diversify their livelihood that led to improved living. A large number of people engaged in agriculture have sold off their land at a better price and invested a part of it in petty businesses. Thus, occupational change has happened significantly in the peri-urban area. The study also found that city impact has significantly transformed the social environment too. This area has witnessed the transformation in family structure. The families that have undergone a change in the occupational structure are increasingly getting nuclear. To access the living standard in the peri-urban area, livelihood asset index (LAI) is devised. The sample survey finds that peri-urban villages have marked influence of city life on their living style and quality of life. This improvement is also evident from their housing condition and household assets. There have been improvements also in sanitation, water supply, electric supply, use of fuel, means of transport to the city, and level of education. Urban amenities are gradually gearing up in the sample villages. Almost all the sample villages are provided with pucca (metalled) and semi-pucca (partially metalled) roads, health facilities and potable water supply. LPG fuel is used in 64% of the households in the peri-urban interface. However, only 42% of the households are living in brick cement RCC house. The study also finds that a peri-urban area is a place of new social class, who are more inclined towards ultra-urbanity. Overall, the transformation and access to infrastructural facilities and public amenities in the peri-urban have greatly improved, as also evident from inferential statistics performed for gauging socio-economic transformation.

CONFLICT OF INTEREST

The author declare that there is no conflict of interest.

ACKNOWLEDGEMENTS

Author is grateful to University Grants Commission, New Delhi for granting fellowship in research purpose.

REFERENCES

Adesina, A. (2008). Socio-Spatial Transformations and the Urban Fringe Landscape in Developing Countries. Resilience and Social Vulnerability. Paper Presented at United Nation University Institute for Environment and Human Security (UNU-UHS) Summer Academy on Social Vulnerability and Resilience Building in MegaCity, Munich, Germany.

Adu, D.T., Kuwornu, J.K.M. and Anim-Somuah, H. (2018). Application of livelihood vulnerability index in assessing small holder maize farming households' vulnerability to climate change in Brong-Ahafo region of Ghana. *Kasetsart Journal of Social Sciences*, 39(1): 22–32.

Agergaard, J., Fold, N. and Gough, K. (2009). Rural-urban dynamics: Livelihoods, mobility and markets in African and Asian frontiers. Routledge.

Ashley, C. and Carney, D. (1999). Sustainable livelihoods: Lessons from early experience (Vol. 7). Department for International Development London, Russell Press Ltd., Nottingham.

Badiani, R., Dercon, S., Krishnan, P. and Rao, K.P.C. (2007). Changes in living standards invillages in India 1975–2004: Revisiting the ICRISAT village level studies. CPRC Working Paper 85. Oxford: Department of International Development, University of Oxford.

Banu, N. and Fazal, S. (2017). A pragmatic assessment of livelihood status in the peri urban interface: A case from developing India. *Asian Geographer*, 34(1): 123.

Bhagat, R.B. and Mohanty, S. (2009). Emerging Patterns of Urbanization and the Contribution of Migration in Urban Growth in India. *Asian Population Studies*, 6(1): 5–20.

Chambers, R. and Conway, G. (1992). Sustainable rural livelihoods: Practical concepts for the 21st century. Institute of Development Studies, United Kingdom.

Dong, Q.H. (2004). Structure and strategy for *in-situ* rural urbanization in China. Urban Transformation in China. Ashgate, Aldershot and Burlington, pp. 57–63.

Dunn, T. and Holtz-Eakin, D. (2000). Financial capital, human capital and the transition to self-employment: Evidence from intergenerational links. *Journal of Labor Economics*, 18(2): 282–305.

Fellmann, J.D., Getis, A., Getis, J., Shrubsole, D. and Hopkins, J. (2007). Human geography: Landscapes of human activities. University of Western Ontario.

Gopi, K.N. (1978). Process of urban fringe development: A model. Concept Publishing Company.

Hagerty, M.R., Cummins, R.A., Ferriss, A.L., Land, K., Michalos, A.C., Peterson, M.S., Andrew, S.M.J. and Vogel, J. (2001). Quality of life indexes for national policy: Review and agenda for research. *Social Indicators Research*, 55(1): 1.

Hulme, D. and McKay, A. (2007). Identifying and Measuring Chronic Poverty: Beyond Monetary Measures? *In:* Kakwani, N. and Silber, J. (*eds.*), The Many Dimensions of Poverty. Palgrave Macmillan, London.

Janakarajan, S. (2009). Urbanization and peri urbanization: Aggressive competition and unresolved conflicts—The case of Chennai City in India. *South Asian Water Studies*, 1(1): 51–76.

Kibwage, J.K., Odondo, A.J. and Momanyi, G.M. (2009). Assessment of livelihood assets and strategies among tobacco and non tobacco growing households in South Nyanza region, Kenya. *African Journal of Agricultural Research*, 4(4): 294–304.

Lee, S. (2018). Social capital and health at the country level. *The Social Science Journal*, 55(1): 37–51.

Mishra, S.V. (2018). Dispossession by appropriation in a global south city: Geography, cartography and statutory regime as mediating factors. *International Journal of Urban Sciences*, pp. 1–17.

Morse, S., McNamara, N., Acholo, M. and Okwoli, B. (2000). Visions of sustainability: Stakeholders, change and indicators. Ashgate.

Moser, C. and Felton, A. (2007). The Construction of an Asset Index Measuring Asset Accumulation in Ecuador CPRC. Vol. Working Paper 87. Washington DC: The Brookings Institution.

Mycoo, M. (2006). Sustainable livelihoods in the peri-urban interface: Anse La Raye, St Lucia. The Periurban Interface: Approaches to Sustainable Natural and Human Resource Use. Earthscan, Sterling.

Pandey, J. (2010). Rural-urban fringe in Indian cities: A case study of Varanasi. New Delhi: Radha Publications.

Pedersen, P.O. (1990). The role of small rural towns in development. *In:* Titus, M. and Hinderink, J. (*eds.*), (1998). Town and hinterland in developing countries. Amsterdam: Thela-Thesis. Ch.3.

Ramachandran, R. (1992). Urbanization and urban systems in India. Oxford University Press Catalogue.

Registrar General, Census of India (1981, 1991, 2001 and 2011). Vital Statistics Division, 2A, Mansingh Road, New Delhi, 110011.

Sen, A. (2011). Quality of Life: India vs. China, *The New York Review of Books*, (May 12 Issue).

Torres, H., Alves, H. and Aparecida De Oliveira, M. (2007). São Paulo peri-urban dynamics: Some social causes and environmental consequences. *Environment and Urbanization*, 19(1): 207–223.

Vyass, S. and Kumaranayake, K. (2006). Constructing Socioeconomic Status Indexes: How to Use Principal Component Analysis. *Health Policy and Planning*, 21(6): 459–468.

Webster, D. and Muller, L. (2002). Challenges of peri-urbanization in the lower Yangtze region: The case of the Hangzhou-Ningbo corridor. California: Stanford University, Asia/Pacific Research Center.

22

Hospital Wastewater and Its Effluent Treatment

Aastha Dhingra[1*], Sirajuddin Ahmed[1], Izharulhaq Farooqi[1], Arshad Hussain[1] and Nadeem A Khan[1]

ABSTRACT

A pharmaceutical is a substance used in healing, relieving pain, or for treating disease. Pharmaceuticals have likely been in the environment since humans or other species have been on the earth. People have accessed and used pharmaceuticals present in natural products such as plants. Ancient to recent history provides examples (or likely often correct assertions) that pharmaceuticals were used by early peoples and were present in plants. Paracelsus tried to assess the potency of pharmaceuticals in the 16th century. There is a report of Neanderthals possibly using pollen containing medicinal to treat themselves approximately 60,000 years ago. Monographs and books document the uses of natural products as pharmaceuticals. Present-day pharmaceuticals have their origins in the environment as documented in regard to their sources from plants. Humans and animals discovered healing substances were in plants since they must have sensed that eating such plants, smelling them, or applying them to the skin helps cure or prevent a malady. They likely also discovered that eating insects, or consuming a species, or a particular food, may have also cured an ailment or otherwise maintained health.

***Key words*:** Pharmaceuticals, Waste water treatment, Environment.

[1]Civil Engineering Department, Jamia Millia Islamia, New Delhi, Delhi 110025.
**Corresponding author:* E-mail: aastha.dhingra@yahoo.com

1.1. HISTORICAL SUMMARY

Pharmaceuticals are biologically active compounds found in prescription medicines, over-the-counter therapeutic drugs, and veterinary drugs. A fraction of the pharmaceutical dose used by humans is excreted unchanged, or as a metabolite, into wastewater. Wastewater treatment systems (WWTSs) are inefficient at removing all of the pharmaceutical products and their metabolites entering these systems. As a result, these compounds are released to receiving waters (*i.e.,* surface waters or even groundwater), where they can adversely affect environmental receptors or become a source of drinking water for people. Drinking water standards have evolved over the last 100 years (USEPA 2000). Just after the turn of the 20th century, drinking water standards were implemented to address the potential for pathogenic bacteria to cause disease. Eventually, drinking water standards were expanded to include aesthetic concerns and the potential for chemicals to cause harm to human health. In the 1960s, with a significant increase in man-made chemical use by industry and in agriculture, it became clear that chemical contaminates in drinking water could have a negative impact on public health and on the environment. Chemicals entering the environment through unregulated factory discharges, street and farm field runoff, and leaking underground storage and disposal tanks were finding their way into surface water, groundwater, and drinking water supplies. Enactment of the National Environmental Policy Act (NEPA) in 1969 and formation of the U.S. Environmental Protection Agency (EPA) soon thereafter gave government the authority to take a more active role in regulating release and remediation of these chemicals.

The release of pharmaceutical compounds and their continued presence in environmental media has for many years gone without challenge by regulatory authorities. The U.S. Food and Drug Administration (FDA) is authorized to evaluate pharmaceutical products intended for use in the diagnosis, cure, mitigation, treatment, or prevention of disease or intended to affect the structure or any function of the body of humans or animals. Although required by NEPA to consider the environmental impact of approving a drug or biologic application, the FDA is not tasked with regulating the release of drugs or biologics into the environment (USFDA, 1998). In contrast, the EPA has authority to regulate the release of hazardous wastes into the environment, but it was not until very recently that pharmaceutical compounds were identified as potentially hazardous wastes contaminating our environment (USEPA, 2009, 2013a, 2013b, 2013c). As countries around the globe are finding that pharmaceuticals in the environment can pose a significant risk of harm to wildlife and possibly even human health, regulations governing the safe levels of pharmaceuticals in the environment are being considered.

Data regarding the occurrence and effects of pharmaceuticals in the environment began to appear in the mid-1970s (reviewed by Pfluger &

Dietrich, 2001). Clofibric acid was detected in a groundwater reservoir that had been recharged with treated wastewater (Garrison *et al.*, 1976). Aspirin, caffeine, and nicotine were detected in wastewater effluent (Hignite & Azarnoff, 1977), and erythromycin, tetracycline, theophylline, and bisphenol A and other suspected endocrine-disrupting compounds (EDCs) were detected in river water (Watts *et al.*, 1984). EDCs were becoming an increasing concern to scientists studying wildlife. Several studies identified adverse effects in wildlife exposed to chemicals with estrogen-like activity (reviewed in McLachlan & Arnold, 1996), while others identified precocious puberty in young children following ingestion of foods or dermal exposure to ointments containing chemicals with estrogen-like activity (reviewed in Partsch & Sippell, 2001). One of the earliest indications that unintentional exposure to synthetic pharmaceuticals could pose a risk of harm to human health occurred in the early 1950s with the observation of precocious puberty in the children indirectly exposed to diethylstilboestrol (DES), a synthetic estrogen used to prevent miscarriage in pregnant women. So when, in the 1970s and 1980s, health practitioners observed epidemics of precocious puberty in Puerto Rico, Haiti, and Italy, they suspected exposure to environmental estrogens (Partsch & Sippell, 2001). Since then, researchers have suggested that environmental estrogens may be one factor resulting in the increase in precocious puberty observed in young girls in the United States over the last 30 years (Biro *et al.*, 2010).

In the 1990s, with several reports of estrogen-like compounds causing effects in wildlife, endocrinologically active compounds in the environment became the subject of intense research. At the same time, researchers were finding other pharmaceuticals (*e.g.*, clofibric acid) were widespread in the aquatic environment (Heberer *et al.*, 1995). Soon, research identified a number of pharmaceutical compounds in wastewater treatment plant effluents (Shore *et al.*, 1993; Hignite & Azarnoff, 1977; Ternes, 1998). Concern about endocrine-disrupting compounds in drinking water grew with the realization that they were being released with sewage wastewater treatment effluent (Mompelat *et al.*, 2011) reaching surface waters (Belfroid *et al.*, 1999; Williams *et al.*, 2003), and even the human drinking water supply (Heberer *et al.*, 2000, 2001). One of the most potent of these endocrine-disrupting compounds was identified as the synthetic estrogen ethinylestradiol (EE2), a component of a widely used pharmaceutical product, birth control pills. Interest in pharmaceuticals in the environment was not fully appreciated until it was discovered that EE2 was contributing to the feminization of male fish in effluent-impacted rivers (Jobling *et al.*, 1998; Deschow *et al.*, 1998; reviewed in Sumpter & Johnson, 2008). It was not long before pharmaceutical industry representatives began to ask whether people were being unintentionally exposed to other pharmaceutical products released into the environment.

The Pharmaceutical Research and Manufacturers of America (PhRMA), representing the country's leading pharmaceutical industry research and biotechnology companies, has supported the production of several reports and presentations regarding pharmaceuticals in the environment (Cunningham *et al.,* 2006; Buzby, 2007). In these reports, PhRMA recognizes that the release of pharmaceuticals into the environment is an emerging environmental concern. Already, the ubiquitous use of pharmaceuticals in developed countries has led to a nearly continuous release of pharmaceuticals and their metabolites into the environment (Daughton & Ternes, 1999). Across the globe, the amount of pharmaceuticals released into the environment is increasing with increasing population growth, monitoring and controlling pharmaceuticals in the environment remains a difficult endeavor, and currently wastewater treatment system technologies are inefficient at removing pharmaceutical compounds before effluents are released to the environment (EEA, 2010). As a result, pharmaceutical compounds ultimately end up in the environment and in drinking water supplies, and the number of people unintentionally exposed to pharmaceuticals and their by-products in drinking waters is likely to increase in the coming years.

1.2. SOURCES OF PHARMACEUTICALS TO THE ENVIRONMENT

The primary route by which pharmaceuticals enter the environment is through excretion in urine and feces (Cunningham *et al.,* 2006; Daughton & Ruhoy, 2009). Many pharmaceuticals entering wastewater treatment systems are incompletely eliminated during treatment (Oulton *et al.,* 2010; Mompelat *et al.,* 2011). As a result, a fraction of the pharmaceuticals excreted by humans can often be detected in sewage treatment plant effluents (Barnes *et al.,* 2008; USGS, 2002; Heberer *et al.,* 2000; Prasse *et al.,* 2010; Foster *et al.,* 2012), receiving waters (Jones *et al.,* 2003; Cunningham *et al.,* 2006; Mompelat *et al.,* 2011), groundwater (Heberer *et al.,* 2000; Mompelat *et al.*, 2009; Foster *et al.,* 2012), and even drinking waters (Heberer *et al.,* 2000, 2001; Mompelat *et al.,* 2011). Secondary routes by which pharmaceuticals enter the environment include bathing and washing, which release pharmaceuticals remaining on the skin and those that are excreted from skin with sweat (Jones *et al.,* 2003), inappropriate disposal of unused and partially used pharmaceutical products, release from pharmaceutical manufacturing operations (Cunningham *et al.,* 2006; Phillips *et al.,* 2010; Reif *et al.,* 2012), release from medical treatment facilities (Brown *et al.,* 2006; Yuan *et al.,* 2012), release from the application of biosolids (*e.g.,* animal waste) to land (Cunningham *et al.*, 2006; Gibson *et al.,* 2010; Gottschall *et al.,* 2012; Reif *et al.,* 2012), and deposition in landfills (*e.g.,* leachate) (Reif *et al.,* 2012). It has become clear over the last few decades that pharmaceuticals and their metabolites are released into the environment, potentially impacting surface waters, groundwater, and ultimately drinking water.

1.3. OCCURRENCE AND CONCENTRATION OF PHARMACEUTICALS IN THE ENVIRONMENT

Many pharmaceutical compounds and their metabolites are resistant to wastewater treatment and have significant persistence in the environment (Heberer *et al.,* 2001; EEA, 2010). As a result, their release in sewage discharges, surface runoff, and through leaching can result in detectable concentrations of these pharmaceutical compounds, typically in the range of nanograms per litre (μg/L) to low micrograms per litre (μg/L), in surface waters (*i.e.,* streams lakes and rivers) or groundwater (WHO, 2012a, 2012b), which may then be used as a source of drinking water (Drewes & Shore, 2001). Advances in analytical technology have been a key factor in the detection of pharmaceuticals in these water systems. Concurrently, over this same time period, however, pharmaceutical use by the general population in developed and undeveloped countries has increased substantially.

1.3.1. Wastewater Treatment Effluents

A large number of pharmaceutical compounds have been detected in wastewater treatment effluents sampled from across the globe. In Greece, Heberer *et al*. (2000) detected diclofenac (200 to 349 ng/L), gemfibrozil (not detected to 159 ng/L), ketoprofen (270 to 870 ng/L), mefenamic acid (80 to 220 ng/L), and salicylic acid (640 to 2,000 ng/L) in the effluents of two sewage treatment plants. In Korea, Han *et al*. (2006) detected wastewater treatment plant effluent concentrations of diclofenac (1.97 μg/L), ibuprofen (0.07 μg/L), clofibric acid (0.31 μg/L), carbamazepine (0.16 μg/L), salicylic acid (2.43 μg/L), and acetaminophen (0.06 μg/L). In the United Kingdom (UK), Ashton *et al.* (2004) reported the frequency of detection and the median concentration in sewage water treatment work effluents for propranolol (100%, 76 ng/L), diclofenac (86%, 424 ng/L), ibuprofen (84%, 3,086 ng/L), mefenamic acid (81%, 133 ng/L), dextropropoxyphene (74%, 195 ng/L), trimethoprim (65%, 70 ng/L), erythromycin (44%, <10 ng/L), and acetyl-sulfamethoxazole (38%, <50 ng/L). A targeted monitoring of sewage water treatment work effluents and receiving waters in the UK detected ibuprofen in more than 84 and 70% of the samples at mean concentrations of 4.2 and 1.1 μg/L, respectively (EA, 2003). Diclofenac was detected at a mean concentration of 0.6 μg/L in effluents in about 90% of the samples, while only appearing at low frequency in receiving waters at a mean concentration of 0.15 μg/L. Propranolol was detected in all effluent samples at a mean concentration of 0.1 μg/L and in receiving waters at a concentration of 0.04 μg/L. Mefenamic acid and dextropropoxyphene were detected in 75% of all effluent samples at a mean concentration between 0.2 and 0.3 μg/L, with receiving waters found to contain 0.15 and 0.01 μg/L of these pharmaceuticals, respectively. Erythromycin, trimethoprim, and acetyl-sulfamethoxazole were detected in about a third of the effluent samples at mean concentrations between 0.1

and 0.2 μg/L, with lower concentrations detected in receiving waters. Sulfamethoxazole was detected in only 9% of the effluent samples and none of the receiving water samples. In Germany, of the eight antiviral drugs (*i.e.,* acyclovir, abacavir, lamivudine, nevirapine, oseltamivir, penciclovir, stavudine, and zidovudine) detected in raw wastewater from two conventional German wastewater treatment plants, only the concentrations of acyclovir, abacavir, and lamivudine were significantly reduced (Prasse *et al.*, 2010). In contrast, there was little change in the concentrations of nevirapine, oseltamivir, and zidovudine with wastewater treatment. Water samples from receiving waters (*i.e.,* the Rhine River, the Ruhr River and Ruhr tributaries, and the Hessian Reid watershed) contained measurable, but very low, concentrations of these antiviral compounds (Prasse *et al.,* 2010). In the early to mid-1990s, analytical analysis identified μg/L concentrations of clofibric acid (used to reduce blood cholesterol) in Berlin wastewater treatment system (WWTS) effluents (Heberer *et al.,* 2001). In Switzerland, Kahle *et al.* (2008) consistently detected fluconazole (28 to 83 ng/L) and clotrimazole (nondetectable to 6 ng/L) in wastewater treatment plant effluents.

In the United States, the U.S. Geological Survey (USGS) identified multiple pharmaceuticals in wastewater treatment effluents and receiving waters from sampling points located across the United States (Barnes *et al.*, 2002; USGS, 2002; Foster *et al.,* 2012).

Current wastewater treatment appears to remove most pharmaceutical compounds with an average elimination rate of 50% (Mompelat *et al.*, 2011), but a fraction of each pharmaceutical compound entering WWTSs is released to receiving waters. While ibuprofen and its metabolites, hydroxy-ibuprofen and carboxy-ibuprofen, are efficiently degraded during treatment at WWTSs (*i.e.,* more than 95% removal efficiency), other pharmaceuticals like clofibric acid and diclofenac (Buser *et al.,* 1999) and caffeine (Mompelat *et al.*, 2011) are not. Even with relatively efficient removal, ibuprofen has been detected at concentrations up to 8 ng/L water collected from rivers and lakes receiving WWTS effluents. In contrast, metabolites of ibuprofen in these same waters have a concentration of less than 1 μg/L.

1.3.2. Surface Waters

Surface waters receiving WWTS effluents have been found to contain detectable concentrations of pharmaceutical compounds, such as EE2 (Belfroid *et al.*, 1999; Williams *et al.*, 2003) and pharmaceutical metabolites. A critical review of pharmaceuticals in global river systems reported the detection of 203 pharmaceutical products in the river systems of 41 countries (Hughes *et al.,* 2012). Many of these pharmaceutical compounds, including antibiotics, cardiovascular drugs, painkillers, contrast media, and antiepileptic drugs, were detected at concentrations known to cause toxic effects in aquatic biota. While the majority of this work has been conducted in North America, Europe, and China (Hughes *et al.,* 2012), less developed countries across the globe, with less rigorous wastewater treatment systems, are likely to also find pharmaceuticals in their environment as pharmaceutical use by their populace increases.

In the UK, the growing number of research papers published in the 1990s reporting trace levels of pharmaceuticals in environmental samples prompted the Environment Agency to commission a review of information on human pharmaceuticals in the environment (EA, 2000). The report identified "trace amounts," at the ng/L and low μg/L concentrations, of contraceptive hormones, lipid regulators, painkillers, antibiotics, anticancer drugs, antiepileptic drugs, and drugs used to regulate blood pressure, trimethoprim, diclofenac, sulfamethoxazole, acetyl-sulfamethoxazole, acetaminophen, mefenamic acid, ibuprofen, erythromycin, dextropropoxyphene, lofepramine, tamoxifen, and propranolol.

A great deal of research is ongoing in China to identify priority pharmaceuticals in the environment (Sui *et al.,* 2012). To date, China has identified 17 priority pharmaceuticals based on their consumption, effective removal from wastewater treatment systems, and potential ecological impacts. Priority pharmaceuticals identified by China include three afforded a high priority (*i.e.,* diclofenac, erythromycin, and ibuprofen), two pharmaceuticals used in China but not mentioned elsewhere (*i.e.,* cephalexin and ketoconozole), and a number of antibiotic, anti-inflammatory, and antilipidemic compounds. Peng *et al.* (2008) reported on the occurrence and distribution of pharmaceuticals in the Pearl River Delta, noting that the most frequently detected pharmaceutical compounds typically range from 100 ng/L to 1 μg/L. In the same Pearl River system (*i.e.,* the Zhujiang and Shijing Rivers), Zhao *et al.* (2010) reported median concentrations of five NSAIDs (*i.e.,* salicylic acid, ibuprofen, diclofenac, mefenamic acid, and naproxen), two blood lipid regulators (*i.e.,* clofibric acid and gemfibrozil), and one antiepileptic drug (*i.e.,* carbamazepine) at concentrations ranging from 11.2 to 102 ng/L. In the Hangzhou metropolitan area and in Linan County in Southeast China, Chen *et al.* (2012) detected antibiotics, including trimethoprim, erythromycin A dehydrate, penicillin G, penicillin V potassium salt, norfloxacin, ofloxacin, cefazolin, cephalexin, and the NSAIDs ibuprofen, naproxen, and diclofenac, liquid-regulating agent clofibric acid, and the beta-adrenoceptor blocker atenolol in surface waters at concentrations ranging from about 200 ng/L to nearly 2 μg/L. A similar result was found in the Chongqing region of China (Chang *et al.,* 2010), where the authors concluded hospital effluents are a more significant source of pharmaceutical compounds into the aquatic environment than are WWTS effluents. In Israel, Shore and Barel-Cohen (2010) report that ethinylestradiol (EE2) can be readily detected in every stream, and that the concentrations detected are affecting fish reproduction.

In Canada, pharmaceuticals detected in surface waters of Wascana Creek, downstream of the Regina, Saskatchewan, sewage treatment system, include antibiotics, analgesics, anti-inflammatory compounds, a lipid regulator, metabolites of caffeine, cocaine, and nicotine, and an insect repellent (Waiser *et al.,* 2011). In Spain, Lopez-Serna *et al.* (2012) reported two pharmaceuticals, ciprofloxacin (5 μg/L) and sulfamethoxazole (27 μg/L), in the surface waters of the Llobregat River, at concentrations that are potentially toxic to algae. Vazquez-Roig *et al.* (2012) reported that the most frequently detected pharmaceuticals in surface waters within the Pego-Oliva marsh in Spain were ibuprofen and codeine at concentrations up to 59 and 63 ng/L, respectively. In Bendz *et al.* (2005) noted the persistence of the beta-blockers atenolol, metoprolol, and propranolol, and the antibiotics trimethoprim, sulfamethoxazole, and carbamazepine.

In Switzerland, Kahle *et al.* (2008) reported lake water to contain as much as 9 ng/L fluconazole, with increasing concentrations in lake water correlating well with expected human impact. In a study of water from Lake Haapajarvi in southern Finland, Brozinski *et al.* (2013) detected the acidic pharmaceuticals bezafibrate (7 to 24 ng/L), diclofenac (22 to 302 ng/L), ibuprofen (17 to 69 ng/L), ketoprofen (not detectable to 106 ng/L), and naproxen (54 to 210 ng/L), and the basic pharmaceuticals atenolol (23 to 98 ng/L), bisoprolol (47 to 195 ng/L), sotalol (18 to 55 ng/L), citalopram (not detectable to 1 ng/L), venlafaxine (1 to 2 ng/L), and carbamazepine (109 to 355 ng/L). In France, pharmaceutical compounds detected in surface waters and drinking waters included psychostimulants, nonsteroidal anti-inflammatory drugs (NSAIDs), iodinated contrast media, and anxiolytic drugs (Mompelat *et al.,* 2011).

Some of the most comprehensive work establishing human pharmaceutical presence in U.S. streams comes from the USGS, which surveyed pharmaceuticals, hormones, and other organic wastewater contaminants in U.S. streams (USGS, 2002; Barnes *et al.*, 2002). This survey identified nonprescription drugs at a mean concentration of 0.1 μg/L, with a maximum concentration of 17.4 μg/L, and a mean concentration of antibiotics in stream waters of less than 0.1 μg/L, with a maximum of 3.6 μg/L. In surface waters, analytical analyses of USGS samples detected azithromycin (n = 1; 29 ng/L), acetaminophen (n = 4; 77.3 to 160 ng/L), caffeine (n = 30; 0.3 to 246 ng/L), carbamazepine (n = 13; 3 to 190 ng/L), codeine (n = 2; 30.1 to 40 ng/L), cotinine (n = 24; 0.3 to 102 ng/L), dehydronifedipine (n = 3; 4 to 19 ng/L), diltiazem (n = 1; 5 ng/L), 1,7-dimethylhydramine (n = 14; 1 to 23 ng/L), fluoxetine (n = 1; 5 ng/L), ibuprofen (n = 1; 270 ng/L), sulfamethoxazole (n = 2; 10.6 to 36 ng/L), and trimethoprim (n = 5; 0.3 to 24.6 ng/L) (Barnes *et al.,* 2008).

In a follow-up study, the USGS analyzed 297 water samples for pharmaceutical contaminates at 12 stream locations upstream and downstream from animal-feeding operations, 28 stream locations upstream and downstream from wastewater treatment plant effluent discharge, 27 stream locations near drinking water intakes, and 32 stream locations targeted for fish health evaluations in Pennsylvania (Reif *et al.,* 2012). The pharmaceuticals detected in the greatest concentrations included caffeine (517 ng/L), acetaminophen (210 ng/L), sulfamethoxazole (146 ng/L), and paraxanthine (101 ng/L).

In the Sacramento River, several pharmaceutical compounds have been detected at the proposed location of a drinking water system intake (TTI 2012), including the artificial sweeteners acesulfame-K (200 ng/L) and sucralose (110 ng/L), the analgesics acetaminophen (27 ng/L) and butalbital (6.5 ng/L), the heart medication dehydronifedipine (22 ng/L), the diuretic furosemide (36 ng/L), the X-ray contrast agent iohexal (110 ng/L), the anti-inflammatory meclofenamic acid (7.9 ng/L), and the antibacterial triclosan (14 ng/L). On the other coast, in Jamaica Bay, a sewage-impacted estuary in New York City, Benotti and Brownawell (2007) reported on the relative abundance of pharmaceuticals detected in surface waters (*i.e.,* acetaminophen, caffeine, carbamazepine, cimetidine, codeine, cotinine, diltiazem, hydrocodone, nicotine, paraxanthine, sulfamethoxazole, and trimethoprim) at 24 sites.

1.3.3. Groundwater

Since 2000, the USGS has been analyzing groundwater samples from multiple sites across the United States. Initially, the USGS assessed pharmaceutical concentrations in ambient groundwater collected from 18 different states (Barnes *et al.,* 2008). In the following year, USGS assessed the concentrations of pharmaceuticals in ambient groundwater from 25 states and Puerto Rico. Analytical analyses of 74 samples of raw untreated groundwater detected acetaminophen (n = 3; 11.1 to 380 ng/L), caffeine (n = 5; 7 to 130 ng/L), cotinine (n = 1; 1 ng/L), dehydronifedipine (n = 2; 20 to 22 ng/L), diltiazem (n = 1; 28 ng/L), 1,7-dimethylhydramine (n = 2; 45 to 57 ng/L), fluoxetine (n = 2; 5 to 56 ng/L), ibuprofen (n = 1; 3,110 ng/L), and sulfamethoxazole (n = 7; 2.2 to 1,110 ng/L).

In Ontario, Canada, three high-volume septic systems were found to have released 10 pharmaceutical compounds to groundwater (Carrara *et al.,* 2008). Of these compounds, detected in groundwater at low ng/L to µg/L concentrations, ibuprofen, gemfibrozil, and naproxen were transported with groundwater flow over the largest distances from the point of filtration. In Denmark, 10 different sulfonamides (*i.e.,* sulfanilic acid, sulfanilamide, sulfaguanidine, sulfadiazine, sulfaimidine, and sulfametrizole) were identified in groundwater as much as 50 metres downgradient of the Grindsted landfill in Denmark (Holm *et al.*, 1995).

1.3.4. Drinking Water

Routine monitoring of drinking waters has not historically included pharmaceuticals or their metabolites. Yet, a variety of pharmaceuticals, including lipid regulators, antiepilepsy drugs, analgesic and anti-inflammatory drugs, psychiatric drugs, and antibiotics, have been identified in drinking water supplies sampled from across the globe, including Canada, France, Greece, Germany, Italy, Spain, the United States, and the United Kingdom (Jones *et al.,* 2005; Mompelat *et al.*, 2011; Vazquez-Roig *et al.,* 2012; WHO, 2012a). While pharmaceutical compounds are generally detected in treated drinking waters at concentrations less than 50 ng/L (WHO, 2012a), several studies have noted higher concentrations. In the 1990s, clofibric acid was detected in tap water in Berlin, Germany, at concentrations in the low µg/L range (Heberer *et al.*, 2001).

3.3.5. Soils and Sediments

The occurrence and persistence of pharmaceutical compounds and their metabolites in soils has not been well studied. This is perhaps because the primary route by which pharmaceutical compounds enter the environment is from human excretion, the majority of which is taken within WWTSs. Other secondary routes by which pharmaceuticals can be released into the environment, such as the agricultural storage or use of animal wastes/ biosolids (*i.e.,* fertilizers) and deposition of unused pharmaceuticals into a landfill, can result in the contamination of soils. While studies have demonstrated that such applications can potentially impact surface waters through surface runoff and groundwater through leaching, very few studies have investigated the occurrence and persistence of pharmaceuticals in soils. In one such study, antibiotics were found to be a persistent contaminate of soils (Tamtam *et al.,* 2011). The quinolines oxolinic acid, nalidixic acid, and flumequine were detected in surface soils and sulfamethoxazole in subsurface soils 4 years after irrigation with wastewaters containing these pharmaceuticals ceased (Tamtam *et al.,* 2011). In an investigation of pharmaceutical compounds in soils and sediments in Spain, Vazquez-Roig *et al.* (2012) reported that 80% of the soils and 94% of the sediments sampled were found to contain carbamazepine and acetaminophen. Calisto and Esteves (2009) reviewed the occurrence and concentration of psychiatric pharmaceuticals (*i.e.,* anxiolytics, sedatives, hypnotics, and antidepressants) in soils, sediments, biosolids, and tissues. Gottschall *et al.* (2012) identified a number of pharmaceutical compounds, including miconazole and fluoxetine, in soils 1 year following application of dewatered municipal biosolids. Similarly, Gibson *et al.* (2010) reports soil concentrations of the NSAIDs ibuprofen, naproxen, and diclofenac, and the antibiotic triclosan in Mexico soils irrigated with wastewater.

1.3.6. Biota

Wildlife, and particularly aquatic biota, can accumulate pharmaceutical compounds released into the environment. The ubiquitous use of pharmaceuticals coupled with their incomplete elimination in wastewater treatment systems has led to a nearly continuous release of pharmaceuticals and their metabolites into the environment (Daughton & Ternes, 1999). As a result, aquatic organisms are continually exposed to low levels of pharmaceuticals, with these compounds potentially accumulating over the organism's lifetime or even from generation to generation (Daughton & Ternes, 1999; EAA, 2010). The accumulation of pharmaceutical compounds in the tissues of aquatic organisms can pose a risk of harm to an aquatic organism's health, but can also become a significant source of unintended exposure to people consuming these aquatic organisms (EAA, 2010). A 2008 EPA pilot study reported detecting several pharmaceuticals in fish tissue collected from five effluent-dominated streams in various parts of the United States (USEPA, 2013d). Specifically, the EPA detected the antihistamine diphenhydramine in fish livers at four sites and in fish fillets at three sites and the antidepressants norfluoxetine and sertraline in livers at all five sites and in fish fillets at three and two sites, respectively. An expanded study of pharmaceuticals in fish tissues, including 150 locations across the United States, is an anticipated part of the EPA's National Survey of Rivers and Streams (USEPA, 2013e).

Pharmaceuticals originating in wastewater treatment plant effluents can be detected in wild bream and roach living in a lake where diclofenac, naproxen, and ibuprofen are present as pollutants (Brozinski *et al.*, 2013). Analyses of bile from these two wild fish species, bream (*Abramis brama*) and roach (*Rutilus rutilus*), collected from Lake Haapajarvi in southeastern Finland, detected naproxen in all six bream (6 to 32 ng/ml) and roach (11 to 103 ng/ml) samples, diclofenac in five bream (6 to 95 ng/ml) and roach (44 to 148 ng/ml) samples, and ibuprofen in three bream (16 to 34 ng/ml) and two roach (15 and 26 ng/ml) samples.

Other researchers have shown that naproxen, ibuprofen, ketoprofen, and carbamazepine can be detected in the plasma of fish exposed to treated wastewater in aquaria (Brown *et al.*, 2007; Fick *et al.*, 2010). In Sweden, Fick *et al.* (2010) determined that a number of pharmaceutical compounds detected in sewage effluent can bioaccumulate in fish plasma (Table 3.1), with some pharmaceutical concentrations (*i.e.*, levonorgesterol at 8.5 to 12 ng/ml) approaching human therapeutic concentrations.

In rivers that receive WWTS effluents, the antidepressant drugs fluoxetine and sertraline and their metabolites norfluoxetine and desmethylsertraline have been found in the liver, muscle, and brain of fish (Brooks *et al.*, 2005; Ramirez *et al.*, 2009; Schultz *et al.*, 2010). Subedi *et al.* (2012) detected two pharmaceutical compounds (*i.e.*, diphenhydramine and desmethylsertraline) in fish tissue samples collected from 14 different locations in Germany.

1.4. FATE AND TRANSPORT OF PHARMACEUTICAL COMPOUNDS IN THE ENVIRONMENT

In 2001, Pfluger and Dietrich noted that there is a significant lack of information about the environmental fate of pharmaceuticals in the environment (Pfluger & Dietrich, 2001). Over the last decade, our understanding of the environmental fate and transport of pharmaceutical compounds released into the environment has not greatly improved. According to Anette Kuster (ERAs) demonstrated that 95% of the pharmaceuticals are not readily biodegradable. Of the human pharmaceuticals tested, 15% were persistent in water and 50% were persistent in sediments. About 50% of the veterinary pharmaceuticals were persistent in soils. In a study of pharmaceutical concentrations in wastewater treatment plant influent, effluent, and in river water samples downstream, Bendz *et al.* (2005) report that ibuprofen, ketoprofen, naproxen, and diclofenac are subject to significant abiotic or biotic transformations or physical sequestration in the river, while the beta-blockers atenolol, metoprolol, and propanol, the antibiotics trimethoprim and sulfamethoxazole, and carbamazepine exhibit a high degree of persistence. A study in Spain by Carballa *et al.* (2004) noted that aerobic wastewater treatment (*i.e.,* activated sludges) caused significant reductions in the concentrations of anti-inflammatory compounds (40 to 65%), sulfamethoxazole (60%), and EE2 (65%). In a similar study conducted in Sweden by Zorita *et al.* (2009), the rate of pharmaceutical removal during wastewater treatment, with an activated sludge step, was over 90%, except for diclofenac, clofibric acid, and ofloxacin, with even higher diclofenac concentrations observed in effluent than in influent streams. Ashton *et al.* (2004) noted other pharmaceutical compounds (*i.e.,* ibuprofen, trimethoprim, erythromycin, and propranolol) may be transported over long distances, potentially exerting effects on organisms throughout an ecosystem. In Canada, a full-scale municipal wastewater treatment system was only able to remove approximately 75% of the EE2 entering this system (Cicek *et al.*, 2007).

Loffler *et al.* (2005) reported that ibuprofen, its metabolite 2-hydroxy-ibuprofen, and acetaminophen are not persistent in the environment. Regardless, concentrations of ibuprofen, in addition to trimethoprim, erythromycin, and propranolol, in surface waters upstream of known effluent sources have suggested to some that longer range transport of these compounds is possible (Ashton *et al.*, 2004). In contrast, ivermectin and oxazepam were found to be moderately persistent, with dissipation times (DT50) of 15 and 54 days, respectively, while diazepam, carbamazepine, 10,11-dihydro-10,11-dihydroxycarbamazepine, and clofibric acid were highly persistent in a water-sediment environment (*i.e.,* DT50 > 365 days) and loperamide was moderately persistent in this environment (Loffler *et al.*, 2005). These authors suggested that elevated sorption to sediments, observed for ivermectin, diazepam, oxazepam, and carbamazepine, plays an important role in the environmental persistence of these pharmaceutical compounds. Conversely, Heberer *et al.* (2000) suggested that polar pharmaceutical compounds in surface waters are unlikely to significantly adsorb to soils.

Unfortunately, current water quality monitoring does not differentiate between soluble and bound pharmaceutical compounds, and therefore may not allow for a complete understanding of the behavior of these compounds in the environment (Maskaoui & Zhou, 2010).

Literature on the fate of pharmaceutical compounds in soils, sediments, and sludges is quite limited. One of the reasons for this is the lack of appropriate analytical methods capable of measuring these compounds at low environmental levels (reviewed by Wilga *et al.*, 2008). Regardless, a number of studies have identified pharmaceutical compounds in solid environmental matrices. Gottschall *et al.* (2012) identified a number of pharmaceutical compounds in dewatered municipal solid aggregates incorporated into soils up to 1 year following their application. Of these, miconazole and fluoxetine were the most persistent, with a reduction in soil concentration of about 50% after 1 year. Psychiatric pharmaceuticals (*i.e.,* anxiolytics, sedatives, hypnotics, and antidepressants) are found in wastewaters, surface waters, soils, sediments, and biosolids and tissues (Calisto & Esteves, 2009). Because of their prevalence in environmental media, their high persistence in the environment, and their toxicity to nontarget organisms, these compounds are some of the most worrisome of the human pharmaceuticals released to the environment. Only in the last few years have scientists begun to pay attention to the potential environmental risk posed by metabolites of pharmaceutical compounds (Celiz *et al.*, 2009; Mompelat *et al.*, 2009). While Mompelat *et al.* (2009) reported that environmental investigations have studied the occurrence, fate, and ecotoxicity of approximately 160 pharmaceutical products, these investigations only included 30 pharmaceutical by-products. In part, this can be attributed to the difficulty inherent in measuring trace amounts of previously unknown or poorly characterized pharmaceutical by-products in complex environmental matrices. Regardless, the metabolites or by-products of pharmaceuticals can have significant biological activity. Several commonly detected human pharmaceuticals in the environment have biologically active metabolites, including gemfibrozil, acetaminophen, carbamazepine, and diclofenac (Celiz *et al.,* 2009). The tricyclic antidepressant drugs amitriptyline and imipramine form stable metabolites that are toxic to test species used in Spirotox and Thammo-toxkit tests (Celiz *et al.,* 2009). In some cases, the pharmaceutical metabolite can have greater biological activity than did the parent pharmaceutical. Norfluoxetine, the main human metabolite of the selective serotonin reuptake inhibitor (SSRI) fluoxetine, is 50% more toxic than its parent compound (Celiz *et al.,* 2009). Detected in wastewater treatment plant effluents at concentrations ranging from 3.9 to 25 ng/L, this metabolite is also known to bioaccumulate in fish (Celiz *et al.,* 2009).

Surface waters used as a source of drinking water are often treated with chlorine or put through some other disinfection process to remove pathogenic bacteria and improve its aesthetic quality. While trimethoprim, sulfamethoxazole, naproxen, estrone, and triclosan concentrations are susceptible to transformation and removal by chlorine disinfection, azithromycin, atenolol, tert-oxyphenol, iopromide, and gemfibrozil are less susceptible to chlorination, and carbamazepine, primidone, fluoxetine, and triclocarban are refractory to treatment in general and specifically to chlorine disinfection (Nelson *et al.,* 2011). In a study of how drinking water processes could affect pharmaceutical residues, Westerhoff *et al.* (2005) reported that the conventional treatment of drinking water by coagulation and chlorine is relatively inefficient at removing pharmaceuticals from finished drinking water. In contrast, these authors found that the addition of powder-activated carbon or ozone treatment, rather than chloride, could significantly improve pharmaceutical removal rates.

Over the last several years, it has become clear that the release of pharmaceuticals into the environment is an emerging environmental concern. The nearly continuous release of pharmaceuticals and their metabolites into the environment is occurring across the globe and is likely to continue to increase with increasing population growth. Monitoring and controlling pharmaceuticals in the environment remains a difficult endeavor. Current wastewater treatment system technologies are inefficient at removing pharmaceutical compounds before effluents are released to the environment where they, or their metabolites or breakdown products, ultimately end up in the environment and in drinking water supplies. The potential impact resulting from these pharmaceuticals and their by-products on human and environmental health is likely to increase in the coming years.

2. CONCLUSIONS

There are now numerous articles demonstrating methods for detecting and reporting on the occurrence and fate with regards to antibiotics and illicit drugs. However, continued research efforts are still necessary for better understanding of the complexity of continual low-level environmental exposures to these chemicals, either singly or as mixtures, and not only their subtle effects on aquatic organisms, but ultimately the consequences to those higher up in the food chain, *i.e.,* humans. The ability to understand the potential for adverse effects from environmental exposure from antibiotics and illicit drugs on human and ecological health is becoming more important due to the increasing multiuse character of wastewater effluent (*e.g.*, snowmaking, golf course irrigation, landscape irrigation, crop irrigation, etc.), and in some cases where it is continuously recycled in a closed loop, such as in Singapore, and Scottsdale, Arizona. This multiuse and recycling of wastewater effluent increases the potential for cumulative increases of antibiotics and illicit drugs into water supply sources.

3. REFERENCES

Ashton, D., Hilton, M., and Thomas, K.V. (2004). Investigating the Environmental Transport of Human Pharmaceuticals to Streams in the United Kingdom. *Sci. Total Environ.,* 333: 167–184.

Barnes, K.K., Klopin, D.W., Meyer, M.T., Thurman, E.M., Furlong, E.T., Zaugg, S.D. and Barber, L.B. (2002). Water-Quality Data for Pharmaceuticals, Hormones and Other Organic Wastewater Contaminates in U.S. Streams, 1999–2000. Open-File Report 02–94. U.S. Department of the Interior, Iowa City, Iowa, p. 9.

Barnes, K.K., Kolpin, D.W., Focazio, M.J., Furlong, E.T., Meyer, M.T., Zaugg, S.D., Haack, S.K., Barber, L.B. and Thurman, E.M. (2008). Water-Quality Data for Pharmaceuticals and Other Organic Wastewater Contaminants in Ground Water and in Untreated Drinking Water Sources in the United States, 2000–01. U.S. Geological Survey Open-File Report 2008–1293.

Belfroid, A.C., Van der Horst, A., Vethaak, A.D., Schafer, A.J., Rijs, G.B.J., Wegener, J. and Cofino, W.P. (1999). Analysis and Occurrence of Estrogenic Hormones and Their Glucuronides in Surface Water and Waste Water in the Netherlands. *Sci. Total Environ.,* 225: 101–108.

Bendz, D., Paxeus, N.A., Ginn, T.R. and Loge, F.J. (2005). Occurrence and Fate of Pharmaceutically Active Compounds in the Environment, A Case Study: Hoje River in Sweden. *J. Hazard. Mater.,* 122(3): 195–204.

Benotti, M.J., and Brownawell, B.J. (2007). Distributions of Pharmaceuticals in an Urban Estuary during Both Dry and Wet Weather Conditions. *Environ. Sci. Technol.,* 41: 5795–5802.

Biro, F.M., Galvez, M.P., Greenspan, L.C., Succop, P.A., Vangeepuram, N., Pinney, S.M., Teitelbaum, S., Windham, G.C., Kushi, L.H. and Wolff, M.S. (2010). Pubertal Assessment Method and Baseline Characteristics in a Mixed Longitudinal Study of Girls. *Pediatrics,* 126: e583–e590.

Brooks, B.W., Chambliss, K., Stanley, J.K., Ramirez, A., Banks, K.E., Johnson, R.D. and Lewis, R.J. (2005). Determination of Select Antidepressants in Fish from an Effluent-Dominated Stream. *Environ. Toxicol. Chem.,* 24: 464"469. (Cited in Brozinski *et al.*, 2013).

Brown, J.N., Paxeìus, N., Forlin, L. and Larsson, D.G.J. (2007). Variations in Bioconcentration of Human Pharmaceuticals from Sewage Effluents into Fish Blood Plasma. *Environ. Toxicol. Pharmacol.,* 24: 267"274. (Cited in Brozinski *et al.*, 2013).

Brown, K.D., Kulis, J., Thomson, B., Chapman, T.H. and Mawhinney, D.B. (2006). Occurrence of Antibiotics in Hospital, Residential and Dairy Effluent, Municipal Wastewater and the Rio Grande in New Mexico. *Sci. Total Environ.,* 366: 772–783. (Cited in Chen *et al.*, 2012).

Brozinski, J.M., Lahti, M., Meierjohann, A., Oikari, A. and Kronberg, L. (2013). The Anti-Inflammatory Drugs Diclofenac, Naproxen and Ibuprofen are found in the Bile of Wild Fish Caught Downstream of a Wastewater Treatment Plant. *Environ. Sci. Technol.,* 47(1): 342–348.

Buser, H.R., Poiger, T. and Muller, M.D. (1999). Occurrence and Environmental Behavior of the Chiral Pharmaceutical Drug Ibuprofen in Surface Waters and in Wastewater. *Environ. Sci. Technol.,* 33: 2529–2535.

Buzby, M. (2007). Pharmaceuticals in the Environment — A Review of PhRMA Initiatives. Presented at 4th Japan-U.S. Governmental Conference on Drinking Water Quality, Management and Wastewater Control. Pharmaceutical Research and Manufacturers of America.

Calisto, V. and Esteves, V.I. (2009). Psychiatric Pharmaceuticals in the Environment. *Chemosphere,* 77(10): 1257–1274.

Carballa, M., Omil, F., Lema, J.M., Llompart, M., Garcia-Jares, C., Rodriguez, I., Gomez, M. and Ternes, T. (2004). Behavior of Pharmaceuticals, Cosmetics and Hormones in a Sewage Treatment Plant. *Water Res.,* 38(12): 2918–2926.

Carrara, C., Ptacek, C.J., Robertson, W.D., Blowes, D.W., Moncur, M.C., Sverko, E. and Backus, S. (2008). Fate of Pharmaceutical and Trace Organic Compounds in Three Septic System Plumes, Ontario, Canada. *Environ. Sci. Technol.,* 42: 2805–2811.

Celiz, M.D., Tso, J. and Aga, D.S. (2009). Pharmaceutical Metabolites in the Environment: Analytical Challenges and Ecological Risks. *Environ. Toxicol. Chem.,* 28(12): 2473–2484.

Chang, X., Meyer, M.T., Liu, X., Zhao, Q., Chen, H., Chen, J., Qiu, Z., Yang, L., Cao, J. and Shu, W. (2010). Determination of Antibiotics in Sewage from Hospitals, Nursery and Slaughter House, Wastewater Treatment Plant and Source Water in Chongqing Region of Three Gorge Reservoir in China. *Environ. Pollut.,* 158: 1444–1450. (Cited in Chen *et al*., 2012.)

Chen, H., Li, X. and Zhu, S. (2012). Occurrence and Distribution of Selected Pharmaceuticals and Personal Care Products in Aquatic Environments: A Comparative Study of Regions in China with Different Urbanization Levels. *Environ. Sci. Pollut. Res.,* 19: 2381–2389.

Cicek, N., Londry, K., Oleszkiewicz, J.A., Wong, D. and Lee, Y. (2007). Removal of Selected Natural and Synthetic Estrogenic Compounds in a Canadian Full-Scale Municipal Wastewater Treatment Plant. *Water Environ. Res.,* 79(7): 795–800.

Cunningham, V.L., Buzby, M., Hutchinson, T., Mastrocco, F., Parke, N. and Roden, N. (2006). Effects of Human Pharmaceuticals on Aquatic Life: Next Steps. How Do Human Pharmaceuticals Get into the Environment and What are their Effects? *Environ. Sci. Technol.,* 40(11): 3457–3462.

Daughton, C.G. and Ruhoy, I.S. (2009). Environmental Footprint of Pharmaceuticals: The Significance of Factors beyond Direct Excretion to Sewers. *Environ. Toxicol. Chem.,* 28(12): 2495–2521.

Daughton, C.G. and Ternes, T.A. (1999). Pharmaceuticals and Personal Care Products in the Environment: Agents of Subtle Change, Special Report. *Environ. Health Perspect.,* 107(Suppl. 6): 907–938.

Deschow, C., Routledge, E.J., Brighty, G.C., Sumpter, J.P. and Waldock, M. (1998). Identification of Estrogenic Chemicals in STW Effluent. I. Chemical Fractionation and *in vitro* Biological Screening. *Environ. Sci. Technol.,* 32: 1549–1358.

Drewes, J.E. and Shore, L.S. (2001). Concerns about Pharmaceuticals in Water Reuse, Groundwater Recharge and Animal Waste. *In*: Pharmaceuticals and Care Products in the Environment, *(ed.),* Daughton, C. *et al*., ACS Symposium Series. Washington, DC: American Chemical Society.

EA (2000). *Review of Human Pharmaceuticals in the Environment. Research and Development*. Technical Report P390. Prepared by WRc-NSF Ltd. for the Environment Agency.

EA (2003). *Targeted Monitoring Programme for Pharmaceuticals in the Aquatic Environment*. R&D Technical Report P6-012/06/TR. Written by Hilton, M.J., Thomas, K.V. and Ashton, D. of CEFAS for the Environment Agency National Center for Ecotoxicology and Hazardous Substances.

EA (2006). *Environment Agency Workshop on Chronic Aquatic Ecotoxicity Testing of Human Pharmaceuticals*. Prepared by Watts & Crane Associates for the Environment Agency.

EEA (2010). *Pharmaceuticals in the Environment. Results of an EEA Workshop*. EEA Technical Report 1. European Environment Agency.

Fick, J., Lindberg, R.H., Parkkonen, J., Arvidsson, B., Tysklind, M. and Larsson, D.G.J. (2010). Therapeutic Levels of Levonorgestrel Detected in Blood Plasma of Fish: Results from Screening Rainbow Trout Exposed to Treated Sewage Effluents. *Environ. Sci. Technol.,* 44: 2661–2666.

Foster, A.L., Katz, B.G. and Meyer, M.T. (2012). *Occurrence and Potential Transport of Selected Pharmaceuticals and Other Organic Wastewater Compounds from Wastewater-Treatment Plant Influent and Effluent to Groundwater and Canal Systems in Miami-Dade County, Florida*. U.S. Geological Survey Scientific Investigations Report 2012–5083.

Garrison, A.W., Pope, J.D. and Allen, F.R. (1976). GC/MS Analysis of Organic Compounds in Domestic Wastewaters. *In*: *Identification and Analysis of Organic Pollutants in Water,* Keith, C.H. and Arbor, Ann (*eds.*), MI: Ann Arbor Science Publishers, p. 517.

Gibson, R., Duran-Alvarez, J.C., Estrada, K.L., Chavez, A. and Jimenez-Cisneros, B. (2010). Accumulation and Leaching Potential of Some Pharmaceuticals and Potential Endocrine Disruptors in Soils Irrigated with Wastewater in the Tula Valley, Mexico. *Chemosphere,* 81(11): 1437–1445.

Gottschall, N., Topp, E., Metcalfe, C., Edwards, M., Payne, M., Kleywegt, S., Russell, P. and Lapen, D.R. (2012). Pharmaceutical and Personal Care Products in Groundwater, Subsurface Drainage, Soil and Wheat Grain, Following a High Single Application of Municipal Biosolids to a Field. *Chemosphere,* 87(2): 194–203.

Han, G.K., Hur, H.G. and Kim, S.D. (2006). Ecotoxicological Risk of Pharmaceuticals from Wastewater Treatment Plants in Korea: Occurrence and Toxicity to *Daphnia magna*. *Environ. Toxicol. Chem.,* 25(1): 265–271.

Heberer, T., Butz, S. and Stan, H.J. (1995). Analysis of Phenoxycarboxylic Acids and Other Acidic Compounds in Tap, Surface and Sewage Water at the Low ng/L Level. *Int. J. Environ. Anal. Chem.,* 58(1–4): 43–53.

Heberer, T., Fuhrmann, B., Schmidt-Baumier, K., Psipi, D., Koutsouba, V. and Hiskia, A. (2000). Occurrence of Pharmaceutical Residues in Sewage, River, Ground and Drinking Water in Greece and Germany. *In*: Issues in the Analysis of Environmental Endocrine Disruptors. Reprints of Extended Abstracts. Symposia Papers Presented before the Division of Environmental Chemistry, San Francisco, CA. *American Chemical Society*, 40(1): 107–109.

Heberer, T., Verstraeten, I.M., Meyer, M.T., Mechlinski, A. and Reddersen, K. (2001). Occurrence and Fate of Pharmaceuticals during Bank Filtration — Preliminary Results from Investigations in Germany and the United States. *Water Resour. Update,* 120: 4–17.

Hignite, C. and Azarnoff, D.L. (1977). Drugs and Drug Metabolites as Environmental Contaminants: Chlorophenoxyisobutyrate and Salicylic Acid in Sewage Water Effluent. *Life Sci.,* 20(2): 337–341.

Holm, J.V., Rugge, K., Bjerg, P.L. and Christensen, T.H. (1995). Occurrence and Distribution of Pharmaceutical Organic Compounds in the Groundwater Downgradient of a Landfill (Grindsted, Denmark). *Environ. Sci. Technol.,* 29(5): 1415–1420.

Hughes, S.R., Kay, P. and Brown, L.E. (2012). A Global Synthesis and Critical Evaluation of Pharmaceutical Datasets Collected from River Systems. *Environ. Sci. Technol.* Just accepted. doi:10.1021/es3030148.

Jobling, S., Nolan, M., Tyler, C.R., Brighty, G. and Sumpter, J.P. (1998). Widespread Sexual Disruption in Wild Fish. *Environ. Sci. Technol.,* 32: 2498–2506.

Jones, O.A., Lester, J.N. and Voulvoulis, N. (2005). Pharmaceuticals: A Threat to Drinking Water? Opinion. *TRENDS Biotechnol.,* 23(4): 163–167.

Jones, O.A.H., Voulvoulis, N. and Lester, J.N. (2003). Potential Impact of Pharmaceuticals on Environmental Health Perspectives. *Bull. World Health Org.,* 81(10): 768–769.

Kahle, M., Buerge, I.J., Hauser, A., Muller, M.D. and Poiger, T. (2008). Azole Fungicides: Occurrence and Fate in Wastewater and Surface Waters. *Environ. Sci. Technol.,* 42: 7193–7200.

Loffler, D., Rombke, J., Meller, M. and Ternes, T.A. (2005). Environmental Fate of Pharmaceuticals in Water/Sediment Systems. *Environ. Sci. Technol.,* 39: 5209–5218.

Lopez-Serna, R., Postigo, C., Blanco, J., Perez, S., Ginebreda, A., de Alda, M.L., Petrovic, M., Munne, A. and Barcelo, D. (2012). Assessing the Effects of Tertiary Treated Wastewater Reuse on the Presence Emerging Contaminants in a Mediterranean River (Llobregat, NE Spain). *Environ. Sci. Pollut. Res.,* 19: 1000–10012.

Maskaoui, K. and Zhou, J.L. (2010). Colloids as a Sink for Certain Pharmaceuticals in the Aquatic Environment. *Environ. Sci. Pollut. Res., 17*:898–907.

McLachlan, J.A. and Arnold, S.F. (1996). Environmental Estrogens. Found Internally, Certain Compounds are Important Biological Signals; found in the Environment, They Can Become Just So Much Noise. *Am. Sci.,* 84: 452–461.

Mompelat, S., Le Bot, B. and Thomas, O. (2009). Occurrence and Fate of Pharmaceutical Products and By-Products, from Resource to Drinking Water. *Environ. Int.,* 35: 803–814. (Cited in Celiz *et al.*, 2009).

Mompelat, S., Thomas, O. and Le Bot, B. (2011). Contamination Levels of Human Pharmaceutical Compounds in French Surface and Drinking Water. *J. Environ. Monit.,* 13(10): 2929–2939.

Nelson, E.D., Do, H., Lewis, R.S. and Carr, S.A. (2011). Diurnal Variability of Pharmaceutical, Personal Care Product, Estrogen and Alkylphenol Concentrations in Effluent from a Tertiary Waste Water Treatment Facility. *Environ. Sci. Technol.,* 45: 1228–1234.

Oulton, R.L., Kohn, T. and Cwiertny, D.M. (2010). Pharmaceuticals and Personal Care Products in Effluent Matrices: A Survey of Transformation and Removal during Wastewater Treatment and Implications for Wastewater Management. *J. Environ. Monit.,* 12(11): 1956–1978.

Partsch, C.J. and Sippell, W.G. (2001). Pathogenesis and Epidemiology of Preconscious Puberty. Effects of Exogenous Oestrogens. *Hum. Reprod. Update,* 7(3): 292–302.

Peng, X., Yu, Y., Tang, C., Tan, J., Huang, Q. and Wang, Z. (2008). Occurrence of Steroid Estrogens, Endocrine-Disrupting Phenols and Acid Pharmaceutical Residues in Urban Riverine Water of the Pearl River Delta, South China. *Sci. Total Environ.,* 397(1–3): 158–166.

Pfluger, P. and Dietrich, D.R. (2001). Effects of Pharmaceuticals in the Environment —An Overview and Principal Considerations. In: Pharmaceuticals in the Environment, Kümmerer, K. *(ed.)*, Berlin: Springer, pp. 11–17.

Phillips, P.J., Smith, S.G., Klopin, D.W., Zaugg, S.D., Buxton, H.T., Furlong, E.T., Esposito, K. and Stinson, B. (2010). Pharmaceutical Formulation Facilities as Sources of Opioids and Other Pharmaceuticals to Waste Water Treatment Plant Effluents. *Environ. Sci. Technol.,* 44: 4910–4916.

Prasse, C., Schlusener, M.P., Schulz, R. and Ternes, T.A. (2010). Antiviral Drugs in Wastewater and Surface Waters: A New Class of Environmental Relevance? *Environ. Sci. Technol.,* 44: 1728–1735.

Ramirez, A.J., Brain, R.A., Usenko, S., Mottaleb, M.A., O'Donnell, J.G., Stahl, L.L., Wathen, J.B., Snyder, B.D., Pitt, J.L., Perez-Hurtado, P., Dobbins, L.L., Brooks, B.W. and Chambliss, C.K. (2009). Occurrence of Pharmaceuticals and Personal Care Products in Fish: Results of a National Pilot Study in the United States. *Environ. Toxicol. Chem.,* 28: 2587"2597. (Cited in Brozinski *et al.*, 2013).

Reif, A.G., Crawford, J.K., Loper, C.A., Proctor, A., Manning, R. and Titler, R. (2012). *Occurrence of Pharmaceuticals, Hormones and Organic Wastewater Compounds in Pennsylvania Waters, 2006–09.* U.S. Geological Survey Scientific Investigations Report 2012–5106.

Schultz, M.M., Furlong, E.T., Kolpin, D.W., Werner, S.T., Schoenfuss, H.L., Barber, L.B., Blazer, V.S., Norris, D.O. and Vajda, A.M. (2010). Antidepressant Pharmaceuticals in Two U.S. Effluent-Impacted Streams: Occurrence and Fate in Water and Sediment and Selective Uptake in Fish Neural Tissue. *Environ. Sci. Technol.,* 44: 1918"1925. (Cited in Brozinski *et al.*, 2013).

Shore, L.S. and Barel-Cohen, C.K. (2010). The Environmental Compartments of Environmental Hormones. *Rev. Environ. Health,* 25(4): 345–350.

Shore, L.S., Gurevitz, M. and Shemesh, M. (1993). Estrogen as an Environmental Pollutant. *Bull. Environ. Contam. Toxicol.,* 51(3): 361–366.

Subedi, B., Du, B., Chambliss, C.K., Koschorreck, J., Rudel, H., Quack, M., Brooks, B.W. and Usenko, S. (2012). Occurrence of Pharmaceuticals and Personal Care Products in German Fish Tissue: A National Study. *Environ. Sci. Technol.,* 46: 9047–9054.

Sui, Q., Wang, B., Zhao, W., Huang, J., Yu, G., Deng, S., Qiu, Z. and Lu, S. (2012). Identification of Priority Pharmaceuticals in the Water Environment of China. *Chemosphere,* 89(3): 260–266.

Sumpter, J.P. and Johnson, A.C. (2008). Reflections on Endocrine Disruption in the Aquatic Environment from Known Knowns to Unknown Unknowns (and Many Things in Between). *J. Environ. Monit.,* 10: 1476–1485.

Tamtam, F., Van Oort, F., Le Bot, B., Dinh, T., Mompleat, S., Chevreuil, M., Lamy, I. and Thiry, M. (2011). Assessing the Fate of Antibiotic Contaminants in Metal Contaminated Soils Four Years after Cessation of Long-Term Waste Water Irrigation. *Sci. Total Environ.* 409(3):540–547.

Ternes, T.A. (1998). Occurrence of Drugs in German Sewage Treatment Plants and Rivers. *Water Res.,* 32: 3245–3260.

TTI (2012). *Sacrament River Water Quality Assessment for the Davis-Woodland Water Supply Project.* Prepared for West Yost Associates by Trussel Technologies, Inc.

USEPA (2000). *The History of Drinking Water Treatment*. EPA-816-F-00-006. Office of Water, U.S. Environmental Protection Agency.

USEPA (2009). *Fact Sheet: Final Third Drinking Water Contaminant Candidate List (CCL 3)*. EPA 815F09001. Office of Water, U.S. Environmental Protection Agency. Available at *www.epa.gov/safewater*

USEPA (2013a). *Pharmaceuticals and Personal Care Products (PPCPs)*. Research and Development, PPCPs. U.S. Environmental Protection Agency. Available at *http://www.epa.gov/ppcp/basic2.html.*

USEPA (2013b). *Pharmaceuticals and Personal Care Products (PPCPs) in Water*. Water, Science and Technology, Surface Water Standards. U.S. Environmental Protection Agency. Available at *http://water.epa.gov/scitech/swguidance/ppcp/index.cfm.*

USEPA (2013c). *Proposal to Address the Management of Hazardous Waste Pharmaceuticals*. Wastes—Hazardous Waste. U.S. Environmental Protection Agency. Available at *http://www.epa.gov/osw/hazard/generation/pharmaceuticals.htm.*

USEPA (2013d). *Pilot Study of Pharmaceuticals and Personal Care Products in Fish Tissue*. Water, Science and Technology, Surface Water Standards and Guidance, Pharmaceuticals and Personal Care Products. U.S. Environmental Protection Agency. Available at *http://water.epa.gov/scitech/swguidance/ppcp/fish-tissue.cfm.*

USEPA (2013e). *Expanded Investigations of Pharmaceuticals in Fish Tissue*. Water, Science and Technology, Surface Water Standards and Guidance, Pharmaceuticals and Personal Care Products. U.S. Environmental Protection Agency. Available at *http://water.epa.gov/scitech/swguidance/ppcp/fish-expand.cfm.*

USFDA (1998). Guidance for Industry, Environmental Assessment of Human Drug and Biologics Applications. Department of Health and Human Services, Food and Drug Administration, Center for Drug Evaluation and Research (CDER), Center for Biologics Evaluation and Research (CBER). Available at *http://www.fda.gov/downloads/Drugs/GuidanceComplianceRegulatoryInformation/Guidances/ucm070561.pdf.*

USGS (2002). Pharmaceuticals, Hormones and Other Organic Wastewater Contaminants in U.S. Streams. USGS Fact Sheet FS-027-02. U.S. Department of the Interior, U.S. Geological Survey.

Vazquez-Roig, P., Andreu, V., Blasco, C. and Pico, Y. (2012). Risk Assessment on the Presence of Pharmaceuticals in Sediments, Soils and Waters of the Pego-Oliva Marshlands (Valencia, Eastern Spain). *Sci. Total Environ.,* 440: 24–32.

Waiser, M.J., Humphreys, D., Tumber, V. and Holm, J. (2011). Effluent-Dominated Streams. Part 2. Presence and Possible Effects of Pharmaceuticals and Personal Care Products in Wascana Creek, Saskatchewan, Canada. *Environ. Toxicol. Chem.,* 30(2): 508–519.

Watts, C.D., Crathorn, B., Fielding, M. and Steel, C.P. (1984). Identification of Non-Volatile Organics in Water Using Field Desorption Mass Spectrometry and High Performance Liquid Chromatography. *In*: *Analysis of Organic Micropollutants in Water: Proceedings of the Third European Symposium*, Oslo, Norway, September 19–21, 1983, Angeletti, G. and Bjorseth, A. (*eds.*), Springer, Dordrecht, the Netherlands, pp. 120–131.

Westerhoff, P., Yoon, Y., Snyder, S. and Wert, E. (2005). Fate of Endocrine-Disruptor, Pharmaceutical and Personal Care Product Chemicals during Simulated Drinking Water Treatment Processes. *Environ. Sci. Technol.,* 39: 6649–6663.

WHO (2012a). *Pharmaceuticals in Drinking-Water*. World Health Organization. Available at *http://www.who.int/water_sanitation_health/publications/2011/pharmaceuticals/en/index.html.*

WHO (2012b). *Information Sheet: Pharmaceuticals in Drinking-Water*. World Health Organization. Available at *http://www.who.int/water_sanitation_health/emerging/info_sheet_pharmaceuticals/en/index.html.*

Wilga, J., Kot-Wasik, A. and Namiesnik, J. (2008). Studies of Human and Veterinary Drugs' Fate in Environmental Solid Samples — Analytical Problems. *J. Chromat. Sci.,* 46: 601–608.

Williams, R.J., Johnson, A.C., Smith, J.J.L. and Kanda, R. (2003). Steroid Estrogens Profiles along River Stretches Arising from Sewage Treatment Works Discharges. *Environ. Sci. Technol.,* 37: 1744–1750.

Yuan, S., Jiang, X., Xia, X., Zhang, H. and Zheng, S. (2012). Detection, Occurrence and Fate of 22 Psychiatric Pharmaceuticals in Psychiatric Hospital and Municipal Wastewater Treatment Plants in Beijing, China. *Chemosphere*. doi:10.1016/j.chemosphere.2012.10.089.

Zhao, J.L., Ying, G.G., Liu, Y.S., Chen, F., Yang, J.F., Wang, L., Yang, X.B., Stauber, J.L. and Warne, M.St.J. (2010). Occurrence and a Screening-Level Risk Assessment of Human Pharmaceuticals in the Pearl River System, South China. *Eviron. Toxicol. Chem.,* 29(6): 1377–1384.

Zorita, S., Martensson, L. and Mathiasson, L. (2009). Occurrence and Removal of Pharmaceuticals in a Municipal Sewage Treatment System in the South of Sweden. *Sci. Total Environ.,* 407(8): 2760–2770.

Subject Index

P

Q

R

S

T

U